D1166871

☆ REVISED EDITION ☆

GETTING THE PART

Thirty-three Professional

Casting Directors Tell You

How to Get Work in Theater,

Films, Commercials, and TV

Judith Searle

LIMELIGHT EDITIONS

Fourth Limelight Edition, October 2001

**Library of Congress
Cataloging-in-Publication Data**

Searle, Judith.
Getting the part: Thirty-three professional
casting directors tell you how to get work in theater,
films, commercials, and TV / Judith Searle.
—1st Limelight ed.

Previously published: New York:
Simon & Schuster. ©1991.
Includes bibliographical references and index.
ISBN: 0-87910-194-6
1. Acting—vocational guidance.
2. Casting directors—Interviews.
I. Title.

PN2055.S43   1995
792' .028' 023—dc20   95-18280
                                        CIP

for Basil

CONTENTS

Part Two

NEW YORK

Part Three

CASTING: A PERFORMER'S PERSPECTIVE

Appendices

Acknowledgments

In addition to the people mentioned in the introduction to this book, I would like to thank, first of all, the casting directors in Los Angeles and New York who agreed to let me interview them. Without them, obviously, there would be no book.

I am also greatly indebted to casting directors with whom I've talked informally over the years about the casting process, and especially those I've interviewed as moderator of several panels on casting that I produced for the Academy of Television Arts and Sciences. These conversations led me to understand what the important questions were.

I got helpful suggestions for my UCLA interviews from Fred Amsel, my theatrical agent, and from T. J. Escott of Cunningham-Escott-Dipene, my commercial agents. For my New York casting class, Michael Thomas and his associate Rozanne Gates were generous with their advice, and I also had help from agents at the CED New York office: Sara Fanning, Ken Slevin, Janey Gubow, Angela Dipene, and Sharon Beirut.

My literary agent, Claire M. Smith of Harold Ober Associates, was enthusiastic about my proposal from the beginning, and also gave me much useful advice about organizing this book.

My friend and colleague, Renni Browne, president of The Editorial Department, encouraged me at an early stage and made many valuable editorial suggestions.

Ed Walters at Simon & Schuster has been enthusiastic and helpful throughout the publishing process, and I feel lucky to have had him as my editor.

Ken Harlin and Bruno Banon made my life a lot easier by transcribing some of the New York interviews.

Finally, I would like to thank Basil Langton, whose practical knowledge of the casting process from both an actor's and a director's point of view made his comments on the manuscript especially valuable.

INTRODUCTION
TO THE SECOND EDITION

Although mine may not be a household name, I represent a kind of success story in show business simply by having earned a decent living at the acting game for most of the past twenty-eight years. Whether you're a professional actor with years of experience or a potential actor looking to develop your career, it may be instructive to look at a few numbers to get some notion of the odds we face.

The Screen Actors Guild (which represents both film and television actors) has 93,000 members. AFTRA (radio and television performers) has 78,000 (two-thirds of whom are also members of SAG). Actors Equity Association (stage actors) has 34,000.

The general public seems to think all working actors earn six-figure incomes. The truth is that in 1994 eighty percent of SAG members earned less than $6,000 from acting. During the same year, less than one percent—fewer than 930 members—earned more than $100,000. On any given day, only fifteen percent of SAG members are employed as actors.

I wish I could have read this book at the start of my own acting career. Since I had no family ties to the entertainment industry, I had to learn the hard way—pounding the pavements making rounds of agents' offices in New York, auditioning for countless roles in plays, films, television shows, and commercials, and making a lot of mistakes.

I spent the first ten years of my acting career in New York, then moved to Los Angeles for the usual reason: more work seemed to be available there. My résumé includes credits on and off Broadway, in stock and regional theaters, feature films, prime-time and daytime television, commercials, and voice-overs.

I've had the privilege of working with such actors as Anthony Hopkins, Tom Hulce, Geraldine Page, Ray Milland, Carroll O'Connor, Bruce Willis, Ben Gazzara, Robby Benson, Lesley Ann Warren, Andy Griffith, James Garner, and Debbie Allen, and I've been cast by some of the casting people I interview here.

On the West Coast I served for ten years on the Activities Committee of the Academy of Television Arts and Sciences, and had the opportunity to produce for the performers' peer group a number of panels on casting, several of which I also moderated.

Like many actors (and especially middle-aged actresses) I know, I turned to a second career in order to meet my expenses. While waiting for the phone to ring, I wrote a novel that was published, then two others that weren't. I edited and evaluated manuscripts for The Editorial Department, a small East Coast company that provides literary services to authors and publishers. Eventually I became their West Coast vice president, and among my responsibilities was teaching a workshop in The Writers' Program at UCLA Extension.

As I browsed through the thick Extension catalog, I was especially interested in the film, television, and theater courses. Nowhere among the extensive offerings was there a course on the casting process geared toward actors, and it occurred to me that my own experience, both as an actress and as a producer of panels on casting, would be a good basis for organizing such a class.

Ronnie Rubin, head of UCLA Extension's Film, Television, Video, and Theater department, liked my idea for" Conversations with Casting Directors," and I started to put together my wish list of the casting directors I wanted to participate. Some were people who had previously sat on panels I'd produced. They represented a variety of casting specialties in film, television, theater, commercials, and voice-overs. Al Onorato, a veteran casting director who had produced most of the ATAS panels with me (and had also sat on several), gave me excellent advice and agreed to be one of my interviewees.

In the spring of 1989, I made one of my regular trips to New York (like many actors nowadays, I'm bicoastal) and approached Lewis Falb, associate dean at The New School, who also liked the idea and agreed to offer an East Coast version of "Conversations with Casting Directors" in the spring of l990.

In the summer of 1990 I repeated my class at UCLA with a different group of casting directors, and eleven of those interviews appear for the first time in this second edition.

Most of the people I interviewed are members of the Casting Society of America or the Commercial Casting Directors Association. CSA currently has 303 members (including 217 in Los Angeles and 53 in New York), while CCDA (which includes only Los Angeles commercial casting directors) has 47 members. These associations aim to improve the status of casting directors and to uphold certain standards and practices within the profession. In order to join these groups, casting directors must have had a certain amount of experience, so CSA and CCDA do not, by any means, include all people now active in casting.

Once I'd completed the interviews, I had to decide in what order to present them, and my choices reflect the main differences between East and West Coast approaches to casting.

I've placed the Los Angeles interviews first, not only because I conducted the original group of them first, but also because Los Angeles— "Hollywood"—is generally acknowledged as the hub of the entertainment industry. Los Angeles is an industry town, and the local industry is film and television. Professional theater, while accorded respect, has never been the "cash crop." Commercials are viewed by most actors as simply a way of paying the rent (though, interestingly enough, many film and television casting directors see them as an important source of new talent). Within the West Coast section, I've placed the casting directors I interviewed for each series in two separate groups (so that all the interviews new to this second edition are together). I've placed them, within each group, in an order roughly corresponding to the prestige of the jobs being cast: first those in films, next those in television, those in theater, and then those in commercials.

The casting scene in New York is different in significant ways from the scene in Los Angeles, and the casting people I invited to my East Coast class reflected those differences. Theater is a major focus of actors' aspirations in the Big Apple, and many more casting directors work primarily on stage productions. In commercial casting, the recent trend in New York, even in the major agencies, has been toward increased use of independent casting directors. As one of the few remaining heads of casting at a large advertising agency explained to me, "The trend is toward independents because the agency can bill the client for an independent casting director's fee." Many New York casting people, of course, work in more than one area, or aspire to (especially those with strong track records in theater who are attempting to expand into television and films).

In the East Coast interviews, the order is significantly different. While New York is not a single-industry town, Broadway represents the epitome of theatrical success in this country, if not in the world, and most actors view a leading part on Broadway as a career pinnacle. A Broadway show is also a stepping stone for many performers to major film and television roles. So, in the New York section, I've placed first the interviews with casting directors who specialize in Broadway theater, followed by those who cast other theater, film, television, and commercials.

In preparing this second edition, I asked all casting directors whose interviews were in the first edition to update their biographical information, and I've included in the introduction to each interview the new credits they provided. There does seem to be a trend for New York casting people to move to the West Coast. Leslee Feldman, formerly Vice President, Manager of Casting at Saatchi and Saatchi Advertising, has moved to the Walt Disney Company, to become Vice President of Casting for Hollywood Pictures. Deborah Aquila, formerly an independent casting director in New York, has become Vice President of Features Casting for Paramount Pictures in Hollywood. And Alice Whitfield, who casts voices, currently spends a portion of her time on the West Coast. These instances are reflected in the increase in CSA members based in Los Angeles—forty-four more in 1994 than in 1989 (while New York has one less).

The increasing competition for casting jobs is also reflected in the dissolution of several long-term casting partnerships and the move of one veteran casting director into personal management.

An interview is only as good as its questions. I asked the casting directors how they got into casting, and encouraged them to discuss their frustrations with the casting process as it now exists. I asked about common mistakes we actors make in presenting ourselves: through our pictures and résumés, our interviews and auditions. I asked about the importance of agents and about how actors can get a casting director's attention. Most of my interviews also included questions about nontraditional casting. Some of the questions included in this book were asked by actors, agents, directors, producers, and aspiring casting directors who attended the UCLA and New School classes, and I gratefully acknowledge their contributions.

As you might expect, there are big differences in philosophies and approaches among casting directors. They come from a variety of backgrounds—most often from acting, but also directing, producing, agenting, cinematography, teaching, and secretarial work—and their personal stories of how they got into casting, in addition to being fascinating on a human level, can be instructive to anyone in the entertainment industry. I think it's also important to mention here one thing that all the casting people I interviewed have in common: a genuine liking for actors and an appreciation of the courage actors need to continually face the processes of audition, performance, and rejection. Several casting directors remarked that the profession of acting is, in a very real sense, the profession of auditioning. *Doing* the job is a lot easier than *getting* it.

In the course of conducting the interviews for this book, I've discovered—to my horror—that even my more than two decades of experience in this business offer no guarantee against making costly mistakes. I've learned a lot about auditioning and effectively presenting myself to casting people, and I believe other seasoned acting professionals will also profit from these conversations.

But the usefulness of these interviews is by no means confined to actors. Talent agents, directors, producers, managers and aspiring casting directors will also find invaluable information here. Since most people in the entertainment industry agree that casting is a crucial element—maybe *the* crucial element—in the success of a project, anyone with a stake in that success would do well to pay attention.

My hope is that this book will give actors a better chance against the long odds they face. I believe these interviews will also be fascinating to anyone curious about this complex, little-understood aspect of show business.

—Judith Searle
December 1994

PART ONE
LOS ANGELES

CASTING DIRECTOR INTERVIEWS: LOS ANGELES

MIKE FENTON, Independent Casting Director, features: *E.T.*, *Beaches, Back to the Future.*

PAM DIXON, Independent Casting Director, features: *The Moderns, Baby Boom, The Music Box.*

AL ONORATO, Independent Casting Director, features and television: *Bagdad Cafe*, "Fame," "Superior Court."

ROSS BROWN, Independent Casting Director, features and television: *The Last Picture Show*, "North and South," "The Burning Bed."

FERN CHAMPION, Independent Casting Director, features and television: "War and Remembrance," *Naked Gun, Police Academy.*

BARBARA CLAMAN, Independent Casting Director, features, television, and commercials: *Days of Heaven*, "Tour of Duty," "Santa Barbara."

STANLEY SOBLE, Casting Director, theater: Mark Taper Forum.

DANNY GOLDMAN, Independent Casting Director, commercials.

SHEILA MANNING, Independent Casting Director, commercials.

ELAINE CRAIG, Independent Casting Director, voice-overs for commercials and animation.

Mike Fenton
_____

Mike Fenton is an independent casting director based in Los Angeles. Among his feature credits are the Indiana Jones films, Back to the Future, E.T., Godfather II, Chinatown, Marathon Man, Beaches, Empire of the Sun, The Freshman, Bird on a Wire, Arachnophobia, Firebirds, *and* Total Recall. *His television credits include "Out on a Limb," "Poor Little Rich Girl," and "Billionaire Boys Club."*

How did you get into casting?

By default. I was at UCLA, majoring in motion pictures. In those days theater arts was divided into theater and motion pictures, and I think there were sixteen of us in the motion-picture division. I graduated as a cinematographer and couldn't get a job. In 1956 if you did not know or have an "in" to a union and you were a below-the-line tradesperson, you had no chance.

I went to law school for a year, hated it, then went in the service for six months because the Army was chasing me. When I got out of the Army, I was hired into the mailroom of MCA on October 5, 1958. Around the end of May in 1959, I became an agent, and I worked with Herman Citron, who was one of Lew Wasserman's right-hand men. So I had a great introduction to the business, and I was trained very well.

All the time I was an agent at MCA, and then later at Ashley Steiner, I kept getting offers from Paramount to come to work as a casting director. And a casting director is just the flip side of being an agent. The difference between a casting director and an agent is that an agent is responsible for his or her own forty or fifty clients, plus all the clients in the agency. A big agency like MCA or, today, Creative Artists represents maybe a thousand, maybe twelve hundred acting clients. The senior agents probably have about twenty-five or thirty clients on their list. It would be the same at William Morris or at ICM. And the casting director is responsible for knowing eight or ten thousand actors, maybe more.

So I went under contract with Paramount in 1963 as a casting director, and I was there until 1965. I cast Hal Wallis's movies and Jerry Lewis movies and Elvis Presley movies and a whole bunch of films that are totally forgotten in my résumé and in anybody else's history of the business. We didn't get credit in those days. This was about the time that Lynn Stalmaster was an independent; if a director wanted to use Lynn, he would say to the director, "I'm not going to do your movie unless you give me billing on the main title."

Fred Roos and I started our company in 1971, and we pulled the same shenanigans—as soon as we got a couple of good clients, such as Francis Ford Coppola and George Lucas, we said, "We're not going to do your movies unless you give us billing in the main title." They said, "What do we care about your billing? You can have whatever you want." So as soon as we made the breakthrough, everybody got on the bandwagon. It was a tremendous battle for all the casting directors at Warner Brothers and Paramount—for whatever reason, those two places never wanted us to have billing.

So Fred and I were together, and then Jane Feinberg joined us, and then Fred got the opportunity to produce *The Conversation*, and he bowed out, and we changed the name of the company to Fenton-Feinberg, and Jane and I had the company together for about fifteen years. Judy Taylor came to work with us as our secretary about two years after we started Fenton-Feinberg, and then Jane decided she wanted to retire in February of 1988. So Judy and I have had the company since then.

Since you were an agent yourself, what advice would you offer to actors about finding an agent? Or about making the most of their relationship with their agent, if they already have one?

I'd like to say that you have three bullets in your arsenal, as an actor. Your three bullets for your weapon are, first and foremost, your agent—probably the most important bullet that you have—and I'll come back to how you get one, and all that. The second is your picture and résumé, and the third is your videocassette. If you have to get along without one of those elements, you should manage without the videocassette. If you have to get along without two of them, you'd probably have to get along without an agent, because if you don't have a picture and a résumé you haven't even started yet. So what you really have to do is find somebody who will take a photograph of you—a black-and-white photograph taken outdoors, under natural light, that does not get airbrushed, that does not get touched up, that is just you. And that's true specifically for women, because if your agent submits your photograph for a part because the Breakdown Services have come out, and you are now thirty-six years old and you weigh 122 pounds—which is fine for your height—but your agent submits a photograph of you when you were seventeen, weighing 96 pounds, and you walk in, there's going to be hell to pay. You really must have a recent photograph. Men, if you have a beard and you shave it off, or if you grow a mustache, you need a picture of what you look like today.

What should be on the résumé?

The format of the résumé starts out with your name in the upper left corner, and in the upper right corner you can list your height, your eye color, and your hair color. You don't have to list your weight, because it may fluctuate. In the middle of your résumé your union affiliations should appear. You might be AF of M, or you might be AGVA—but that doesn't go on an acting résumé. If you are Actors Equity Association, if you are SAG, if you are AFTRA, if you are ACTRA—a Canadian union—that might go on your résumé. We cast films in Canada, and if you live in Los Angeles and we know of you as an actor in our area, we would be much happier to hire you and ship you to Canada if you are ACTRA than we would be to go up there and find a Canadian.

The first heading on your résumé should be "Film." And that means motion-picture film. If you've never done a motion-picture film, you can list "Film" and just put a colon there; it shows that you at least know the format, and someday you're *going* to do a motion picture, we hope—if you stay in the business long enough.

The next category is "Television," and the television category encompasses network, syndicated, or first-run syndicated—not cable in this particular area.

The next category is "Theater," and theater is all the theater work you've done, wherever you've done it. For a lot of you, your résumé will be primarily made up of theater. If you have a lot of theater, then you have to be discerning about what you list there. If you wish to list only plays you've starred in, then list plays you've starred in.

The next category is "Other Film"—a very important category. It includes university film, industrials, AFI film, and cable television. It's all of those areas where you've probably had a real chance to strut your stuff, but it's not quite mainstream the way the "Film" and "Television" categories are.

After "Other Film," you can take your choice. You might put "Commercials: List upon Request." You may never do a commercial in your entire life, but at least you know the format. And then you can list "Special Skills and Abilities," which is all the things you can do and all the things you are licensed to do—and that means licensed as a scuba diver or licensed as a skydiver or licensed as a pilot. You should be current in these areas—because if you once went skydiving seven years ago, and someone is doing a television movie about skydiving and you go up for it and it says "skydiving" on your résumé, and the casting director says, "Yes, we'll take you," and the director reads you and loves you and you get the part and they take you up and throw you out of an airplane, it could be a problem for you. So make sure you're current at whatever you say you're licensed to do. Under "Special Skills and Abilities," list any languages that you speak—and that's real *skill* in speaking a language, not a language that you studied for six months in high school twenty years ago; it means that you are fluent in the language. If you say that you play baseball, you don't have to play at the semipro level, but you sure as hell better be able to hit the ball if someone pitches it to you. So, again, in putting your résumé together use your head—because if you prevaricate on your résumé, it can come back and bite you in the bottom, and if it does it leaves teeth marks. Then, either in that heading or the next heading, is "Education." And the only reason for that is that I like to know where you went to school, what you studied, what degrees you have, who your acting teachers were, if you're studying currently, and if you're in a workshop. Those things are of interest to me because they show professionality—a lot of casting directors couldn't care less.

I mentioned before that film is a director's medium. In terms of your résumé, you can leave the producer's name off, you can leave the distributor's name off, you can leave the name of the movie off—but *put the director's name on.* In a blind submission, let's say that your agent sends your résumé in for a picture that Dick Donner is directing. Dick Donner's memory is not as long as mine—which isn't very long—but if I get a picture and a résumé that says you worked for Dick Donner eight years ago, I'd be a fool not to go to Dick Donner and say, "Look, here's Joan Smith; you used her eight years ago. She looks perfect for this role. Let's get her in." So list the director's name—very, very important.

So you list the director's name for film. Should you do it for television and theater, also?

Yes, for film, television, and theater. Television directors graduate, and go on to do film. Theater directors graduate, and go on to do AFI films or whatever. Your AFI directors go on to be motion-picture directors and heads of studios—also guys at UCLA, guys at USC, guys at Carnegie-Mellon who make film. One year they're a senior in college or a graduate student, and four years later they're running Tri-Star.

Do you have any advice about how actors should conduct themselves in interviews?

If you have an interview with anyone who is in a position to hire you and you've had a psychological trauma, don't go to the interview. If you blow the interview, you may never get in again. We have very, very short memories when we see you do something great—we might remember it for one year, three years, nine years. But if you do something awful, we'll never forget.

Works begets work. And even if you star in a motion picture that's not mainstream—if you star in a motion picture at USC or at UCLA or at AFI and the picture gets great notices—and if John Milius asks you or asks your agent, "Gee, would he do this terrific three-minute scene in my movie?" you'd better think about it, because Milius's films, whether they're accepted by the public or not, are seen by the inner circle—because Milius is a good filmmaker.

You should also think about the dollar involvement, because when you're young it doesn't make any difference what they pay you. You are looking for exposure, and money is not the end-all. If money is your end-all, you are in the wrong business.

And so it really is better to think, from the beginning, about building a career, rather than just making a living?

If you need a job to pay your rent and you come in and sit opposite the interviewer, you've got about as much chance of getting that job as I have, and I'm not going up for it. Anytime you need a job, the chances are you won't get it. I don't mean that you should come in and kick back and take off your shoes. There is a happy medium, but if you're comfortable in the interview process, if you can work yourself to that point, then the chances are that if you're in there and you're right for the part, you're going to get a fair shake.

And I will tell you this—directors don't interview six people and then turn to us and say, "Ugh, those four were just horrible; I couldn't stand them. And the one with the orange hair—yuck! But I'll take *her.*" It doesn't happen that way. It usually comes down to making a decision between two people, among three people. And that decision is based on a lot of variables, not the least of which is the hair color of the star of the film. If she's blonde and you're blonde and there are only two women in the film, guess what? The chances are that you will not get the part, and the brunette who read against you *will* get the part. Is there much difference between the readings? Probably not. Is the one so much a better actress? Probably not. Hair color, chemistry. How do you look with the lead in the film? How do you look with the male lead in the film? How do you look with the person you're playing the role with in the particular scene you're doing?

Are you aware of a big difference between the casting scene in New York and that in Los Angeles, from an actor's point of view?

One thing that happens in New York is that most actors come to an interview or a reading totally prepared. Now I'm not suggesting that if you have a reading in California for a motion picture you be off the page, but if you *were* off the page and still held onto the script, the director could do a lot more with you. So my suggestion is that if you want to be very, very comfortable in a reading with a motion-picture director, then you should have your words.

Let's talk about videocassettes. What do you like to see on an actor's cassette?

With any luck, your videocassette will have some work on it—a body of work that you are pleased with. But when you are very young, or when you are just starting out in the business, you are not going to have a test with Dustin Hoffman and a reading for a pilot at ABC and a movie-of-the-week opposite Victoria Principal. We're reasonable people; we understand that. So your first videocassette, if you're lucky, may have one thirty-second commercial on it. But it's a place to start. I work very often for a man named Steven Spielberg, and when he's in the editing room, what does he watch during the daytime? Soap operas. He loves them. While he's cutting a film, I'll probably get no fewer than two calls a week to find out who's on this soap opera, who's on that soap opera, who is the girl in the Pepsi commercial, who is the guy in the hang-gliding commercial. Steven Spielberg looks at commercials and soap operas. And so do many other directors. Commercials give you great exposure.

What should go on your videocassette? Well, one thing I can tell you *not* to do: don't spend six or seven hundred dollars and go down to the corner production house and do a soliloquy from *Hamlet* or *Hello, Out There,* because it's not professional and it looks crummy. That videocassette is your calling card, and obviously you want it to be as good as it can possibly be. If you don't have anything to put on a videocassette, then don't put anything on a videocassette.

How do you get stuff for your videocassette? Well, first, say you get a job—let's say you go up for a movie at AFI and they say, "We love you and we're going to use you, but we're not going to pay you." So you cleverly go to the director—or if you're *really* clever, you go quickly to the editor—and you say, "Hey, I'm not getting paid for the job, but I will pay you to get a composite of my scenes." And the editor says, "Don't worry, I'll take care of it." But you've got to do it *before* you shoot the scene. Go to the editor—and if you can't find out who's going to cut it, go to the director and say, "Look, I'm doing you a favor, and I'm doing it for nothing. I've got a two-and-a-half-minute scene. I want the film from that or I want a videocassette copy of it, because if I'm going to give you my time and my energy, I want to be repaid." There isn't a director or an editor on the face of the earth who will say, "No, I'm not going to do that for you." The same goes if you do "L.A. Law"—if you have a scene that matters. I *don't* mean a scene in which you open the door and someone hands you a flower and you say, "Thank you." You have to look at it realistically. Even if you're just starting, you've got to have a scene that's got something in it—something that's going to give the viewer something to study, something to look at, something that shows your ability to handle dialogue and what you look like on film at that moment.

About the format of your videotape: your videotape master should be on three-quarter-inch tape. The videotape that you send to your agent—or, if you don't have an agent, your prospective agent—should be half-inch VHS. No matter how large your body of work is, the cassette that you send to an agent or a casting service should never exceed eight minutes in length.

Now, about the order of what you put on it: I can't tell you the best order. If you have a body of work, look at it—look at it with a friend who's an editor, a friend who's a director, a friend who's a writer, a friend who's a cinematographer, a friend who's a still cameraman. You have a wife, you have a mother, you have a father, you have a husband, you have somebody. Sit down with that individual and say, "Look, here are my scenes." You write them down on a sheet of paper, and say, "Here's a scene where I laugh, here's a scene where I cry," or whatever. Figure out an order that makes sense. If you want to gussie it up, have someone make little titles for you. Use the main title from a show that you did, so that it says, " 'L.A. Law,' featuring *Joan Smith.*" At least they know who they're looking at. And if you're clever, and if the director is somebody who really matters, put " 'L.A. Law,' directed by so-and-so, featuring *Joan Smith.*" It's a director's medium. A director looking at that piece of videotape says, "Aha, this person appreciates directors." Since directors are our lifeblood, they're very important to you as an actor.

Let's talk about agents. How should an actor go about finding the right agent?

An approach to getting an agent is to go to the Academy of Motion Picture Arts and Sciences Library and get the *Academy Players Directory*—either the male or the female volume. And sit and open it to where the pictures are. Every time you see and recognize a face, write down who the agent is. You'll have a legal pad, and you'll end up with about thirty agencies, and those thirty agencies will have most of the tick marks next to them because the people you recognize are going to be working actors. And then you'll look at that list and say, "Well, CAA isn't going to sign me, and APA isn't going to sign me, and William Morris isn't going to sign me." And then you'll look down, and you'll see that there are sixteen small and medium-sized agencies left.

The way to get an agent is to talk to actors who work, submit your picture and résumé, and submit a videotape. And if you have anything at all on the videotape that sparks their interest, you might get signed.

Women, if you walk into an agent's office, and the agent is male and is sitting behind the desk, and you pull up a chair and sit down, and you're in there about four minutes and then the agent says, "Yes, I think I should sign you," you say, "Well, let me think about it. I've got to talk to my dad about it." And then get up and leave. If an agent has not seen your work and doesn't know what you can do, how can the agent possibly represent you? And if the agent doesn't know what you are capable of, that agent is not going to sell you for work, and therefore it's foolish to sign with that agent. So if you don't do a scene for an agent, or you don't show the agent your videotape, what do they have to go on? And in this city, agents *sign* actors. It's not a freelance marketplace—it's not like New York. So if you are signed with an agent here, you're stuck for nine months—unless you don't work. If you don't work you can get out.

It's hard to get an agent whom you trust, and it's hard to get an agent who is a good agent. A good agent is somebody who is able to get you the proper kind of exposure to the proper kind of people for roles that will build a career. If all an agent wants to do is send you out for day work for the rest of your life, that's probably where you are.

We use a wonderful agency in the Valley, called Feature Players, which represents day players. They represent all the faces that you see. Everybody on their roster has probably done a minimum of fifty films. And they're all just regular-looking people who've had enormous amounts of training and study, and they study all the time in workshops and they work constantly. And why do they work constantly? Because they've created a niche in the marketplace, and they're very satisfied working three days a month, four days a month, at six or eight hundred dollars a day. And they have another job—they sell real estate or cars or whatever—and they're very happy. They're actors, they get their health insurance paid for—which is no mean task today—and they're enjoying themselves. But they don't kid themselves. They know that when they're with Feature Players that's where they're going to be. And whenever we're stuck—when we get that horrible phone call at four-thirty in the afternoon from someone saying, "We just wrote this new part, and we need somebody, we need a day player who'll do it for six hundred dollars," we call Feature Players.

What are some of the problems of casting kids? How do you find a little Elliott in *E.T.*?

Let me tell you how we found little Elliott, because it's kind of a clue about the difference between Steven Spielberg and me. We were looking desperately for someone to play Elliott, and Kathy Kennedy had seen some footage on a film called *Raggedy Man*, and Henry Thomas had been in *Raggedy Man*. And Kathy said, "You all should see this guy!" So we trooped into the projection room and looked at this film, and Steven said, "He's terrific. Get him here." So he flew all morning from Texas, and with the time change he got up at four o'clock in the morning and got to MGM and had lunch. I met with him after lunch, and I gave him a scene. And for Steven's movies we don't use a scene from the movie; Steven has a scene written to test people with. So I gave Henry the scene, and he looked at it, and I ran the scene with him. I directed him in the scene, I acted in the scene with him—and nothing was happening. The scene just sat there. And I'm thinking to myself, "Well, this kid's been up all day, he's traveled all this way—but this scene is deadly." So I called Steven down, and Steven looked at the scene and said, "Yeah, you're right." And he said, "Henry, go in the video room." So Henry goes in the video room, and Steven turns to me and says, "Look, get off the page, and when the page ends, I want you to go for his throat—go for the jugular. You just stay right after him. Barrel in and say you're going to take E.T. away from him." We start the camera, and I do the scene, and the scene is going nowhere. Henry's energy is just nil. I get to the end of the page, and Henry puts the page down. I turn to him and I say, "I am taking the E.T." And he says, "What?!" I say, "I am taking the E.T. away from you. I represent the United States government. The government is bigger than you are, and we are going to experiment on the E.T." And he looks at me and says, "You can't do that. He's my friend." And he starts to cry. And Steven, standing right next to the camera says, "Henry, it's okay, you got the job. Cut."

When we did *The Bad News Bears*, it was like madness. With *Honey, I Shrunk the Kids*, it took weeks to get those kids. It's very difficult to cast children. But again, it's like casting adults. You work with somebody long enough, something comes through—or nothing comes through. It's the luck of the draw.

Pam Dixon

Pam Dixon, an independent casting director based in Los Angeles, casts films. Her credits include Forget Paris, Tank Girl, Safe Passage, Angels in the Outfield, City Slickers I *and* II, WaterDance, The Music Box, *and* Baby Boom.

How did you get into casting?

I started at CBS Television as a trainee after I graduated from college. I went to all the different departments and landed in the casting department, where I stayed. I went from a very low-level entry position as a trainee, to a secretary, to an assistant, to a casting director—all at CBS. And then in 1975 I became head of casting for ABC Television. In 1980 I left ABC and went to Paramount Pictures as a production vice president. Then I got pregnant and had one child, and I got pregnant again and then had two children. At that point I decided that I didn't want to work in a corporate situation anymore—I really wanted to work for myself. And so I went back into casting and formed my own company, which I'd never had.

What makes a good casting director?

Having good taste. The basic dividing line between casting directors is their ability to choose. And that's something you can't really teach. It's something you either have or you don't have.

Are there certain types of films that you, with your particular tastes, have a special ability to cast?

I've cast a wide range of films. I've done a lot of art films with directors like Costa-Gavras and Alan Rudolph. I've also done commercial films like *Revenge of the Nerds,* which is very different from anything I'd ever done. I also just did a film for Universal—kind of a horror film in a funny way, produced by Gale Ann Hurd, who did *Terminator* and *Alien.* I've really done everything from comedy to drama to art to very commercial films.

Could you describe the way you work on a casting project?

A typical project goes like this: You get a script. You have to break it down according to the characters, and basically you start with just the leads. Very seldom have I ever done a film where someone comes attached to it. I'm usually the person putting in the stars first. So you go through all the big names, and finally you come to some people that everybody agrees upon—the director, the producer, and the studio.

From there you go down, and, depending on where you're shooting the film, you may see actors in Los Angeles if it's convenient to take actors from Los Angeles, or if you're shooting in Los Angeles. If you're doing a film that's closer to New York, you go to New York and you see actors in New York for all the other little parts. And then you'll see people locally in whatever town you're shooting in. Sometimes when you do a film you're shooting in two or three locations. So you travel from one location to the next.

A typical day is really spent getting a list of all the actors, having someone in your office look up who the agent is, and then calling that agent to see if the actor is available on the date that you need him or her. Then often they'll come in to read. They'll come in to read for me first sometimes, and often they'll come in to read for both me and the director. So then they're given a side, which is a copy of a couple of pages taken out of the script for the particular role that the actor will be asked to read. You have actors coming in to read about every five to fifteen minutes, depending on who your director is and how fast he is.

Part of your day is spent on negotiation, because once you find the actors that you want, you have to negotiate the deal, which involves the amount of money they'll get paid and the number of days they'll work on the film. Then someone in your office has to do a cast list and type up a contract. And then the actors have to be cleared as members of SAG. Most of the day is really spent on the phone, because you're always gathering more information, and you're dealing mainly with agents who are suggesting their people, or else you're calling them to have their people in.

How much time do you usually have to cast all but the tiniest roles in a film?

The longest amount of time, really, is twelve weeks, and the average amount of time today is between eight and ten weeks.

We've been talking about film so far, but you do occasionally cast for television, such as for "The Phantom of the Opera." I'm curious to know your relationship to network casting departments when you work on a miniseries or other television project. Since you've been head of casting at a network yourself, I think this is an interesting area to explore. For example, is the relationship different with different networks?

It is different with different networks, but I've never had any problem dealing with the networks. I have found, basically because I'm only in the two-hour movies and miniseries—I'm not in the pilot area at all—that the people are quite cooperative and have really always left me alone, and have just been there to help me when I've needed them. What happens is that the vice president of talent, whether at ABC, CBS, or NBC, is basically a clearing person and works, in turn, with the head of whatever department is doing the project, whether it's the head of two-hour movies or the head of miniseries. And I've found them to be very helpful, because they're kind of a buffer between you and the department you're dealing with. So sometimes you can get something through that is quite terrific, and you wouldn't if you didn't have that person as an ally.

How far down the cast list does this requirement for network approval usually go nowadays?

In a miniseries—say, in "Phantom of the Opera"—it was basically the four leads—which included the Phantom, who was Charles Dance; and the father of the Phantom, who was Burt Lancaster; and, interestingly enough, the role of Christina, the lead, who is a totally unknown girl. While they had approval, she's not a name. And the young boy, the fourth lead, is also not a name. So it doesn't always mean you're going with names, just because they have approval. It just means that on a part like that of the young girl I often bring several people to read at the network. But we didn't even do that. We brought one person, the person we wanted, and she got approved—and that was it.

How many people did you see before you arrived at her as your choice?

Actually, I didn't see all that many people, but I did see them in many different places. I saw them in London, I saw them in L.A., and I saw them in New York. But in each place I was basically there for only one day—I saw people in the morning, had callbacks in the afternoon, and moved on.

Were you mostly dealing with submissions from agents?

Actually, a manager had sent me the picture of the girl we ended up casting. He didn't even call me, he just sent me the picture. And I knew who the manager was, and I just decided that I'd meet this person when I went to New York.

When you met her, did you see right away that this was possible? What was the process of her getting the part?

Well, we were only there for a day. So we saw people every five minutes, from ten to noon. We called back four girls. At two-thirty, this girl was going on a plane that evening to Los Angeles. That's how fast it was. And the truth is that when she came on the plane to Los Angeles, she had to come totally prepared to go to Paris for ten weeks—if she got the part.

What had she done? Did she have any credits at all?

She had done a small part on a series, and that was really it. And she had been a ballerina, trained as a dancer.

And you got her through a manager. Did she also have an agent?

Yes, she did. But it was just that this manager knew me, and he sent me the picture. If I had gone to New York and called this agent, maybe I would have seen her, also. But that came so early on that I'll never really know. Because the minute I saw the picture, I just said, "I want to meet her."

In general, is it useful for an actor starting out to have a manager as well as an agent?

It's hard to say, because managers are not really allowed to negotiate; they're not allowed to solicit employment. So it has to happen in conjunction with an agent. But sometimes what happens is that a manager can give more time today than an agent in a big agency. Because sometimes the agents are so busy, they have so many people, that a person—especially a young person—doesn't get as much attention as he or she would like to have. So sometimes it's helpful. But I don't deal with that many managers. This was a very flukey situation.

How important is it for an actor to have a powerful agent in order to get to see you?

It depends what your definition of powerful is. To see me, actually, I don't think you need to have a powerful agent, because I'm very open-minded, and I do so many projects that are for young actors that I don't really meet people just because of their agents. I tend to see a lot of people, and I don't even have to like the agent to see some of their people. I don't believe in that, either. If I'm doing a "young" project, I try to meet everyone I don't know. If I'm doing an absolute lead in a film, and a person's got to carry a film and they've never done anything, then chances are that I'm not going to see them for the lead in that film. But if they've done some theater and maybe one television thing, and I look at their picture and I think they're right, then I will meet them.

Is there any chance at all for an actor who doesn't have an agent?

Sure. I think it's harder for them, because I think they have to call you a lot; they have to be *very* persistent. There are some people that will never see that person, but every so often you'll get that one person that will give you a shot. I think those people should really contact people who cast episodic television, rather than people who do miniseries or two-hour movies, because if you're casting episodic television, your job is so hard—you can't find anyone to play those parts. No one wants to do them. And so what happens is that you're thrilled to meet anybody, because if they can do small parts and they're just starting out—even if they're older but just starting—you have somebody new to use on your shows. Most episodic casting directors are pretty good about meeting people because they need the actor as much as the actor needs them.

Let's talk about the kind of theater you might go to, trying to get to know new actors. Do you go to Equity-waiver productions, showcases?

I will go to a play that's Equity, non-Equity, Equity-waiver, whatever. I will not attend a showcase where the actors have to pay to be seen. I think that most of the time a showcase is a little unfair to actors—it's much better to be in a play, as opposed to a short scene. I don't see scenes in my office. I prefer going to see a small theater play in which a group of actors have gotten together and rented a theater for a couple of nights.

Will I go see the graduating class at Cal Arts? Sure. Will I go see the graduating class at USC or UCLA? Yes. I'll go to anything that's legitimate like that.

What about videotapes? How important are they in the casting process for you?

Sometimes they can be very helpful. They're most helpful with the director, because sometimes a director doesn't really like to see a lot of people. And that may be just because they're a little shy, and they're uncomfortable with the process. So often if you have videotape that's from a real movie or a real television show, that's better than sitting in one of those video studios and doing your own video. I don't think that helps because it never looks good. But I think it's helpful, if you've done a lot of television shows or a lot of movies—or commercials, even—to edit a video of different roles.

How long should a video be?

No longer than fifteen minutes.

What impresses you in a picture or on a résumé?

To tell you the truth, I very seldom look at a résumé, because résumés are not always true. Usually I just look at a picture. And if I think there's a quality that's right for what I'm doing at that moment, then I'll bring the person in. And sometimes they'll come in and they look totally different from this picture I have. I wish people would try to take a more realistic picture of themselves, rather than a glamorous or artsy picture. It's nice to have a natural picture, because then when you come in, the people you're meeting are really seeing the person they thought they were going to see. Some people don't photograph well, so you can have a very interesting person who doesn't have very good pictures. A still camera and a camera used for film are very different from one another. And sometimes you can look really good on film and not so good with a still.

How many submissions are you likely to get for, say, a major supporting role on a film you're casting? How many pictures will be sent to you?

I've never counted them, but we get a lot. I mean, you figure there are, what, a hundred agents, roughly?

There are about 240 franchised agents in the L.A. area.

If you figure that each agent is submitting anywhere from two to five people per role, then it adds up. So you literally have, like, bookcases.

We're talking about thousands and thousands of pictures for each role, then?

Oh yes. But the nice thing is that they don't all come in on one day. A hundred agents won't all do it on the same day.

Is there a particular kind of training that you think is useful for an actor in films?

Not really, because I think a lot of great actors have had no training. So I don't know. I think it's whatever works for that person. Some people work well with training; others don't work well with training at all.

I think what is helpful in television is some kind of course that teaches the technique of reading. And I don't consider that an acting course, really, because I think you can learn the technique of reading very well but not necessarily be a good actor, and vice versa—a good actor may never learn the technique of reading. But I think that if you're interested in doing television, the ability to learn that technique is very important.

Movies are a little different, because in movies often you'll meet somebody—and I've worked for three directors who don't even read actors at any point, which I think is great.

They'll just interview the actors?

They hardly even interview them; they really just talk to them. And from that conversation, they get a feeling about them and make a decision. Woody Allen works that way; a lot of directors work that way.

What are some of the biggest mistakes you commonly see actors make in an audition situation?

The biggest mistake actors sometimes make is stating anything negative before they've begun. And by that I mean coming in and saying, "Well, I read the script, and it's interesting, but I really don't know about . . . and I'm not sure . . ." Directors really don't want to hear it, even though they try to be nice. And what I've found is that no matter what you say thereafter to try to win back favor, the director has formed an impression, and most of the time you cannot get him to think differently. And it doesn't mean the person is not a good actor. But half of it is the acting, and half of it is the way the other person feels.

How important is it to memorize the sides, to know the scene?

I don't think it's important for the people you're doing it for at all. I think it may be important to you, depending on how you work. Even if you've memorized it, I think sometimes it's better to hold it, and not let everyone know—because no one's going to be impressed, really, that you've memorized it. And in fact most of the time we'll say to actors, "Don't memorize it." Because sometimes if it's memorized it loses something; sometimes doing it cold is better.

Let's talk a little bit about nontraditional casting. I'm not sure that this really applies a lot to feature films, because we are dealing not so much with acting as with being, in a sense, on film. But, as you know, the Screen Actors Guild has committees devoted to furthering the casting of minorities and women. In your view, is there anything a person in your position can—or should—do to have an effect in this area?

Well, I think that last year I had a really good effect on it. I did a film called *The Moderns*, and put John Lone in it. He's won four awards for that. What was interesting is that that was a part that in no way called for anything ethnic. It was written as a totally average white American. Was it our absolute first idea? No. But we started going through things, and when I threw it out the director said, "Oh, that's kind of interesting."

Often you also get a script that's written for a male, which you can change to a female. It doesn't happen with just minority groupings—I do that all the time. I did it in *An Officer and a Gentleman* with Lou Gossett's part, which was not written black. In fact, they wanted to cast it with a white person, and the studio wasn't too thrilled with the person they wanted to cast. I said—kind of as a joke, actually—"Why don't we do it black and make it Lou Gossett?" And they said, "That's kind of interesting"—and that's exactly how it happened. We never even interviewed any black actors for it. Lou Gossett came in the next day, and that was it. So you always try to think of that, because sometimes it can make a role a lot more interesting.

You were talking a minute ago about sometimes casting women in roles that were written for men, and it could work the other way, as well. I'm sure you're aware, as I am, that career patterns for women are quite different from those for men, particularly in the feature-film business. For example, Screen Actors Guild did some research a few years ago and determined that women over forty have only ten percent of all roles, while men over forty have thirty percent. Why is that? Would you talk a little about the career patterns for men and women in terms of film?

The most interesting thing, really—and I guess this has been true for a long time—is that there are very few roles for women over thirty-five. And if you had to name stars—male on the one hand and female on the other hand—you're very limited by the females. You could name fifteen, twenty men who are stars, from Tom Beringer to Paul Newman to Jon Voight. But when you get to the women—Debra Winger. And then a few up-and-coming younger girls, but they're very limited. I have a film that I'm casting right now with a male and a female lead—and the truth is, when I try to think of male stars, I could do it forever. And when I get to the female side, I'm really sitting there saying, "Isn't there somebody else? There must be somebody else I haven't thought of." And it's sad, because after eight women, that's it. Women who really have the ability to get a film made, which is something else. I don't mean someone who you can just cast, either—there are a lot of people you can cast. But when you're doing the leads and they want somebody that gets a film made, you're hard-pressed. And it's because women haven't had the opportunity.

You mean actresses we call bankable, in other words. We can raise money if we know that Debra Winger is in this movie.

Exactly. If you look at the films that have come out in the last few years, there are very few women who have done well at the box office, which is probably why there aren't a lot of scripts being written for women. And I don't really know why that is—except that, if you look at the films that have been very successful, a lot of them have been hard-action films, and women don't play, except girlfriend-type roles, in hard-action films. And, with very few exceptions, there really have not been relationship films with older women in the past few years. Most of the time they've been young—a bunch of guys with girls going to high school, or how I got into college, or whatever.

And yet a film like *Terms of Endearment*, which you had a great deal to do with when you were at Paramount, was one of the great film successes of that moment. Why are there not more like that?

The thing that's interesting about that is that it took a long time to get made. It was not a film that anyone thought would be successful, while it was being made. And after it got critical acclaim, everyone said, "Oh, yes." But it was very hard to make. There are definitely more roles written for men than for women. There's no question about that.

Al Onorato

Al Onorato, *currently a personal manager, was for many years an independent casting director. His credits include a stint at Columbia Pictures as Vice President in charge of Talent and Casting. In partnership with Jerold Franks, he was responsible for casting the series "Fame," the* *four-hour miniseries "Deadly Intentions," the syndicated series "Superior Court," and the feature film* Bagdad Cafe. *His present company is Onorato/Guillod Entertainment*

Al, how did you get into casting? How did it all begin for you?

It began on the other side of the desk. I wanted to be an actor. I found out early on, luckily for the acting profession, that I wasn't very good, and I also didn't have the necessary calling that you have to have to be an actor. I loved the industry, but I found out that I really didn't have the talent and that desire to stay for all the punishment that you have to take. I've done all those jobs that supposedly get you into the industry. I was a page at NBC in New York. I worked in the mailroom at Universal when I first came out here. And most of the people who work in that area have a lot of film background, either from UCLA or USC. And I didn't have that. So I persuaded the people at Universal to get me into a job that would utilize my performing background, and they put me in the casting department as a male secretary. At that time practically all the casting assistants were women, but they were very kind to me. I eventually worked my way around that studio into the new talent area, and then went to work at CBS for Ethel Winant. I went to MGM after that. Then I went to work at Columbia when it was still Screen Gems. Eventually we became The Burbank Studios, and then we joined hands with Warner Brothers. And then, in 1980, I split away from all that, and we started our own company.

And you've been at it for nine years, and extremely successful.

We're in the same situation that a lot of actors and producers and directors are in. You're always concerned whether, when one door closes, the next one is ever going to open—are you ever going to get another job? It's the same with us.

I'd like to talk a little about the casting director's position both now and in the past. I believe you're the treasurer of an organization called the Casting Society of America, which is the professional association of casting directors. What changes over the past ten or fifteen or even twenty years have you observed in the professional position of casting directors in the industry?

The three founders of the society were Mike Fenton, Joe Reich, and me. And prior to all this, we had tried to form a union, but the casting directors in general were very resistant to becoming part of an organized group of people who were going to dictate terms to them. So that fell apart. We waited a couple of years and then talked about this society, the Casting Society of America.

When was it actually founded?

This is our eighth year now. The idea was to try to upgrade the position of the casting director in the eyes of the industry. For a long time, people who worked at various studios were never able to get their name on the screen—acknowledging that they did the casting. So we were trying to improve our visibility in the industry and in the world. It seems as though the casting director has suddenly become an important entity in the business, in that he or she is much more the liaison between the agent and actor and the producer, writers, and directors. Very often now on movie screens you'll see front billing for a lot of casting people. It seems to be an area in which the independent casting director has emerged. We have in our organization 223 members across the country.

How many of those are in Los Angeles?

About 150—maybe a little more now. There are people in Chicago, New York, Miami, Dallas, and various other cities where filming is done. We have people who have been in the business a long time and meet the requirements. But it's now the independent who has taken over, whereas we used to have staff casting people at most of the studios. You'd go to Universal or Columbia or Paramount, and they'd have the head of the casting department, and then various other people beneath them who worked on the various shows or projects. Somewhere along the line, someone realized that the overhead the studio was carrying for the casting people or for any production people was an unnecessary liability for them. So, for the most part, when the hiatus period came along into television, they just laid everybody off. They found it was much better to hire per project and not have that overhead. So in the past ten years I've seen an enormous emergence of the independent casting director's prominence in the business. In fact, this year [1989] will be the first that a casting director will be eligible for a television Emmy. We're also going to be eligible in 1989 for a cable award. The next step, we hope, is that we would become eligible for an Academy Award.

Does the Casting Society have a code of ethics or behavior that is promulgated among the members, a code that members are required to adhere to?

Yes. At one time, casting directors were casting director-managers—who also got into the area of managing an actor or actress they found, whom they expected to be really successful. They would sign the actor on the dotted line and say, "I will now work as your manager and try to get you work elsewhere, in addition to the work that I do." We thought that would be a real conflict of interest, so we ask that anyone who is a member of the Casting Society of America be prohibited from being a manager.

Two years ago there was a big uproar between SAG and the CSA about the teaching that had suddenly been proliferating around the city—cold-reading seminars and cold-reading workshops and such, which are quite prevalent all over. It's a new area that had never existed before—I guess no one had thought of it before. Anyway, it started, and we've tried to set down terms.

What sort of terms does the Casting Society establish for its members with regard to teaching workshops?

There are those situations in which actors get together and put on an evening of scenes. They put together prepared scenes and invite casting people or members of the industry to come and see it. There had been a time when actors, in order to induce us to come, were offering money. So we said, "No, no, no. That's part of our research. That's like going to a movie or watching television."

It's part of your job, so you shouldn't be paid extra for doing it?

Exactly.

Some of the other code requirements for Casting Society members: to become a member of our organization, we like somebody to have been in line casting—that means casting a television show or a movie—for at least two years. Also, we do not have commercial casting people in the organization. It's not that we're snobs, it's just that they have an organization of their own, and the two so far have not joined together. It possibly could happen, but we have not come together yet.

I'd like to talk a little bit about the process of casting in the various areas you do. First of all, I'd like to talk about "Superior Court," which always struck me as a kind of tour de force in casting, with a syndicated show that's on five days a week in most markets, and each show having a whole new cast of characters except for the judge. And you cast this show for three years—how did you do it?

Actually, we did five shows a week the first two years, and then the last year we did six shows a week. And that was in one day—they taped all the shows in one day. As the producers become more comfortable with you, it becomes easier because they trust you more; they'll listen to you. We cast forty to fifty actors a week on that show. We did another show this past year in a similar way, called "Family Medical Center," also syndicated around the country, and they also taped six of those in a day. And we would cast approximately thirty actors a week on that show. So we used a lot of actors.

With very little repetition.

And almost no crossover. The producers wanted it to seem as though these shows were actually taking place somewhere else; they didn't want it to seem like these were actors moving from one show to another. So that you almost always had to be aware that, if someone had worked on one show, he or she couldn't work on the other show. You also had the situation in which there were a certain number of actors who didn't want to work on the show because they felt the work was too fast. You had to learn a lot of dialogue in a very short amount of time.

And most actors were paid minimum for it, weren't they?

Yes. It was a favored-nations situation, where you were paid minimum scale for the show, and there were no negotiations—that was it. I found out that what Jerry and I both had to do was keep extensive files of people. We saw somebody in a show or we saw somebody on television or we met somebody who was interesting to us—I had my "interesting" file and my "quirky" file and things like that.

How many actors would you normally bring in for each role?

We usually would bring in three or four actors per role. And then often what would happen is, the producer would say, "You know, I don't think it really works this way. Let's try it that way, and bring in some more people."

You must have gotten to know almost the entire membership of the Screen Actors Guild. Did you ever count up the number of actors you cast over three years in just this show?

Last year we cast fifteen hundred actors in the courtroom show. I've never counted up over three years—I would suspect it's three or four times that many. And in the medical show—that was only one year, so it was probably not quite as many.

In searching out the people for these shows, did you habitually go to a lot of Equity-waiver theater?

I go to a lot of Equity-waiver anyway—so that was just an extension of my job.

Is that a pretty valuable source of exposure for actors? Especially for someone starting out?

Absolutely. I think it's enormously important. In the long run, it's one of the things you have to do. In New York, one of the things actors do all the time is participate in off-Broadway shows, in Equity Library Theatre plays, and it's really no different in L.A. Again, hopefully you're going to get industry people in the audience who are going to be able to give you a job. So I think it's really important that actors and actresses avail themselves of the good showcases that are done around town in theaters, as well as making themselves available to the film schools that do good work—UCLA, AFI, USC, Loyola, Columbia College. Each of those places generally has an evening or a couple evenings when they show the major industry at large, who will come to see them, the films that they do. I know a lot of actors and actresses who have gotten agents or jobs out of those shorts, because they're not just schlock movies—they're the forerunners of the Spielbergs and those people who do big movies.

So the procedure would be to call up the film departments of those universities and say, "Who do I send my picture and résumé to, to be cast by your students?"

Definitely. And look in *Dramalogue*. A lot of the students are now advertising in there for actors to come audition for those films.

What about workshops? I don't mean the kind where casting directors are paid to come, but I know you teach a workshop that has a fine reputation. What should an actor look for in a workshop?

I think you should find out what that person has done. Try to audit one of the classes. Whenever you plunk your money down for anything, there should be something that you're going to get back from it. Try to get some background on people—see where they've been; maybe what schools they've gone to; do they go to Equity-waiver theater; do they know anything about the theater? Whoever is conducting these classes—is he or she a member of our organization? Call the CSA office and try to get some background on that person.

It's the same when you go to see a casting person or a director or a producer or a writer. It behooves you as an actor to get some background on the person you're seeing, so that you're not going into an absolutely cold situation without any knowledge of who the person is and what he or she has done. It automatically enhances your situation with that person if you can say, "I loved such-and-such a program, or such-and-such a thing that you worked on and did." Automatically, you have connected with that person, and you're not so much an outsider in the industry. It's no big secret what we all do. If you want to know about people who work in the film industry, you call the Academy of Motion Picture Arts and Sciences. If you want to know what people do in the television industry, you call the

Academy of Television Arts and Sciences. What we've done in the theater you could probably find out from the Equity office here.

Let's talk a little bit about the process of casting a film—say, *Bagdad Cafe*. How does something like that work?

What happened with *Bagdad Cafe* was that Percy Adlon, who directed it, and Eleanor Adlon, who wrote and produced it, came over from Europe, and Percy had never worked in America before. When I first read the script, it was a delight to me, because all of a sudden I was able to cast something in which it would matter to cast the textures and get people who were going to be interesting on the screen. So, after I'd read it, Percy and I met, and he admitted that he didn't know many actors in America. He knew of the movie stars, but this was not going to be a movie-star picture. He already had Marianne Sägebrecht, who was the heavy lady in the movie. And that was the one role that was precast as far as he was concerned. Beyond that, he said, "Here's my script. I need you to cast these people for me." We started casting the movie in February and finished casting it in June, and they started shooting in July.

Let's talk a minute about résumés. What should be on these? What impresses you on a résumé?

What impresses me on a résumé is background—someone who has trained for the profession, who has worked at his or her profession doing theater, studying. Acting, to me, is very much like athletics. Athletes are constantly working out, constantly trying to stretch their muscles and their abilities. And I think it's important that actors do that as well.

What kind of training do you think is particularly valuable?

One of the most important kinds of training for actors is improvisation, taking improv classes. One of the things that sometimes actors don't do as well as they might is listen. So often you have a script in front of you, and you'll give the dialogue back and forth, not really listening to what the other person is saying. In an improv class you have to listen to what the other person is saying, because you have to respond to it.

I would be remiss if I didn't say that certain theater training impresses me.

What, for example?

If someone has studied at Goodman Theatre in Chicago, if someone has studied with Sandy Meisner, if someone has studied in the Neighborhood Playhouse in New York. The major universities—Northwestern, the University of Southern California—have excellent theater departments. UCLA has a good theater department—not a great theater department, a good theater department. Cal State in Northridge is another good one, and Cal Arts is wonderful. If someone has studied at LAMDA or RADA in England, if someone has studied up in San Francisco at ACT—those are some of the places I'm going to know of. That's not to say there aren't a lot of others. There's a place in New York called the HB Studios—Herbert Berghof Studios—that still, I think, charges only ten dollars a class, which utterly mystifies me when I see what some of the other teachers around the country charge. And they've got some of the best teachers in the country there.

What advice would you offer a person who's just entering the business with a limited résumé—really few or no credits?

As much as possible, avail yourself of the work that's available to you. Try out for the Mark Taper Forum lab. They have auditions once a month there, and that's one of the best experimental theaters in the country. Go to see the theater in town, and find a place where you like the work they do. The Odyssey Theater in West Los Angeles, the Matrix Theatre on Melrose—those are just off-the-top-of-my-head examples, but they do very good work there. So take advantage of those Equity-waiver playhouses. If you can get a group of actors together and put on a showcase yourselves, that's a good way to be seen. The student films that are being done are good work, so you should avail yourself of that.

About the stuff you shouldn't do: you shouldn't become involved in things that you're not going to be able to show me. The chances of your showing me a nudie movie that you've done are nil. You're not going to show me, you're not going to show your mother—because it's not going to get you any work, for the most part; it's just going to be something that you did.

Something that you have to live down when you become successful?

Exactly. You always hear those situations: "I wish I hadn't done it. I wish I'd known better." You do know better. You're not an imbecile. You know what's right and you know what's wrong. You've got to go with your gut instincts. If this is a sleazy person you're talking to, and he or she is going to make this movie, you don't want to be part of it. It's not going to help your career—it's going to hinder your career.

That's a very good caveat.

Also, once you get in the union, do not do nonunion films. You're going to endanger yourself later on with Screen Actors Guild and with any of the other unions. It's going to be a situation in which they could cast you off, and you're not going to get back in easily. So don't endanger that situation.

However, if you're not yet in the union, and a picture comes along with a meaty role that's going to show you doing something you're going to be able to utilize—like some of the student films—you've got to consider that. But, again, make sure it's not schlock that you're going to be ashamed of later on.

So, if we sum up how a performer whose work you don't know can best get your attention, it might be: get in an Equity-waiver play and let me know about it?

Exactly. Try to find something good. There's a theater in North Hollywood that grinds these things out—loosely called Equity-waiver productions— and they're just terrible. Make sure that what you're going to do will show you in your best light. If you do something and you don't think it's the best work, don't start inviting a lot of people, because you're going to turn us off. Wait until you're doing something that you think is worthy of your talent and of you, and then put the big push on. And you do the push with postcards, with phone calls—you almost have to inundate us with the information.

What do you like to see in an actor's picture?

Something that makes me smile, that intrigues me about this person, that makes me want to meet this person. Something going on in the eyes.

It's really difficult to say exactly what that is, but when I respond to a picture, I'm drawn to that person; I want to know who he or she is. When I see it, I put the pictures aside and say to Greg, who works in my office, "This is a group of people that I want to meet."

When they come in to see you—these people whose pictures you liked—do they do a scene for you? Do they just talk with you? What happens?

The first thing they do is talk to me. What I try never to do is put somebody on the defensive right away—and I find that once you ask people to read right away, you're automatically putting them in a situation in which they have to prove something; they have to prove their worth as an actor or actress. And that's really not what I'm trying to find out. I'm trying to find out what he or she is all about; trying to get some sense about whether what I saw in the picture is really inherent in the person—or is it a lie?

I go a lot with my gut instincts on people. I can look at a résumé sometimes, and the person may not have much on the résumé but has a lot going as a person, and is going to bring to the part what he or she is all about. Some of the best movie stars ever were people who were not great actors or actresses, necessarily, but who had qualities that just transmitted across the screen. People like John Wayne and Spencer Tracy and Gary Cooper and Humphrey Bogart were always accused of being themselves all the time, but it was that self we wanted to go to see because it was an interesting self.

After you've seen the same scene ten or eleven times, it's so "middle ground" that it becomes mush. So you look for the person who's suddenly going to take a risk and sing it or something, so that it's completely different.

When you go in for an audition, don't play it safe. Playing it safe is not going to get you a part. You've got to take risks, and the risks are not always going to pay off. You're not always going to get the job, but, hopefully, it's going to show us, the buyer, that there's a creative mind and a creative soul, and that you have something interesting going on inside you—that there's an ability that we would want to tap.

So doing something off-the-wall, if you can do it with conviction, is a good idea. Even if it's wrong, at least it'll be memorable.

That's exactly right.

What about videotapes? Are they an important casting tool at a certain level?

It really has become very important. I don't have the time to sit in my office and watch scenes any longer. So I ask, when actors or actresses have tapes, that they present their best ten minutes. And don't worry if you've got a couple of commercials interspersed there. If you've done a lot of commercials and that's the crux of what your work has been, put a composite tape together of all those commercials you may have done.

But be careful, when you put a tape together, that you don't go out to one of these places that charges you a hundred dollars, and it's like Mickey and Judy in the back yard putting a movie together. Then you'll start apologizing that the sound isn't too good and the lighting isn't too good, but here's what I look like.

So professional production quality is important.

Yes. I had someone who presented me with a tape of a staged production that he was in. And, unfortunately, the person who was taping it was way in the back of the theater, and I could never see anyone's face. And obviously, in television and film, what's going on in the face is important, so that really was of no value to me.

So a bad tape may be worse than no tape at all?

Exactly. If you don't have one, don't manufacture it. Don't put something together that's going to make you look bad.

Let's talk a little bit about the pet peeves that you may have about actors and about the way they conduct themselves in auditions. Is there anything that you would say is a big no-no—something never, ever to do?

One of the requirements that the Screen Actors Guild made in its last negotiation is that a script should be available to you at least twenty-four hours prior to the time that you are going to go and read for a part. I experienced this a lot on "Superior Court," when we were reading people for parts and they couldn't come to pick up the material during the day prior to the day they were scheduled to read. We'd say, "Okay, we have a building that's open twenty-four hours a day, so we'll leave the material downstairs at the desk for you to pick up after six o'clock." We'd go back at ten o'clock the next morning, and the material would still be there. The people did not bother to take responsibility. You can make excuses, but you hinder yourself when you do stuff like that. You're not taking advantage of the things that are presented to you.

Today we had a situation in which an actor came in to read for a part. And he had just gotten off the plane, literally got off the plane and came into the office, found somebody in the office—an actress that he knew—and they talked the entire time that he was there waiting to go in for his reading. He came in and was terrible, because he had no preparation.

Other things not to do: mispronounce words. These two shows we worked on—the medical show and the courtroom show—obviously contained a lot of medical and legal terms that we don't use in everyday language. If you don't know how to pronounce a word—be it a foreign word or a legal term—find out how to pronounce it. Nothing sounds worse than someone who comes into the room and is reading through the script, and they get to the word they don't know, and all of a sudden the Champs Élysées becomes the "Chemps de l'easy." It takes just a second to ask, "How do you pronounce such-and-such a word?" And if you're in a situation where you're not comfortable with what's going on—either with the person you're reading with or how your own concentration is going—stop it. Say, "I'm sorry; I lost my place," or whatever, and "May we start again, please?" Because we, too, are human beings once in a while, we will forgive that idiosyncrasy. Don't get in your car and go home and say, "I wish I had done such-and-such." It's too late. Right then and there is when you should do all the discussing—with the casting person you're dealing with.

Ross Brown

Ross Brown is an independent casting director in partnership with Mary West (Brown-West Casting). Among feature films he has cast are The Last Picture Show *and its sequel,* Texasville; Paper Moon, Pennies from Heaven, Planet of the Apes, *and* The Windwalker. *He is also known for such television classics as "Eleanor and Franklin," "North and South," "Toughlove," "The Day After," "The Burning Bed," "The Jerico Mile," "Attica," "The Andersonville Trial," and "Silence of the Heart."*

How did you get into casting?

I've been doing it for twenty-two years. I went to work with an advertising agency called BBD&O. I happen to speak several languages, and I came out to the West Coast and met a man named Selig Seligman, who was producing a show called "Combat." There was a casting director by the name of Marvin Paige, and he said, "Ross, by any chance do you speak German?" And I said, "Uh-huh." So he said, "What we do with actors is, everything is written in English and we translate. So many actors say, 'Yes, I speak German.' Would you just see if this person speaks German?" In fact, it was Lloyd Bochner. So we spoke in German, and I said, "Yes, he speaks German." I was offered a job, and I thought, *How wonderful.* I was being paid close to a thousand dollars a week in advertising, and I left that job to answer the phone at Marvin's for fifty dollars a week. Getting paid to learn—I mean, that's amazing. I worked with Marvin for a year.

I came from a very wealthy family, so money wasn't that important to me. But I decided that it was numbers to people here and that on the fifteenth of October I had to have a two-hundred-dollar-a-week raise. That was just whimsy—this is a very whimsical business we're in. So Marvin couldn't afford me—that's why I went to 20th Century-Fox. Every fifteenth of October at Fox it was a two-hundred-dollar-a-week raise. I realized that when people couldn't afford me, I would start my own business.

When did that happen?

1970. When it happened, there was a wonderful casting director named Jane Murray, whose work I just loved. Jane had left MGM, and we had lunch one day, and I said, "How would you like to go into business?" We discussed it, and I said, "Can you support yourself for a year without taking any money?" And she said, "I think so." So I called Bob Sweeney, who was doing "The Doris Day Show." I said, "Bob, I hear you're looking for a casting director," because I had done a show for him before. And he said, "Are you available?" I said, "Yes, I've just formed a company." And he said, "Why don't you come on over to the office and we'll discuss it?" And I said, "I'll bring my partner over." So the two of us drove over there, and he said, "Fine, you got it. Where are your offices?" And I said, "Have you got an office?" And, bingo, we ended up with the most wonderful suite you ever saw. Then Jane and I dissolved our company after two wonderful years, and I went out on my own and found out how much I loved it. I've been offered so many different areas of the business, but none of them appealed to me except this one.

What makes a good casting director?

Heart, humor. I think I'll put it the way my partner Mary West did about actors: the difference between an actor and a star is one who dares. And that's what's exciting about a special casting director.

A couple of years ago we were doing a show called "The Day After." It was about the end of the world. I remember going into a meeting, and after we'd been talking for about an hour and a half, I said to Bob Papazian, who was the producer, "Bob, I have to leave and go over to the blood bank and give two pints of blood." And he said, "What are you talking about?" And I said, "I'm going to go over and give two pints of blood and get two pints of black blood." And he said, "Ross, what is this?" I said, "If the end of the world is going to come, the only people that are going to die are white people. That's all that's in your script. If I don't get some black blood in me, I'm going to die." That's how we got ten of the leading roles black. And that's often how you have to do it. You have to make people aware.

Do you feel, then, that a casting director has not only the power but also the responsibility to increase casting of minorities?

Not just a responsibility—an obligation. In the CSA minority committee, what we've been doing for the last six or seven years is going to the Writers Guild and talking to them about how, when you've got this twenty-two-year-old blonde bimbo who comes in to serve the hamburger, please don't *write* that—write a nondescript character. The minorities consist of four groups—first is the handicapped, the disabled; second is the ethnic, which includes blacks, Hispanics, Asian-Pacifics, and Native Americans; third are women over thirty-five; fourth are men and women over forty-five. Those four categories get the least work in the business. So, if somebody's done their homework, if somebody's worked at a craft for a great deal of time, then should that mean that because they hit a certain age we don't hire them? The whole point of it is to create an awareness.

Do you feel that the CSA committee has made a difference?

Darn right. I've seen it. In fact, where I've seen it more is that we're working with different organizations and groups, and it's making the minorities realize that they are valuable.

Could you describe for us the process of casting a film?

In the beginning was the Word. Obviously, you start with the script. You get a script. You read it. The first thing producers like to do is pick your brain. I'm going to a meeting tomorrow at three o'clock. I will not have a pencil or a piece of paper on me, because I'm not going into that meeting to say who I think would be right to play this or that person; I'm going into that meeting to find out if I read the same script they read. It's concept—because they may be saying, "Wouldn't this be great for Robert Redford?" and I'm thinking it would be wonderful for Herve Villechaise. So we just don't belong together.

Let's assume your concept and the director's are compatible on a film. What happens then?

Let me put it this way: most people are confused about the expression "show business." Most people think it's one word, but it's not—it's two. It's a business, folks, and if you don't take care of business, you're not going to be able to show anything. It's all negotiation. I negotiate everybody's deal.

So you try to set the leads first, then, and make deals with them?

Without a doubt. First of all, it's a blank canvas. Let's say you're going to spend anywhere from one to five million dollars for a star. So what you do is throw a color up on that canvas. Now that color had better be a cardinal—it had better be red, yellow, or blue. Because that's what you're spending money on. Whether you like this person or not, that's what people are going to pay to come into the theater for. So let's say, for instance, that's a blue up there. You happen to be a red—a wonderful red. You cannot be in this film. It has nothing to do with your work or your abilities. It's not that red is a bad color, it's just that you don't fit our picture. It visually doesn't work, because many times you contradict. If I'm paying that much money for the star, it's my responsibility to make him or her look good. A lot of actors think the reason they didn't get the role is that "they didn't like me." No. It's that they're the wrong shape, the wrong size, the wrong "color"—it's going to detract.

So you get the stars set, and they're like jewels, and you build the rest of the cast like a setting around them, based on what will best enhance the "coloration" of the star.

Most definitely. And one of the most tedious things is having actors who come in and act. Because I think one of the hardest things in the world is to see someone *act*. In other words, you should not show your seams. Once you start showing your seams, I know where you're going to go. Why pay seven bucks to know what's going to happen? The only advice I ever give an actor is, when in doubt when you're doing a reading, smile. And the reason for that is that you're reading the script and you're emoting, and we all know that you don't know what the hell you're doing—we know this bloody script inside and out. But if all of a sudden you put a smile in there, we're either going to look at you and say, "That person's stupid," or "What do they know that we don't know?"

Those people that have a little bit of make-believe in them are the people we hire. The best actor doesn't always get the role. If you're imaginative, we'll be, too.

The unfortunate part of my career is that I've spent all these years giving actors roles. In my life as a casting director, I've had maybe twelve actors *take* a role. Because you know, the hardest part of acting is not doing the job; it's *getting* the bloody thing.

For a reading, is it a good idea to memorize the scene if you can?

Don't memorize. Don't turn this bloody thing into granite. I've never—and this is God's honor—I have never seen an actor get a role when he's reading for the director without the script. It is a reading—you're judged by a reading. If you have memorized it, it is a performance. Let the director see something that he can work with and mold. He can't mold brick. That's what you come in with when you've memorized the script. *Unless*—the only time when there's a change—you've been *asked* to memorize it.

Now this will sound very cold, but it's very true. The way we work in our office is that you'd better make us look good, or else you don't come back a second time. Before you go out on any interview, you're told how to get the role. We know who's going to be there. We'll tell you what to wear—not only to make you look good, but to make us look good. I mean, it's a business. You know, people think that we're the buyers. Well, we are. But the minute we buy you, we turn right around and sell you. We do more of the selling job than your agent or your manager.

Before you walk in the door, we want you to have the bloody job. Why? Because we don't want to do this anymore. There are a hundred other things to do. So whoever's behind that door, everybody wants. Door opens, you come in. Out of a hundred percent, we take off eighty-five percent for nerves. Of the fifteen percent that's left, if you can hit a seven, you've got the role. Most people hit between three and five, and that's on callbacks.

What I hire are communicators—people who can take this script and make it come alive; who can communicate to me and to others.

You seem to see the casting director's work as more an art than a craft. Is that a fair description of your approach?

Well, it's kind of interesting, because my mother was a concert pianist. Neither my brothers nor I played the piano. And I remember my mother saying, "Ross, it's all right if you don't play the piano. What's important is that you appreciate those that do. Because we need you. We don't need a world of piano players."

Many times when we're looking at a script, we know what roles we're going to lose—and win.

Lose in what sense?

That we're not going to get the right actor for it—because it's a business, folks—if it's a television movie, if we've got to sell Noxzema, or whatever. But then we home in on the roles that we know we're going to win. So we fight. There's an old expression that is very important to our office—and has been very important to me all my life. And that is, "If you don't stand for something, you'll fall for anything." When you start taking stands in your life, you may find out you're wrong, and then you can switch. But if you're on your back, waiting to see what other people are going to do, you're just going to let it happen.

Do you put out breakdowns on all your scripts?

Every single one. In fact, we just put out a breakdown. This is very interesting, because it's a *huge* script. So what we decided to do on this recent breakdown was just put it out for the first twelve roles, because we were going to be inundated anyway. We had the descriptions of the twelve roles go out—we usually like to do it on a Wednesday. We had boxes and packages come in. And after everybody had left on Friday, Mary and I were in the office until about three in the morning. We go over every photograph. There were about thirty-five hundred that were sent for those twelve roles. And I understand shotgun—because for one particular role I had said, "I don't care if he's black, green, blue or orange—just give me somebody interesting."

Sometimes putting a breakdown out is rather strange. The last show that Mary just did, a show called "Hollywood Detective," she unfortunately put the whole breakdown out. And there were six thousand photographs to wade through! The reason we usually put it out toward the end of the week is so that we can have Friday, Saturday, and Sunday to go through the submissions. And what we culled out of all those photographs was sixty pictures—and most of them were people we didn't know. So we'll see what will happen.

Each show is totally new, and we start from scratch on every show. And that's what is exciting for us. It's important to us—if we can't have the excitement for the film, how dare we expect you to be excited about our film? It's all reflected in our work.

Now I'll read the script, I'll make my notes, and I'll say, "That role won't play. There's no way that role will play." That's what our meetings are for. "That won't work, but if we did this . . ." And that's what we do. "Why don't we cut out this role and add a role here, or . . ." Yes, we *do* go through the photographs.

What hours do you work?

I don't know. I try not to get into the office before ten. I'm many times at a breakfast meeting. Many times I put in a good twelve, fourteen hours a day. It's all according to what my schedule is that day. When I'm on location I have very little time, because I'm always looking.

When casting directors get together, you know what we talk about? It isn't, "I'm doing the new Dudley Moore film" or "I'm doing the new Nicholson film." Actually, it's, "There's a guy that I saw who was really kind of interesting." Or "What's-his-name has been doing this kind of role for so long, wouldn't it be interesting to see if we could change his whole M.O.?" That's the mark of the casting director.

Mary wanted to make a mark, and she said to me, maybe thirty-five or forty films ago, "Ross, from now on, in whatever film we do, in one of the first five leads I want a new face." So that's what we've done. It's more of a challenge for us; we have fun doing it.

I'm asked, day in and day out, if I think this guy is sexy. Well, I happen not to be gay. The only way I judge a man's sex appeal is: Do I feel competitive? True. And it doesn't matter if he's got any hair on his head or if he's fifteen years old or seventy-five years old. You *know*. I mean, would you like an eight-by-ten of Yves Montand? That's scary. The man is . . . whew!

The essence of a true man is a *gentle*man. Gentleness is the key. When people say, "Well, he's not really too butch"—give me a break! If he's gentle, it doesn't matter.

The most wonderful thing is contradiction. I mean, if all of a sudden you're playing Nellie the Nun, give her a little sensuality. You know, there's a sexual point in all of us, and that's what we buy. That's what you go to the movies and pay for—a sexuality. And most people are asexual or neutral—truly, truly.

When I look at a leading man, my first thought is, "Would I let this person lead me into battle?" Or with a lady, it's the idea—let me put it this way: I love women. It has nothing to do with makeup or anything like that. The difference to me, between a girl and a woman, is that a girl giggles and a woman laughs. You could be a woman at the age of twelve or you can be a girl at fifty. Men happen to love girls. We buy girls the baubles, we escort them, we can bed twenty of them and never know the color of their eyes. A woman requires one thing that most men are afraid to do—and that is to talk to her. Girls are used to being talked at. So it's very interesting—when we're looking at roles, we say, "This is a girl role" or "This is a woman role." And there are very few roles out there for women. You see, the thing that is so interesting about a woman is, that a woman can have a face that, as they say, "stops a clock." I mean, she could be ugly as sin, but if she has a sense of who she is, there won't be a head that won't turn for her. I happen to think one of the sexiest women is Colleen Dewhurst. But my point regarding the female of the species is that she's hardest hit. So many times you, as actors, represent humanity.

Fern Champion

*F*ern Champion *is an independent casting director whose current credits include the films* The Mask, Mortal Combat *and* Keys to Tulsa *and the TV series "*Legend.*" With her former partner Pamela Basker she cast* Pet Sematary, Troop Beverly Hills, Naked Gun, *the* Police Academy *films,* Saturday Night Fever, *and* All the President's Men. *Champion-Basker's television credits include the miniseries "*War and Remembrance*" and programming for the HBO Comedy Channel.*

How did you get into casting?

I started out in New York as an actress, and my first husband was a producer. At that point most producers didn't hire their wives as actresses, so I decided that I would help him in another area, which was casting, since I felt that I had a really good eye for actors.

Do you think a performing background is helpful in casting?

I do. Because I was on that other side of the table, I can appreciate the nerves and the sweaty palms. So I'm a little more relaxed, as opposed to jumping right in and getting someone just to read.

What was the second step in your getting into casting—after you worked for your producer-husband?

I divorced him. And casting was something that I really did enjoy. There were many, many terrific actors in New York at that time—it was ridiculous for me even to think about going up against them. And I enjoyed the other side—I liked putting together that ensemble of people, and looking at my work when it was finished. So, when my husband and I separated, it was an area that I knew I wanted to work in. And I was very fortunate at that point because Sidney Lumet, whom I'd met earlier as an actress, heard that I was going into casting. Sidney loved actors, so he could only think that as an actress-turned-casting director I had it all. He let my former partner and me cast *Network*, and that was really the beginning of my career. And then we went on to do *The Wiz*. All of a sudden there's great acceptance, when you work with such a prominent director.

What makes a good casting director?

I think it starts with what we casting people call an "eye for talent." It has a lot to do with recognizing an actor coming into a room on a cold reading—that there is magic, the stuff that makes it interesting.

How is casting in L.A. different from casting in New York? Could you talk a little about how these differences affect the actor?

In New York there are a lot of agents, but they don't necessarily handle each person individually. In other words, the actors free-lance. Most casting directors' doors in New York are open. You can almost walk into any casting office and drop off a résumé—the reason being that there is only one union. There is only Screen Actors Guild in New York. There is no Screen Extras Guild. Everyone, whether they have a walk-on or the silent bit, is an actor. They might get a smaller rate, but they are all considered actors. There are no people in New York who belong to an extras union, where it's just a job. There's a difference when you watch a film shot there, rather than here. Here it's a job for the extras. In New York they're waiting to get a line—they're hoping the director is going to pick them and say, "You know something, there's a line. Come up and do it." And they're all under the SAG ruling, so it's much easier for the director to have that freedom. Besides that, a director takes more time with his background there because, again, they're actors. There's just a different feeling. I mean, when that actor walks on the set, he's working. It's not just a paycheck. And therefore, back East, when I was doing the background casting, I was much more careful because it mattered more. Here the extra casting people have them all on computers, and it's a meat market—there's no thought process to it—whereas in the East, you really want to know the person. If there's a chance of an upgrade, you want to make sure you give them a good actor. I used to work in New York with Jimmy Woods and Brian Dennehy and Richard Masur. I mean, these were my *background* players. They were actors, and they would do these small bits, and it worked.

Would you recommend that a new actor in L.A. do extra work to gain experience?

No. No, I don't— because first of all, from what I hear, background people here are not treated well. It's a job, a computerized job. I'm not saying it's anybody's fault; it's just that awful separation between an extra and an actor, because the bottom line is that extras here are not actors.

I'd like to talk a little bit about the casting director's professional position in the industry. Have you observed changes over the past ten or twenty years? Has the Casting Society of America played a role in this?

We're still babies. CSA is a club, at this point. We really don't have a whole lot of substance, but we're trying. Casting directors have finally been nominated for an Emmy for the first time this year, and that's long overdue. There's so much expertise involved in putting together the ensemble to make the movie. The CSA is trying to get us recognized in the field, where for so many years we haven't been. We're the only people who don't have a union. I think that most directors and producers are listening to the casting people much more than they ever have.

You've observed some progress over the past ten years, then?

Yes. Absolutely, as far as credit is concerned, because in this town credit is the name of the game. We all strive for that. We all strive for that main title credit, and we've gotten that, over the years. It's been a tough haul. I mean, for the casting people, just as for the actors, it's a fight, every step of the way.

What advice would you offer to a person who was interested in becoming a casting director?

It ain't easy. It's very competitive. I mean, there are more people than I would ever have believed there could be. And there are just so many jobs. You really have to know what you're doing. You have to be so aware of actors out there—from the smallest community theater to the stand-up comedians—it's an enormous spectrum.

What's a good place to start?

Coming from the East, I love theater. It doesn't matter where you work—get involved with the small productions. Start as what production companies call a "gofer." You go for this, you go for that, you do everything you can with your eye geared toward the casting. And you watch the casting process. Maybe you assist the director, so you're in on the casting sessions. You make your own copious notes, so that on the next job you can offer suggestions. I think that's a fun place to start. I think interning is a great experience.

When I think about the process of casting a miniseries like "War and Remembrance," it seems to me that it must have been only slightly less formidable than putting together the landing plan for D-Day. Would you tell us a bit about the process as you experienced it?

"War and Remembrance" will never happen again. Looking back on it, it's a process that I'm glad I was involved with. We had thirty hours, seven hundred roles. I don't know where you start. So, in order to make our job easier, we asked the agents: "If you really want to play with us, and know what we're going through—read the book, read the scripts. And if, after that, you still want to play, we're here." So we started it that way—and we sent out the breakdowns. And then Pamela and I thought, "How are we going to read people?" There aren't enough hours in the day—it's impossible. Not only that—how are we going to have Dan Curtis sit there and listen to all of these people? So what Pamela and I devised was that we taped everybody. It was a concerted effort on our part to make it right, because we knew it was our major career break. And the actors were very eager to work with us. If you saw any part of "War and Remembrance," you know there were some lengthy dialogues. To walk in and do a cold reading was impossible. So the actors in town really appreciated being able to pick up the material. We scheduled them two days later, and they taped. They were prepared, they had an actor reading with them, and they were in wardrobe. And Dan Curtis saw a performance, rather than a reading. If he didn't like an actor, he could fast-forward. And there was no risk of the actor seeing the director's lack of interest—because after hours of casting, you really get a little bleary-eyed. And that was the way Pamela and I got through "War and Remembrance."

I'd like to get into the relationships that you and Pamela have with network casting departments. What kind of relationship did you have with ABC's casting department on "War and Remembrance"?

Well, you have to understand that it was a different situation with "War and Remembrance." Dan owned most of it—it was a Dan Curtis production. It was not a new kid on the block. Dan had done "Winds of War." So ABC was very supportive of whomever we came up with.

How is it different on other projects—say on your typical movie of the week? On an MOW, to what level will the network require approval?

Well, Pamela and I have only done one TV movie. So it's relatively new to me. The movie of the week that we did for NBC required running names past them. You wonder why, but you don't ask why. You just say, "Okay, fine," and then you do what they ask you to do. I can't answer for sure, because I don't have that mentality. However, what Pamela and I think is that they have certain shows on their network that bring certain ratings. And if it's a high-rated show—"L.A. Law," "Dear John," "Murphy Brown," the hits—they'd like to use those people because people want to see Candace and Corbin and this one and that one again and again and again. Which is why sometimes you O.D. on the same person. I *think* that's part of the mentality—otherwise I don't understand why they want some and not others. They don't say no absolutely, because that's blacklisting and they don't do that—but they strongly recommend no. The only thing that does make it difficult is when you find somebody that's great, and the person has no ratings and hasn't done diddley. But it's gotten easier over the last five years because you now have heads of casting that have gone beyond the network shows, that have seen theater and film.

Would you talk a little about the general process of casting a film? How is it different from, say, casting a movie-of-the-week or casting a "War and Remembrance?"

Well, you don't have the network. With film it's the casting person, the director, and the producer. And the decision is made in that room. It's not that step-process that makes actors crazy by the time they get to the network because they've read God-knows-how-many times. They've read for me, they've read for the director, they've read for the producer, they've read for the head of casting. Now they're going to read for that *room* at the network. However it's done—I don't care if it's in a sweet theater—it's mind-blowing. It's the most uncomfortable process.

As far as a film is concerned, I have more time, to start with. I have more time to explore the theater groups and to see that many more actors for a role—because I have eight weeks, usually, to cast.

How do the submissions work on a film? Do you put out breakdowns to the agents?

They work the same way. Everyone's aware of the breakdown process. Except there are actors who will only do film. Low-budget or not—they will do a small-budget film, as opposed to an episodic—one of the weekly TV series. There is something about film that actors enjoy. Is it seeing themselves on the big screen? I don't know. I'm not talking about "L.A. Law"—there are the exceptions. There always will be.

Do you think that an actor who does episodic—or even, say, a soap opera—is getting himself or herself into a category that's hard to get out of, in terms of being considered for a feature?

I think that's a silly actor—because it's not what category it is that's important; it's the quality of the piece. If an agent sells an actor that way—not to do television—I think that's a bad agent. Every situation is different. I don't think you can just lump it all together.

So you're not going to eliminate someone from being cast in a feature because he or she has done a soap opera, then?

Absolutely not. You can't.

Do you feel there are casting people who do that?

Are we talking about soap operas now? Daytime series? I think what happens to actors sometimes on a daytime serial is that they become—we all know the word—soapy. Because of the script and the dialogue and the way it's directed, an actor falls into that kind of false reading. And I think, after three years on a soap, they get soapy. I don't know any other word for it. If you heard it, you would know, because there are those *pauses*. It's not even a stage thing; it's just this *long* pause, because they are making *a statement.* I think daytime experience is terrific—it's the greatest learning. But don't stay on it too long, because that's just what happens. You can't help it; you get into bad habits.

It's like that with some stage actors. When I first came out here, Joel Thurm and I had this big argument. I had this actor—"Look at the stage. He won a Tony, he won a this, he won a that." And Joel very simply said, "He cannot work on television." I said, "I don't get it. What do you mean he can't work?" He said, "He's bigger than life. You can't bring him down." I said, "Prove my point. Please let me bring him in." And we brought him in. And it was true—this actor talked to the back of the audience, but he never just *talked,* which is what television and film is. And I knew Joel was just sitting there saying, "You see?"

So in your experience there are some actors who may have a major talent for the stage, but don't fit in film and television?

Yes, unless they can really take those classes to bring them down—because if you've done theater, you know it's bigger than life. And television and film is conversational; it's much smaller.

How can an actor whose work you don't know best get your attention?

I've gotten burned so many times with showcases that I'm gun-shy. Pamela and I procrastinate terribly about seeing them, but we're getting better. There are certain acting coaches in this town that I respect, and so we do go. I do like the theater—with certain organizations.

What are some of the ones you go to?

We go to the Coast, the Tiffany, the Matrix—the smaller, better houses. And they have good productions—not these dated things that you've seen thousands of times before.

Do you ever hold general auditions?

I don't know what generals achieve. I mean, we can talk, but I don't know if you can act. I'd much rather bring you in on a part, with your picture submitted for a role, than sit and talk.

To what degree do you have to trust an agent to bring in someone you don't know, who's represented by them, for a role you're casting?

It's trust over the years. Just like every other situation, you go back to the well, and if it keeps feeding you and the water's good, you'll keep going back. And then you go back, and it's dry—and about the third time, you don't go back to that well, because the trust is gone. If someone gives me a list of six actors that are great for a role, I'll know that this is not the agent for me. This is not the agent for most actors.

How can an actor find the right agent?

I don't really know how to answer that. It starts with a personality—you have to click there. Take a look at their client list—ask who else they have who is like you. You hope they'll be honest, and you hope you'll know the names if you're looking at the list. If not, take a look at their pictures in the Academy Players Directory, and if there are too many like you, then this is not the agent for you, because they're not going to be able to give you the attention you deserve.

Choosing an agent is like choosing a mate—you really have to be careful. I'm not saying that once you're committed you're in for life; there are papers that can marry you and divorce you. So don't feel that because you've gone with an agent, that's it for the rest of your life. Make the best of it—go through every avenue to make it better. Then, if it's still not working, you've got to think about moving on.

What about managers, as opposed to agents? When does an actor need a manager?

I think you need a manager only when your career has reached a plateau where you don't want to be doing the same role anymore, and you want to branch out and be considered in other areas. And the agent sometimes will only sell you in one kind of role, because they know you do it well. A manager has more time than an agent. Usually a manager has only a handful of people, so they read a script very carefully with only you in mind. And if it's something that you've done to death, sometimes the manager will say, "Let's not do this one again. But there is a role—and you've never done comedy—it's not the first lead, and it's not the second lead. And therefore the onus won't be on your shoulders to carry the film. But there is a moment that you have in one scene. Do it." An agent will not necessarily always pick up on that, reading the script—because they have the people that can do that comedy, and that's the way they're going to sell it because that's their job. A manager nurtures a lot more than an agent.

So if we're talking about building a career, a manager might be very helpful, as opposed to just obtaining the next job?

Absolutely. Sometimes at a certain point in life, you don't need the agent any more, because the scripts are coming to you. And that's where the manager is deciding yea or nay, for just you.

Is there any point in an actor having a manager at an early stage of a career?

I don't see why. I don't understand why you would have a manager at that point, unless a well-established manager sees you in a show and is very excited about what you did and wants to plan your career. But understand, this is not some Joe off the streets—this is a person with a track record who knows how to make a star. *Then* you consider a manager.

Are there any absolute no-no's for actors in an audition situation— common mistakes you see actors make that you wish you could advise them against?

Yes. If you read once, and a casting director says, "Thank you very much— that's fine," don't ask, "What did I do wrong?" You might say, "Do you want to see it another way?" That's okay. But keep the word "wrong" out of your vocabulary. We get really uncomfortable if you say that word to us, and we start saying, "No, you didn't do anything wrong. It was really fine."

Don't challenge us. Trust us; we know what we're doing—or most of us do. And if we're ready to dismiss you, don't come walking back into the room. *Unless* you feel you did it *so* badly that you know if you can do it one more time that you can do a whole different reading. Then I'll accept it. But you'd better show me something that is entirely different and much better.

The other point is, if you're in the middle of a reading and it's really bad—it ain't going anywhere, and your energy is just off—stop. Don't finish it. Say, "I'm sorry. I'd like to do it again." But don't make me sit there for four pages and watch you drown. If you know it's bad, stop yourself. Don't keep going, hoping it's going to get better. Once you're off, you're off. And understand that—you never really catch the ball again unless you start fresh. I don't care what you do—if you jump up and down, if you go in a corner and scream, whatever method you're using—but start it over. Don't go through the whole thing, then say, "I really wasn't happy with the way I read that. Can I do it again?" That's really annoying.

Other no-no's? "I'm not really right for this part, but I can do that other part really well." I brought you in for this part—stay with it. I'll know if you can do the other part. That's my job.

Let's talk for a minute about pictures and résumés. What impresses you on a résumé or in a picture enough to make you want to meet an actor you don't know?

There are certain photographers that do a shot that only fills half the eight-by-ten page. It's beautifully set in, very natural, very striking. You really stop and look at this kind of picture.

Whatever you do, get a straight-on shot. Don't start with cutesy pictures—a profile, airbrushed. Don't. It's awful. I'm sure we all say the same thing to you, but invariably a lot of the actors do it anyway. It's so touched-up that it's not you.

I also don't recommend wearing white—white fades in. I know that most of the casting people out here like studio lighting. I like natural lighting. Pamela and I like a natural shot, a picture that looks like you.

On a résumé, what kind of background impresses you?

I look at the East Coast theater credits, the better summer-stock credits, the off-Broadway credits.

I like to see that you have studied with different teachers for different things. I know it's a lot of money to get involved in so many classes, but it's necessary. You have to pick the ones who are best at what they do. We see the coaches and the classes so many times on a résumé, we begin to know who the better ones are in this town. I think smaller classes are better for certain things. Larger classes are better if you're doing scenes—you get a better audience.

Are there any particular teachers you could mention who you think are good?

I think Candy Hearst is terrific, and I think Vincent Chase is terrific. Vincent is wonderful for private coaching—he rips apart a script, tears you down, picks you up. He's a rough coach, but he's wonderful. He's got great classes—Pamela and I have sat in on a lot of them. I think Tracy Roberts has really good classes. And of course the Strasberg Institute is wonderful. You really have to go in and audit a class to see if you can understand it. But Vincent and Tracy and Candy are people who teach the way I read.

Let's talk a little about the area of nontraditional casting. The Screen Actors Guild has committees devoted to furthering the casting of minorities and women. In your view, is there anything a person in your position can—or should—do to have an effect in this area?

Well, we're doing it, and unfortunately, even with Breakdown, we have to remind the agents. When they read a script—it's so elementary—and they see a doctor, a lot of agents still just submit the he's. They see a nurse, and a lot of them just submit the she's. They forget that a doctor can be a woman. She can also be a minority—she can be Eurasian, she can be black, she can be Hispanic. We're trying to educate the agents about that. We're trying to educate ourselves about that. We're trying to say to the producer, "Can it be a woman? Why not?" Sometimes we don't even ask—we just bring the people in. I know Pamela and I do that. You have to take the gamble. It's not an easy process, because there are a lot of people who are just dead set in their ways. But we're trying.

What are your major frustrations with the casting process? Is there something you would like to see changed or done away with completely?

I don't think the process will ever change as far as readings are concerned—cold readings. The Screen Actors Guild has tried to make sure that scripts are available to actors so that they're more familiar with them, that material is available, so you're not walking in ice-cold. But I think a class for reading is so key—because you have to read for us; that's just the way it is.

So cold-reading classes are useful, you think?

I am absolutely for them. When you're outside in the waiting room, looking at other people, you're going to get nervous. And I think you need that cold-reading class to deal with it. In addition, if that outer office makes you nuts, walk out into the hall. Tell the receptionist you're in the hall, ask how much time there is until your reading, but get out of there. Walk out; take a breath. Pick up the material early. Come in the day before and read the script. Do anything that's going to alleviate that pain and that horror of sitting and looking at everybody else up for the same role. You don't have a choice. That's how we have to play the game. And that frustrates me.

Casting people who have not earned their time in this town—that frustrates me. New people that think they can cast that aren't ready. But the CSA is trying to do something about that. And I think the stronger we get, the less riffraff we'll have casting.

How can an actor break out of being known for a certain type of role in which he or she gets cast again and again?

You almost have to get yourself involved with a theater production in town, where you are showcasing a character that you've never done before. I don't know how else you're going to do it—unless the agent has got such a tight relationship with the casting person that the casting person trusts the agent.

Would you talk a little about how you get your casting projects? Do they all come to you, or do you have to go out and pursue them?

At this point, we're given every comedy script around, from *Cheech and Chong* to *Police Academy* to *Naked Gun*. We do know comedy. But I still have to fight for the drama. It's not unlike the problem that an actor has with being typecast.

Barbara Claman

Barbara Claman *is an independent casting director who casts features, television, and commercials. Among films she has cast are* Days of Heaven, Lost in America, Modern Romance *and* Defending Your Life. *Her TV credits include the miniseries "Burden of Proof" and "Guts and Glory: The Rise and Fall of Oliver North" and the series "Wolf," "Tour of Duty," "Equal Justice," "Silk Stalkings," "Renegade," and "Santa Barbara" (which she cast for four years).*

How did you get into casting?

Well, I'm out of New York, and I came to L.A. ten years ago. I started out as a production assistant for David Susskind and Eli Landau, and I was doing the Play of the Week, and I was enjoying myself. But then I got married, and my husband didn't think it was a wonderful thing for me to come home at nine o'clock in the morning, after a night of editing. So I thought, *Why don't I get a nine-to-five job in show business? Maybe casting.* And here I am.

What was your first step in getting into casting?

My first casting job was mainly in commercials, because I had gone from production assistant on *The Three Sisters,* the Lee Strasberg Studio's production, and we were doing it at the Videotape Center in Manhattan. They were just getting into commercials in 1966, and I got a job there as a casting director for free-lance advertising agencies that didn't have their own casting departments. And it just grew like Topsy.

What do you think makes a good casting director—what kind of background or training?

Thorough knowledge of theater. Going to a lot of theater. A lot of people call themselves casting directors, but they have no idea of theater; they have not seen any shows in New York. I was a Broadway baby. You grow up in New York City, and going to theater and then being in show business and seeing theater every other night, you grow up believing in what is the best. And I think a casting director really has to know the territory—they have to know actors. It just isn't good enough to see them on a television show and say, "I know that actor"—because usually what happens in television is that you get stereotyped. An actor looks a certain way, he gets one kind of job. It's very, very hard to see a person do one kind of job and see them do it over and over again, and know what else they have to bring. And on the stage you get to see actors doing all kinds of things. I first saw Jeff Goldblum coming out here and playing psychological crazy killers because he had those funny eyes; I saw him do *El Grande de Coca Cola* in New York and knew from the beginning that the man was a comedian. I also feel that going out to regional theater is a must for somebody who's casting.

From an actor's point of view, how would you characterize the difference between New York and L.A.?

Well, I think the difference is training, basically. I think there are a lot of bad acting teachers here that take advantage of actors. I think there's a lot of bad everything here, and an actor is really at the mercy of advertisements. Actors don't really get a chance to be trained as well here as in New York.

What, in your view, constitutes good training? What, if you see it on a résumé, makes you think an actor is well trained?

I'm impressed if they've gone to Yale, to Juilliard, to Northwestern, to Chicago. If they've done theater in Chicago, off-Broadway or off-off-

Broadway, I'm likely to be impressed. I don't want to name anyone except the best people—we all know Stella Adler; we all know Herbert Berghof, and Lee Strasberg when he was alive.

Good actors, to me, are those that stay on the stage, that go back to the stage, that hone their craft. And certainly people like Dustin Hoffman keep doing that—and that's important.

Dustin Hoffman is a good example of someone who's a fine stage actor and also a superb film actor. There is a kind of mythology that says that some people who are great stage actors find it impossible to bring themselves down for film. Do you find that's true?

No, that's not true. A good actor is a good actor in any medium. I think it probably takes a stage actor a movie or two to get that under his belt, although the movie is much easier than a television show.

I think the whole thing is experience—and what makes a good stage actor good is the time he puts into it. He didn't get good the first day he got out on that stage. He got good over a period of time doing stage—the experience of doing regional theater, the experience of doing good theater and working with good theater. Now that stage actor is going to learn the same thing in relation to screen acting, but it takes time. And if the director has to get it in the first shot for a half-hour TV show, I understand their problems about casting a stage actor. Bill Hurt can do *Eyewitness* or *Body Heat* as his first movie and be brilliant, because he had three months to do it. But a television show has only a week.

I'd like to ask you about the process of casting "Santa Barbara." Would you say that the types or age ranges of actors used in a soap are different from the types or age ranges used in a typical television movie or feature?

Absolutely not. Kathleen Turner was on a soap. Major actors and actresses in this business have been on soaps. And the reason is that they could get the job. It's very simple. I could not get the better actors to come and audition for "Santa Barbara," because they didn't want to do daytime. Now in New York, when an actor is just doing commercials and doesn't have a job, he does daytime. Everybody in New York needs to work, so they take a soap opera. Tom Berenger did a soap. But nobody of that ilk stayed with a soap opera for more than three or four years. And I'm not saying I didn't get good actors for "Santa Barbara," but I'd have to get the new ones. I got an actor who was either on his way down—you know, maybe some kind of a problem of one sort or another, and was in the mood to do a soap because he needed some self-esteem—or was from New York and on his way up.

But what happens in a soap opera is that most everybody who's been on for fifteen years or whatever gets very flattened out, and I think they lose all sense of proportion, of what acting is all about. Unless they're doing other things, like somebody such as Robin Strasser, who certainly worked in the soap opera business long enough. She comes in, and I'm always surprised. It's like the exception to the rule; her readings are wonderful, and she's still there. And then I realize that she spends most of her summers doing the-ater. So I think it's a big danger to stay with a soap for any longer than three years—but those three years are a terrific way to learn how to be a very fast read, fast on your feet. I mean, there it is; you are on tape. It is the closest thing to being on stage, in terms of discipline.

What is the process you go through in casting a major soap role, a continuing role on a soap?

Well, first, you want them pretty—and anybody who says otherwise is crazy. Soap opera is about fantasy. And in the fantasy world people are rich, or they're the "poor family." I mean, people who sit and watch television all day don't want really, really unattractive people to watch. So the opening gun is that if you are getting a person for a contract role, they need looks.

Pretty in what sense? Are we talking about P & G?

It all depends what the role is. If the role is the bitch, then it's pretty in the *Cosmopolitan* magazine sense. It really depends—if she's the housewife who's the victim, then it's going to be a Procter & Gamble type. But the bitch is going to look like a bitch, and is going to have a lot of hair. And the new guy in town, hopefully, has a lot of muscles and is very handsome. And it's always a problem, because very often they are not very good actors. So you may notice on soaps that they come and go very quickly. You hire them. Thirteen weeks later, you don't see them. People at home don't understand that their thirteen weeks were up, but that's the way it goes. And that's the way they get hired and fired. But, again, you have a better chance of getting better people in New York than here, because that's where they're starting out.

If you're casting a continuing role on a soap, how many people would you normally see for it? How does the process work?

A lot. I mean, I have seen 150 for a role that is hard to cast. And one of the reasons it's hard to cast is that agents in this town do not want their people to do soaps. You don't get enough money on soaps—they don't get enough of a commission. You know, on a soap, big money is fifteen hundred dollars a show—I'm talking about coming in. Two thousand is very high.

I'm not saying that those people who are on soaps for three years, four years, five years aren't making a lot more money than that. But a quarter of a million for a year's work on a soap is very big money, and agents don't consider that very big money. I mean, they're thinking millions for their people. So soaps are not where major agents put their up-and-coming people.

Let's say you've seen 150 people in this process. Out of that number, how many would you do a tape test of?

Five.

So what do you do? Put it out on breakdowns?

Put it out on breakdowns, I'll tell you that that's the one area where the smaller agents really get a break; it's where actors get a break if they come into town and they've had a lot of work in New York or Chicago and they really can't get a major agent. Soap opera casting people see *everybody*. They don't miss a soul. And if they do, it's out in *Dramalogue* or in *Variety*.

On a soap like "Santa Barbara," would you cast strictly from West Coast people, or would you put it out in New York as well and get submissions from there?

They don't go to New York unless they can't get it here. They don't go to Chicago or Dallas or whatever, unless they can't find it here. So most of the time you find it here. And then—let's face it—the networks all have people working for them in New York who can put people on tape. And at the last minute if you're really stuck—there's a part you can't cast here—then the casting director for NBC or CBS or whatever network your show is on will put some people on tape for that role.

Speaking of the networks, what is your relationship to network casting departments when you work on a miniseries or other television projects?

You're working with CBS or NBC or ABC or even the Turner network, and there are certain characters that they have say-so over—it's their decision. If they don't like the person, then the person has to come and read for them, or you have to show them tape, or you have to do something. But they must have the network approval.

To what extent do you sense TVQ or some such measure of a performer's popularity is a factor with the networks?

Of course it's a factor with the networks.

Its existence has been denied here by a number of people. That's why I was curious to get your opinion.

I mean, it stands to reason that CBS has CBS people who they owe shows to. You make a deal—you do "Simon and Simon" for seven years—you don't think that those people don't have a deal with the network to do a show, two shows, or something?

What we call a "network commitment"?

It's a network commitment, and every network has network commitments.

When you're casting episodic, like "Tour of Duty," are you able to get in new people for each episode without having to get network approval?

Oh, nobody gets approved on "Tour of Duty," except by the director. Once you have episodic, they don't care.

How is casting a feature film different than these areas we've talked about—soaps and other television?

It's completely different, because in a feature film the director is the man. You go to the director, although I must say that now it's getting a little different because when it comes to the leads, the studios want to put Patrick Swayze in everything—right, wrong, or whatever. It used to be much more that the director was the boss. Now the studios are the bosses. If it's an independent film and they've got their own financing, that's the best way to get just wonderful actors in the film. And there the director is in charge.

Is that your favorite kind of project to work on—an independent film with a director you feel compatible with?

Yes, but even in that, these days they always have to have *a name,* in order to finance the films. It's getting more and more like that.

Are there certain agents that you habitually call when you're in a spot, and can rely on?

You betcha.

About how many of them are there—agents you pretty regularly are in touch with and whose clients you will see if they recommend someone strongly?

Well, that depends, too. Because there are agents that bring you day players. I would say there are ten of those. They're not the same as the people who bring you the guest stars. Of the guest-star variety, there are about twenty-five. And of the featured-player variety, there are about ten.

What's the best way for an actor whose work you don't know to get your attention?

Probably with a very good picture. Not a tape, because I don't have time to see all the tapes that are sent to me, unsolicited. So, for me, a picture and an impressive résumé. You know, besides all the pictures that come in on all the various jobs that we do, I get about sixty pictures a day from strangers. And what impresses me, again, is a New York background, a lot of stage, impressive training credits, and regional theater. I will see every picture and résumé that comes into my office, and a picture that intrigues me is somebody I will want to see on a general.

What happens on that general interview? Do they just come in and meet you and talk to you?

No, they do either a scene for me or they do a monologue.

What sort of guidelines do you give them for the scene or the monologue? Length? Type of material?

Well, in monologues, I ask for a comedy monologue and a dramatic monologue. It shouldn't be longer than two or three minutes—most monologues aren't. It's the same kind of thing that you would do on an audition for a Broadway show. Because I also teach a cold-reading class, I have a great many scenes, and I can look at an actor and decide which, in my bag of tricks, is a scene that he should read.

So you give him something to read and have someone from your office read with him?

No, I read with him.

What about pictures? What in a picture will attract you and make you want to meet the person?

A real picture—nothing that's been airbrushed. I hate glamour pictures. I hate full-body photos. I like a picture that is real, that I can recognize. The person's eyes should be alive. I should be able to really see some personality in that face and not just some kind of a plastic photo. So many actresses come in, and their photo is about their clothes and about their hair—not about the person. I want to see a face—an eight-by-ten head shot is just that. It should be a person's head. I want to see what the eyes look like. I want to be able to look at that and recognize a person when they come into my office.

Since you cast commercials as well as all these other things, are the composites of any use to actors?

Oh, absolutely. Since so many commercials are M.O.S.—"mit out sound"—the look is the most important thing. And what I always tell people to do who are going after a composite picture, is to spend two weeks just looking at the commercials. Turn off the shows—just look at the commercials. And what you will see within two weeks' time is everybody that does commercials. What do they look like? And they really are quite specific. That is to say, the man who is a "nice daddy" has those crew-necked sweaters and he's got the picture with his tennis racket, and another picture carrying bundles, and a third picture with his kid on his shoulder. Don't give me a picture of yourself in a leather jacket and an earring. It is quite specific what they're looking for in commercials—the regular daddy, the beer-drinking guy, the football-player type. I think you should look at yourself in the mirror for two weeks straight and look at commercials for two weeks straight, and make absolute decisions about the kinds of characters that you really are, and go for it.

Knowing yourself is very, very important—knowing what kind of a product you can sell. And knowing your age range is very important. Don't try to fool anybody. Don't airbrush your pictures. And about the age range— "I'm eighteen to thirty-five"—nobody's eighteen to thirty-five.

How much of an age range should one claim to have?

Well, it's eighteen to twenty-four, twenty-five to thirty, thirty to thirty-five. I'm not saying that a woman of forty-five can't look thirty-eight, but don't give me the age range that goes that far. I think, once again, it takes looking in the mirror and really knowing.

Do you attend workshops, showcases, Equity-waiver theater? Is this a way an actor might get your attention?

All of the above. I find the little scenes are ofttimes not very good, so I'm very careful about the showcases that I do attend. But I go to a lot of Equity-waiver theater, as much as I can. I like good theater. I really get very grumpy when I see bad theater, so I try to keep it to the South Coast, the Matrix, the Zephyr, the Odyssey—to good stuff.

And if an actor is in something and wants you to see it, what's the best way? Send you a flyer? Send you a note?

Yes—send me a flyer and pester me until I'm too embarrassed not to go.

Let's talk for a minute about auditions. Are there any absolute no-no's for an actor at an audition?

Never touch the casting director. *Never* touch the casting director. That can be fatal to an actor's performance. I never really experienced that because if I was with an actor and I'd find him leaning over me or doing something like that, I'd stop the scene and start again. But what happened on "Santa Barbara"—and I never really expected it and it just kept happening until I said very clearly, "You will do the callback exactly the way you did it with me." Actors would come in, they would do a wonderful scene with me, and then they would read for the producers because I'd called them back. And then they suddenly wanted to *act out* the entire scene. And whenever that would happen, and the directions would say, "he grabs her and kisses her" or whatever, they'd be grabbing me. I'm moving backward, and the producers now stop looking at the actor and are only looking at me, to see what I'm going to do next—whether I'm going to punch him out or whatever. So that is the end of the actor's performance. Part of the problem is that I read well with actors, because I believe you should. I believe that if an actor is going to give you anything, you've got to give them something back. Otherwise they could be reading to a stone wall. So I like to act it, and I like to read with an actor. But that doesn't mean that the next step is to really reenact the scene with me.

And I hate when an actor comes in for an audition loaded with props. They come in, and it's "I'll put the apple here. Would you move your telephone?" It's definitely not necessary.

What about dressing for the part? How important is that?

Only to the extent that you are like something. In other words, if you are playing the part of a floozy, you're not going to come dressed in a tailored suit. I mean, that just doesn't make any sense. So yes, I think you should dress the type, but you don't have to go all out.

What about callbacks? Assuming you're on a callback for a commercial, should you wear the same thing you wore to the first audition?

Yes, unless you're told otherwise. I mean, you're usually told what to wear: "She's a housewife, something simple." I think that most of the casting directors tell you whether you dress sophisticatedly or not.

How useful is it to memorize whatever it is you're auditioning for—commercial or otherwise?

I think it's essential, but I think you should always have the paper in your hand, and I'll tell you why. You can go up in your lines once you have the job, but you cannot go up in your lines in an audition—that's fatal. But, on the other hand, and especially if you are reading for the producers, you want to have all of the emotional thing going for you, so that they know you can do a part. And let's face it—the directors and producers of episodic shows really want the actor's audition to be the final performance, because they don't have time. Again, they're shooting five days, they're shooting seven days; they don't have time to tell an actor how to do the job. So very often people say, "Don't give it all away in the audition." When you're talking television, give it all away. Because they want it. They want to know, *I'm solid with that person. I don't have to worry. Now all I have to worry about is getting the job in on time. So* memorizing is very important, but hold that paper.

So if you can get material the night before, the day before, it's a good idea to do that?

Oh, it's essential. And it's essential, if it's a large part, to get more than the sides. The sides may only show you one side to the person's character. So if you are up for a large part—a guest star or a major role—you've got to get the whole script.

What are your major frustrations with the casting process as it now exists?

It's a very barbaric custom, because so much of the auditioning process is based not only on whether the actor reads well, but on the choices he makes. Now an actor goes home, he doesn't have a director in front of him; he makes a choice, and he reads it that way. That's why I like to arm them with as much as possible—like the script, all the sides, everything.

Then he meets the director, who sits there and says, "Thank you very much." The guy leaves the room, and the director says, "Boy, he made him so hostile." And I say, "Boy, why didn't you tell him?" But they don't. They usually do not say a word. "Thank you very much." And anybody who made a wrong choice gets hung by his wrong choice.

I find that a lot of good actors lose jobs because they either audition badly or don't know how to make the right choices. Don't get yourself in such a mode that you can't pull back and do it a different way.

Stanley Soble

S *tanley Soble is casting director for the Mark Taper Forum, the Ahmanson, and the Ahmanson at the Doolittle in Los Angeles. His Broadway credits include* Angels in America, Kentucky Cycle, *and* Jelly's Last Jam.

How did you get into casting?

I'd been an actor and a director, working six months out of the year and working in offices the rest of the year. A friend of mine asked if I wanted to be an agent. I said yes, and I became a commercial agent. I was working in a relatively prestigious agency, and my boss said that they were looking for a casting director for "Search for Tomorrow," a soap opera that is no longer on the air, and I went over and interviewed and got the job.

This was in New York?

This was in New York. I'd never cast anything before; I'd never worked in a casting office. But I was aggressive enough to get the job, and I learned from that point on how to cast.

How did you get from casting a soap opera to casting theater?

I think it's very important in this business that you maintain friendships, because you never know where the person that's sitting next to you is going to wind up. I had a friend that was casting for the New York Shakespeare Festival—which is the theater that Joseph Papp produces—and she was leaving, and she called me at the soap opera and said, "Would you like to interview for this job?" and I said, "Sure." They offered it to me and I took it, and that's how I started casting for the theater.

How long did you stay at the Shakespeare Festival?

I was at the Shakespeare Festival for four years, and then I opened my own business in New York where I did television. In New York it's very different doing television. They come to New York to find actors in the theater. So sometimes, when they cast a show out here, they'll go to New York to look for certain roles that they can't find in L.A. I cast a series in New York that ran only for a year, I cast the Broadway show *Big River*, I cast a couple of other Broadway shows, I did all the students in the movie *Lean on Me*. And then I got a call from Gordon Davidson, who's artistic director of the Mark Taper, and he said, "Would you be interested in doing this?" The idea of moving all the way across the country without knowing the actors in California was a little frightening, but I thought, *I'm going to do it.* And I did.

So you've been here in L.A. how long now?

Since October 1988. And it's fascinating, having lived and worked in New York for twenty-seven years, to suddenly find yourself out here. The strange thing is that most people from New York are coming out here now, too.

How do you see the difference between the casting scene in New York and the one here, from the actor's point of view?

In New York there are still actors who are interested in the work, and I think most people out here are most interested in the career. I think there are very few people in what we call our industry—show business—who do it because they're interested in doing the work. It's much more a career-oriented market out here than it is in New York. New York doesn't have television the way we do out here—it's there, but it's not accessible. The commercial market is moving out here. Most of the industry and most of the business is out here. Most people that want to work in the theater stay in New York, because that's where the theater is—although that's having difficulty, too.

Is the theater in L.A. really a kind of second-class citizen?

Try third-class. When an actor's résumé says, "Movies, Television, Theater," in that order, the writing's on the wall. It's a luxury. What you get is people saying, "I'd like to do a play. Can I have an out? Can I leave for a movie? Can I leave for a television show?" Whereas, nobody has ever uttered these words on a film set: "I want to leave for a play." I don't think those words will ever be said in Los Angeles—or even in New York. I think that we're all victims of a socioeconomic thing that affects everybody in this industry.

So even professional Equity theater here, such as the Mark Taper, is seen to a degree as a showcase for film and television?

Yes, it is. When I cast a play here I start out the way any casting director starts out—I make a list of actors that I know, and the list has nothing to do with East Coast or West Coast; it's just every actor I know that I feel is right for a role. I turn the list over to my assistant, and we try to find out whether the actor is here or available or is interested in doing a play, and the first thing we have to find is the agent, because most agents don't want to commit their actors to a play unless it's a new talent they feel will somehow get the kind of showcase they wouldn't get anyplace else. The most frightening thing for the agent is to learn that if the actor commits to my theater they can only get out with six weeks notice. That is, if a project comes up, they have to let us know six weeks in advance that they're going to drop out. There is, however, one other way—they can buy their way out of the contract. In other words, they have to pay for X amount of weeks that they do not fulfill their contract. So that's a possibility, too. But I have to fight with agents all the time, because they realize that if they give over this talent, the talent is going to be lost to them for X amount of weeks, and they're not going to be sending them out on calls. And that's how agents make their living.

What bothers me is established actors not coming back to the theater—people who already have millions and millions of dollars, who could come back and give a period of time, not necessarily to my theater, but to any theater.

The way a lawyer or a doctor does *pro bono* work?

I think so, yes. Because it's not about making money. I think theater is one of the few places left where it is essentially about the work. This is not to denigrate the other media, but I don't think one gets the same sort of feeling one gets from doing a play—where you're working for, let's say, two and a half hours on performing and doing an arc and creating a character in front of an audience.

What makes a good casting director? Is a performing background helpful?

I think it is. For me it's helpful because I know the anxiety an actor goes through when he comes in to perform an audition. I want people to know that there's someone on their side when they come into the room. I spent so many years as a performer that I understand the isolation an actor goes through the minute he walks through that door, and I don't know whether every casting director really understands that.

What's the best way for a performer whose work you don't know to get your attention?

We have two Mondays every month where we do one day of open calls for non-Equity actors, and one day for Equity actors. The nonunion people are on a first-come-first-served basis. We put a list up, and we see three hours' worth of people. The Equity actors can call our office—I believe it's the first Monday in the month—and give their names and sign up, make an appointment. What we ask them to do is two contrasting pieces—it doesn't have to be classical and contemporary, it can be anything—just to show the differences in their talent.

They can do monologues or bring in a scene partner?

Monologues. They can bring in a scene partner, too; I don't mind that. I've always believed that monologues are a very synthetic situation. The best you can tell from that is whether a person has a quality. Sometimes they choose the wrong material—sometimes you can see through that, sometimes you can't.

You're in a room. You have to make it as if it's a performance. You have to walk from the doorway to the center of that room, turn it on, do it, and walk out of the room within four minutes. And that's very difficult; that's a technique in itself.

It's just a total of four minutes of material, then?

It's four minutes of material, right. And the reason for that is that I'm the only casting director at the Mark Taper Forum. I cast no less than seven projects, all going at one time. For me to take even two hours out of my day to see actors is really difficult because everything gets backlogged. But the feeling of the theater—and I applaud it—is that we have to be an open shop for people to get in.

Do you go to performances at other theaters?

I find the theater in Los Angeles very discouraging. The problem is that a lot of it is just not very good. But I try to go to at least three or four things a week. If there's one person in the whole evening, that's all I care about—if I find somebody I can use, somebody that I think is talented.

What are qualities of a stage actor that you look for in the Equity-waiver shows or the general auditions—a stage actor as opposed to a film or television actor?

Technique.

And what does technique mean to you?

Someone who knows how to handle himself or herself on the stage. I always go back to the first time I ever saw Meryl Streep, and she no more than came on the stage—it was at Lincoln Center, a play called *Trelawney of the Wells*. She had an entrance stage right, where she came center stage and then immediately walked downstage right, and I can still see it. And I didn't know who the hell she was—but I just knew that there was something incredible.

The one thing that drives me crazy in auditions more than anything is that so many people come and do an audition as if they're auditioning for a television show or a film, where the voice is *this* big. The thing I hear from most theater directors is, "Does this person have the ability to project in a house?" And that's something that really bugs me.

I don't know how to answer your question except to say that, because I've been involved in this business now for a very long time, nine times out of ten I'll know almost right away—someone comes into the room and you're just pulled to them.

Magic?

Yes, it is magic. Something that just shines. And the thing that I've learned over the years—Laurence Olivier said once that knowing who you are is the hardest struggle of all. You have to look at yourself in the the-ater, I think, as a product in an industry, and you have to know how to market that product, how to use that product to its best advantage, how to dress it the best way it can be dressed, how to use it vocally the best it can be used. Most people do not realize that when they look in the mirror in the morning—honestly look in the mirror—that's what the peo-ple sitting across the desk see. It comes down to the knowledge of your physical self.

It's very important that when you come into an audition you're as sure as you possibly can be about what it is you're auditioning for and what it is that you're going to show this person. That's very important.

So an audition should make a strong statement, even if it's a wrong statement?

It has to make an impression.

What kind of training should an actor have, to be able to do this?

It's hard, it's really hard. Because I think that's one of the things that's sorely lacking in the business today—really good teachers. I think if some-one is serious about being a theater actor, a conservatory program is still a very good place to learn. And that's a four-year program where you're taught everything—you're taught fencing and dancing and speech and how to talk and how to walk and how to do a character and how to research a character and how to talk to a director and how to do it all on your own, because sometimes you really have to. And then what has to happen is that you have to come out of that school and forget everything that you learned, so that it becomes subconscious. Because a lot of times actors come out of that environment and you can tell the paint is still on them.

But the thing that happens is that a year or two down the road when they're suddenly confronted by a director who doesn't know what he's doing, it's the most glorious thing in the world because suddenly they know that they can always turn to themselves.

Let's talk a bit about agents, particularly since you know this situation from the other side. If you were an actor looking for an agent, what qualities would you look for?

I think that's very difficult to say, because the actor is hungry. I use myself as an example—it didn't matter to me who the agent was; I just wanted an agent. That's the only thing I thought about. And New York is much more accessible than California—that's another thing.

How do you mean, more accessible?

If you wanted to be in a Broadway show, this is how you do that: at seven-thirty—which is half-hour—you go to the stage manager of the theater, and you gulp a lot and you're scared to death because you're afraid the stage manager'll say, "What the hell do you want? Get out of here." But you just say, "I'm interested in replacing in this play," and you give them a picture and résumé. My picture went from the stage manager to a casting director named Shirley Rich, and that's how I started out in this business.

It's hard. I would say that if you have to talk to somebody, you shouldn't feel intimidated by them. For example, I say to an actor, "Why did you come on this audition unprepared?" "Well, my agent only told me this, and I didn't know what to do." I say, "Well, why didn't you call your agent back?" "I didn't want to bother him." I say, "Yes, but you don't have the knowledge of what's going on here. It isn't bothering if you want to get true information." "Yes, but you don't understand, it's the first audition I've had in a month, and I'm afraid that if I call . . ." Well, that's a bad relationship to begin with.

Finding an agent is the same thing as finding a therapist—you have to make sure that you connect with this person. It's really important, because this is the person that will, in some way, run your life for a certain period of time and help you make decisions that could be right or wrong for you. So you have to feel that you really trust this person. Don't forget, you've also got a whole covey of people on the other side saying, "Is that what your agent said? Your agent's a louse." Usually that's somebody who's unemployed and hasn't worked for about three years.

Do you have favorite agents you habitually call if you can't think of any actor who's right for a particular part?

I'm just learning who I can trust, and I have an open-door policy. So the agents call and say, "You've got to see this person," and I say, "Fine, I'll see him." And we schedule a prescreen. A lot of times we put cast breakdowns in *Dramalogue* in addition to sending them to agents through Breakdown Services, so that people that are not represented by agents can send their pictures and résumés in, too.

Assume you've got the pile of résumés and you're casting some roles. What are you going to look for? Let's say the picture looks right for a part. You turn it over—what are you going to look for on the résumé?

A lot of times out here, because there's not a lot of stage credit, I look to see how much television work they've done, how much movie work. I look to see if they've played a role in a film I might recognize. I still look at the training. I look to see how much theater they've done, what roles they've played. And a lot of times I just look at the picture and I think, *This person interests me.* And I bring them in. I do a lot of prescreens.

How does that work?

Before the director will see people, I'll see actors that I think are right for the roles or actors that I don't know. And then, having heard them read from the play, I'll bring them in to meet the director.

So it's like a callback when they meet the director?

Yes, it is. But basically it's the first time, because it's the first time with the director. And sometimes I'll suggest something for them to do that I think is appropriate for what the director's looking for. I try to give as many pointers as I possibly can.

On the question of general auditions, when an actor brings in a monologue, are there certain monologues that you are utterly sick of hearing and would rather never hear again in your life?

I don't think I ever want to hear *The Woolgatherer* again as long as I live. It amazes me that with thousands of years of drama, people ultimately opt for the short circuit, which is to buy those little books that have all the scenes in them. What they don't realize is that they're not the only person buying that book. Lots of people buy it.

I think the best thing to do is try to find something that you don't have to explain. In other words, I don't think you should come into a room and say, "This is a scene where the Trojan horses have just come down the hill and this woman's husband has just been killed."

If you can find a scene that says it all in one minute and shows your quality, then you're really ahead of it. The shorter the better, because all a monologue audition will show is your quality.

The other bit of advice I'd give you is, if in an audition situation a casting director or a director or a producer strikes up a conversation, let them lead the conversation. Don't, because you feel, *Oh my God, it's a chance to talk,* spend five minutes telling a story. Answer the question, and don't be abrupt, but don't say anything that isn't necessary to the conversation, and don't ask any question that isn't necessary to the audition. I mean, it's very important to ask, "Can I use you?" Which means, can you relate to the person who's sitting there—because a lot of people are very uncomfortable with that. I'm not. So that gives you somebody to look at. A lot of times you might not want to do that because people will yawn at you and scratch and look down at the paper. But there are some people who are very good about letting you use them. If you have questions about the room—like can you use a chair, or do they mind if you use the side of the room—then questions like that are very important to your audition. Never go into a situation without asking a question of importance, but make sure it's a question that is essential to the audition.

Are there other no-no's for auditions? Are there terrible mistakes that actors habitually make?

If it's a theater audition, it's very important that you give yourself what I call aesthetic distance between you and the person you're auditioning for. Don't stand right on top of the people. Don't try to do a theater audition the same way you'd do a film audition. Because most film and television auditions are really sitting in a room and reading with someone across the table from you.

Try very hard to dress for what it is that you're auditioning for. I mean, don't come in dressed as Lady Macbeth, obviously, but it's very important that you dress reasonably well for what you're auditioning for. And don't spend a lot of time talking unnecessarily. Get right to your work—that's the most important thing.

The other thing is, I think a lot of people are disturbed when actors come in and say, "Do you mind if I have two minutes to prepare for this?" Don't do that. Come in prepared to do it. You've got time in the waiting room. If you've got to do that, go to the restroom. If it's a matter of someone giving you a script to read right away, don't sit down in the area where everybody else is sitting. Get up, take the script, go down the hall, go out in front of the building, go anywhere. But don't wait with all those other actors, because their vibrations are going to bleed over onto you.

I've had actors do things in auditions, where they'll be hostile or angry but they're not really hostile or angry, and the director or producer will say, "I don't want to work with that person; he has problems." People are looking at two things in auditions. They're not only looking at your talent, they're looking to see whether or not you're going to make problems.

How do you feel about nontraditional casting—about casting mixtures of blacks and whites in Ibsen, say?

I'm for it. I really wish that more of my directors were for it. I have a tough time convincing them, but I'm absolutely for it. I think that with the theater in the state that it's in, it behooves us to take the most talented people to play the roles that they should play. And it's interesting that people talk about it all the time in theater, but in film it's never talked about.

What are your major frustrations with the casting process as it now exists?

Time. Time is a major frustration. I'm also frustrated by the people that make a really good living in film and television but won't come back to the theater. I don't mean people that haven't done theater—I mean actors that I know and have known for years.

If you could change something about the casting process, what would it be?

I'd have everybody that ever makes a movie—and I don't mean just stars—I mean that if you make a movie, it would say in your contract that you have to do a play.

Can an actor today survive just doing theater?

Yes and no. It depends on which city you're doing theater in. If you were a member of the company of, let's say, the Guthrie Theater, which is in Minneapolis, Minnesota, the Guthrie pays its actors a thousand a week—that's its top salary. I think you can live on a thousand a week. But that's a theater that employs an actor year-round. There aren't many theaters that do that. There are actors in New York that live on doing only their work. The way they do it is—and this is the "no" part of the answer—they can't survive just doing theater in New York. Because they want to stay in New York, they will take work that a lot of actors here probably wouldn't take. For instance, it can be a stigma out here for an actor to do episodic television. In New York you can get almost anyone to do episodic television—from someone who's playing a lead in a Broadway show to someone who's just come to New York—because there's no better way to make money in New York than to do television or commercials.

So the answer is *yes*, if you're in a repertory company where you're hired all year 'round; *no* if you just want to go from job to job—it's impossible. And it's *really* impossible in Los Angeles.

Danny Goldman

Danny Goldman is an independent casting director in Los Angeles who specializes in commercials. About forty percent of his casting involves children, and he also does some voice-over casting.

How did you get into casting?

Well, I'd been a professional actor for a million years. And then somehow I started directing plays at La Mama, and then I directed a lot of plays at different theaters like the Odyssey Theatre, the Company Theatre, and other Equity-waiver theaters. A friend of mine who was a screenwriter had written an educational film about cults, and he asked me if I would cast the film. And I said, "Why don't you just hire a professional casting person?" And he said, "It's not a matter of money, it's just that I always love the way you cast your plays. So I would really like you to cast this film." So I asked a friend of mine who was working in commercial casting, a neighbor of mine, and she said, "Well, it's an educational film, so you can call the commercial casting agents"—which I did. And we did this job, and one of the first actors that walked in was Michael J. Fox.

And did you cast him?

I don't remember, but he was one of the first actors I remember auditioning. That was in 1980. I started working for my friend, because she would get busy and I lived two doors away. She'd say, "Could you come over and make calls to a couple of agents for me?" And before I knew it I was working for another casting director, and she was really gracious and terrific in that she was going away for a month and she said, "Just answer my phones. You know more about this than I do. Just take the calls." And a local ad agency was doing a campaign, and I cast it for them, and they insisted that I cast all their projects for a while—which got me into meeting a lot of directors and a lot of producers and a lot of other people that I never would have met. And before I knew it, this little business that I thought I'd do one or two days a week turned into a full-time job.

Do you think being a performer has been particularly useful to you as a background?

Indeed it has, because I think I have a certain perspective on the talent, and when people come to our office we try to be as pleasant as we possibly can. We try to give them their best shot. I also have the ability to direct the people on-camera, to actually see what they may be doing, in terms of the acting, that can be improved.

We speak the language of the actor. A lot of people don't—a lot of the directors in commercials, unfortunately, are directors of cinematography. And talking to an actor, to them, is the most terrifying experience they have to go through. They'd rather die than talk to an actor. Yet they're given these huge projects to direct, and they have to talk to the actors. A lot of what we do is dialogue and comedy spots, and we're hired for that. And what I feel we're doing is showing the director how to direct the spot, because in about sixty percent of the cases they really cannot improve the spot with the actor. They'll just put pressure on the actor, make the actor more and more uptight, give the actor less and less confidence in himself or herself, and get a worse performance. This is what we're up against.

Do you feel a casting director has a responsibility to bring in minorities, to bring in nontraditional people for roles?

Of course we do, and we try to do a certain amount of that. A lot of it comes from lack of thought on the agency's part. And I'll say, "You have four reporters. Shouldn't one of them be black? Shouldn't one of them be oriental?"

Shouldn't one of them be a woman?

Very often I'll say that: "Why can't this be a woman? Can I bring in a couple of women, and let's try it and see what happens? Can we change your mind?" And often we do.

Let's talk a little bit about the odds in terms of commercial casting. How many actors do you see for the average commercial?

I don't want to tell you. You don't want to know. I mean if anybody gets work, I think it's a miracle of God.

I do, too. But let's know what magnitude of miracle it is.

Well, it depends. There are certain casting directors that do those fifty-people spots like Michelob. And the directors they work with do quick cuts of this couple, that couple, five people, seven people getting out of a convertible, two people going into a theater, eleven people in a nightclub. We don't do those. With the directors we work for, we usually get two people, four people—for us, ten is a lot to cast in a spot. So I have the luxury of seeing a lot of people—and I do, for a lot of reasons. I see a lot because I want to see at least twenty percent new people, that I don't know.

The other thing is that, even though this spot may not have Judith Searle's name on it, I don't want Judith to get rusty by not going out and auditioning. You know what I'm saying? Because when your number does come up, if you haven't been on an audition in two years, you're going to be so freaked out that you're not going to get your best shot. But if you go out on a regular basis and you handle the rejection, then when the one comes up that you're perfect for, you're ready, you're primed, you're cooking.

I had a case of this the other day. The guy was so perfect for it. And I was in the room, directing, which I don't, unfortunately, get enough chance to do. And he's sitting worrying, "Should I do glasses? Should I do a bow tie?" I said, "No, no, no, no, no. You have to own this material. You have to be this character. I don't know whether you should wear glasses or not. These are your choices. You know, you have to feel: What is this man? Who is this man? Deliver who this man is, and they will buy it." Because they don't know what they want until they see it—and once they see it, then *that's* what they want.

So for that spot, for example, did you see five hundred people? One hundred people?

For that spot—it was a campaign—we saw one day's work, which was seventy people, for one part.

How many would you typically call back out of that number?

I don't have any control over the callback. Except a little bit lately—I've been very naughty.

Tell us about that.

What happens is that we send the commercial tape out—we send it to the ad agency and also to the director. The ad agency looks at it, picks the people they want on callback; the director picks the people he wants on callback. These guys can get distracted in a minute. A guy calls up the director while he's watching the tape and says, "You lost the location." Well, for the next five guys on the tape, they could be Marlon Brando, Laurence Olivier, Robert Duvall—he wouldn't notice them, because all he's thinking is, *I lost my location. What am I going to do?*—while at the ad agency they could have gotten the bad news that the legal department won't allow them to make this comparison between Scope and something else. So while they're viewing the tape, they get the call: "We're going to have to rewrite this." The next five guys or women go by; they don't even pay attention to them.

So sometimes I'll look at the tape—I keep a safety dupe—and I'll think, *Gee, so-and-so gave an awfully good performance and is terribly right for it.* And I'll put that person on the callback. Sometimes these very officious producers will say, "Well, I didn't see Joe Whip's name on anybody's list." I say, "You didn't? God, I must have made a mistake. Oh, I'm sorry. Well, Joe's here. What are we going to do? I can't just send him home. Why don't we just let him audition? Please, if you'd just give me the courtesy—I feel terrible. He lives all the way out in Saugus." A lot of times people have booked the spot.

Let's talk a little bit about how people can get your attention if you don't know them.

Since I'm a prisoner in my office anyway, I don't mind if people come in and drop off a picture. And what I'm doing with agents whose talent I may not be that familiar with is, I will call them and I will say on a given day, "Tomorrow we're not terribly busy. Between the hours of twelve and two you can send anybody by." Now I'm not going to sit and interview you for hours. But I am going to look at your picture, try to get it into the mental computer, try to see where you fit in, try to find out who you are—a little something about you. I have been making some nice discoveries—so I am willing to do that. And, you know, I'm always open to an agent's saying, "I really would like you to see . . ."

We have a lot of studios, and a lot of different casting directors also rent from us. Very often an actor will come to the door, and say, "I want to go in on the so-and-so spot that you're casting." Depending on what my mood is, sometimes I'll say, "Go in." And I'll put the guy on tape. Sometimes they look at me, and I think, *They really want to go in on the spot, and the agent might have had a reason. Maybe they had a conflict.* You know that in our business you can't advertise two competing products during the life of the commercial.

Let's talk a little bit about conflicts. We haven't actually talked about that.

Let's say Joe books a national McDonald's, and I have a Skipper's Restaurant in Seattle, and I think Joe would be perfect. They want a guy with a beard, they want a guy who looks artistic, and he's just perfect for it. I call up his agent, and say, "Does Joe have a fast-food on the air?" They say, "Yes, he has a national McDonald's." What they're paying the actors residuals for is holding them exclusive to that product category for the run of the commercial. All commercials are done in twenty-one-month cycles. So, while he's got that national McDonald's, he cannot do another fast-food commercial, and he's out of the market for that period of time. So we call that "conflicts." We always ask the agent, "Does he have a conflict? Does she have a conflict?" Meaning, is she on another ad that's competing with this product?

And what can happen if the actor does two spots in the same category?

They can sue the actor for the cost of the commercial. Not the agent. And agents have screwed up and sent us people who got callbacks, who went to the callback. But actors also have to be aware of what they have on the air and what's running—and what the conflicts might be.

Let's talk a little bit about pictures and résumés and composites. What kind of thing do you like to see?

I'm a composite man—for a lot of reasons. If I know who the person is, all I need is the name on a piece of paper—Judith Searle. I don't even need to see a picture, because I know Judith, I know what she looks like. But if we don't know who you are, I think a composite really helps.

For example, we do a lot of beauty work. Some women look great head-on. Others don't look great head-on, but at three-quarters are beautiful. A lot of the people who do beauty and fashion are former still photographers, and they can see the angles. And they can see how they can light someone to her best advantage. They can also see where the weak angles are.

In terms of background about the actor, do you also like to see what is on most commercial composites—which is sort of a little bio, a paragraph about the person? Or do you prefer a résumé?

I like a résumé. Everybody these days is liking résumés. I like to see the background and training. I can tell an awful lot about an actor by the résumé.

So the person should provide you with a composite, with a résumé clipped to it?

Yes, if I don't know them. If I know the actor, I certainly don't need to read the résumé.

What impresses you on a résumé?

Not only acting credits. Special things, like "Worked as a missionary in Guatemala, 1962 to 1965." That I like. You know why? I'll never forget that. The tenth production I see of *Summer and Smoke* done I don't know where doesn't interest me quite as much as some of the things you might have done outside of the business—or even within the business. Anything unusual or different: "Studied in Japan for two years." "Modeled in Uruguay." I find that interesting. "Was a VISTA volunteer." "Worked in the Peace Corps."

Is there any particular kind of training that impresses you?

Well, I look at the names of the teachers, and some teachers are more impressive than others, let's face it. Every now and then I can spot the product of a certain teacher.

Are there some teachers that have had consistently good results that you can see?

Yes. Roy London is one of them. I'm talking about theatrical now. There are an awful lot of good people in Milton Katselas's classes. Joan Darling is a wonderful teacher. There are a lot of very good teachers in town.

What about commercial workshops? How useful are they?

Well, they're useful and they're not so useful. One of the not-useful things about a lot of commercial workshops is that they teach a lot of phoney acting. This is my pet peeve right now. I was once in bed with the flu, and I made a study of what commercial acting was like on television now. It was something like fifty-seven to four, the four being the old holding-up-the-soap-winking-at-the-product, and all this cutesy stuff that they haven't been doing since the 1960s. And there are still teachers in town teaching that crap. Now I don't know whether they're hyping you up so that you can get your energy up, because, yes, commercial acting is a little bit different in that it's compressed. But it's still truthful. I sit with clients all the time, and they say, "I don't believe a thing that's coming out of her mouth." I say, "Right. It's fake. You're absolutely right. On to the next—fast-forward." They don't know anything about the actor's process, they don't know anything about what we do, they don't understand that much about it, to be perfectly honest with you. But the one thing I do consistently hear is, "I really believe him. I really believe her." And that's really what it's about. And yet we only have thirty seconds, or however many seconds, and yes, you have to compress it. But all those acting beats have to be there. They just have to happen a little bit faster, that's all.

What are the biggest mistakes you see actors make?

Sometimes actors don't listen to what we say. We'll let you do the first rehearsal yourself because basically we're interested in your instincts. Sometimes I see the actor's purest instincts on the rehearsal, and I think, *This is really great. She's using every instinct she's got.* Other times I see that what she's doing is acting her *plans.* Out in the lobby she had this plan that wouldn't it be awfully cute if she giggled on this line. And, boy, you can read that on the videotape—you see it coming. She's anticipating the moment that she planned it, she does it, and you see it. So, yes, you have an agenda, you have pretty much what you think you want to do when you go in the room. But then you have to be open: the room is going to be different, the area is going to be different, we may tell you something completely contradictory to what you thought we were going to ask you to do. And sometimes, when we're hip enough and smart enough and together enough and good enough, we'll come out and explain it to you so that you can actually prepare it in the lobby. But a lot of times we don't want you to prepare it, because we're looking for that little spark of genius that the individual actor is going to bring to the part.

How useful is it to memorize the copy on a commercial?

Not all that useful. Sometimes I've done it with children when it's very difficult copy. Sometimes we'll give it in advance. But I can tell immediately if the concentration is on the memory. The eye just kind of goes upward, as though it's written up there, or they're trying to re-see how it was on the page. So we always have a cue card there. But sometimes we'll give the scripts out in advance because it's complicated or tricky. And sometimes we'll say to the agents, "If the actors want to come, and they're in the neighborhood and they want to pick up the script . . ." But basically, on the first audition, they're not expecting you to memorize it.

I know on a cue card, for example, if you're dealing with dialogue and a scene with somebody, it can be very helpful to be able to look at the other person.

Yes, it can be very helpful. There are people that teach a cue card technique in which, as I'm talking to you, I'm also looking around the room trying to gather my thoughts. So they use the cue card as the place to go to gather your thoughts. You pick up the line, and then you come back to camera and say the line. Like you're thinking for a second. You pick up the line off the cue card and come back.

Let's talk a little about the question of dressing for the part. How important is it in commercials?

You dress indicative of the part. You dress suggestive of the part. For example, a lot of times we cast policemen or postmen or whatever. All it is is a uniform work shirt. And jeans would be fine. Or a uniform work shirt and work pants for men. For women, when there's a waitress thing, a little skirt might be better than slacks. A blouse that speaks a little bit of waitress, without actually . . . There was a girl, who's pretty well known as an actress now, who used to come in full waitress drag. Some casting directors look down on that. I don't—I mean, if you feel that's your best shot, do your best shot.

What about slates? How important is the actor's personality when he introduces himself, says his name to the camera before the audition?

It's fairly important. It's important that the slate be nice and simple. Do not slate your agent—and I don't know where they teach it, but all over town they slate their agents. Why would you want to slate your agent? It's *your* name that's important, not who represents you.

I like it simple, and I want to get a sense of the person behind it. And I wouldn't pitch myself, like in music, more than a half step above how happy I feel on that particular day. You know what I'm saying? Sometimes people come in and go, "Hiiii!!"

Yards and yards of teeth.

Yes, for no reason. I mean, you know they don't mean it; you know they're not feeling it. Some directors are so cruel—they just fast-forward from the slate. Right after that, you're dead meat. They don't look at the performance. So you could have given the greatest performance of your life on the tape, but if they hated your slate you're gone.

Let's talk a little bit about types. Is there such a thing as a general "commercial" type?

There was at one time a commercial type, and it was called the standard Procter & Gamble. Procter & Gamble liked blondes. It used to be that moms and dads in their thirties were probably the most common thing in casting commercials. Now America is aging. The bulk of the population is moving upward in age. All of a sudden, advertisers are becoming aware that the people with the largest amount of disposable income are men and women over fifty. So now you're going to see commercials for people over forty—what they call "nonspecific over-forty." I'm casting the same moms and dads I was casting eight years ago for thirty-six. So these people are forty-four. Of course they're keeping themselves nice and trim and fit and whatnot. But I'm casting a lot of them.

Let's talk a little bit about the question of casting children. What are some problems you tend to run into?

The parents. The parents try to rehearse the children in the most canned, automatic response, so that they have no life as actors. A lot of boys have been doing this since age two and four—by ten and eleven they'd rather be at the Little League game. The parents know this is the only way they're ever going to be able to afford to get their kids through college, so they keep them working to the last possible commercial. Some of these kids do twenty or twenty-five commercials a year—they make hundreds of thousands of dollars, which are put in trust, and, you know, they're set. Everybody wants their kids to do commercials, because nobody can afford college anymore.

Do parents try to get training for their kids?

Yes. Open *Backstage*—there's a lot of training available for kids. And the jury is out on whether this training really improves them. What might help them is to understand the business and to understand the process of auditioning a little bit better. I'm inclined to like a child that's studying, because that means to me that they're trying. But some kids are so natural they don't need it, and the training will only mess them up.

Sheila Manning

Sheila Manning is an independent casting director who specializes in commercials.

How did you get into casting?

I was recently divorced. I had a neighbor who was an agent, whose wife was one of my best friends, and we were trying to decide whether I should become an extra or deliver pizzas. Extras were making thirty dollars a day then—and this was not to be sneezed at. We went dancing one night and his wife said, "Dance with him—he's a rotten dancer—let me dance with your date," and I did and he hired me. I worked for him for about eight months, and a casting director that I had dealt with all day on the telephone offered me half of her business to come in with her, so I did. I stayed there for about three months, and we were both interested in the same director—not as a client—and I ended up with him and she ended up with the business.

How long have you had your own business here?

Twenty-five years.

What would you say are the most important qualities for a casting director to have?

Most casting people are one-time performers. I wanted to act until I was about nineteen, and then I thought, *Ugh, why would anybody want to do this?* I guess an objectivity is the most important thing, an ability to step outside and give a really objective assessment of somebody.

Is there any particular quality you think the area of commercials calls for—say, more than television or theater casting?

Speed. Not necessarily accuracy, but definitely speed. Commercials are a great business for people like me who have a very low threshold of boredom. Where a feature will take six weeks if you're lucky—that's a short length of time to cast a feature these days—you have three days to cast a commercial. You prep one day, you cast the next day, you do callbacks the following day, and they shoot it the day after that. You have to do it right the first time.

How many actors do you see for the average commercial?

It depends on the director. We will see anywhere from fifteen to three hundred people for a part. But those fifteen to three hundred will be culled from a stack of about two thousand eight-by-tens. And that's on almost every part.

When you're going through two thousand pictures that are submitted to you for a particular commercial, how do you decide what people to bring in?

On the vignette commercials, where you don't know the people, you try to pick out faces that are interesting. This is probably the single best tip I can give you: you look at the eyes. And if they're not living eyes, that actor doesn't have a shot in hell of coming in. So when you get your pictures back, cover everything else and look at the eyes, because if they're not warm and alive—and it's easy not to be—then you won't have a shot at coming in on an interview.

Do you ever see actors who aren't in SAG?

Oh yes, all the time. I'm casting a nonunion film right now, for actors who aren't in SAG.

Assuming you see the maximum—say, three hundred people for a spot—how many of those actors would you normally call back for a final audition?

Again, it depends on the director. I have one director who's spectacular who brings back three. I have another director who's even more spectacular who brings back those people that he wants to use—and only brings them back for the ad agency's approval and the client's approval. I have other directors who don't know what they're doing, and they sometimes bring in twenty on callbacks—and twenty should be a casting session, it shouldn't be a callback session.

How many agents do you regularly call on a commercial?

We put it out on Breakdown Services. That's a company that was formed by a young man named Gary Marsh twenty-some years ago. Gary's mother was an agent, and in those days the agencies would go to the studios, and they actually read the scripts all by themselves and broke them down and figured out who their talent was, and then submitted them to the casting people at the studios. So Gary started doing this for his mother, and two other agents in Gary's mother's building said, "Gosh, that's great. If we can have copies of those breakdowns you're doing for your mom, we'll give you X amount of money." And Gary, being not too dumb for a nineteen-year-old kid, thought, *Hey—maybe other agents would do that,* and started the whole thing.

Now he uses electronics, and all the commercial agents have machines in their offices that are like teletypes. We call Breakdown Services to give them the breakdown in general terms, and they get it out to all the agents. The agents submit pictures and/or names to us, and we see who comes in. We've been using this service pretty exclusively for the last few years, for almost everything we do. That has changed the number of agents that we can get pictures and names from, and has increased the amount of talent that we can see from other sources.

But we have what we call the Top Ten—actually there are fourteen of them—and if we have a last-minute rush thing and I need actors who can read dialogue, then we call just these fourteen and get the names from them.

Is a performer from one of those fourteen agencies likely to go out on more calls, then, than someone with a small or new agency?

Yes.

Would you tell us who these major agencies are?

This is not necessarily in order of preference: Special Artists, Sutton Barth and Vennari, Abrams Artists, TGI, Joseph Heldfond and Rix, Commercials Unlimited, Abrams Rubaloff, CPC, Cunningham, William Morris, Tannen, Wilhelmina West, Tyler Kjar, and Cassel Levy.

What criteria should an actor use in choosing an agent? If you were an actor choosing an agent, how would you go about it?

I would check with other actors and see who gets out a lot. If I were attending a class—which I think is always a very nice idea—I would find out from the other people who they liked. A good agent is one that works hard for you. You know, there are many actors who were with a smaller agent, and then they got hot and they moved to a bigger agency. Suddenly they were one of many, instead of being the star of the agency. Sometimes it's better to stay where you are, if you're getting out, if you're getting jobs—and, in our area, if you're getting callbacks.

For us, getting callbacks is exactly the same thing as getting the job. It just doesn't pay as well. This is what you guys do for a living—what an actor does for a living is go on interviews. That is your work. If you do your job of going on interviews very, very well, we reward you by letting you come to the set and play with us for a whole day, and then we give you lots of money. But that's not the job. The job is getting that day on the set, and that's the hard part.

Is there any chance for an actor who doesn't have an agent to get seen for commercials?

Oh, sure, there is a chance. It is harder because we are human and we would rather make one phone call to an agent and get three people than make three phone calls for three people. Let me tell you how to go about getting an agent. You go to Screen Actors Guild. You give them a dollar; they give you a list that has every franchised agent. You only want to be with franchised agents. The list even has them broken down into which are children's agents, which are commercial agents, which are theatrical agents.

And then you have one picture—one decent eight-by-ten head shot—preferably, if you're going for a commercial agent, smiling or looking pleasant. And if you're going for a theatrical agent, have it half-lit and mysterious. Then you mail the picture with a little covering note and a résumé—and even if you've done nothing except study or high-school plays or whatever, make a résumé—and don't lie. Or if you lie, at least read the play, because I may question you about it.

The agents will generally contact you. You could follow up a few days later. It doesn't really help, but it might if they liked you and they've lost the phone number. And that's the best way to get an agent. Make sure the picture looks like you, not how you *want* to look.

What do you like to see on a résumé? Assuming an actor has had some experience, what do you look for?

There is a specific form to résumés that you can get. It starts out with your name and your union affiliations and your agent's name. Then height, weight, and hair and eye color. Depending on your thrust, usually you start with films, and then TV, and then stage. You never list commercials. Ever.

Why is that?

Because, if you list a Chevy—even if you did it some years ago—when you come up on Ford they're going to dump you. They don't care when it was. You're aware that you can't do both a Chevy and a Ford, a McDonald's and a Burger King, a Levi's and a Lee Jeans, that there are product conflicts and that you can only do one of each particular thing. And they're very sensitive about that, so you just never list that. You put "Commercials upon Request."

Should you list special skills on your résumé?

The real skills: unicycles, languages. But they should be native languages. When we're looking for a person who speaks French, I really want a native accent. Something like skydiving—stuff that other people can't do—you should list.

Do you have any preference between a head shot and a composite? A composite has a head shot on the front, usually, and on the back there will be three or four smaller pictures showing you in different situations— maybe one as a businesswoman, one as a housewife, one in a glamour shot, maybe one in a bathing suit if you look great in a bathing suit.

And one with a baby, and one stirring a pot. Unless you're a guy. Then they have one with a dog and one showing some short of athletic piece of equipment. You probably can guess that I despise composites with a passion. Composites are from the old days when no actor would do a commercial. None of you remember this, but in the early days of commercials there was no dialogue because they couldn't get anybody to say words. So you cast really on a look. But those days are gone, and therefore the composites should be gone. We no longer have to see if you can smile, frown, hold a baby, and stir a pot. You need a good picture with a résumé.

We want to know if you can act. You have to act in commercials, and if you start thinking of commercial acting as a separate technique, you're dead. Because acting is acting, and it may be instant characterization, which we require in commercials—we don't have the luxury of allowing you to build a character because we have you for thirty seconds on camera. So you have to have the character built and ready to present when that camera rolls, and that's harder. But we want to know that you can do that. So always, always, put a résumé on the back of your picture. And have it already stapled.

What about dressing for the part? To what extent should a performer carry this? I know actors who have car trunks full of wigs and costumes and sporting gear, hard hats, nurses' caps, stethoscopes, glasses, brief-cases.

For me, if you have to prop and wardrobe, it means you can't act. It is a dead giveaway that you are relying on externals instead of yourself, instead of the internals. You should dress to suggest a character. Certainly if it's a doctor you're not going to come in sweats. If it's a cleaning woman, you're not going to wear a suit with a frilly blouse. If it's a businesswoman you're not going to wear jeans and a sweatshirt. But you're going to do something somewhere along the line that won't make them wonder, "What is that person doing?" Or, worse, "What part is he in for?" Which is a little scary, because they can fast-forward.

The worst thing that ever happened to actors is fast-forward. And the best. It gets more people seen. But this is now how they watch the videotape. And they will sometimes stop for your slate. You know about slating—where you say your name at the beginning of a reading for commercials. The slate is the most important thing you can do. If you're going to practice anything *now* for commercials, practice saying your name in a warm, friendly, believable, likeable manner. You know how, when you meet somebody, the second you meet them you know if you're going to like them or hate them? That's how they react to your saying your name on camera. And it shouldn't be a "Hi! I'm . . . ," although sometimes that works. But if there are three of you doing the same scene, and all three of you go, "Hi, I'm Judith Searle," "Hi, I'm Sheila Manning," "Hi, I'm Danny Goldman," it's like, "Oh, shut up!" So if you just practice saying, "Sheila Manning," or whatever, an affirmation of who you are, it's better.

Let's talk about etiquette at the audition. Are there any particular things actors do at auditions that mess them up, that make them less than likeable, that irritate you a lot?

Scatology and true sexual innuendo are out. Be careful of your political statements. You can always feel free with me, but generally it's not a good idea with casting directors because you don't know where they stand.

The biggest gripe at the last Casting Association meeting was actors or models who don't show up or who are late. They drive casting people crazy. On rainy days, when we're dealing with models, I wake up and I think, *Oh, no, they're all going to wake up and say, "What chance do I have to get this anyway," and go right back to sleep.* It's true—we have about a forty-percent attrition rate on rainy mornings. And by afternoon they're all calling: "Cheryl didn't make it this morning. Do you think she could come in this afternoon?" And we always say yes, because we're working. But it's annoying.

What else? Don't be late; don't borrow the stapler. I've heard more casting people say that it pisses them off when you borrow their stapler. I'm fairly loose about running the office, but there are casting directors that are on the phone if you're a minute late.

I'll tell you the worst thing you can do—the single worst thing you can do: crash an interview. We have a rule in my office that every actor that ever tries to crash an interview is told the rule immediately: You try to crash an interview, you will never be seen here. We keep your picture and put it in the file. You will never be seen here again. It's that simple. It has eliminated crashing to an enormous degree.

I'm paid to bring in the people that are right for the job. If you're really wrong, and you happen to get on the tape past my video operator and you look really horrendous, I'm the one who's screwed. It doesn't matter to you guys—you don't even know about it—*I'm* the one that the client doesn't use on the next job. So it's not just ego involved, it's practicality. It's also my ego—if I thought you were right I'd have brought you in, and frequently I'll say that to people. So do not crash—it's the worst thing you can do.

Apart from these areas of etiquette, what mistakes do actors make in presenting themselves, besides the bad slate? What things do you constantly see actors do that you wish you could tell them not to do?

Acting. Actors who act in commercials—or probably in anything—are dead. You have to look like it's real. You have to look like it's a moment we just lifted out of time. It's the hardest kind of acting. If you start falling into the trap of thinking, *Gee, I'm doing a commercial; I'll do it like a commercial,* then it's all over. I'd rather you erred on the side of underacting.

What about memorizing copy? As we all know, the Screen Actors Guild requires that you have cue cards with the copy written on them now for actors. Is it a good idea, anyway, for the actor to memorize the copy so that he's not looking from the camera to the copy back to the camera all the time?

Oh no, don't waste your brain cells. If you memorize the stuff, especially in an audition situation where you haven't had time to work out this thing, you're more concerned with dredging up what the next line is than with what you're saying. There are some classes that teach you to memorize the first and last line of the commercial so that you can then look directly at the camera. I think that's dumb, too, because going back and forth like that doesn't look real.

Suppose you got really lucky or were really skillful, and you got a callback. Should you dress the same way at the callback as you did at the first call?

This is one of those superstitions actors have that I'm touched by. It doesn't matter. Frequently, we've called you back for another part. So if you wear the same thing, you're probably not dressed right, anyway. But your clothes should not be of paramount importance. We're very fond of saying "nice casual."

There used to be a theory that you can't wear white. You still can't wear white if you happen to be black, because the cameras don't adjust well for wide variations. Don't wear vertical stripes because they strobe—they make us crazy. Small geometric patterns do the same thing. Solid colors are always safest. Pastels are really nice, especially for women of a certain age. There are no rules. The winter uniform for men seems to consist of chinos and a sweater with a shirt collar sticking out. And for women, if they're being "awfully Connecticut," it's the same thing. Clean is always nice.

Let's talk for a minute about types. Is there such a thing as a general "commercial type?"

Not any more. There used to be, but now with the advent of things like Levi's 501 Jeans and all this vignette stuff, the most interesting people are the ones that are able to give to the camera who they really are. Because whoever you are is what they're buying in commercials right now. There's a saleability for heavy people right now. I think that we fat people are about to be the next minority that television discovers.

I'm going to be fifty this year, and I like it when I get a breakdown like this: we've got a "young male executive, around forty-five" and an "older woman, forty-eight to fifty." And this is common—and that's still how they look at it. That's one of the major problems that we do have.

So we have sexism and ageism and racism. While we're talking about minority and nonsexist casting, is there anything a person in your position can—or should—do to have an effect in this area? To bring in, say, a black person for a spot that isn't described as being for a black? Or bring in a woman as a spokesperson when they ask for a man?

We do it all the time. I got complimented on it the other day by a client who actually used the phrase "color-blind casting"—which I thought was sort of interesting, because I hadn't even considered that that's what it was. We not only do that, but we also make it a point to ask the client. Sometimes I just do it, and make my point that way. And frequently there's no malice intended; it just never occurred to them that there are other people in this world. On the other hand, there are agencies that *always* give you a color-blind breakdown, which is really kind of nice.

What about seeing new people, in general? Do you make an effort to see people you haven't seen before?

Always.

So when an agent suggests somebody you haven't seen, you're willing to take a chance on the basis of a picture sometimes?

Sometimes I do. I have several directors that want new faces from me all the time. Fortunately, we're in a city that can provide a never-ending supply. The fun thing is when they want a new face at seventy. We say, "Okay, we can do that"—and we can. There are new faces out there that have retired and want to do it now, suddenly. The hard ones to find are new forty-year-olds, because at forty to forty-five, if you really aren't making a living as an actor, you should be doing something else to keep yourself alive. So that's a hard area.

In the search for new faces, do you attend Equity-waiver theater, workshops, or showcases? How valuable as a source of exposure for actors are things like that?

They aren't very important, and I hate going. Do you know what it's like to have theater-going turned into work? What I don't go to—and I have a personal morality about this—are things where actors pay casting people to come see them. I think it's the most immoral new game in town. Or maybe it's an old game now, but I refuse to take part in it. We're supposed to see new actors; this is what we do for a living. I do go see things that are not that kind of showcase—I try to go to little theater. But I must tell you, there's so much bad stuff around that unless you're in something that's good—or unless you're in something that's bad, but you're in the first part of it—I'd rather have you come to my office. If you must do a scene, come and do it in my office.

How valuable is something like a commercial workshop for someone who has never done a commercial and wants to get some idea of how to do it?

It can be incredibly valuable, if you already are an actor. It will not teach you how to act, but it will teach you how to do this form of acting, if it's a good workshop. It will teach what they say about you behind the scenes. If it's run by a casting director or someone who's active in the business, that person can tell you—and I don't have one, so I can say this very objectively.

Are there particular ones you would recommend?

There are some I recommend. Stuart Robinson is the best commercial teacher in this city. Most of the agents send their people to Stuart now. The Diviseks give a very good workshop—they're casting directors. I understand that the Tepper-Gallegos workshops are very effective. I've never attended them, but I know that they always are very full.

I find that most workshops taught by talent are taught by people who don't work. And my attitude about that is: if they can't get the jobs, how can they teach you how to get the jobs? So you want to make sure that the person who is teaching is an active professional. I think actors are very good at teaching other forms of acting, but not commercials. I think you have to have a knowledge of what goes on in the choosing process, to see what to do in the front part—and that's why casting people can be effective.

What are your greatest frustrations with the casting process?

Lack of time. I left the office to come here tonight, and a client had called at five o'clock and said, "We got the Sprint job. Can you start at ten o'clock tomorrow?" I said, "I'm not sure," and tried desperately to pull together at least a morning session. And then I'll go in early tomorrow and set up the afternoon.

On your side of it, if you're getting calls from your agent the same day, it's hard for you, too. You should all have beepers, by the way, because we get these rush jobs more and more. It used to be that seventy percent of the business was shot in New York and thirty percent here, and now it's gone quite the other way. There are places in New York folding. In the summertime they are coming here to shoot on stages because we have better talent and generally a more cooperative atmosphere. So right now we are very busy. So you should all have beepers. Frequently what happens is—like tomorrow—I'll be putting out calls at ten o'clock for twelve o'clock, and if I can't reach you you're going to miss the call at twelve. Actors tend to assume that if they get a last-minute call they're a replacement for somebody who couldn't make it, and I tell you this so you'll know that's not always the case—in fact it frequently isn't the case.

What part, if any, does the *Academy Players Directory* play in your business?

I think every actor should be in the *Players Directory*. I think it's very, very important, and I think you should keep it updated. And while I'm on this subject, all of you think that the minute you sign a contract with an agent, it goes by magic into the computer of Screen Actors Guild—so that if we casting directors want to find you, we just call the agency department and ask them how to reach you and they will give us your agency. But that is not the case. You must go individually and put yourself in the computer at Screen Actors Guild, so that they will give us your agency. You must also do that with your home telephone number, which we can get from the SAG agency department. But you have to keep them updated—that's a really important thing. As for the *Players Directory*, we use it as a reference. If an agent suggests somebody and I can't bring up a picture in my mind, I'll grab the *Players Directory* and look for a picture in there. Or, when an agency uses a prototype and I can't think what that person looks like, I'll check to see who looks like the prototype.

Elaine Craig

E*laine Craig casts voices for commercials, animation, and film narrations. Her recent credits include "The Simpsons" (syndicated launch), MCI "PolitenessMan" TV campaign, Budweiser Ice Draft, Honda, The Disney Channel, 7UP, Saturn, Coors Light, Delta Airlines, Jeep Cherokee, and FTD.*

How did you get into casting?

I started out with the William Morris Agency, as a secretary. A year later, an agent trainee position in the voice-over department opened up. My degree in college was in speech communications—speech and drama—and I always liked the directing side. I was also fascinated with the other side of the business—the talent agency side, and with voice-overs I was able to put the two things together. I was able to direct as well as represent talent, and I liked that. From William Morris, I went to Special Artists Agency and represented voice-over talent there, and then went on to open my own casting company three years ago. I did a couple of free-lance jobs, and it started rolling and took off.

How does the audition process work in voice-overs?

In voice-overs, there are basically three different ways of getting a job. One is to send in a demo tape, and sometimes you get booked just from that. But more often a producer from an ad agency will send the copy to your voice-over agent, and the agent will bring you in on whatever copy they feel is appropriate for you. So you actually audition in your agent's office, which is very different from most on-camera casting. The third way you audition is by going to a casting director's office.

What advice would you give to an actor who has never done voice-over work and wants to break in?

I would say the first thing is to take a voice-over workshop. Any acting background is great for voice-overs, but voice-over is a very, very specific skill. So I suggest that people take voice-over classes—take several, if they can. There are a lot of really good people in town that teach voice-overs.

Who are some of them?

Thom Pinto, Kat Lehman, and Joanie Gerber all offer very good commercial voice-over classes. I do workshops myself, and get very good feedback about them. For animation, Susan Blu and Andrea Romano teach an excellent workshop. I'd suggest that anybody who wants to get started in voice-overs buy a book called *Word of Mouth,* by Susan Blu and Molly Ann Mullin. It's the only book I know of on the subject, and in the back of it is a list of maybe ten voice-over workshops. And what I would suggest is that if you know anyone who does voice-overs, ask who they studied with. But call around to the various places, find out how much they charge, what they teach specifically, whether they have beginners' classes, daytime, nighttime, whatever fits your schedule. I can't stress enough that studying in a workshop is really the way to go, in the beginning.

However, let's say you think maybe you want to get into voice-overs, but you're not sure you want to invest three hundred dollars for a workshop, which is pretty much what they cost—three hundred for a six-week workshop. My suggestion would be to buy Susan's book and read through it. In it, she describes a basic process of how to break down and interpret copy.

Another thing you can do is go through magazines—the copy in magazine ads is often the same copy that you hear on the radio. So you can tear that out and practice—get your microphone and your tape recorder at home and just listen to yourself.

And listen to the radio. A lot of people do a lot of little voices, which is great. But not everything is commercial, and that's why you really need to listen to TV and radio spots. Most people turn down the volume on TV commercials between shows. What I suggest you do instead is keep the volume up and close your eyes and listen to how they interpret the copy. That's a way you can begin to study on your own—do some exploration and listen back to yourself. And if you still like it and want to pursue it, then take a workshop.

How long do you think the training should be—six months, a year?

In very general terms, I would say a year. I would say train for a good solid year before you even think about putting your demo tape together. And then it depends. That's when you need to get a lot of feedback. Ask people if they think you're competitive. Sometimes it's hard to hear back, "No, you need more training." But talk to as many people as you can. Ask your friends or people in the workshop or your teachers—your teachers are really the best. They're usually pretty honest with you.

How should an actor go about getting a demo tape made?

First of all, I would stress that you don't make your tape until you really, really feel that you're ready. Because they can be very expensive. They range usually between two hundred and fifty and seven hundred dollars—and that's just to make your tape. That doesn't include tape duplications or cassette labels. When you're ready, there are several recording studios that produce demo tapes. Call around for price quotes. Ask your friends who they've worked with.

What should be on this tape? What kind of variety of things? How many spots? What sorts of things do you like to hear on a demo tape?

First of all, there are two different kinds of tapes—people generally do an animation tape or they do a commercial demo tape. Or possibly they do both, if they're that versatile. Let's talk first about the commercial tape. In this area, some people only do one thing. If you do one voice, and you're really good at it, that's fine—put that on your tape. And do it five times if you need to. I mean, not exactly the same thing—you can change your attitude, you can put yourself in different situations. But there are people who pretty much do one voice, who work a lot.

Dialogue with another person is a good thing to put on your tape, and if you do that, I suggest you do it with someone of the opposite sex. What can happen is that if you hear two men or two women on the tape, it can be confusing as to who is who. Having dialogue on your tape is good because a casting director can tell if you have good comedy timing, if you read well with other people, things like that.

How long should a demo tape be?

Two to three minutes—no longer than three minutes. This usually consists of seven or eight spots. In terms of what to put on the tape, pay attention in your classes and listen to your radio to find out what's marketable out there, what works, and then zero in on what type of commercial copy is appropriate to your age and vocal range. Let's say you're a thirty-five-year-old woman—well, you could be a mom, a businesswoman, a spokes-woman for cosmetics, and you can have all kinds of attitudes within your role. By the way, a lot of people who are thirty are doing fifteen-year-old voices for me, so when I say an "age," I'm talking about the age that you *sound.* If you sound like a teenager, maybe you can do one spot as a counter girl, you can do one talking about or to your boyfriend or girlfriend, talking about teenage products and topics like food, zits, and Magic Mountain. If you're a man you can be anything from a hard-sell announcer to a sensitive father to—all kinds of things. But on a commercial demo tape I would stress that your first spot should be something that is very natural and believable. One mistake a lot of people make is that they think, *Okay, I'm going to blow them away right at the top.* And then they do their Donald Duck voice or whatever. And it's just not something that's used very often for commercials. What I suggest is that you put just your own natural voice on the tape, reading something that feels natural to you—within commercial copy, of course.

Something that's really straight down the middle?

Yes. What you hear a lot on the radio and on TV now is just a very natural approach; you're talking to your best friend. It's not about being a big authoritative announcer, and the FM deejay sound on commercials is really out. Being an exceptionally good actor is the key thing, I think. Being natural is really just getting in touch with yourself and what you like about the product. Making extremely specific choices about Who am I? Where am I? Who am I talking to and why? All those things. And you'll find the answers in the copy and in your imagination. So I think you should put that real-person kind of spot on your demo tape first, then show your range. Then show you can also do a fast-talking thing, or a bit of dialogue—whatever you feel you're exceptionally good at and is commercial.

Segueing into the animation tape, if you do a lot of different voices, I would suggest that you do two different tapes: one commercial, one animation. Because what can happen is that it can be confusing to a casting director if they're casting a commercial spot and they put the tape in and they want to hear someone's natural voice and instead they hear a lot of cartoon voices. I suggest that you make two demo tapes and send the animation tape to the animation houses, and send your commercial tape to casting directors and producers at the ad agencies. With animation tapes, that's where the variety can come in—you can put in all kinds of things. I'd still keep it about three minutes long at the most, but with animation you can just go for it. The one suggestion I'd make is that you not make each little section too short—a casting director wants to hear that you can sustain that character a little bit.

How long should it be? Twenty seconds?

Yes, for each character, about twenty seconds—probably not more than that. Not less than five or ten and not more than twenty, I'd say.

How do you classify voices?

By age, by texture, by vocal range and pitch, by attitude—things like that.

Approximately what percentage of the work is for men and what percentage for women?

About fourteen percent is done by women—eighty-six percent is done by men. It's actually a little better than it was. A few years ago it was ninety percent men and ten percent women.

A few years ago the Women's Voice-Over Committee of the Screen Actors Guild in New York paid for some research to determine whether, in two different categories (Nestle's Morsels and Listerine were the products), men's voices or women's voices sold the product better. Would you tell us what they discovered?

In the test, effectiveness was defined according to whether the voice changed the consumer's attitude toward the product. And they found that men and women were equally effective—that's what it said in the study's conclusion. But if you read through the statistics, the actual numbers showed that the women were actually slightly more effective than the men. But in the conclusion they didn't really rub that in. I think the reason men get more of the work is more-or-less out of habit. People tend to think of men for voice-overs, and heads of corporations tend to think a male voice is more authoritative, more dynamic, that it's going to cut through. It isn't necessarily so. As we've been seeing recently, there have been some changes in that women are starting to get more voice-overs. In the last couple of years the Lindsay Wagner spots for Ford have been very effective and very successful. I think that's opened a lot of doors for women. I don't think it's going to be fifty-fifty in the next year or two; I think it's going to take a little while.

To get back to the question of categories, what are some examples of categories you use for male voices and for female voices?

For male voices, a lot of it is according to age. Generally, I'll get a call and they'll say, "We want a fifty-year-old storyteller" or "We want a grand-father" or "We want a dad, age thirty," or "We want a good, authoritative announcer, forty to fifty." Sometimes I go according to texture—who has a real raspy texture, or who's very gravelly, those kinds of categories. It's usually according to age, pitch, texture, and attitude—you know, some-times I'll have the warm-and-friendly versus someone who's a little more authoritative. I even have another category that's separate from authorita-tive, which is informative. And for women, it's pretty much the same thing. Men and women generally have the same categories within those kinds of qualities.

Let's get onto the subject of agents. Are there certain agents you regu-larly call for voices?

Yes. There are fifteen voice-over agents, most of whom represent both voice-over and on-camera talent. If I'm pressed for time, I will typically call the five or six agencies who have consistently sent me good people in the past. However, when time permits, I will call all of the agents and scan the city for new talent.

How important is it for an actor to have a powerful agent—say, one of the big five?

I don't think that's necessarily the most important thing. I think what's important is that your agent is doing all they can to get you out on auditions and working. The advantage to being with a big, powerful agent is that, obviously, over the last fifteen or twenty years, they have established so many contacts all over the country that whenever somebody wants a voice, they're going to call there—as well as some of the other agencies. But I'd say the bigger ones are probably going to get a little more copy, which means that you then get more opportunities to read. However, someone who's starting out can get lost in the big agencies. What I sometimes suggest, if you're starting out, is that you start out with one of the smaller agencies, because they're just as aggressive—in fact, sometimes a little more aggressive, because they're a little hungrier. They could represent you very well, because they're going to get you out there—they're really going to try and hustle the copy and get you work. So there are pros and cons to both, really. The important thing is that you *and* your agent have a marketing strategy to get you out there and known in the voice-over world.

Is there any chance at all for an actor who wants to do voice-overs but doesn't have an agent?

Yes, there is some. I have to say that, as a casting director, ninety percent of the time when I'm looking for talent I'll call the agents. But you can send in your tapes if you don't have an agent. It helps a lot if you're in the unions—that's the first thing. With AFTRA you can just pay your dues and you're in. Screen Actors Guild is a little tougher to get into, but it's not impossible. Those are the two unions that you need to be in for voice-overs. AFTRA covers radio, and Screen Actors Guild covers TV.

You had asked me whether you have to have an agent to get work. My favorite story about that is that a couple of weeks ago I was casting a CBS special, "Betty Boop." It's basically the characters from the old Betty Boop animation series. They're bringing it up to date, but were looking for the character of Betty Boop, as well as a lot of other voices. They'd been having a lot of trouble finding people—they'd tried New York and here, and then called me. The day before they called, I happened to go across the street to an office where I had a meeting, and the receptionist, as I was going out, said, "I'm pursuing voice-overs." And I thought, *Oh, that's nice.* I don't mean to sound callous, but I go to parties and people come up to me and say, "Do you like my voice?" It gets to a point where it's ridiculous. And people don't realize that you actually have to train for this—it sounds easy, but it isn't. So when the receptionist told me that, I didn't think a lot about it. I said, "Do you have a tape yet?" And she said, "No, but I've done a couple of things." So I said, "Great. When you get your tape together, send it to me." So the next day I had to go back there—actually that was the day I got the call for Betty Boop. I heard her talking on the phone when I was walking out, and all of a sudden I stopped—you know, like in a movie: "Ah, that voice!" It suddenly struck me that she sounded very similar to Mae Questel, who was the original voice in the series. I went back in, waited until she got off the phone, and said, "Melissa, have you ever tried to do Betty Boop, by any chance?" And she said, "Yes, I've been working on Betty Boop." And I couldn't believe it. I said, "Do you sing?" And she said, "Yes, I sing." And she seemed very professional. But the thing was, she had that voice naturally. I didn't know what her acting ability was or her singing, but I could hear that she had the basic quality that was close to that voice. It's a very high-pitched, slightly nasal, young and innocent kind of voice, and it was something that a lot of actresses weren't getting because they were trying to force their pitch, and she was just there naturally. So I decided to take a chance and gave her an audition time along with twenty or so other actresses reading for the part.

She came in the next day, and the producers had flown down from San Francisco for the audition session. And she was wonderful. She brought a lot of life to the character, she sang beautifully, they loved her, and she got the job! So you can get a job if you don't have an agent. She didn't have an agent, but she did have a personal manager, and she'd obviously been training, and it was one of those situations where opportunity and preparation met, and it happened. The other point to this story is that it's a good idea to tell everybody you know, "This is what I'm doing; I'm pursuing voice-overs." Toot your own horn a little bit. You never know what opportunity may come along. To put it into perspective, that's a rare instance. Only about one percent of all the casting that I do happens that way. But you never know.

How many people will you normally bring in on a role for a particular commercial?

Generally, I bring in around fifteen per role. If I have a dialogue, and it's men and women, I'll bring in thirty people, fifteen couples. It depends on what the client wants, but that's usually the maximum number they have time to listen to—which is part of the reason people hire me; it saves them a lot of time. Everything in commercials works so fast that you usually don't have time to hear a hundred people. So they'll call me and say, "This is what we're looking for, and we'll leave it up to your judgment to bring in the fifteen people that you think would be right." And then I call all the different agents and request certain people, and sometimes I take suggestions from the agents.

Do you ask them to send the person to your office, or to put the person on tape in their office?

Generally I will ask them to send the actor to my office, because that's pretty much my job—to direct the talent. For instance, I'll call up Cunningham and say, "I'd like to see Judith Searle," and they'll say, "Okay, great. But do you know we have so-and-so, too? Would you like to see her also?" And sometimes I'll say, "Yes, great," and sometimes I'll say no, and they get real mad at me for a day or so. I try to see as many people as I can from each agency, but there's always a time limitation.

How does the agency normally introduce you to their voice-over clients?

A couple of different ways. There's a thing called a house tape. Every voice-over agent has a male house tape and a female house tape, and on that they have each talent, in alphabetical order, one minute of their voice. You put together your minute for them. Let's say you're with Sutton, Barth and Vennari, and they call you and say, "We're putting our house tape together. You need to get your minute together." What that means is, you need to take your tape that you already have—your three minute tape—and edit that down to one minute. And you try to put on that what you feel really represents you and what you feel strongest in. So then you submit that one minute to your agent, and they put together this compilation on one reel—it's usually a cassette, actually. And that is then sent out to all the ad agencies across the country—all the major ones, anyway—and to the independent casting directors and to anybody that's looking for talent. So that's one way of introducing the talent to me. I listen to the house tape.

I also listen to the individual cassettes. Believe it or not, I listen to every tape that comes in—either I do or my assistant does.

We also do general auditions, from time to time. We will call the agent, and we'll say, "Here are five times—every ten minutes. Please send in new people that we haven't met yet." And that is an excellent way to meet new people. I'll give them copy, and they'll read, and I'll give them direction. And that really is the best way to find new talent. Because sometimes your demo tape is not as good as you are—sometimes you did it a few years ago and you've gotten a lot better. Sometimes it's better than you are— sometimes I hear a tape that's terrific, and you get the person in there and you realize that they must have had editing on every other word to get a sentence together.

What is the time frame on casting a typical voice-over? How fast do you have to cast?

To give you an idea: on Monday they'll call and say, "We have a script we'd like to send and have you do some casting on it. Can you do this tomorrow?" And sometimes, if they fax the copy to me, and if I'm not booked up, I can cast it the next day and have the tape in by the end of the following day. So sometimes it's a twenty-four-hour turnaround.

Our casting session will start about ten o'clock in the morning, because I'm not a very good early-morning person myself, and most voices don't wake up until at least ten o'clock. So then the talent comes in—and they're scheduled every ten to twenty minutes, usually, so you don't have time to dawdle. You really have to get there early and rehearse what you're doing and try to be as prepared as possible, so that when you get in the booth for your ten minutes, you're ready to do a run-through, record and possibly hear playback, and record a take two. And then at the end of the day, I usually dub it onto cassettes—because everybody likes cassettes now, instead of reels—and then the cassette goes out to the ad agency.

Then they decide—and usually, before it gets to the client, the ad agency has picked out their one or two favorite people. Sometimes they'll call me and say, "This is who we're presenting. We don't have approval on this person yet, but this is who we're going to recommend to the client. Could you find out if they're available on Friday?" So sometimes this will happen in about a three-day period: I'll get the copy on Monday, we do auditions on Tuesday, they call me on Wednesday to book it, and it records on Thursday.

Do you have any particular no-no's for voice actors in regard to their auditions—things that some actors do that are big mistakes?

Yes. Sometimes actors don't show up, and that only happens once, because I won't see them again if it happens, unless there's a really good excuse. So not showing up is a major no-no.

Showing up late consistently will really annoy a casting director because, when we're doing something every ten minutes, if you're paired with someone to read and that person is waiting for you, the whole day gets thrown off. So it's important to be on time.

Other mistakes you can make: Generally your attitude is so important in an audition. Everybody's nervous—even the casting director, because if I bring in fifteen people and one of them just doesn't hit it, I've got to answer to my client. So just know that casting directors want you to be good. They're on your side. And attitude is so, so important. I mean, some people have a bad day, and they carry it in with them, and I don't need that.

Also, being prepared is really important. When you go into a casting director's office, generally there's no receptionist there, but on the board or in a fairly obvious place there'll be the copy and what the direction is— "warm and friendly" or "authoritative," or whatever. A lot of them are buzzwords: "friendly but authoritative," "put a smile in it"—all those things that drive actors crazy. And take that time—get there early, look at the copy, read the direction, and pay attention to what you're there for. Because two minutes after you get there your best buddy's probably going to walk in—the person you see at every audition because you two are in the same category. And he's going to want to talk about the game last night or his last three jobs. But just remember, you can say to him, "Hey, I need to look at the copy." Go out in the hall if you need to. Because one of the biggest frustrations for a casting director is when you hear everyone out there talking, and that's fine, but then you go out and you say, "Okay, John

Doe, it's your turn," and he says, "Oh, no, I haven't even looked at the copy." Well, why not? It's five minutes past your audition time. So being prepared is really important.

I think if you come in on time and you have a good attitude and you prepare as much as you can, there aren't all that many mistakes you can make. You may not be right for that particular job, but you might be right for one we're casting next week.

Is it okay in an audition situation to ask for a playback?

Oh, absolutely. With me it is. I think it's smart to ask for a playback. Most people will do it. Sometimes they'll say, "I'm sorry, I can't" if they're casting a lot of spots on that day. But most of the time it's to everyone's benefit to play it back, because so much of voice-over is instinct. It's not always something someone can tell you to do; it's more that you hear it and you just know what to do. So if you think hearing the playback might help you improve your audition, by all means ask.

NEW INTERVIEWS
LOS ANGELES

New
Los Angeles
Interviews

PAMELA BASKER, Independent Casting Director, features and television: "War and Remembrance," *Naked Gun, Police Academy.*

REUBEN CANNON, Independent Casting Director, features and television: *Who Framed Roger Rabbit?, The Color Purple,* "The Women of Brewster Place."

DON PEMRICK, Vice President of Talent for Feature Films and Television, I.R.S. Media, Inc.: *Dead Weekend, Tom & Viv, Shakes the Clown.*

JERRY FRANKS, Independent Casting Director, features and television: *Bagdad Cafe,* "Fame," "Picket Fences."

EUGENE BLYTHE, Vice President of Television Casting, Walt Disney Television: "St. Elsewhere," "Newhart."

JOHN LEVEY, Director of Television Casting, Warner Brothers: "China Beach," "Head of the Class."

ROBIN NASSIF, Director of Casting, West Coast, ABC Entertainment, television: "Ellen," "Grace Under Fire," "Roseanne."

LACY BISHOP, Independent Casting Director, theater: Los Angeles Theatre Center.

BEVERLY LONG, Independent Casting Director, commercials.

PAUL VENTURA, Independent Casting Director, commercials

BOB LLOYD, The Voicecaster, voice-overs for commercials.

Pamela Basker

Pamela Basker is an independent casting director who casts film and television in Los Angeles With her former partner Fern Champion she cast the mammoth miniseries "War and Remembrance"; the films Pet Sematary, Troop Beverly Hills, The Naked Gun, Police Academy, *and* Screwface; *and the MOWs "Semester at Sea" and "First Impressions." Champion-Basker also cast for the HBO comedy channel and the series "War of the Worlds," "Friday the 13th," and "Mamma's Family." On her own, Pamela cast the feature* Millions *and the MOWs "Storm and Sorrow" and "The World's Oldest Living Bridesmaid."*

Pamela, how did you get into casting in the first place?

Probably like most casting directors, I started off acting but only lasted about a minute and a half. At the same time my former partner was casting extras in New York, so in between my calls I would go to her office and watch what she was doing. She would sit there all day long and interview people—different personalities, never the same person twice—and that seemed more fascinating to me than what I was doing. But I stayed in my acting class to figure out what actors are all about and how they work, and I think that helped me in the long run as a casting director because it gave me more compassion, more patience.

Since you've worked on both coasts, how would you say the casting scene in New York is different from the one in L.A.?

New York actors are constantly working on their craft, and they have a background in stage and singing and dancing—they can do a little bit of everything. In L.A. the résumés don't seem as full.

I myself go for the training, how much theater they've had, where they studied. But I think it's an advantage for a New York actor out here because when they come in and do a performance it has a beginning, a middle and an end. I'm not saying there aren't good coaches in L.A., but they tend to teach one specific thing. In New York you learn all sorts of different things about yourself, so that when you come out here you probably have a better shot at a role than an actor from L.A.

What kinds of training on a résumé would impress you?

The thing that impresses me the most is when I ask an actor if he's studying and he says, "Yes."

As far as teachers go, what I tell actors is: audit as many classes as you can and take as many different classes as you can. And if they don't allow you to audit then don't go. And don't stay with one teacher too long—experiment. I mean, sometimes you get caught up in a pattern where you feel real comfortable with that teacher, but then you don't keep learning things.

What about taking part in small theaters, showcases, workshops? Do you go to those yourself? Do you think they're valuable as a source of experience or exposure for actors?

I do go to them. I must caution everybody to be careful which ones they get into, especially Equity waiver. L.A. has a real bad rep about theater. Even when you do plays, be careful that the production values are good and that everybody there is as committed as you are. The other important thing is to make sure everybody knows about your theater and that they've come to it before. Some theaters people just don't go to anymore because they've done too many bad productions.

The casting of "War and Remembrance" must have been a marathon. Would you describe how that was done? How many hours was it?

Thirty-two. I think they only showed thirty. It was a very tough project. First of all, there was one director who was also the producer—who was also the guy nobody challenged. It was a 128-month shooting schedule, most of it in Europe. There were 450 speaking roles. The casting process went on for three years. We had a thing called the War Room: bulletin boards on every single wall, all kinds of video equipment

Unfortunately, our director didn't really love actors. He was also a little hard of hearing and too vain to wear a hearing aid. The actor would come in and, since Dan was hard of hearing, he'd go, "What?" and scream and growl—and the actor would be intimidated. So we started telling the actors before they came in, "Project. Talk loud. The man can't hear."

Then after a couple of months we figured that wasn't working either, so we came up with a plan of putting all the actors on tape—because then Dan couldn't embarrass anybody. We could sit down and talk without the humiliation of the actor sitting there and Dan getting bored and cutting him off in the middle of a sentence.

One of the things that interested me about this project is that after "Winds of War," several major parts, which ended up being played by John Gielgud and Jane Seymour, got recast from the original miniseries. Would you talk a little bit about how that happened and how the search took place?

Like I said, Dan is a very hard-headed kind of guy, and if he'd had his way, he would have brought back Ali McGraw and Jan Michael Vincent, and they were too old for the first one. He wanted to bring John Houseman back, too. There were so many wonderful people out there that we could have had in the roles, but he in fact was extremely rigid.

We won a couple of small battles, not real big ones. Like Jane Seymour. She was good in it, but there were people who were better. We didn't want to hire Jane Seymour then because she was queen of miniseries. We would have much preferred seeing an unknown, like in *Gandhi*. Dustin Hoffman was going to play Gandhi, and Attenborough said, "No way. I have to have somebody that nobody has seen before so you believe the character and you're not just watching Dustin Hoffman."

So we were trying to get that across to Dan—to no avail. The person that should have played it actually tested twice. She did a fabulous screen test, absolutely phenomenal—and he just didn't get it. So we had to go on, and Jane, who wanted this part very much, tested, and she never tests for things. She took a cut in price because she really wanted it. And she did a nice job, but it wasn't as exciting as it could have been.

Sometimes you have to give in. You can only tell the director so many times in so many different ways why somebody is right. If it comes down to a screen test and they still don't see it, you have to back off as a casting director. Otherwise they'll just fire you or stop listening to you.

When you cast a project for a network, how much of a role does the network generally end up playing?

My personal opinion is that networks have way too much say. They take away the strength from the director. They take away the vision of the producers. They are ninety percent not there when the actor does it for the producer in a room, which is usually the second callback for the actor. And then—assuming this is a pilot—what happens is the producers bring their choices to the network.

Now, I think the easiest one is probably ABC. But at CBS you walk into a huge, impersonal hall with all these network executives sitting around in a half circle, and ninety percent of them don't belong there, but they're there. And then you have this poor actor come in and sit right in the middle of them on a very hard chair, and some casting director is off to the side reading with them. Now this actor has to put on a performance to impress twenty people. Twenty people who are never going to decide on the one person.

And what usually happens after all the actors leave, the network people sit down and start talking about it. I have heard some of the strangest things come out of their mouths—things having nothing whatsoever to do with the actor's ability. And unfortunately, since it's their show and their money, they're able to dictate this mess. But I think it usurps the ability of the director and the producer and takes away from their vision about how they see it.

Now you have producers who are the exception—like Bochco—who basically tell the network what they're doing. But unfortunately that's not true in most cases.

It sounds like a real trial by ordeal for an actor. What would be your advice to an actor put in this situation?

What you should try to remember is, it's all fate after a certain point. You have to go in totally focused and do the best job you can and walk out and leave it to luck. Because I'm telling you, luck has so much to do with it. It has nothing to do with your ability. You can be brilliant in your performance and then somebody in the room can say something incredibly stupid and somebody else agrees with it and you're out.

How would you say the audition process for feature films differs from the process for television—especially on callbacks? Should you always try to do your audition exactly the way you did it the last time?

In film you should always change a performance slightly every time you go back. Because in film you have so much rehearsal time. A director usually asks for a week or two weeks before you even start. He needs to know that he has things he can work with.

But in television it's different. When you read it in the office, that's the way they want it on the set. Don't change it. Don't change anything about it.

Some people even say you should wear the same outfit you wore for the first audition.

For a film audition, how many times will an actor likely have to come back before the answer is yes?

Not as many times as in television. If you have a good director who knows what he's looking for, three times max. And usually the third time he pairs you up with someone he's considering for another role to see chemistry. And that's when, if you know that (and this is something your agent should tell you beforehand), you get that other person's phone number as soon as you can and start working on it together. Because the two of you don't want to go in there and start upstaging one another. You want to go in and give him just what he wants, which is chemistry.

So the other actor is not your adversary. The other actor is going to help you get the part.

And hopefully you'll help him get his part. Absolutely. And sometimes they'll change you around with somebody else because of coloring or the way you look or whatever, but make sure that you have the opportunity to work with that actor beforehand. Call up your agent and say, "Call the casting director. I want that person's phone number. I need to know who I'm working with."

You say with a feature one might go back three times. How many times might one go back for a role in television that one ultimately gets? What would be typical?

Seven. And by that time the poor actor is so burned out they don't know what anybody wants. That's why I say you have to focus.

So the point is, if you're the actor you shouldn't think: What didn't they see that they want from me? Maybe they did see what they want.

And they want to see it again. Unless, of course, the producer or director pulls you aside beforehand and says, "Look, change it this way." But I guarantee you the reason you come back so many times is that one executive went to lunch. He missed it and he's got to find out what it's about. Unfortunately, it's that inane.

And Screen Actors Guild has a ruling that after the third time you should start getting paid for it, but nobody ever adheres to that. And it's too bad the union is that weak. In Canada, they stick to that. Third time back you have to pay them or else they aren't coming.

That's true in commercials here. With commercials, if you go in for your third audition, you do get paid. Pamela, how can an actor whose work you don't know best get your attention?

Well, I'll be honest with you. The stuff that comes through the mail—unless of course they have a very interesting résumé and interesting face and good picture—I usually don't call them in. Because in casting we're so busy dealing with the agents and their submissions. What we do is, when we get the submissions in we put all the pictures in one character file—"The role of the jeweler." And you have a file six inches thick. And that's a lot to get through, so when you're working you don't have time for things called generals, which I personally think are a waste of time, because I can't remember an actor by sitting and talking about the weather. I need to read an actor on a character so I can see what the choices were. Were they good? Did I like them? Do they fit into the role? All those different things. Unfortunately, in Los Angeles you really do need an agent and a strong one. You need an agent who, as soon as the breakdown is out, is calling or sending off their pictures. Hopefully, a good agent will also pick up a script and read it. Because breakdown doesn't give you that much information. Agents need vision on their clients and how to best serve them. But I think you need a very good agent. In New York agents aren't really all that necessary.

You cast a lot of comedy. What do you have to say to us about actors auditioning for comedy, as opposed to a dramatic audition?

I think there's more movement involved in comedy. In comedy you have to be able to move comedically as well as talk comedically. Comedy is more full-blown, and usually the character is exaggerated if the comedy's broad, as the *Police Academy* films are. The timing is so hard, especially if you're reading with a casting director and they're not being funny. They're not helping you and you have to do it all on your own. Comedy is probably the hardest kind of audition to do. So actors really have to go in much more focused than if they were doing dramatic.

Are there any mistakes in general that you see actors make a lot in auditions that you wish you could warn them about?

Don't hang out too long. It's a business. Everybody's got a limited amount of time. Get in, do your thing, and get out.

Present yourself the best way possible: make sure your clothes are fresh; make sure you have a fresh face on, you are well mannered, you are polite to everybody—and just do your thing.

I find it terribly disarming when an actor comes in in character, because you don't know what that person's like and the camera's not always rolling. And if this person is in character, you have no idea who they are. So I like to see a line of demarcation between the person who comes in and the performance.

Probably the biggest mistake actors make is when they start off on a scene, find themselves floundering because they've lost concentration, and keep going because they're afraid to stop. You have to stop yourself and say, "I'm sorry. I want to start again."

And they'll generally let you?

They'll always let you. They're as nervous about the process as you are. It's very uncomfortable for everybody. If you can walk in looking totally comfortable and in control and can work the room, you can actually put those producers and directors at ease and they feel better about it. It's a tough thing to do, especially if the room is small and you have twenty people stacked up. But I've seen actors do it so well that a lot of times they don't end up reading—because they have shown bits of their personality that are so right for the character that directors have said, "I got it. I saw what you have and you got it." And then they get the role. I have seen actors come in and just totally enchant everybody.

So we're talking about charm, not nervous chatter.

Charm, not nervous chatter. Nervous chatter just makes the whole room more nervous. If you're not good at it, don't do it. Just go in, be polite, do your scene and leave.

Is there anything in terms of etiquette that actors aren't aware of that you would like to caution them about?

One of my pet peeves is actors who come in with way too much perfume. You shake hands with somebody and that smell is with you for the rest of the day, and you're not listening to the actor because it's so overpowering.

What are your major frustrations with the casting process as it exists? What would you change if you could?

I think the biggest frustration is that casting directors are looked at as the block—that we keep actors from getting work as opposed to helping them get work. But the truth is, a good casting director is only an extension of your agent and we only want you to look good when you get to the director. We're rooting for you because when you look good, we look good. And a lot of times agents and managers put it into their client's head that a casting director will stop you before you have a chance to get to the director. And that's part of our job. We're there not to bring him a hundred people but to bring him ten really good different choices for a particular role.

Reuben Cannon

Reuben Cannon is an independent casting director turned producer. His background in casting includes a stint at Universal, where he cast the series "Ironside," "The Rockford Files," "Baretta," and "Tenafly," which was the first drama series to have a black leading man. Also at Universal Reuben cast the classic MOW "The Execution of Private Slovick." Moving on to Warner Brothers, he cast "Roots 2: The Next Generation" and" A Death in Canaan. "In 1979 he founded his own company, Reuben Cannon & Associates, which was responsible for casting the series "The Lazarus Syndrome," "Moonlighting," "The A Team," "Hardcastle & McCormick," and "Hunter." He also cast the mini-series "Winds of War" and "Amerika" and the features Who Framed Roger Rabbit?, The Color Purple, and A Soldier's Story. He also produced the series "Amen" and "The Women of Brewster Place."

Reuben, how did you get into casting in the first place?

I started at Universal in the mailroom. And from the mailroom I went to casting as a secretary to the head of the department at that time. Casting was absolutely a blessing because in my working life I'd had only three or four jobs in my life outside of entertainment. I started out as a child actor in theater, and once my voice changed they dumped me. So I said, "Well, I must arrange my life so I'm never rejected like this again." So I went behind the scenes in theater and I loved it.

How were you involved in theater?

In producing. First Community Theater in Chicago.

So your ending up in producing now is something you've had some preparation for.

I'm now, twenty years later, getting back to my original purpose of coming to Hollywood—which was to produce. But I still love casting. Casting encompasses so much of the process of film making. I believe that the work of filmmaking begins with a good script and good casting. Basically, what I refer to as producing is taking more responsibility for what's on the screen and the ability to marry good actors with good material. The only thing more difficult than finding good actors is finding good material.

The Screen Actors Guild, as you know, has committees devoted to furthering the casting of minorities and women. Recently I spoke with Rodney Mitchell at SAG about some of the current statistics, and things do seem to be getting a little better for minorities.

Not as dismal as they used to be?

Well, they were pretty dismal. In 1984 thirteen percent of all roles were for ethnic and racial minorities. In 1989 sixteen percent of all roles were for this group. So it's getting a little bit better. Do you feel there's anything a person in your position can do to have an effect in this area?

Well, I've had less of a problem with this for an obvious reason—because when I'm in a room with a director, I have no hesitancy about recommending that we cast a role or a show to reflect society. Unless it takes place on a different planet, you're going to have people from all cultures. In urban America you're going to have a heavy black population. So I've been pretty aggressive and convincing in doing that.

The reason I joined CSA was to beat up on my colleagues to take a similar approach. It begins in the room of the casting director. If the script is going to be written lily white, it is upon you to put the color in. You have to sit there and say that this script can be played by this actor. But if you don't say anything, then you've got a script that takes place in L.A. and you've got no Latin representation, no black representation. But forget about that. What about the lead when you make up your list of suggestions? When we did "Lazarus Syndrome," it was originally written for Dennis Weaver. Dennis said no, and Dennis sent it to Tony Franciosa, who said no.

And Lou Gossett was the one who got it.

And not one word was changed except the name of the character. Lou Gossett's name was discussed from the very beginning and the receptivity was lukewarm. But once these other guys started saying no ... what Lou did, I think, was elevate the material, because the casting was unexpected and the craft was there. But had it not been for me, his name would not have been on the list.

That mind set should exist with all casting directors. There are certain directors who have that attitude, others that just read the script and cast the way it was written.

Do you think there has been any improvement in this in recent years, Reuben? From the point of view of somebody who is looking at this casually, there does seem to be more opportunity. Is there a real chance for minority performers in leads of series—more than there used to be? Because statistics can lie so easily—they could all be walk ons.

There are more opportunities, but hardly any cause for celebration. We have James Earl Jones and we also have "In Living Color" on Fox. We have certain networks like Fox that are a little more innovative in taking chances. "In Living Color" is a comedy. But black dramas, like James Earl Jones's show "Gabriel's Fire" are still a novelty in television. There have been maybe five series that James Earl's been in in thirty-five years. Five dramatic series with black subject matter. Comedy's been around since "Amos & Andy."

While we're on the subject on actors who are under-utilized in television compared to their representation in the population, let's talk a little bit about the situation of women, particularly women over 40. These statistics, unlike those for minority performers, are going in the wrong direction. For example, women 40 and over in 1986 had ten percent of the roles. In 1989 they had 8.8% of the roles. Why is this? Women's roles are declining all across the board—not just for older women, though older women are the most invisible of the lot in terms of their representation in the population.

Well, maybe ten years ago I saw a report that spoke to the ratio of roles written for women or women cast—and it was like one out of ten, ten years ago. That spoke to no specific age or complexion. It was for all women. So that meant that at the top it was one out of ten. The minute you changed the complexion, the ratio got higher and the minute you changed the age it got worse. So at some point if you were a 45-year-old black character actress, the odds were like one out of 2,500. And as I look around today, I think the odds are probably one out of fifteen across the board.

Drama often seems to consist of what the man does, and the woman is the prize for the man who does it best. Is that a fair way to describe television and film?

Yes. Very often the woman is there just to sell the heterosexual nature of the man—she's not driving the material. It's a business that is male driven.

And of course we see some complaints in the press by people like Sigourney Weaver about the fact that even if a woman does drive the story, as in *Alien*, she gets paid less than a man who drives a comparable story.

And sometimes by women producers. One does not assume that there is equal opportunity among those of the same gender who employ them.

Women producers are as beholden to a bottom-line mentality as male producers, there's no question about that. But I suppose what we're talking about here is that, although a casting director can raise the question to a certain extent, the basic prejudices of our society are very deeply ingrained.

And I think there's a certain lack of effectiveness on the part of casting directors as they fail to realize a role can be cast with a person of a different color. They also fail to visualize how the sex of a character can be changed without affecting the script—and in fact possibly improving it. Two factors are missing: imagination and courage in the casting profession.

Let's talk a little bit about the casting process. When you're casting a film—*The Color Purple* or *Who Framed Roger Rabbit?*—would you describe what the process is?

As the Bible says, first there was the word. So, of course, we get the script. I'll give it a cursory glance and then I'll read it again in detail. And while reading, I'll first just look to be entertained and then look to the casting possibilities. While I'm reading I'll either jot down names or very often I'll give my associate Carol Dudley a copy to read and get her sense of it. Then I'll start making a list drawing from my experience, the Academy Players Directory, audition papers, actors I've seen recently in a theater, actors I've heard about but haven't seen. Just possibilities. And then I look at just the basic framework, and it's like alchemy. How does this actor combine with this actor? We could really create something explosive here. Or is there a sameness to this cast? Is everybody redheads or everybody blonde?

So you're looking for visual as well as emotional contrast.

Exactly. What's the physical look? How can we make it better? And at some point you get to where it doesn't get any better. You hit on certain names. You write down Robert Duvall.

And one of the other things casting really demands is that you act instinctively and have the courage of your convictions so you can go in and talk about an actor who is unknown, if the director is open-minded. In the case of *The Color Purple*, Steven was very supportive and very open. When I got involved in the project Whoopi Goldberg was the only actress that was committed. Anyone can pick names out of the book, but when you're told, "Let's make it as fresh as possible," that's when you really get to show your stuff.

Tell us a little more about *The Color Purple* and your relationship with Steven Spielberg and how you arrived at the rest of the cast—how you arrived at Oprah Winfrey and the other wonderful actors that were in it.

I never worked with Steven. Mike Minto was really Steven's casting director and, fortunately for me, he was sensitive to the fact that if you have a project that is telling a story that involves the black perspective, then you'd better surround yourself with some black people. There are many studios and directors that don't think that way, but Steven was sensitive from the very beginning.

I read the book, loved the book and approached it as you would put together an all-star jazz band of unknowns. Finding a Wynton Marsalis who isn't a star yet but who has all the talent to be there. The first search started for Shug, which was really key.

Margaret Avery.

Margaret Avery. And we had met with Tina Turner and Patti LaBelle, and when it comes to casting, I believe the best way to get people for a movie is to have the actor read.

Did Tina Turner read?

Tina Turner did not read and did not respond to the material—which was ultimately the best thing for the film. Because if we'd done a movie with basically a balanced cast of unknowns—Whoopi at this point was unknown—to put a name like Tina Turner in there would have really distracted, I felt.

How many actresses did you see for the part of Shug?

Oh, maybe a hundred, and maybe I directed thirty, from Patti LaBelle to unknowns on video tests. Steven was busy doing something else, so I would do the videos and he would go home at night and look at the videos and say he liked A, B, or C. He would call and give me some notes: "Direct them again, test them again, and do it this way." And when I do the video tests, I try to catch as much as possible of the person performing a scene. "Let's put the scene aside and see how much you can ad lib, see your personality."

Now Margaret had written me a letter. She was touring Japan as a singer because she couldn't find work in Hollywood as a black actress. I had known Margaret for at least fifteen years or so when she worked in theater and I was casting for Warner Brothers. She said she really liked the project and would I see her. I said I would, so she came in and read for me. Based on her reading, I put her on tape. Steven saw the tape, and there was this wildness about her. The thing we were looking for was a wildness about this character, and she had that.

It certainly came off the screen.

In the case of Oprah, I was casting *Jo Jo Dancer,* and Quincy Jones was in Chicago testifying in a deposition. While there he was watching a local talk show hosted by Oprah Winfrey—a local Chicago show. He called and said, "Reuben, I saw a lady in Chicago that may be right for the subject." I said, "I'm headed to Chicago because I'm looking for a young kid to play the part of the child and I need an urban child to do that." So I called and told them I was coming, and what was sent to me prior to my arrival was a videotape of Oprah touring the South doing a show on black historical figures. I looked and said, "That's impressive," and I was also impressed because here was an actress I didn't know, and I kind of pride myself on knowing about a lot of actors. So I called them up in Chicago and said I want to meet with her.

I arrived in Chicago on one of the coldest days in history. I'm from Chicago, and I really was so cold I never left the office I was using to cast *Jo Jo Dancer.* Michigan Avenue and my hotel was a half block away, so I was living in this hotel and working in this office and I didn't dare go to the south side to see my family because it was just too cold. And they wouldn't come to see me because they said it was too cold.

Oprah was living at least a block away, and I was interviewing by myself, and she came and said, "I'm here to meet Reuben Cannon." I said, "I'm Reuben Cannon." She said, "Look, mister, I have a 101 temperature, I got out of my bed, I want to meet Reuben Cannon, so let's not play any games." I said, "I am he." And she said, "Reuben Cannon's black?" I said, "And his mother and his father and his uncle and all his brothers and sisters."

And that kicked off a wonderful conversation about who she was and her detour from acting into journalism. I listened to her read and said, "If you come out to L.A. I will definitely put you on tape." She did her test on tape, and it was very impressive. At the time, Alfre Woodard was also a candidate, and Alfre tested well, Alfre was smokin'. But what Oprah had was that thing you can't define, and so from that Steven directed her. He came out and directed Oprah for Sophia and Margaret Avery for Shug along with two other actresses. And that Saturday with him directing the videotapes we cast Sophia and Shug. It was exciting and exhilarating, because I have never had any faith in luck. I believe in preparation for the opportunity. And that's what happened there.

When we talk about preparation in terms of a videotape audition, what are we talking about? Are we talking about memorizing the script?

Yes, but not to the point that you forget to bring who you are to it. You learn the lines but also, you know....

Still be flexible enough to be directable.

Absolutely. I must tell you, if I were an actor today, and some guy who woke up this morning and decided to be a casting director was directing my test for a lead, I would ask to do it twice. Do it once based on stage directions, based on the input from the casting director—and hope he has some experience and knows what the director is looking for. Then do it the second time based on my own imaginative awareness.

Really taking it some distance from the first?

Yes, because we're always searching. We don't know how rich this character can be. We wait for the actor to show it to us. And the degree to which you bare your soul is the degree to which the material comes alive. I had an actor once come in for the role of a blind soldier. And whenever you play blind, it has all the built-in traps filled with all the clichés. And this actor in the audition not only played the character blind but also crippled—he stumbled and had a limp. A twist like that can make all the difference.

When I found Bruce Willis for "Moonlighting," we had read—between the network and the casting directors—over 3,000 actors for the part. And they all read the same scene! So after a while, the scene started to sound the same. But it never fails—when someone says it right, it gets your attention. Because you've heard it, you know where the beats are. And Bruce came in and read, and it was like you had never heard it before.

And that's what you have to do with your material. You have to take it and make it sound like something nobody had heard before. The only place you can get that is from inside.

What kind of training impresses you?

Theater. I think the essence of all good training begins with theater. Workshops are important in absence of theater. Class is important. But you can look at a résumé and see if the person has invested a certain portion of their life in acting for the love of acting. It shows. The thing theater gives you that workshop doesn't give you is a character you can take from beginning to middle to end. On stage you have an audience that demands something of you. And the feedback is right there. And that's what assures you that the actor can give you more than what's on the page. There's no substitute for it in becoming professional.

How important is it for an actor to have a powerful agent?

Oprah didn't have an agent. Margaret didn't have an agent. Bruce Willis actually had an agent. In fact it was his agent who called me and said, "There's an actor who's in town on vacation. Would you see him?" I said yes. But it wasn't because of this agent's power, it was just that I was looking for this role.

Don Pemrick

Don Pemrick, *whose credits include film, television, and theater, is currently at I.R.S. Media, Inc., where he has been Vice President of Talent for Feature Films and Television since 1990. His feature credits include* Dead Weekend; Pocahontas; Venus Rising; A Sailor's Tattoo; Tom & Viv; The Beans of Egypt Maine; Bank Robber; One False Move; Shakes the Clown; My New Gun; December; Blood and Concrete: A Love Story; Me, Myself & I; *and* Natural Causes. *Before coming to Los Angeles to work for I.R.S., he and his former partner Deborah Aquila were casting consultants to NBC in New York. Earlier he was a staff casting director for Universal Television. His television credits include* "Three's Company" *and* "Dynasty." *On Broadway he cast the musical* Welcome to the Club, *and he is currently directing a theater group in L.A.*

How did you get into casting?

I was not an actor, which so many casting directors were prior to becoming casting directors. I come from upstate New York, the son of a surgeon; my mother's an R.N. and my sister is an R.N., so I was groomed to go into the medical profession. I said, "No, I'm going to be a lawyer," just to mess them up. I did my undergraduate work in biology and government and got my degree from St. Lawrence University. When it came time to decide on either law school or medical school, I pleaded with my dad to give me six months to go skiing and think about it.

I did ski for a week, but I knew I was only sixteen hours away from Los Angeles. I got in my car, and I came out here and just knocked on doors. I got on a lot, and I talked my way into a job at Marble Arch Productions in the mailroom. I always wore a coat and tie to work, even delivering the mail—that's that prep school upbringing, I guess. So I was at the receptionist's desk one day, and a gentleman came in to meet the President of the company. At the time there were three huge films being cast out of there—Diane Crittendon was doing that. And I used to deliver the mail, so all these submissions came in, and I was totally intrigued by it.

This gentleman and I got to talking, and he obviously didn't think I worked in the mail room because I was wearing this coat and tie and just hanging out, talking to the receptionist. He said, "What do you do? You work here?" I said, "Yeah," and he said, "What do you do?" I didn't want to say "Mailroom." I'd just come from Diane's office, so I said, "Casting." He said, "Well, I know they're looking for a casting director on *Annie*. I'll give them your name." So I gave him the number, which was my extension in the mailroom, and, sure enough, a week later they called me and I went over and met with them. I told them I had no experience, but it was something I thought would be a lot of fun and if they'd give me a shot I'd try to do it. Garrison True, who was the casting director, needed an assistant, and he said, "The job's yours if you want it." I said, "Great," and I started casting on *Annie* in 1980.

One thing led to another and I loved it. We went all over. We did a sixteen–city search for the little girl, and I started learning agents and realized I knew a lot more about the business than I thought I knew. After that ended, I did a short stint on "Archie Bunker's Place"—twelve episodes as a P.A.—realized I didn't like that, and in the meantime met with Barbara Claman at BCI casting.

Barbara gave me my first real job in casting. *Annie* was a fluke, in that it was this huge thing and we were only looking for the little girl. I went to work for Barbara in the summer of '81, and it was in Barbara's office that I really learned on-hands casting, the business of the business. She was really terrific. So I've been doing it ever since. I was out here for eight years and basically did the studio thing.

Then I went to New York in '88 and hooked up with Debby Aquila, and we worked together for about sixteen months, and that was just terrific because I was weaned on television out here, and going to New York was a whole new thing—getting weaned more on theater. Then I ended up getting a gig with I.R.S. media to do six pictures for them on a non-exclusive basis, so that's what brought me back out here.

How would you say the casting scene in L.A. is different from that in New York?

Ninety-five percent of all the casting is done in California and only five percent in New York. But the process is basically the same both places. I get a script, I read it before I even discuss it with the director, and as I'm reading I'm writing ideas down. Then I talk to the director and the producer and get their input—I don't want their input before I come up with my ideas. And then we have a creative meeting and discuss the roles. Then I send the script to Breakdown Services and they break it down and send it to all the agents, and the agents make their submissions and I start the interviewing process. Or we start making offers if we're going after star names.

We're talking film and television.

Film and television, correct. The majority of film casting that I ended up doing in New York was for one or two roles in each of the films. We didn't do the whole movie. When they couldn't find it in California they would come to New York.

We did *Wild Orchid* and *Lord of the Flies*, and the roles we cast were usually the lead roles or lead supporting roles. And we did a couple movies that shot locally there.

Is there such a thing as a New York actor?

Yes. When people graduate in theater from colleges and universities throughout the country, it seems to me there is a mentality thing. You go to California to become a star. You go to New York to work on the craft. I don't want to say there aren't serious and dedicated actors in Los Angeles, but there are 40,000 "actors" in Los Angeles. Out of that 40,000, maybe 12,000 are extremely dedicated to their craft and work on it on a continuous basis. In New York you've got 8,000 actors. Out of that 8,000, 7,500 are dedicated actors. And they're doing primarily theater.

And by "dedicated," you mean they want to do it even though they get paid next to nothing for it?

Right. They're there busting their tail trying to support themselves as well as pursue and work on their craft. Whereas out here there are a lot more commercials, there is a lot of television, there are a lot of episodic shows that support the actor. They are "acting," but they're not really working on their craft. I think episodic is great to pay your union dues and get your insurance. But you're not really working on your craft, let's face it. And that's nothing against television, it's just that you have absolutely zero time to prepare and you really don't have the creativity that you do on a film.

How can an actor in Los Angeles work on his or her craft?

There is the theater here. You have the breakdown in *Dramalogue*. There are the theater groups that you can get involved with. Barbara Claman actually said this to me: "Theater-trained people will never let you down." And she was right. And I pull primarily from theater, as I did when I was doing television. The more episodic, the more television credits you have on your résumé when I get it, the less likely I am to bring you in. For whatever I'm doing—even television.

So what you're really interested in is seeing that somebody has paid their dues in theater?

In theater and training. And I don't mean just New York. I mean dinner theater—Seattle, Florida, Pittsburgh, Boston. Really gotten up there on stage and broken down all the barriers and really worked.

Do you ever run into a situation where a stage-trained actor is performing in too large a size for television and film?

Well, TV is a little box, but I would rather have someone who is too big—to bring them down is easier than to bring them up.

Today I just came from film tests we're doing for *Helena.* and we did something that is absolutely wonderful. *Helena* is a feature I'm doing based on Helena Rubenstein, the cosmetic baroness, but it's more of a love story because it only goes for the first twenty-five years of her life. And we have F. Murray Abraham and Shelley Winters in the cast, and they are completely willing to go with an unknown in the female lead. And I've auditioned 478 actresses on both coasts. Today we got down to the actual, old-fashioned, full-blown film test. We tested eight actresses today, and it was really exciting.

What happens in a film test?

I don't think these actresses have ever been through something like this. Most actresses today rarely go through a full screen test, with hair, make up, camera—the whole works, the director there. My point in bringing it up was that one of the actresses was so down it was like pulling teeth to get her to come up to where we needed her. Whereas two of the actresses were so over the top, we just brought them down a notch and they nailed it. But the other actress ... we did three or four takes and she just never got up to it. So that's what I'm saying. I would rather have somebody a little too much larger than life.

These eight women who came today for the big test for *Helena,* how many times had they been seen before and under what circumstances?

Most of them probably had three or four or more preliminary auditions. They would have read for me first. We talked about a lot of star names, and we thought a star name would actually be a detriment because it would be like, "Oh, there's Meryl Streep playing Helena." And I think that's a problem. I saw *Steel Magnolias* in New York Off Broadway, and I saw it three times and absolutely loved the play because there were five unknown theater actresses up there, and I got totally lost in the story and it was terrific. When I saw the film, I saw Shirley MacLaine, I saw Dolly Parton. We realized that might happen in *Helena,* so that's why we shifted and went unknown. I released it in Breakdown, we released it in *Variety,* I got pictures from all over—pictures from New Zealand, Poland....

How many submissions were made for that role?

About three or four thousand. And I honestly looked at every one of them. A lot I eliminated on age, because I got a lot of pictures of women in their 30s and 40s. Based their photo, they would have come in and read for me and then come back—usually again just for me.

You wanted to see if they could do it twice?

Yeah, so I wasn't fooled the first time. And then they'd go in to the director, and we usually had another call back for the director, and we just today tested our eight actresses.

How can an actor whose work you don't know best get your attention?

Every piece of mail that is sent to me, I read myself. I think that's only fair. You've taken the time to write a letter, I should take the time to read it. I have always loved to find new people, that's been a thing with me. Even if it's a one-line role, I'll read fifty people for one line because you never know what you're going to find. And I also will bring in to my director a variety of ways and types. Everybody today said the eight women couldn't have been more different, physically.

You will not see when you come into my office six clones of yourself waiting to go in to see me. To me that's boring.

So to get your attention there has to be a picture?

Yeah, I'll look at the picture, but let's face it. You guys never look like that—especially the women. So I look at your picture first, but then I really do flip it over immediately and I look at where you've studied, who you've studied under, who you've worked with—which is why it is essential when you put down the theater that you've done, you don't just list the play and the role. List the director and where you did it. It can only help you because I might know one of the directors you've worked with, and I'll go: "Oh gosh—so-and-so hired you. I like his or her taste." I'll bring you in. Or it's a certain theater that I know puts out really above-standard work, that's what's going to jump out at me. I do see the agents' people that are submitted and I also have my ideas, but I try, out of my generals—people whose résumés I've saved—to bring in many of those people also.

So those people might not necessarily have agents?

There are about four people in *Blood and Concrete* that didn't have representation. And on *Shakes the Clown* there are about another five that don't have theatrical representation and three of them are standups. I went to Igby's and the Comedy Club and brought them in.

How do you feel about showcases? Showcases being a series of scenes, as opposed to a production of a play.

There are pros and cons to both. I'm forming a theater group here now because I'm segueing out of casting into directing. I see that's an avenue that's the next step for me. I don't want to become a "frustrated casting director"—I think there are a number of them out there and I think you see it in a lot of the work.

What are the frustrations of being a casting director, as opposed to being a director?

I have always said to myself the day I wake up and I don't want to go to the office is the day I take another job. I'm not at that point. I love casting, but I see that more of what I want to do is to direct. I love working with the actor in my office because I know when the actor comes in and reads for me how much I'm responsible for his getting the role.

By the direction you give him, by the way you read with him?

By the way I read with him, by the adjustments I give him. So to me that's kind of a rush and I like that.

How do you feel about an actor memorizing the scene for a film audition? Should the actor try to memorize it?

Absolutely not. Because you will lock in to that way. You will not be open to me throwing some suggestions at you. I'm not saying all of you, but with the majority of actors, in my experience, that happens. What I like is for you to be very familiar with the role, very familiar with the scene, and keep it open. This case today—obviously I wanted the women with the film test to be off book because we did blocking and we did movement, and that's difficult if you're holding a book.

But when I meet the actor now and you've read the full script, I don't give you any indication of what I'm looking for. I'll ask if you have any questions and if you do I'll answer, but I try not to give you any direction ... because I respect every actor as a creative individual. I want to see your interpretation, and it may be completely different than the one I had in mind, but I love it. Or you may have some colors of the character that I want and we'll work on it a little bit. When you come in and you've memorized it, it's really hard to shake that out of the person.

Especially with kids. That was a real problem because when I did "Charles in Charge" and *Annie* I met more stage mothers. We auditioned 12,000 girls for Annie. Do you know how many stage mothers and aunts and grandmothers that is? But I was adamant. I would not let the children take the scenes home with them. There's an age from about 6 to 12 where kids are just kids. They're not acting. And they're just spontaneous, wonderful, creative, fun little people. You never know what they're going to do. After 12 they do start getting a little actory and they understand more of what you want and you can talk to them more on an adult level. I can pretty much tell right away when I read a kid whether I'm going to have him back or not. It's just a gut feeling, and I won't let them take the sides because they'll go home and grandma and mom will coach them and inevitably ruin their performance.

Are there common mistakes you see actors make in auditions that you wish you could warn them against?

Obviously, just keep yourself open—and most people are. If they have it memorized and they're pretty open, I can throw them an adjustment. And many times when you come in and I love what you've done, I'll throw you a curve just to see if you can take it.

A big adjustment.

Yes. Especially if I don't know you and I'm meeting you for the first time. Because when you get on the set, many times the role changes. I need to know that the actor I'm bringing to my director is capable of that.

How important is video tape in the casting process these days?

I don't think video tape is important. I hate watching it. That's why we spent $5,000 today and screen tested these women on film, because film does it for me. Video tape is the biggest liar in the world. And I get mad that actors think they have to have video tape on themselves.

So many agents demand producers and directors see tape on you. Well, I think that's horrendous, because tape is not going to tell you anything about an actor, it's really not. The only time tape is useful to me is if I have worked with you and I know your work. You have either worked for me or auditioned for me a number of times, and I'm a fan of yours and I know what you can do. And say I'm casting a role that has to shoot in two days and you're in Cincinnati doing a show; on my say-so I can just show a little bit of your tape to the director, so they get the sense of you, and I can hire you off the tape. But that's the only time I've ever used tape. I don't like it.

Jerry Franks

Jerry Franks is an independent casting director who, with his former partner Al Onorato, was responsible for casting the series "Fame" and "Barney Miller"; the mini-series "Deadly Intentions"; the feature film Bagdad Cafe, *which won an Artios award from The Casting Society of America; the pilot to the HBO series "Vietnam War Story" and many other projects. He also cast the television movies "Long Road Home," "Kids Like These," and "Matters of the Heart," and the series "Picket Fences." Former casting positions include a stint as Executive in Charge of Talent and Casting for Twentieth Century Fox and one as Director of Talent and Casting for Columbia Pictures Television. He is President of the Casting Society of America.*

Jerry, how did you get into casting in the first place?

Well, I came out from New Jersey in 1964 and went directly to work for Universal Studios. In those days it was easier than it is now to obtain work. I really walked into this dumpy personnel office and filled out an application. And fortunately I was—and still am—a very adept typist, and they immediately grabbed me and I started there.

After two and a half years at Universal I went back to UCLA to finish my graduate studies and went into private practice in psychology for five years. But I couldn't deal with the negativity. So at 28 I quit—sold my practice and quit my job at the V.A.—and I went back to Universal and became a secretary again and just sort of worked my way up.

You find less negativity in casting than you did in psychology?

Well, it's like exchanging one set of nuts for another. I find more rejection in casting from the actor's standpoint, but less negativity because there's so much more creativity, as opposed to dealing with drug addiction and alcoholism. They didn't have Antabuse at that time, and there are some other drugs that weren't on the market then that help somewhat now. I don't know that it's any less disheartening, but it's easier if you want to get over an addiction today than it was twenty years ago.

What about an addiction to acting?

One never gets over an addiction to acting.

Do you think it has been useful in terms of background for a casting director to have trained in psychology?

It has given me a lot of insight. I think there are a lot of people in casting today in New York and out here that are not sensitive to the actors' needs and egos, wants and desires. I think it's unfair to bring in a caster who is not compassionate. Because you guys are in a profession that is full of rejection. That's all it is—rejection. And you have to learn how to address the fact that it is not you. There are so many variables in casting. So you could be the next Meryl Streep or Harrison Ford in terms of acting, but you have blue eyes and they need somebody with brown eyes. There are a lot of variables that actors don't understand.

Is there any advice you can offer actors about this whole question of rejection?

I think you need to leave the interview and know that you've done the best that you can do and go on with your life. You cannot sit at the phone waiting for the call that you got it or you didn't get it. And more times than not you didn't get it because of other variables—like the lead of the series or the feature film will not work with an actor taller than himself. Or the leading lady will not work with someone prettier than she. They're casting a daughter, and both parents have dark hair; you have blonde hair. You're either too tall or too short, too old or too young. There are so many variables that actors don't know about.

And actors generally leave a casting session thinking they should have done this or that. But you did what you did and that's the end of it. Don't run home and beat yourself over the head thinking what you could have done or didn't do.

Sitting in a waiting room, waiting to go in for an audition, don't do one of these "Why am I here? This lady is blonde and this lady is black and this lady is tall and this lady is short." You can never outguess what the producer, the director, the casting director are looking for. And you can psych yourself right out of a job by going into a reading with all this negativity. What you need to do is really concentrate on blocking that out and just addressing what you're going in there for. That's the bottom line. And when you leave the room, forget it. Don't drive that negativity around with you.

You've been active in CSA. I'd like to hear you talk a little about how the casting director position has developed and changed over the past few decades. Also what CSA consists of and what your criteria for membership are.

Forty years ago casting directors were called Talent Scouts, and they would go around the country and spot certain looks. In those days there was not the competition there is today, and in the last ten years it's like. . . wow! I used to know ninety-five percent of the actors in Los Angeles, and I just can't keep up with them anymore.

Within the last ten or twenty years, casting directors have begun to receive credit on the screen, which they never did before. CSA started ten years ago. Before it was CSA it was the American Society of Casting Directors, and acceptance was by interview only. We then expanded, and the criterion is now two years on-line credit—which means that your name has to have appeared on screen for two years at some point during your career. And recommendation by two other members.

What advice would you offer to a person interested in getting into casting?

Anyone trying to get into casting must sit at the front desk for a minimum of two years, sometimes three.

Be an assistant in a casting office?

Be an assistant, which means they learn all the agents in town, they know who the agents are, they know a multitude of actors because the pictures come across their desks, the actors come in and hound them. They know who their employers are casting and what they're looking for. We ask our assistants always to read the scripts and get to know our taste.

But prepare to pay your dues. You cannot sit at the desk for two months and then say, "I'm ready to cast a feature film." It would be comparable to going to the UCLA School of Medicine and taking two biology courses and learning how to hold a scalpel and saying, "Well, I'm ready for surgery."

It's a very arduous job. It's not glamorous. And once you make it, it's even harder. You've got to constantly keep up with who the actors are. I just went to New York and met 120 actors I had never seen in my life.

Tell us about the project you were doing and how that worked.

The project was the Jane Seymour television movie "Matters of the Heart," and we saw actors out here for about four weeks for the role of Jane Seymour's 17-, 18-year-old daughter. Based on the fact that the script takes place in upstate New York, where there's a completely different attitude, I had an instinct that actors in New York might be more likely to have a feel for it. As it turned out, the actor we hired grew up in a small town and was aware of the lifestyle and the challenges and the frustrations involved in breaking out of it. I grew up in a small town myself, so I was totally aware of who this person was.

So we're dealing with a situation in which life experience may be more crucial than acting ability.

Yes. Acting is not acting. Acting is just being. Acting is just life experiences, and that's why Meryl Streep, Hoffman, Pacino and all these people run around to prisons and hospitals and do whatever they do to get into the knowledge of what the role is. If one has not had a life experience, one must learn or observe.

In terms of your casting experience in New York, are you aware of a difference in attitude between New York actors and California actors?

It's like a shot of adrenaline when I get into New York because I feel that New York actors are so serious about their craft. Now I interviewed 120 17-, 18-, and 19-year-olds, and they knew theater, they knew plays, they were all studying and working two jobs, sacrificing.

In Los Angeles, with the exception of the people who have come out from New York, it's like Be-Bop City. People get off the bus from Iowa and they think here they are, they're going to be a star tomorrow. They're not prepared to study, they're not prepared to sacrifice, they're not prepared to go out and do theater. I think a lot of people in Los Angeles slide through on their looks or their charm. And I say to actors, "If you're having a tough time, don't worry, because talent always comes through. It always surfaces." And you have to hold on to that or else address getting out of this business.

At what point should an actor think about getting out of this business?

Well, because I'm such a positive person, I think that if you have a goal you should stick to it. But I think you must be honest with yourself at a certain point in your career. If you're 40 and it hasn't happened, you might think about staying in the business but in a different area. It's just not there for you.

How can a performer whose work you don't know best get your attention?

I recommend that actors go out for theater, for plays. There's so much good theater in Los Angeles, it's unfortunate that a lot of actors are too lazy to go out for roles. If you are on the stage, you never know who's going to pop in—agents drop in, casting people drop in. Al and I are notorious for going to Act One at one theater and then rushing over to Act Two somewhere else. And we alternate, so we catch four plays a night.

I do not suggest making tapes at home. I call them Loving Hands of Home tapes. The lighting is wrong, the sound is wrong, and you don't know with whom you're acting, and you could be the world's greatest actor and it would never come across.

What are some of the major mistakes you see actors make in auditions time after time?

The most major mistake is attitude. The actor will walk in with a cigarette in his hand and walk over and do this cocky number, walking in as the next Meryl Streep of the industry. And that is like Turn-off City. I can tell in a flash. And having a modicum of background in psychology, I know that they are really the most insecure.

Another problem is that they think they're ready to work and they're not. If you get an agent to take a chance on you based on your look or your experience or maybe just your general attitude toward the profession, and if they send you out when you are definitely not ready to read, that's the kiss of death. Now I don't preclude actors from coming back, but I wait at least six months to have them back.

That's why I keep saying wait until you feel ready. I know actors that have told me they don't want to go out for two more years, and I cite the example of Richard Chamberlain. He was just not an actor when he did "Dr. Kildare." But he left Los Angeles and went to London to study arduously for two or three years, and came back and really is now an actor.

In New York it's much more common for actors to be studying, no matter where they are in their career.

Yes. It's called honing your craft, or exercises. I mean even wonderful dancers still take class every day. George Chakiris is a friend of mine. George Chakiris was a star of *West Side Story*. He has never not taken a dance class every day in his life. And that's dedication. It's like the physician who doesn't stop reading every journal that comes out. It's a profession. You must treat it like a profession.

Here in L.A. are there particular teachers that you have a lot of respect for?

There are, but I'd rather not name names. I can tell you ten people for whom I have a great deal of respect as coaches or as agents, but I'm not the client and you may hate them. It just doesn't work if the chemistry isn't there. And that's why I say, when the time comes to take classes outside of normal schooling, go out and audit as much as you can.

What about things like cold reading workshops run by casting directors, run by directors? In general, are those useful?

They're very useful in terms of technique, of knowing what to do and what not to do in a cold reading. I think you have to be very judicious about where you're going. But if you're just going in to meet a casting director, thinking that you're going to get a job, don't go to those things. You've got to go and work with qualified people who will honestly tell you what it's all about. We have had in the last two or three years a major brouhaha over this.

I know there has been a lot of controversy over whether members of CSA should, in effect, be paid to go and watch a workshop.

Watching scenes, we are not permitted to get paid. Teaching a course is a different situation, and there are several casting directors in the city that do teach and they are credentialed. But there are also actors who teach. I pick up the *Dramalogue* every week, and I see So-and-So is teaching and I think So-and-So can't act himself. So you have to know with whom you're getting involved, because they can really give you information that is dangerous and then you have to undo it.

I think the best way is to talk to your friends. Talk to people that have been in class with whomever. Like going to have pictures taken. You don't just say, "Oh here's a list of photographers. I'll take that one." You go to see their portfolios and you ask people, "Who took your pictures? They were wonderful." And then go in and interview that photographer and see what he has in mind. Because your picture must look like you. Period. You don't want color shots and you don't want artsy fartsy.

Let's talk for a minute about this whole question of the camera loving certain faces.

We're talking about a face that jumps on the screen. If you take Meryl Streep and put her on a television screen that's very small, there's something about the chemistry—you have to watch! It's like Katharine Hepburn said about Michael Jackson: "No matter whether you like him or you don't like him, you cannot take your eyes off him." There's something that jumps off. And Meryl Streep can then go to the large screen and she's bigger than life. She's really there, as opposed to other actors who just do not translate. They're great on television or in the theater, but they just don't come across on the big screen. Television is much less threatening to a lot of actors than feature films because in features your face is blown up hundreds of times.

So there has to be a proportion and an energy ... something going on.

Is that a quality of energy you can pick up from a photograph sometimes?

I can pick up a photograph and know in a second. I had this experience with Mickey Rourke. Mickey Rourke walked into my office and my heart started pounding. This is magnetism. And he wasn't a member of the Guild. He was brand new, no SAG card, nothing. No experience. And I was at Columbia in those days and ran him down to this producer who said, "No, he's just not the right type." But I knew that he was going to hit any second and he did shortly thereafter. I think you're born with part of that, but I think it's also developable.

If you do have this, how could you best develop it?

Self confidence. And I think actors must carry themselves with the attitude ... not that they are better than everyone else, but that they are secure within themselves. They like themselves and don't feel that if they lose a role it's because of their lack of acting ability. It was because of a look or a matching problem.

Don't go in and act desperate. You cannot give off the vibe of being desperate, because then it will never happen for you. You've got to go in and acknowledge by attitude that you don't need this job—I'm not talking about an attitude of nose up in the air, but that you don't need this job to pay your rent. You've got to go in saying, "If I get this, fine. If I don't, I really like this role and it's too bad, but it's not the end of the world."

I love it when an actor comes into the room and meets the producer and the director and stands up—and you always know it's a good actor when they do this. They'll pick up the side and say, "Oh yes, it's so nice to meet you all." And then they'll go right into the scene, as opposed to doing sixteen exercises, breathing and stretching and shaking. They're serious and they know what they're doing.

Jerry, what are your major frustrations with the casting process? What would you like to see changed about the way it's done?

I would like to see more trust from the producers so we can be more creative. We recently had a role of a pimp, and the producer wanted a black actor with an open shirt and chains, and I said, "I know a lot of white pimps. Why can't this be an Asian pimp?" He was adamant about using a black actor because it was a certain story theme that went through this, but I insisted and they listened to me. The guy I was pushing for looked like a banker. And in real life most pimps really do not look like the stereotypical pimps we have seen on television. Why be boring?

Eugene Blythe

*E*ugene *Blythe is Vice President of Television Casting for Walt Disney Television. In that position, he oversees all casting for network television projects, including movies of the week, pilots for series and series. Before joining Disney in 1988 he was Director of TV Casting for MTM, where he cast* "St. Elsewhere" *and* "Newhart." *His feature credits include* Zoot Suit *and* Just Between Friends.

Gene, how did you get into casting?

My career actually started in the Army, where I was an entertainment specialist. I directed plays for the Army and coordinated the USO program in Korea. While I was in Korea, Helen Hayes came and she picked me and two other guys to tour with her to do scenes from American theater, and I did a bit from *Death of a Salesman*. And that's how I got the theater bug. Then when I got out of the service I went to New York. I still consider that the bulk of my career took place in New York. I started out as an actor in the 60s, and I was on Broadway in a couple plays, and then slowly my interests went another way.

I started out as a Production Manager in theater in New York, and one of the last places I was production manager was Taft Playhouse in Huntington, Long Island, which at the time was the only regional theater in America that did only original plays—*Vanities* came from there; *Gemini* came from there. While I was there, I wound up casting plays. I was there for three years and then I got two offers from California—one to go to ACT in San Francisco to be Production Manager and the other to work in the Casting Office at the Mark Taper Forum. So I came out here and started working.

Is it useful for a casting director to have been a performer?

I personally think so, for a couple of reasons. Not only can you read better with actors, but I think you understand the process and therefore can take shortcuts to get the best out of actors. Because you've been there, you'll go to greater lengths to make sure the actor is comfortable so they can relax and give their best. Also, because your eye's a little keener, you can tell if someone is forcing or pushing. I also think it helps you spot instincts for acting in green or novice talent.

What do casting people, directors, producers in California mean when they say, "Get me a New York actor"? What is a New York actor?

It doesn't really apply in New York. There was a time in the late 60s and maybe into the 70s where there was so much happening in New York that New York actors primarily stayed in New York because there was enough theater and other work to keep them there. Now everybody comes out here. We don't even have to go to New York that often anymore. But at the time I think it meant someone who takes their career seriously enough to dedicate a certain portion of their life to learning the skills and techniques it takes to be an actor and spend some time in regional theaters to learn what it means to work in an ensemble group. Theater training was especially good for "St. Elsewhere" and other productions like that—because it not only teaches you the discipline to sustain a performance, it teaches you the whole concept of ensemble playing which I think makes a more rounded performer, as opposed to someone who might be more presentational. I have always respected actors who were willing, for example, to give two years to the Neighborhood Playhouse or give three years to another drama program, as opposed to those who try to sort of build a career as they go along. Actors who take the time to set a foundation. In television especially, because time is of such essence, you have to be able to do the same thing twice. And that may sound simple, but there are a lot of people who can't. And the meter is always running because it's so fast. The director usually has no time to talk to an actor.

So you almost have to be able to direct yourself?

To some extent, absolutely. Because a lot of television directors are technicians. There are very few that are what I would call an actor's director.

That's been my experience acting in television. Do you think people who are trained for the stage find it difficult to bring their performance down to television or film size?

Sometimes you do get theater actors who are new to the television medium, and it takes them a while to be able to bring things down and not lose dimension. But I think good actors just sort of adapt.

What about the reverse—actors who have worked in television trying to work on stage without having had basic stage training? Is that as easy a jump to make?

No. That really involves technique. You have to have that training in voice. I would think it's much harder to bring a small performance up than to bring a large performance down, especially if you haven't been trained in that way.

Gene, what does the job of casting for a large production company like

Disney involve? How does it differ from the job of, say, independent casting director?

Well, it's totally different. I oversee freelance casting directors who actually cast episodic. So I'm not involved with Cop #1, Cop #2. What I am involved with most of the time is the stars or the regulars in a series and the concept with which we want the casting to go. Other than that, and because I'm able to attract really capable casting directors, it's not my style to treat them like assistants and put myself in the middle of their process. So I'll always be an added opinion and a consultant and the person that the company looks to. I'm now "The Suit." I'm a nice Suit—I think everybody likes me—but I am the person who comes in and says, "Gee, are we really thinking about this in the right way?"

At what stage of a project do you usually get involved?

From the beginning, before a casting director is ever assigned. As a matter of fact, these days I'm more involved with development and packaging. I'm usually involved from the moment we have a producer and/or writer who has an idea. So when it's just an idea I might come up with a list of names that might inspire the writers to think a certain way in terms of the parts. When we do have a script, I probably will be the person who comes up with the initial list of the people to star in the vehicle before a casting director is assigned.

What is your relationship to the network casting departments?

I try to treat the networks as partners because in theory we are partners. They're paying half the bills and the studio's paying the other half. So I try to keep it on an even keel. However, I am looking out for my studio's best interests and that may clash with what the networks feel they need or want—and often does.

Does the relationship differ from network to network?

Yes. Again, it's a matter of the personality of the network and also the tastes of the casting office. In some cases you have strong producers who just go on a direct course and say, "This is what we want," and until they redirect us we go on that way. But usually networks like to see choices.

What do they mean when they talk about choices?

When we're going in for regulars, they want to see three or four people for the same part. They don't really care whether they see one black, one white, one Hispanic or one ethereal lady as opposed to one stronger woman. They just want to see three or four choices so they're part of the process. The problem with bringing in choices is that they may choose someone you don't want. So you have to finesse that. You have to finesse it in a way that everybody feels good about. At MTM we would proceed with our choices until they vetoed them. If they vetoed them, we would bring them somebody else. And that's pretty much what I try to do now, as opposed to just opening up the field.

I also think that bringing in the studio's first choice on roles gives the network the opportunity to see the concept realized—not only the words but the casting concept—how we view the project. Maybe the network will say, "No, we really weren't seeing the show this way, and this is the way we were seeing the casting." So then we can straighten it out. But I think it's important to at least get the point of view of the studio and the writer across first.

Now when you go into the network with actors, on what level does the network have to approve for a series? All regulars?

Yes, usually. Unless they say, "We don't need to see that person." But usually they want to see all regulars.

With many new series these days I'm aware that the leading performers aren't very well known. Often the whole series will not have a single actor I've heard of.

Indeed. Most of the time, especially with the hour format, we're out there looking for new people. I describe television as this huge machine. We're constantly feeding it bodies and it needs more all the time. And the networks are always looking for new people—not the tried and true, because in recent years very few established people who have had one hit series have another hit series. People like Cosby come around once in a lifetime. Television is the maker of stars—that's why some people who have been doing movies and whose career sort of stalls want to come into television.

This is a different situation than twenty years ago.

Oh, absolutely. In that sense it's a very exciting playground to play in. In terms of casting, that's where the casting director gets his payoff—in discovering that new person who takes off.

Over the years you must have seen an awful lot of auditions—bad ones and good ones. What are some of the common mistakes actors make in auditions that you wish you could warn them against?

They talk too much. I think it's nervous talk. There's never anything wrong with an actor asking a question that's pertinent to the material before them. There's never anything wrong with discussing an opinion or approach to the material—making it concise and moving along. But a lot of times actors are too chatty. They're trying to ingratiate themselves and for that purpose, for the audition purpose, believing that saying the words effectively is what's going to get them the job.

My opinion is that the audition is not about getting the job, it's about establishing the idea that you deserve to be in the business. Because seventy-five percent of the time the reason an actor is not chosen for a job has nothing to do with their skills. It has to do with their hair color, their height, how the producers want to go. It's such a competitive business that we can get a 5'2" redhead man to match up with a 5'2" redheaded woman. So most of the time I think your concentration should be on preparing and looking at an audition as an opportunity to act, an opportunity to show that you belong in the business because we do so many projects that if you want it and you're working in the right way at it, it will happen.

Another mistake actors make when auditioning is bringing props. Props are almost never necessary. And time is of the essence. If you're chatting on or setting up props, the producer's mind starts to wander. So it's best to seize the moment, keep them interested. Get in, do your work, ask them if they need to see anything else, thank them for the opportunity, leave the room and go to a movie.

How important are pictures and résumés to an actor?

Well, in terms of the first contact with the casting director, it's very important. I look at every piece of mail that comes to me, and I make decisions based on résumés and pictures if I don't know the actor. I'm constantly astounded at how many times I respond to a photograph and it pays off in an interview. And in an interview with someone, I can get pretty good information as to whether or not they can act, mainly because they have a presence about them which, to my mind, is the most important element of acting. It's not so much whether you have a pretty face. It's whether or not you are in touch with your essence. I think an actors who are in touch with their truth and can reflect that are usually magnetic people—like Robert Duvall.

Is it true that the camera is in love with certain faces?

Yes. Sometimes it astounds me because certain people who are not particularly attractive in person just sort of fill out in front of a camera. I'm told that John Depp in person was not someone anybody really wanted to hire. Nobody was really crazy about the way he looked in person, but when he did the test, he just came alive.

How does a videotape test work and how important is it?

The taping process is a frustration most of the time for casting people. First of all, it's very static situation, very non-dimensional. They're not really interacting with another actor. It's a very unnatural setting. I think we can miss acting potential in the tape process. We just put a kid in a show, "The Fanelli Boys," who is probably going to be a huge star. And last year when I put him on tape for three or four projects nothing happened. But all of a sudden one day he woke up, I guess, and said, "I know how to do this now." And the next two auditions I had producers fighting over this guy.

As you know, the Screen Actors Guild has committees to further the casting of minorities and women—blacks, Hispanics, native Americans, women—to get them represented on television in proportion to their numbers in the population. Is there anything a person in your position can do or should do to further this?

Well, every time we have a casting session, we suggest a different way to go with the parts. For instance, on "St. Elsewhere," the Alfre Woodard role was never written as a black role. That was my suggestion. So I think the casting director's influence is to always be in there punching and saying, "Couldn't this be a female lawyer?" or "Does this have to be an Anglo?"

Do you find the networks are generally open to that?

Most of the time they're open to those kinds of suggestions. Sometimes it works conversely. On "St. Elsewhere" we had written a black couple into one of the scripts and the guys just never thought about it while they were writing. But this was about a wife abuse situation, and after it was written they said, "You know what? We can't do this. This is not right." So we changed it to an Anglo couple.

Given the fact that you are a couple of steps up from where most actors would enter the casting process, what's the best way for an actor whose work you don't know to get your attention?

The mail.

Send a résumé? A picture?

Yes. And as you're doing things, send me cards. I look at every piece of mail that comes across my desk, and it doesn't hurt your image for me to see you in a special context every week of my life. So if anything ever does come around, I say, "You know what...?" Or let's say a casting director will mention your name to me. I might say, "I know her. She's done a lot of stuff around town. Maybe this is somebody worth reading."

How about phone calls?

It's not really worthwhile, because I'm not going to take the phone call and there's really nothing for us to discuss. You're going to say, "I want to work," and I'm going to say, "When I have something for you I'll call you." You're not being realistic anyway, so you're not really respecting my time. And I can't take unsolicited tapes, because if I did I would never have time to look at any tapes.

Do you have any favorite outrageous stories of ways actors have attempted to get your attention or maybe gotten it in ways that didn't do them a lot of good?

The most embarrassing audition I ever had to sit through was at the Mark Taper Forum. The first Monday of every month, they have an open call. And so a woman came in with a bag of props and a throw blanket and proceeded to do the enema scene from "Sybil." And she screamed and wailed for like five minutes, and when she was through I just opened the door and explained to all the actors out there that I didn't touch this person.

Let's talk for a minute about agents. Do you have favorite agents you habitually call?

I always try to keep, more or less, an open attitude towards everybody. but yes, we all have our favorite people. What you really look for in an agent is someone who exhibits some taste, who has some kind of eye, who goes about their job creatively. And once you develop a relationship like that with somebody, you're not going to give it up, because we need agents. Especially the week-to-week episodic casting director needs agents because they need as much input as they can get. There are a lot of jobs to fill.

Is there ever a chance for an actor without an agent to get to you?

Oh, it's always been the case with me. Even in generals that I hold now, based on my response to the photograph and the résumé.

And when you have them in, what do you have them do? A scene?

When I went through the transition from theater to film, I hated doing general interviews. And I realized how many thousands of people are out there and that I don't have the time to read all these people initially. So I made the general interview pay for me in terms of trying to develop instincts for it. I never have anybody do a prepared scene now, because it tells me nothing about them. Because it doesn't matter if you can work on a part for thirty days and come up with something credible. I need to know that you can look over material in twenty-four hours and come up with something that will get you hired and not embarrass me or the producer. I think it's a little different in theater because you have more time for the rehearsal process, so you can see if someone can get to something. But in terms of television, it doesn't pay off. But in general interviews, I do try to make evaluations as to whether I think people can act or whether it's worthwhile in terms of their type, personality and that sort of thing to call them in for parts.

You can get a feel for them even if you've only talked to them for five, ten, fifteen minutes? How long is it generally?

Usually fifteen minutes, and then if we really start talking about fishing or something interesting, a half hour. I always try to get actors not to talk about acting. I always try to get them to talk about something else to get them to open up to me because that's really how I get in touch with their essence, with who they are. Sometimes I will throw them by saying, "So what do you want to do with your life?" and get them talking in a larger scale so I can get a sense of them. You're not going to get them to react when you talk about all the projects you're doing and the projects they've been doing. So I will try to talk about fishing or cooking.

What are your biggest frustrations with the casting process? What would you really like to change, if you could?

Well, on a personal level I regret that I couldn't respond to a lot of actors quicker because there was no material to bring them in on. There are so many people that we discover, and we just know they're going to take off and they do take off, but I can't do anything quick enough. That's a constant frustration.

We're not always casting simply on ability and the uniqueness of someone. A lot of times we are casting for cosmetic purposes, and sometimes I wonder if that's not just the lazy way to go and not really what the public wants. Because you are reminded daily of people on television that were not a pretty face but were so unique that they took off and people responded to them. Holly Hunter or whoever. Features seem to be able to do more of that than television. And that's a sort of frustration— not being able to approach my craft in a purely aesthetic way, having to pay so much attention to commercial considerations.

John Levey

*J*ohn Levey *is director of Television Casting at Warner Brothers, where he's in charge of casting for movies of the week, miniseries, sitcoms and drama series. Of all the projects he has worked on, he is proudest of the pilot and all the episodes of "China Beach."*

John, how did you get into casting in the first place?

By accident. I spent fifteen years directing in the theater before I got into casting. Had the National Endowment for the Arts scholarship at the Mark Taper Forum here in town and directed up and down the coast—South Coast Rep, The Old Globe in Seattle and other places on the West Coast. And was doing reasonably well and enjoying myself pretty much, although I was shocked to discover that the National Endowment for the Arts director's scholarship at a prestigious theater like the Mark Taper Forum pays $17,000 a year. Which is below the poverty level, actually. I mean, it was an incredible dream come true and I was thrilled, and then reality set in.

I had spent a little time in my early years directing in Los Angeles working for Breakdown Services, and during that time I had gotten to meet a lot of casting directors. I began to get a sense that it was a community that it might be fun to be part of, and it seemed clear that people made a living doing it. Then I directed a production here in town, *"The Dining Room"* by A.R. Gurney. And it was a bomb.

It happened that along about that time my wife got pregnant with our second child, so I got a job. During the year and a half I was at the Taper I was probably responsible for casting 150 to 250 roles for the readings they did. And then one night Barbara Claman came to see "The Dining Room." She had come to a number of plays I had directed at the Taper, and I'd gotten to know her reasonably well. We went out for a drink after the show and I was moaning about having gotten such a dreadful response to work that I thought was pretty damn good. And she said, "Why don't you come to work for me? You can start on Monday, $200 a week." So I did and I worked for Barbara for about ten months.

From Barbara I went to work for Marsha Kleinman, who for my money is the best casting director in the city and in television. Many casting directors don't really have a working understanding of the actor's process. Marsha does and insists that the people who work for her think of themselves as much more than list makers and availability checkers. I feel casting is an important part of the rewrite process and an important part of the rehearsal process—that I am the eyes and ears of the writer/producers and the directors.

Tell us about your current job. How does the job of casting for a large production company or studio like Warner Brothers differ from independent casting?

Greatly. I'm in the embrace of the largest entertainment corporation in the history of the world, Time/Warner, Inc. We are an enormous conglomerate—almost terrifying in some respects, especially for a child of the 60s. It's different in that respect. I never have to look for work—it's put on my desk on a daily basis. An independent who is getting a lot of work can make a very good living in this day and age in Hollywood. But as a staff casting director I get what I need because I'm a husband and a father—I have two children—and I get a decent living that is guaranteed by a contract, so I'm an executive.

When I first went into television I thought: Okay, it's time to join the whores. But now that chip on my shoulder from years in the theater is gone. I'm working with the smartest people I've ever worked with, people who care about what they do more than anybody I've ever worked with, people who are passionate, people who work hard, people who are a lot of fun.

Tell us a little bit about the beginnings of "China Beach." You cast the pilot for it.

Along with Phyllis Huffman I did, yes. It happened off-season. Interestingly enough, I think a lot of projects that happen off-season have a better shot of getting on the air than many projects that happen during the so-called pilot season. Pilot season is an insane institution, a feeding frenzy. One year it's 35-year-old leading men who can play comedy, and every single damn project is that. And then the next year it's "Murphy Brown" clones, and the next year it's "Batman" clones. Maybe actors don't want to hear this, but a series lead in television is a very rare commodity. Someone who can actually carry an hour drama on their shoulders every week for twenty-two weeks.

How did you find Dana Delaney?

Well, Dana had read for me for a Hallmark Hall of Fame Movie of the Week that I did when I worked for Marsha Kleinman. They were shooting it in Oregon someplace and they already had a bunch of girls in Oregon that they thought were okay, but they wanted to see some people down here.

So Marsha and I suggested that they read Dana Delaney, and she came in and it was unforgettable. For economic reasons, the studio insisted on using somebody at scale plus ten percent in Portland; Dana didn't get the job, but I was overwhelmed by her bravery as an actress.

And I knew that "China Beach" was going to require talent, a certain level of beauty because it was network television, a wide range of qualities—but the main thing it was going to require was bravery, because it was going to put an actress into circumstances that nobody else on television was going to be in. Phyllis and I each got a copy of this script and we went into our respective offices to read it and we finished it at almost the same time. And when we came out we both said, "Dana Delaney?"

Tell us what Dana Delaney went through to get this role. How many times did she have to come back?

Well, she came a day early to the first audition. It is actually kind of interesting, because she and John Young, whose office she was coming to, met and talked and spent maybe twenty, twenty-five minutes chatting, and then the next day when she came back, they already had laid the groundwork about the character. Some people say that was an accident, some people aren't so sure. She read for us. We read a lot of other people. She read for us again. At a certain point in the process we went over to the studio executives and said, "Here's where we think we are." They said, "She can stay in the mix. Keep looking." They nixed a lot of people for the other roles.

So we're looking at what period of time from the first time she read to when they said, "You're it"?

Four months.

And she had to hang in there and do a performance ... how many times?

She probably read ten times by the time she went through the networks. And then finally another wonderful young woman and she were the last two at the network. They read at the network live. The network wanted the other person. We really wanted Dana.

Did she change her performance in the course of these ten readings?

Actually, as people get closer and closer to jobs for series, they get worse and worse. It's almost axiomatic. Now Dana was working. She wasn't working a huge amount, but she was working—maybe making $35,000 a year. If you get a series at fifteen grand an episode and you start multiplying it times twenty-two ...your life changes. Completely. And so does the level of tension.

First you read for the casting director—there's just two of you in the room goofing around and it's easy and friendly. And then you go in and meet the directors and the producers and it gets a little harder, and you meet the studio executives and it gets a little harder, and you meet the network executives and it gets a little harder and a little more impersonal, a little scarier. You're really close to a job that's going to change your life, maybe forever. Then you have to do a screen test on top of that. Boy, it's a nerve-wracking process.

And it's a nerve-wracking process for casting directors because it's the only time of the year where your work is assessed publicly. Because when I cast an episode people may look at it and go, "I really hated that girl you cast." But they don't say it out loud in front of me. But here you go to the studio or you go to the network and say, "Here are our choices," and they say, "You ain't got it. Go back." That's hard to take. Especially when you think you have got it.

What advice would you give an actor in Dana's position, going back again and again and probably thinking: *Why aren't they saying yes? Am I doing something wrong? Maybe I should change it.*

Focus on your work. Don't let any of the rest of the bullshit get into your life at all. It's not possible, but just do your work. That's how you got past the first reading, the second reading and the tenth reading. Just try to breathe and do your work. It's very, very hard.

I've talked with a lot of casting directors about the problem of roles for women on television and the fact that roles for women very rarely drive the show. And in "China Beach" they do, as in "Cagney and Lacey," "Golden Girls," "Designing Women."

Well, television is the only place where women have a real opportunity to play ongoing, wonderful roles. You look at most of the feature films, it's shocking. It's Neanderthal. It's unbelievable.

Do you see any hope for that changing?

I find it pretty hard. There is hope, but I'm not quite sure what it's based on. A lot of people in my position are always saying, "I want to leave television and go do features." But I want to do television. I love the pace of television. I love it that decisions get made. And I love the opportunities for women and for minorities that are developed. I still think feature film opportunities for blacks in this country are shockingly limited to the worst element, because we want to see these disgusting crime movies—the "blaxsploitation" movies. And on "China Beach," because the Vietnam War was fought mainly by poor blacks and poor whites from urban and rural areas, there are wonderful roles.

Do you feel in general, John, that casting directors can have a serious effect on the under-representation on television of groups like women and minorities?

Yeah, sure. Only if you have taken the time to have a relationship with your producers where you can go in to them and say, "How about a black woman in this part for the judge?" "How about a handicapped man as the clerical person at the hotel in the financial department?" Why do we only have to hire people that it's written for?

And there is a great inverse racism on television. For example, I've got a nasty guy on "China Beach," a real shithead. "We cannot use a black here. It's a negative image." So that's a job that a black doesn't get.

When you're casting "Head of the Class," and you hire young people on their first or second jobs, do you find them through agents primarily? Do you see them in little theaters?

I have to admit that I don't go to the theater as much as I used to. It's kind of like seeing an old lover: "I wonder what I ever saw in her." It's very hard for me to sit through bad plays now. And I hate leaving at intermission, but I do it, because I hate being bored more than I hate leaving. So I don't see a lot of people in plays, although now I have an assistant, and they're covering stuff for me. I have very good relationships with agents, so when they sign somebody who they think is really cool and new, they'll call me and say, "I just got this new person and I think they're really terrific. Why don't you meet them?"

So they'll come to your office?

They'll come to my office and maybe I'll just talk to them and get a feel for them or maybe they'll do some work for me or maybe I'll have something they're right for right away.

They might do a monologue for you in your office?

Sometimes, if they have one. You talk to them for five minutes and *you* say, "Do you have something in your bag? Jump up and do it for me." And most of them don't have anything, which I think is fairly shocking.

So it's a good idea to have something ready.

Yes! You never know when someone's going to ask you to jump up and work.

A couple of monologues? A comedy and dramatic number?

Yes. I think you should be working all the time! Working harder than the next guy. A lot of people go into acting because they're the prettiest girl in the class or they're the funniest guy in class or somebody gives them that kind of positive attention that creates that need for more attention. They grow up and say, "I should do this. This is a nice way to make a living."

But they don't get the kind of discipline and training that a dancer gets—you can't dance for Twyla Tharp or Merce Cunningham if you don't have your chops up. It can't be done! And a lot of you slide around through your time, partly because you can't afford to study. But I think every actor should be reading out loud every day, I think you should be getting together with groups of friends every week and reading plays out loud, whether you're right for the part or wrong for the part. You should be driving yourselves. You should be playing scales. You should be stretching muscles every day of your life. I mean, there are a zillion actors ahead of you, further along than you are right now. And you may be talented, but if you aren't going to work as hard as they are, they're going to work more than you are. I promise. And it is shocking how lazy actors as a group can be.

I would like to talk about the importance of video tape for an actor, a demo video tape that an actor has of scenes done in other shows or put together from monologues. How do you feel about video tape? Is it an important factor in getting a shot at something?

It can be. It can change my mind sometimes. But it also can be the kiss of death, if the tape is a wrong tape. I think home videos—your made scenes and monologues—are essentially useless from a casting director's point of view because they're nothing you would show to a producer—the quality is so dreadful. Also, actors, in my experience, tend to choose the wrong material. I went to a college showcase last year where two actors in their early twenties did a Pinter play about people in their late 60s looking back at their relationship. I wanted to run screaming from the theater.

So choose something that's appropriate age-wise?

And also to what you are. If you're gorgeous, you should be playing the leading lady. If you're not, you shouldn't. You're not going to get a job as a leading lady in commercial television. It may not be fair, I know. I found a woman I love and I'm not Robert Redford, so it's possible for regular-looking folks to fall in love in real life. It's very unlikely for them to fall in love on television.

Be realistic about yourself. It's critical. Even when you have the advantage of a wonderful agent who's a great salesperson, actors are the product and the salesperson at the same time. I don't care how good a salesperson you are, if you don't know how a vacuum cleaner works, you can't sell it. If you're trying to sell it as a water fountain, you're not going to do very well. You've got to know what it is and how it works. And you have to understand the commercial marketplace, understand where you fit into it in order to successfully market yourself.

John, what are your major frustrations with the casting process? Is there something you would like to see changed or done away with?

I don't think it can be changed. As hard as we try in my office and as hard as I insist with the people who work for me that we respect the humanity of actors as a ... really a sacred thing, my major frustration is that it is impossible, given the constraints of time and money that television has, to really respect the humanity and the performance.

Robin Nassif

R obin Nassif is Director of Casting, West Coast, for ABC Entertainment. Since 1984, she has supervised the casting for many pilots and on-air series, including "Ellen," "All American Girl," "On Our Own," "Grace Under Fire," "Roseanne," "The Wonder Years," "Perfect Strangers," "Growing Pains," "Home Improvement," "Coach," "The Young Riders," and Life Goes On." Prior to joining ABC, Robin was a Staff Casting Director for Embassy Television, where she was responsible for casting "One Day at a Time," "Facts of Life," "Silver Spoons," and the pilot of "Who's the Boss?"

How did you get into casting, Robin?

Well, I graduated from U.C. Berkeley, and my college roommate's father was an actor, and he was doing a show for Norman Lear called "Hot L Baltimore." And he got to be friendly with the lady who did all the costumes for the Norman Lear shows and they needed a runner, so he recommended me to be a runner. I started off doing odd jobs, picking up and delivering costumes. Eventually I become a key costumer and had my own show called "One Day at a Time." But I was horrible at this and it was sort of mutually decided that I would leave, finally, because it was really not my cup of tea.

I had made friends with the lady in charge of personnel for Norman Lear, and I said, "I want another job." So she called me about this job in casting. It was a huge cut in pay, and I moved back in with my parents and sort of started all over again.

Over the next six years I was a receptionist, casting assistant, casting associate and then finally I became a casting director in 1982. And that's when I worked on "Facts of Life," "One Day at a Time," "Square Pegs" and various pilots. And then I followed my boss over from Embassy to ABC. I went to the network in 1984 and have been there ever since.

I know you had a particularly dramatic day today. Could you tell us about what happened? I think it would probably tell us a lot about a network casting director's job.

This started last night actually. I got a call from my boss, Donna Rosenstein, who said, "I hope you had a nice weekend because I didn't." I said, "What happened?" and she said, "Well, Connie Selleca [star of an ABC show called "Baby Talk"] quit. Or was fired." She had a huge screaming fight with the producer on Friday. She's not coming back to the show, and the show is in production. We've shot one show already, and we must find a person to fill her role this week. So Donna said, "We're having a meeting at 8:30 in the morning to come up with ideas, and obviously you'll be there."

So I was there at 8:30 this morning, and we came up with a whole list of names. I went through lots of folders of other shows I've worked on and listed everybody I could think of. My boss went over to have a meeting with Ed Weinberger, who is the producer in question. They didn't come up with anything in the meeting, so when I came back from lunch there was a note on my desk: "Call me immediately at Ed Weinberger's office." I called her and she said, "You're moving over here. We're casting this show out of here this week."

So I had to take all my files and my secretary and move over to Raleigh Studios—which has never happened in the history of my working at ABC. I'm literally there as his casting director because he didn't hire his own casting director. So we have a session set up tomorrow from one o'clock to five o'clock with various and sundry leading ladies coming in to read for this part. We're under a lot of pressure.

So that's what I was doing today. I was sending out scripts and checking availabilities and making sure he was going to have a set full of actors. And I'm doing a lot of pre-reads in the morning. I'm reading actors to see whether or not they're good enough to go to him. I'm doing that from 9:30 to 1:00, and whoever's good out of that session we'll add to the session that we already have set up. We have to find somebody who's beautiful, who's funny and who Ed can get along with.

In the process of trying to come up with lists, what role do agents play?

Agents are so important. I cannot stress how important agents are. What I did was, I sat down, and we made a list of people we wanted. We make an A list and a B list. Then I called all the agents for all the actors, and while I was talking to the agents I said, "Not only are we interested in this person, but is there anybody else you represent that you think could be right for this?" So they had an opportunity to give me other ideas of people I might not have thought of. Then, after we did that, I went back again and sat down with the agency book, which is really important to have. It lists all these different agents and what they're in charge of at the agencies. And I went through every single agency that I knew of to see if I'd left any agencies out.

How many agencies did you get in touch with?

I probably will have contacted about a hundred theatrical agencies over the next few days.

So what happens then when the first group comes in in the morning—the ones you're not sure about?

If I see something there that looks like it could be right, I'll probably recommend that they work on it a little more, I'll give them some direction and I'll have them come back for the afternoon session to read for Ed. But they'll have to be really good because he's very picky and he demands funny. So I have to be really sure of who I'm sending to him.

In a situation like this, Robin, is it a good idea for an actor to memorize the scene?

It's not necessary, but it's always helpful. But the thing I hate to see is an actor who comes in and has tried to memorize it and hasn't and keeps stumbling over the material. I'd rather have them have it in their hand as a security blanket and just refer to it every once in awhile. Producers who write their own material do not like it when actors ad lib and try to change it around. They like it the way they wrote it. So it's an insult to them if you don't do it that way. Obviously Robin Williams can improv, but most people don't have that comedic genius, so it's better to leave it to the writers.

I have noticed in comedy shows I've worked on that they're much more particular about the line being absolutely accurate than in any other kind of show—and with good reason. Because the timing and the rhythm are so crucial.

That's true. Absolutely. Another thing I always say is, "When you come in and you do it and you get a callback, please do it exactly like you did it when you came in." Because that's what they want. They want to show it to another group of people to see how they feel about what you did. If they want you to do something different, they'll tell you to do something different. But don't make something up or change it or embellish it. I've seen more actors blow parts through trying to make something different the next time they come in. Wear the same thing, read the same way, do everything as close as possible to the way you did it the first time.

I think a lot of us have the feeling if we were perfect we would have been cast the first time round. But that is not so, given the situation in television. Could you explain why that is?

Well, the first person you read for could be the casting director or a casting assistant. The next people you're going to go to are the writers and producers of the show. The next group will be the studio heads, the people who run that studio. And then you go to the network.

So you are reading usually for different people each time, and what the casting director wants to show eventually to the network is that this person is right for the role. And they want you to do what they saw you do. So that's why it's really important to give the same thing. Sometimes they'll have you come back in again and usually, if you're coming back in again for the same people, they'll tell you what they want you to do differently. Because maybe they didn't see the comedy, or maybe you were talking too fast or maybe they needed to see a side of the character that they want you to portray. But if you are coming back in a second time and there's no reason for it, then just do the same thing you did before.

Let's talk a little bit about network approval in the casting process for, say, a pilot for a new series. For what roles does the network require approval of an actor?

At ABC we have approval over all the series regulars. We do not get involved with the recurring roles. We do not get involved with the guest stars. And we do not get involved with the small speaking roles. We let the producers pretty much do their own thing.

Now that doesn't mean that we tell people who to bring in and who to see. We all sit in a room at the end of the process and talk about who we think is right. It's not like they call us and say, "Can we have so-and-so?" and we say "NO!" We never say, "You can't bring that person to network."

But every once in a while if there is a really important producer, like a Steven Bochco who is tried and true and knows every actor in town, sometimes that producer will make a certain deal with the network development people ahead of time and say, "Look, I don't want to schlep actors over to the network. I'm just going to send you videotape on the actors I want. You will look at it and tell us if you will approve these people." And that's happening more and more too. But the greener a producer is, the more we will supervise them and work with them.

By the time an actor is actually presented to the network by a producer, the deal is usually in place, isn't it? Could you explain that?

Yes. We have what we call a test-option deal. No actor reads at the network before his test-option deal is signed. No one. ABC has a very strong policy about that because what has happened in the past is that occasionally an actor would come in, they would be someone we would all be interested in seeing, they would not sign their deal, they would read, everybody would become wildly excited and then the agent would say, "Oh no, we want three times more money."

So now we make sure that every single actor's deal is in place before they walk through that door to read. And if we have to hold up readings, if we have to sit there and wait for faxes to come through, if we have to wait for contracts to be delivered, we do. Nobody reads at the network without a signed deal.

I think this is common to all the networks, not just ABC. And we may be talking about a seven-year deal with a series.

And for the same part there can be an actor who has a test-option deal for $15,000 a week and one that has one for $65,000 a week. It depends on how much the actor has done, how much experience they have, how strong the agent is, how cutthroat the agent is. You can have three different people reading for the role and very different deals. We really don't cast someone because they're cheap. We cast someone because they are right for a role. And many times we end up going with the most expensive actor because they are the one that is really reading the material correctly.

Robin, recently I know you've been involved in casting children in "Who's the Boss?" and "Growing Pains." How do you feel about workshops for children? Training them at an early age?

Well, I think if there is a child who has an amazing personality who is very focused and very bright, that it's terrific. If the mother has the time and the energy to take the child around and take them to the acting classes and do all this stuff, I think it's great. I think that certain kids have a very hard time and end up in a bad place, and certain kids come through it great. Obviously Todd Bridges didn't do so well. Obviously the kids on "Growing Pains" are doing great. They're not on drugs and they're very happy and they're very well adjusted and they're nice kids. It depends on the family structure and it depends on the upbringing and it depends on the way the parents deal with it.

When you seek out a child performer, do you mainly go through agents? What is the search process for you?

Yes. We call the children's agents. There are many of them. And we have the children come in and read. Sometimes we'll go to schools. We did a TV movie last year starring Mare Winningham, about a young mother who had a child and who was homeless. And the boy who played the teenage boy in that, Dante Smith, had never acted before in his life—we found him in school in Brooklyn. And we brought him in and he read and blew everybody away and got the part.

We look everywhere for kids. You never know. And kids are so natural they don't have to study. Some of the ones that study are great. Other kids never took a lesson in their life and they're just naturally wonderful. Gary Coleman never took an acting class in his life.

Talking about adult actors now, how can a performer whose work you don't know best get your attention?

I've been asked this question a lot. People say, "Should I send a silly letter? Should I send balloons? Should I send something outrageous?" The way an actor gets my attention is if I get a really interesting, really good headshot. And I call in actors—in fact just recently, out of the blue, I got a picture sent by a young lady, 15 years old, who didn't even have a résumé, but her head shot was really good. She looked really interesting and really pretty and I set her up and brought her in, and she's a really good actress and I'm going to try to find something for her. I meet a lot of people through pictures that are submitted to me, but I don't meet everybody. Some of the pictures are absolutely horrendous, and they go in the trash can because 1 can't even tell what the actor looks like.

Is it a good idea to write a cover letter of some kind?

Yes, but please, when you write a cover letter, get the casting director's name right. I've had so many letters addressed to Robert Nassif and Robin Nassar. It's really a pet peeve of casting people not to have their names spelled correctly.

We're talking about a brief cover letter?

A brief cover letter that's personalized: "Dear Robin, I just got in town from New York." Tell me about a play that you just co-starred or starred in. Tell me about something that I would be interested in. "I just worked with Joe Papp doing Shakespeare in the Park and I played the role...." Boy, I'll take a second look at that. That to me is interesting. Or "I just guest starred on the pilot of such-and-such." Or mention anything that you think might catch my attention in an acting way.

Let's talk for a minute about résumés. What impresses you on a résumé?

I don't like a résumé that's really, really crowded. If you have a lot of credits, make your résumé nice and concise, and don't put on a bunch of stuff that nobody's ever heard of. What you want is a short indication in each category of what you've done and hopefully the best known things. I would much rather see a résumé with five things I've heard of on it than with twenty-five things I've never heard of. Obviously, when you're starting out that's really hard. But that's eventually what you want to get to.

I love to see theater on a résumé. That is more interesting to me than all the television and film. If I see a strong theater background and I don't know the person and I recognize the theaters they've worked in, I'll be much more likely to call them in than if they have a few TV credits and no theater.

How do you feel about actors doing extra work? Is there a prejudice against them as serious actors?

Absolutely. Don't do it. If you want to be an actor, don't do extra work. Don't do stand-in work. I know of only one instance where an actress worked as a stand in for me and now is doing guest-starring or featured roles. It's okay to do small speaking roles, day-player work, under fives. Don't do extra work, because you will get typed, and you will get into a rut of doing the extra work and not really focusing your career on being an actor with lines. You're not going to learn that much being an extra.

How important is a performer's videotape for the kind of casting you do?

It's very important. For example, today when I was talking to agents and I didn't know a particular actor, they said, "I will send you a videotape tomorrow so you can see this actor's work." And I said, "Great." But a lot of actors don't have videotapes—it's hard when you're first starting out. That's when you have to get yourself in the door and be ready for people and get yourself on shows, meet casting people and have them give you small parts, and that's the way you get tape. The more credits an actor has, the more important the tape becomes. It's really good to have a nice composite tape of three or four things that you've done—really short, really succinct.

How short is " really short " ?

Well, casting directors lose patience after about five minutes. So have your best stuff in the first five minutes. Two minutes of a drama, two minutes of a comedy, two minutes of a soap—however you have it set up.

If you don't have any shows you've actually done on television or film, how do you feel about going to your neighborhood production house and getting one made up, or having your friend with a camcorder do a scene of you?

The only time you can get away with that, in my opinion, is when you're a standup comedian and you have somebody come in and film your standup act. And even then you need to be close enough, you need to have good volume, you need to be able to have a few close ups. I don't like watching stuff that was done in somebody's apartment.

Let's talk for a minute about auditions, the audition process. Do you have any absolute no-no's in advising an actor how to conduct himself in an audition?

My pet peeve is lateness. Never—I repeat, never—be late to read for a casting director in a studio or for producers or writers, because if you keep them waiting they're not going to be in a good mood when you're seeing them.

How useful are things like cold reading classes for actors?

Great. An actor should never stop studying. Ray Liotta goes to acting class every single week. Always take class. Cold reading classes, scene study classes, improv classes are invaluable. If you have any interest in comedy, an improv class is invaluable to you. It teaches you to think on your feet.

Lacy Bishop

Lacy Bishop at the time of this interview was head of casting for the Los Angeles Theatre Center, formerly one of the two regular Equity theaters in L.A. While at L.A.T.C., she founded the Women Artists Group (W.A.G.). Her work as a casting director also included numerous regional theater productions as well as several pilots for television series and a stint on "L.A. Law." As a director her credits include David White's Dyeing *at the Los Angeles Playwrights Festival and* La Fea, *a one-woman show by Diane Rodrigues, and* Sister Girl, *a one-woman .show by Brandon Barbara Artis, both performed at L.A.T.C. For L.A.T.C.'s New Works Festival, she staged readings of Han Ong's* In a Lonely Country *and Mira Lani Oglesby's* Increase after Completion. *Also as a director she staged* W.A.G. Works, *a collective piece performed at Highways and* Prideaux Pieces, *for which she won a Dramalogue award.*

Lacy, how did you get into casting in the first place?

A sort of crooked path. I didn't get interested in theater at all until after I did a year of college. I'm a 60s person, so at that point I took my knapsack and my $200 and I started roaming around Europe, and I wound up getting a job at the Royal Shakespeare Company. I stayed there for two and half years, made a round of all the drama schools in England, decided if I could get into school in England, I would become an actress. If not, I would come back to the States and go to college. I got called back everywhere. I got in nowhere. I came back, went to San Francisco State, got one degree. Did a lot of acting in community theater, went back to San Francisco State and got another degree and got involved in directing. I did a lot of directing in graduate school, and then I got out of graduate school and decided after about six months that if I was going try and make a career I might as well do it in Los Angeles.

So I came to L.A., and in the back of my mind was always tucked the notion of casting, partially because women directors don't work a whole lot and also because I always felt that was one of my main strengths as a director. I enjoyed working with actors.

Right after I got to L.A., somebody told me that they were opening this place called the Los Angeles Theater Center. I came down and got a job in the production department, and about a month into it, the then casting director, who was all by herself trying to cast, started pulling her hair out and saying," Please, please come help me." And that's how I started, as her assistant. When she took a leave, I ran the whole department. I then left to do more directing and try out TV for a very short period, then got invited back after about a year. So I went back to the Theater Center and have been there close to three years—four years altogether.

Could you tell us the about the process of casting a typical production at LATC?

Right now I'm trying to put together two musicals back to back. I haven't done a whole lot of musicals. In both cases the directors are going to try and get certain names, and in a struggling, not-for-profit theater that never hurts. But it doesn't always work, and I have to make sure there are talented people around in case that doesn't happen.

The people that you're seeing now you're basically screening?

Exactly. Ideally, I would like to always have the freedom to do that. You know, actors reach a certain juncture in their career where they no longer want to come in and audition for casting directors. I'm totally sympathetic to that—I think acting is the one profession where you never gain any credibility. You have to keep proving it over and over. So sometimes, if I know people, they just automatically go into The-Director-Should-See-These-People category. But people I don't know well or people who are just starting out or people that are new in town, I like to pre-screen them. And I think it's frequently to the advantage of the actor.

Why?

Because I will have had a chance to talk to the director, I'll have a pretty good idea of what the director is looking for. And so often directors don't work with actors in auditions. Sometimes I can give hints to an actor as to which way to head, what way to go with it, so they'll have their best shot.

What mistakes do you find that actors consistently make? Let's talk first of all specifically about musical auditions.

Many, many singers don't chose material that really complements their own voices. In this case I'm working with a musical director, and we have the people come in and sing two songs, because both of these shows are essentially ninety percent music. Then the musical director has been working with them. And several people will have these incredible voices that will suddenly appear when the musical director asks them to do certain things—voices we never heard when they were singing material they prepared and brought in.

Could you talk a little about non-traditional casting?

Sure. L.A.T.C. is an organization that is committed to interracial casting, so as far as myself and the producers are concerned, it's a non-issue. Except that sometimes I find myself being more militant than they are. Every year we do a festival of new work—five or six new works. I had to do all the readings at the same time. And the directors, oddly enough, all lined up outside my office one day to get their session. And each one of them— mostly East Coast white guys, Yale-types—came in one at a time and sat down, and I said, "Do you know anything about non-traditional casting?" And we would be off and running. And not a single one of them said, "I wouldn't do that. What is that?" But each and every one of them had reasons why their particular play was not appropriate for that. And ultimately we managed to get some of it done.

But a lot of people just haven't thought about it. A lot of times it just has to do with getting people to think about it for the first time. I think there is a growing acceptance of it in theater. Television and films are much tougher, especially television. But in theater, there is beginning to be an overall acceptance of the notion. I still think the hardest one is what is called color-blind casting. And that's when you break up a family.

You're casting *Long Day's Journey Into Night*. Can one of the sons be very black if both the parents are white? Can the audience accept that without asking questions that are beyond the scope of the play?

That certainly is always the discussion. It seems to me that, if you're going to do color-blind casting, what you do is explode it altogether. I mean, you don't cast three white people in a family and one black person. You cast an Asian person, a black person, a white person, an Hispanic person—and then it's so confusing that people just have to let go of it. They go: *Obviously this doesn't mean anything.* And then they can tune in and just go ahead and watch whatever they're watching. But I think you have to explode it. That pulls it out of naturalism and makes you accept things on a more universal level.

There's also just cross-cultural casting, which means you can do any play you want black or Asian or Hispanic, and that's sometimes done as well.

Let's talk a little more about the audition process and the mistakes actors make in presenting themselves. Are there some particular no-no's that you would caution us against?

If you've had a really rotten day, bringing anger in with you—which is understandable and human but not helpful. If it's big enough, it can't help but interfere, because you think: Is this person going to work well with the director? Is this person going to be able to work with other actors?

That's an important factor in the casting process, then—how personable someone is, how easy to work with?

Yes and no. One of my producers says, "If you're going to be difficult, you'd better be damn good." And I have a tendency to agree with that.
Another thing: I think the biggest single mistake actors make is not respecting themselves enough. And that includes trying to do what you think is wanted rather than what your instincts tell you to do. Caring too much about getting the job has a tendency to undermine your work.

I think another mistake actors make is getting so focused in this business town on the business that they aren't paying enough attention to the work. Their energy is going into getting the audition and not into doing the work. I think if you're good, your work will ultimately be recognized. And I think actors who get to a comfortable place with that in themselves bring that into an audition. They are not apologetic, they're not overly solicitous, they're not angry. They're just good, and they know it.

Are there certain general audition scenes, pieces of material, that you hope you never have to see again?

My particular audition speech that I hate a lot is the bird speech from *Woolgatherer*. If somebody starts to do it, I actually stop them. It's about killing animals, and my particular bugaboo is animal things. There's another one about a dog that eats glass. I could live forever without ever hearing that one again.

In terms of length of each monologue or each scene, do you like to see things that are three minutes or less, five minutes or less?

Two minutes or less. You can see an immense amount about somebody's work in two minutes—usually in ten seconds. If you do two minutes and the two minutes are fantastic, you leave them wanting more. If you do two minutes and it's not so great, at least you haven't put somebody through a major episode of discomfort.

What about all of those books of One Hundred Scenes for Actors? Is that the place to look for material?

I think from an actor's view that's unconscionable. How can you possibly prepare a piece of work if you don't know the context that it comes from? That's lazy. That is a person who is not taking their work, their career seriously.

So if you do find a wonderful scene in one of these books, the first thing might be to get the play?

Absolutely. Go read the play. And then you may find out that you don't even like the character.

What kind of preparation should an actor make for an audition for a play? Is it a good idea to memorize the text of the scene if you know you're going to read a particular scene?

I think it depends on the kind of actor you are. It isn't mandatory—it never matters to me much one way or another whether people memorize things. I usually give them a brownie point for having taken the effort to do it, but in the final analysis it's how well prepared you are. In other words, if you are an actor who is not going to be able to lose this piece of paper unless you've memorized it, then memorize it. If you're an actor who is really uncomfortable with a cold read, then prepare really well. If you're got the material and you don't have enough time and you know that you're good off the top, I would hardly look at it at all and just wing it. I think that's part of your job as an actor—to diagnose your own process and learn how to show yourself to your best advantage.

Apart from the material and the skill with which we do our audition, are there any lapses in etiquette at auditions that you would like to warn actors against?

I think bringing too many props into an audition is a lapse of taste and a lapse of etiquette. In extreme cases people bring in entire living room sets—tablecloths, candles—and you're sitting there thinking: *You'd better be good.* And usually they're not.

I think a mistake actors make is that they frequently don't ask questions if they have them and that they will say they understand when they don't. But, on the flip side, spending too long grilling a director or casting person about every moment and nuance is also a mistake.

We've heard the phrase "working the room" a fair amount in relation to television and film auditions. Does this have a place in theater auditions, or is it basically a different kind of context? Do people get cast on the basis of their charm?

No. I think shmoozing has almost no importance in theater at all. Because I can indeed make a note that someone is incredibly nice but can't act. You have to put it out there on the stage, and if you can't act no amount of charm is going to save you.

It has often been said that Los Angeles is an industry town and the industry is not theater. How much difference does this make in the availability of performers to you? Is the town so strongly focused on film and television that professional theater has a second-class status?

Well, I think it has a very confused status. Interestingly enough, most of the important agents care about having their clients do theater more than the less successful agents—probably because all concerned can afford it. There is a respect for it. There is also a knowledge that you get a wonderful actor who's incredibly excited about doing a play and he'll ditch it in thirty seconds or less when he gets a major part in a feature film, and everybody goes: What do you expect him to do? He's going to get $25,000 to do this and $3,000 to do that. What would you do?

Clearly the actors that we can expect to begin and finish a run at the theater are those who don't need the money at all. On the other hand, I think there are so many actors out there who would rather do theater than almost anything else and who get in fights with their agents for doing theater when their agents think they should be doing something else. Casting directors are notorious for calling actors at home and skipping agents.

Has this been a useful modus operandi for you?

At times, when I know an agent is lying to me. There's one I have to track down today. We called an agent and asked whether an actor was interested in doing a play. The answer I got from the agent was "no." Then after the weekend I came back and the actor had signed up for the play. Now that means that the producer—Bill Bushnell—went and talked to the actor and got a different story than he got from the agent. So that indeed goes on, and I understand why agents do that. Agents don't make money when actors do theater. It's their livelihood they're protecting.

Do you think it's wrong of an agent to turn down an offer without telling an actor?

I think it's wrong of an agent to turn down any offer without telling an actor. I don't care what it is. They are there to offer options, to work for an actor and indeed to have an opinion about what the actor should be doing. But make decisions about it? No, no, no. But that, indeed, happens.

Do you think there is a big difference between the attitude on the part

of agents and also the performers toward work at L.A.T.C. or the Taper compared with the ninety-nine-seat theaters?

Yes, I do. I think there's almost as much difference from those theaters to L.A.T.C. as there is from L.A.T.C. to feature films, in terms of interest and respect. I don't run into any agents, unless they're really dumb, who don't want to deal with the theater somewhere. As I said, they get angry if we go around them, whereas with the small theaters a lot of agents say, "I'll get so-and-so to call you. We don't deal with this stuff." They don't want anything to do with it. Because again, it doesn't matter to them at all. With L.A.T.C. people sign a contract. At the Taper they sign a contract. They make a commitment.

And I think one of the problems with the way the ninety-nine-seat theater works is that everybody ditches it at a moment's notice. It's something that we do until ... whatever the until is. Bingo! You're out of there. Instantly! Which I think is a bad professional standard to establish.

Are you aware of major differences between East and West Coast casting situations for theater?

I haven't done any casting at all on the East Coast. The only difference I can tell you is that there indeed seems to be a difference between a New York actor and an L.A. actor.

What is the difference? What is a New York actor?

I think the difference is again in attitude. Let's say an actor goes to Northwestern. When he gets out of Northwestern, does he go to New York or L.A.? It tells you an enormous amount about what his attitude towards his work is, whether he chooses L.A. or New York.

Usually actors who come out of New York have spent a lot of time doing theater and take theater work seriously. Actors in L.A. sometimes take their theater work seriously, but frequently they're doing it to get exposure so they can get television work. The ones, in a way, that I feel for are the sort of talented young actors who come up in film or television and make a name for themselves. People watch everything they do, and now they have to go back to the theater and try to learn to act, and they have to do it publicly. I admire their chutzpah for doing it, but I think that the theater as a foundation is a really good starting place. And people who come at it from a different direction have a whole different way of working.

Would you say, then, that it's easier to make the transition from stage work to film or television than to make the transition from screen acting to the stage?

Yes, I think it is. I think the talent comes from the same place, but the techniques are different. Film acting technique and stage technique are very different. But I think it is easier for a stage actor to translate that onto film than it is for a film actor to translate it onto the stage. If you have great technique, you know how to use your voice, which is a really important thing and a big problem for most American actors—they don't have proper voice training. You also know how to use your body, you understand language, you understand how to communicate language on stage, and you understand how to sustain a part for an hour and a half. If you know how to do all those things, you can probably make a career on the stage.

On film, if you are just born with great, great instincts—like Marlon Brando was—you can make a wonderful career on film because you just do it and it's great and it's right here.

If you want to be a really great actor, you have to have both, and there aren't that many people who have both. But I think it is easier to translate that stage technique and figure out how to take all those things that you know about how to play a character and put it way down inside yourself and let that little bit come out. Using your voice, finding the arc of the character, using your breath to say a Shakespearean monologue—all those things are much harder to learn than simply how to be honest.

To reduce the size rather than pumping it up?

Yes. And I think it's more than reducing the size. I think you can get away with being pretty false on stage a lot of the time, if your technique is good enough. It's like spectacular and people will go: "Wow, look at that." It's like watching somebody jump through fire hoops or something. The actor on the stage who brings an incredible sense of truth to the work is the exceptional being, whereas on film you get caught telling a lie immediately.

Beverly Long

Beverly Long is best known for casting commercials, but she has also cast features, including When A Stranger Calls, a series for the Disney channel, and Michael Jackson videos.

Beverly, how did you get into casting?

As we do most things in life, probably by accident. If somebody had said to me at the age of 18, "What are you going to be when you grow up?" being a casting director would not have been top on my list. I was going to be an actress first, and I did that for a long time. Then I had three kids and a divorce and I had to grow up and get a real job. So I became an agent, and I really liked being an agent. The only problem with being an agent was sitting at the same desk every day. I am fairly restless, and after a while it got to me. Then I got to know a casting director who was going crazy because she was way too busy. I said, "I can do that," so I became her feeble-minded assistant for about a year, and she threw me right into the deep part of the pool and I started doing commercial casting because she hated it. I had to just do it, so I learned very fast. That was in about 1975.

Do you think it is useful for a casting director to have been a performer?

I think it's fabulous, because a lot of the casting directors I know came out of advertising or something else, and they haven't got a clue as to what actors do. I think it's just great having done all of it. If you're an actor, it's sort of a basis for anything that you want to become later on, and especially in this business—whether it's production, becoming a director or producer. If you're an agent, having been an actor, you know what actors go through and how they suffer and how difficult the rejection is— so you're kinder.

Let's talk a little bit about the odds. How many actors do you see for the average commercial?

Lots. It used to be, in the old days, that we would see—like they do theatrically—maybe six, seven, eight guys who show up for the part of Officer #2, if that many. But in commercials—whether it is a speaking part or not—as long as it's a principal, we see between thirty-five and a hundred people per part, depending on the part. But sometimes it can go on and on, and they will see 200 or 300 people. And it's just overload sometimes, just ludicrous. Sometimes we'll see 700 people for one commercial and maybe there are eight or ten parts.

Out of the couple hundred that you might see for a part, how many do you usually call back?

It depends. I think really smart, really secure directors—guys and women who have been in it for awhile—or secure agency people bring back maybe six people per part. Very new or insecure people bring back half the original casting take. It's insane.

The whole thing is because of the invention of the video tape. In the old days, directors and agency people had to come and actually be there in person and take their entire day to interview people. They don't have to do that anymore. They want to get their money's worth—they figure it's an hour video tape, three-quarter-inch, let's fill it full of people. So that's why you see so many people, even on call-back. Sometimes I think that insecure directors have to prove themselves to the agency people.

Do you see any more people for national commercials than for local spots?

No, not really. It's amazing. The national spots, everybody wants to be there, you just get the first team—you get more of who you want because the agents are pushing them and they want to show up. I just finished a huge package of Hallmark Card commercials for their Christmas and Halloween commercials, but those are prestigious commercials, so everybody showed up.

Would you explain how conflicts work?

Well, you can only do one fast food, right? And if you get a Wendy's and it's a regional playing in Salt Lake City, you're in deep trouble. They have a right to hold it for twenty-one months—for the life of the twenty-one-month contract. So if you get stuck in one that plays in one little market someplace, you get a very tiny amount of money.

Scale, right?

Scale, but you get the residuals, and they're just dreadful. For thirteen weeks there would be maybe another $600, $675. Whereas if you got a national—a national McDonald's, for example—it would play a short period of time, but you would make a few thousand dollars. So it's always a gamble, but those hot areas are for national products like fast foods. Or, say, during car season, everybody in the world goes out on twenty-five car auditions for Chevys and Toyotas and Hondas and Jeeps—everything. And if you land one, that's it. You can't do another car commercial until they release it. Usually cars they release every year—you wouldn't be doing that car commercial for twenty-one months. Or if you go out for Pepsi Cola and you get that, then your agent has to take you off the books for doing any other kind of soft drink, and you can't do anything from 7-Up to Gatorade ... or sometimes milk.

That's why agents have so many clients, because if they have all of these wonderful little Burger King and McDonald's counter girls—darling college or high school types—several of them get conflicted out and then they have to hunt around and find new ones.

To what extent do agents ask for and get guarantees of a certain amount of money on some of these regional commercials?

They try, they try, they try. But it's very hard.

Does it cut out their clients to a large degree if they won't work for scale?

Oh yes. For the most part, commercials actors are scale people—except models. I do a lot of beauty stuff too, and I'm sending some people to Mexico City this week to do some commercials for perfume. Now, they're for the Mexican market, but those are models, and they get big bucks. They get $1,500 to $2,500 a day and more. $3,000 a day. A lot of money.

But they have a very short shelf life. You do well in modeling from the time you're 16 to 26 or 27 and then it's all over. And some of the people can make the cross-over into young mom or young dad, businessman—things like that. They can alter themselves a little bit. In my class this time I have a couple of girls who were wonderful models, but they see the handwriting on the wall and it's going to be all over very, very soon. Once you turn 30, that's it. Thank you very much. It's like being a baseball player. Rarely are there people who pitch at 42.

In terms of agents, how many do you regularly call for a spot that will come up?

Well, I don't put all my things on Breakdown Services because it makes me too nervous to get 4,000 pictures in the mail. I look at all those little actor faces and it breaks my heart. But a lot of casting directors do everything on the Breakdown. That means it reaches a tremendous number of agents all at once.

So, assuming you decide that you don't really want 4,000 pictures on your desk, what do you do? Who do you call?

Okay, suppose I need a spokesman for an insurance company—a big national spot. I'm not going to put that on the Breakdown because I already know how many spokesmen there are in town and what they can do. A little computer in my brain goes off. I have been in this business so long, I just sort of spit out names and faces, and I just call the agents then. I call the agents that I know have their coterie of spokesmen, and that is thirty to forty spokesguys.

How many agents would you typically call in that situation?

I would probably call more than the average. Depending on what it is. If it's a small casting, where I'm only going to see twenty-five guys or something like that, I would probably only call eight or ten ... or maybe even fewer.

Is there any chance for an actor in commercials who doesn't have an agent?

No. Very hard. I do it because I teach class, and I bring in my students who I know don't have agents. Because I know them—I have their phone number—and I would kill them if they didn't show up. But it's too scary—what if you cast somebody without an agent in something and then they didn't show up ... what would you do? And you have a half-million-dollar production sitting there waiting for this person who decided to go to the beach that day. You see, if they're not in the union and they have no agent, they can do whatever they want. And we're talking about millions and millions of dollars here. We're not talking about a little Equity-waiver show. So the responsibility is enormous. See, if you didn't show up and you had an agent, we could sue somebody. There is somebody who is responsible for you, even though the Screen Actors Guild, if you didn't show up, would say, "Oh, that wasn't very nice." That's about as far as they'll go.

Is there any chance for somebody who isn't a member of SAG or AFTRA?

Well, sure! Nobody was born with a SAG card in their hand.

So agents will sometimes send people to you who are not yet union members.

Sure. I've had it happen, and I do it all the time. I just Taft-Hartley'd seven people, but they were all little people. They were all between the ages of 1 and 3.

Should actors make themselves available for extra work in commercials?

It used to be in the old days of Hollywood it was sort of a stigma to be an "extra." If you wanted to be an actor you didn't do extra work. I don't know that that's so true anymore. I mean, who cares? A lot of people, young people particularly, put themselves through college. My son put himself through school doing extra work, although he didn't want to be an actor, but he did well being an extra because you could study on the set.

I think if somebody needs the bucks and they don't talk about it a lot .... I don't think you should put it on your résumé. If you're going to do extra work, do it—show up, do your job, don't try to get another job while on that set. Don't say, "Hi, I'm an actor. I'd like to do your next movie." Don't try to push yourself. Just do your little job of extra work and go home.

Let's talk a little bit about auditions and the auditioning process. What are the biggest mistakes you continually see actors make in commercial auditions?

Not taking enough time to prepare and being late ... and being harried and having their minds elsewhere—on the next audition or the fact they're going to get a ticket, or the fight they just had with their girlfriend. The inability to concentrate on the job at hand—the audition, that moment. It's like I say to people in my class who are actors: You call yourself an actor, but what you really should call yourself is an *auditioner*. If somebody says, "What do you do for a living?" you should say, "I audition." Once in a while you're an actor. Most of your life is going to be spent auditioning, so you should learn how to do that, and that's the hardest thing.

Actors are often nervous, and they've got the dry mouth and all those things. But if you are concentrating, blocking out all of those other things—you can't pay your rent this month—all those horrible other things that crowd in upon us all day, you can take that moment out to look at that copy. Try and find out what is it saying. Who is he talking to? Why are they saying this? Why would I be the one that they should cast in this part? What could I bring to this that nobody else has? How could I be uniquely wonderful on this copy instead of just being generically safe?

You have to really take a risk.

Take a risk. Be there. Give yourself enough time to look at it, try to dress appropriately. You don't have to go to Western Costume and rent a cop suit if you're going to be a cop or a soldier suit if you're going to be a soldier. I just did some soldiers, some recruit-type young guys. Now the smart guys came in khaki pants and a khaki shirt or a khaki t-shirt, like you buy at one of those Army supply places. It's no big deal—it's not a uniform, but it kind of gives you the feeling of recruit.

Say you have gone to another audition and you have a suit and tie on, and you are coming here and your guy is out playing golf or your guy is at a poker game. Don't go crazy and make everybody crazy that you have the wrong outfit on. Take off your coat, take off your tie, roll up your sleeves and do it. Just pull it together and do it.

Have stuff in the trunk of your car. Have a sweatshirt in your trunk. Or have a tie to put on, just so you give the essence of whatever it is. Commercials are so competitive and there are so many people who want to do them because you can make big bucks doing this stuff.

What about memorizing the copy if you can? It is a good idea?

There are some people who have a facility for memorizing and that's great. I don't knock it. They are always going to have a cue card for you, by the way. It says in the Screen Actors Guild contract you must be provided a cue card.

If it's one or two words, I'm assuming you're going to memorize it, but otherwise what I would do if it were wall-to-wall copy, as we call it, I would memorize the first thought—real important. Because if you start and they slate your name and if you give your name kind of bored ... a lot of people don't get that auditioning for a commercial is very different than any other auditioning, because your slate—meaning saying your name—is equally as important sometimes as the copy.

Because if they don't like your face, they have this little fast forward button. Directors and people in the advertising agencies are very busy people and they're very restless. They have locations to scout, they've got this happening and that happening and they just got off a plane ... whatever. Anyway, they sit there and they look at these casting tapes, and they read everything very quickly because commercials are very fast, so I would say you don't have more than four to five seconds tops to get their attention And if you say your name quickly and are waiting to give this great drama that you are going to do for this commercial audition, it's too late already. They won't watch you, because your first little image is critical.

Then going into that first thought on the commercial copy—nailing that lens, zapping whoever is watching you. If you're not zapping them—if you haven't gotten across to them in that first moment and nailed them with your eyes and really talked to them—you're out. The first line is always the hook. Something to draw you in.

Then you have, as I call it, the shitload of information in the middle—where we talk about the EPA mileage of blah, blah, the overhead cams and all that. That stuff you can a lot of times get away with reading, or at least having your eyes pretty much on the cue card.

Then they have that little button at the end that is always cute and wonderful and dear. So you can then look into the camera—make sure you nail that lens again with your last line, the last thought. And then you're pretty much there. You don't have to kill yourself memorizing.

Paul Ventura

Paul Ventura casts features, television and commercials. Films he has cast include The Kid *and* Teen Wolf.

Paul, how did you get into casting?

A friend of mine used to be an aficionado of movies, and every time a group of us in college would go and see a movie—something obscure like *The Culpepper Cattle Company*—he would see somebody and say, "Oh, that's Jeffrey Lewis. He had five lines in this other movie." And I'd be going: *Right.* "And there's so-and-so"—and he'd come up with some obscure name I'd never heard of. But I never saw a movie the same way after that. And when I first got into casting down here, every time I'd see somebody come on, even if they had just one line, I'd know their name, I'd know their agent, I'd know how much they'd made.

It's amazing the number of different things casting incorporates—I've acted and directed and written, but I also paint. And a lot of times in a sense, whether it's a commercial or movies, you're providing different—I don't want to say colors or forms—but if the movie's the canvas, you're providing the paints in a way. If you give them the wrong texture, it screws up the movie.

Every time you bring people in—whether it's how you schedule them, who you put in different combinations, what you do with the people once they're there to audition—you are in a sense utilizing all the things you've done before.

One commercial I was casting was dealing with different relationships. The producers gave me free rein to do whatever I wanted, but basically all people had to do was say their name to the camera and look like themselves. So I had a poker table set up with chips and cards and special lighting, and I brought in seven people that I played poker with that week. Two of them were actors, the other five didn't know anything about the business. Well, I had them just playing, and I'd take close-ups and group shots of them dealing the cards and playing with the chips for a few minutes, and I'd finally have them slate their name. Everybody got cast in the commercial from that except the two actors.

So commercials casting is a total crap shoot. You're not just competing against every actor in your category, you're competing against my gardener, people I play poker with or softball.

There was a cruise ship commercial we were casting, and they actually wanted to see husbands and wives or people who were living together—because they were too cheap to spring for separate berths. They needed people who could stay in the same room on the cruise ship. One couple that I know of got ten days in the Caribbean with all sorts of golden hours and overtime. They cut the commercial into about five different spots, and that one couple took home, by the end of the run, a quarter of a million dollars.

So there are a lot of fallacies about casting, particularly with commercials. One fallacy is the actor thinking: "I want to be with a small select agency that's out there hustling for me." The problem is that the reason they're out there hustling for you is no one will return their phone calls. There are just so many actors and so many agents commercially.

How many actors would you see for an average commercial?

A lot of times we bring in 100, 150 ... sometimes 200 people a day. So in a five-day a week, that's 1,000 people that come through on tape. But a lot of times you don't get to bring in all the people that you would like to. A lot of times they just cut you off after a day or two or three days.

Who are the first agents you call?

The agencies that will have their submissions opened first, the ones that the calls will go out to first are TGI Talent Group; CU; JH&R; SBV; CED; Special Artists; Abrams Artists; Abrams, Rubiloff & Lawrence—there are a lot of agencies out there that are very good. I know I'm missing some.

Who makes the final decision as to who is cast in a commercial?

There are certain times when I'm dealing with a director on one side and the agency on the other side. Sometimes the director doesn't get what he wants. The agency will come in saying, "This is who we want. We get who we want." Other times there's horse trading.

Many times in callbacks there are five people who could do the job, and the director and the agency will say, "What do we do? We have five people who could all do the job?" Well, I have to know who my first choice would be, and sometimes it makes a difference. I can say, "All right, look. If you want a very good actor that's done a lot of commercials, this is the person. Or if you want somebody who is a tremendous actor nobody knows about—he or she is from Chicago and just got out here, starring in some movie that's coming out with Robert Duvall—this is the person. Nobody knows this person." The directors commercially all have the hots for people they haven't seen do this over and over.

Are there certain mistakes you often see actors make in auditioning for commercials—things you wish you could warn them against?

More people lose the job before they ever walk in to the audition. First of all, they're sitting there looking at other people and they're thinking: *He's perfect for this role. What am I doing, here?* Or: *Everybody else is ten years older than I am. My stupid agent sent me out on this.* When in fact they're one of the three people I called to get him in immediately because he's now the way they're going, and all those other people are probably wrong. So you sometimes can be your own worst enemy.

Psyching yourself out of a job.

Yeah. There's one instance where I was casting Michael J. Fox's first movie called *Teen Wolf.* Two stories from that. We were casting it at the

Professional Artists Group, where they were also doing a commercial down the hall. We were casting the part of a teacher. A woman walked into the movie audition and said, "I'm sorry. Is this for Colgate?" We said, "No." But she was dressed right, she looked perfect for the part, had her résumé there; we could see that she had done a lot of things, and we started talking a little bit. The director and producers were in the room, and we thought: Wouldn't this make a great story? Somebody walks into the wrong room and actually gets the job? So we gave her the script. She read the sides and came back and got the part. I found out a week later that she was asking every woman that came out of our audition, "What's the part? What are you reading for? What are they looking for? What do they have you do?" She went to her car, she dressed differently. She calculated and manipulated the whole thing.

The other story: This is the only time I have ever experienced this, but it was overpowering. Someone came in for another role, and something he did—literally a split second—got him the role right then and there, and the director and producers wouldn't consider anybody else who came in. They totally forgot anybody who came in before him and wouldn't even listen to anybody who came in afterwards. There was this scene where this very pompous high school drama teacher is trying to seduce his student. This beautiful blonde who can't act a lick is doing this horrible scene, and he's trying to encourage her and make her think she's great. So what's happening is, all of a sudden in the middle of the scene there's this crash on stage. Michael J. Fox plays this hardware store guy with paint cans and stuff. The drama coach says, "What was that? Can't you see I'm trying to rehearse? Oh, you're from the hardware store—the paint. One can of cocoa, one can of mauve, right? Right." Basically that was that moment in the scene. Well, everybody was either doing it as Orson Welles or with an ascot or like kind of a John Malkovich in *Dangerous Liaisons*.

But this guy did this: Crash! "What was that? Can't you see I'm trying to rehearse? The paint—my paint—one can of cocoa, one can of mauve. Right? Right." He became this visionary just by adding that split second of "the paint—*my paint.*" Everything became clear about that character, and it was a brilliant choice and they added the line for the movie. It got him the part.

Being inventive, being ready to pick up on a moment.

Being inventive and also listening. Because it's rare that a director will actually say something to you beforehand. Usually you say, "Is there anything you want to say to me?" And they say, "No, just do what you're going to do. If you're missing anything we'll come back and let you know." Well, they very seldom do. If there are fifty-seven ways of doing it and you do fifty-six-A and they want fifty-six-B, you're out the door. The best you can do is hope that they see a good actor, recognize a good actor and say, "Listen, you're slightly off on what we're looking for. Try it this way."

But if somebody comes in and they've been working on this Cajun accent and the director says, "Listen, we're telling everybody, eighty-six the Cajun accent. It's terrible. We're going a completely different way. Just play it naturally," it has happened that an actor has said, "I worked hard on this. I'll still do it my way," and he does a Cajun accent. And the director has wasted his time, the actor hasn't listened.

There are fifty people who can do any role. Your job when you come in on an audition is, in a sense, to make these people around you feel comfortable. They want you to be good. The idea that they're the enemy is another fallacy. They don't want you wasting their time. They love the idea of you coming in and getting the part. "Oh, thank God. We got this one out of the way." So assume they're on your side.

One person came in for a commercial who literally had a car accident five minutes before she got there. She was shaking and she said, "Can I make a phone call?" I said, "Yeah, are you okay? Do you want to come back later on?" She said, "No because I've got to deal with this." So—car accident, car totaled, made a phone call, came back, left it outside the door, came in and relaxed, made everyone feel comfortable. She got the part. It was a big national commercial. She's probably made twenty or thirty thousand so far on it. When you're dealing with this kind of money, you can't let the fact that you didn't get any sleep the night before or somebody flushed your cat down the toilet or your car is totaled get in the way.

Here's another thing. In the waiting room. You walk in and you haven't seen somebody in six years. "Hey, how you doing? I haven't seen you since New York. How's the family?" And for some reason they call you in before the person that's chatting you up, as it were, and you go in, you're unprepared, you don't really know what you're doing—you just lost out on a part. I'm not saying the other person will get it, but there's all sorts of subtle subterfuge. You know?

And there are all kinds of tricks that you play on yourself to screw it up. Like sitting there going: *Oh, he'd be perfect for this role.* Or somebody's older or younger. Or: *Why is it that everybody's blonde and I'm brunette? They must want a blonde.* Maybe the blondes were scheduled at a different time but they all got lost and showed up at the wrong place. Don't assume that because somebody is in the room that they're in the right category and you're in the wrong category.

A psychologist I knew once said, "Show up as what they're looking for." The mental attitude of that sounds like what you're talking about.

Usually it's better to not come in character unless it's something that is close to your character to begin with, and you can kind of feel how it's going in the beginning.

If you're dealing with a situation either with the network where you have fourteen faces across the room or a callback on a commercial, it's best not to shake everyone's hand because you're not going to recognize their names anyway on the way out, and it gets embarrassing. Plus the fact that if it takes five minutes to do that, and if they're seeing twenty people on a callback that's a lot of time taken away from just seeing you be at your best.

By the way, one fallacy about callbacks that people don't talk about. If you're one person out of ten for the callbacks, you would figure your odds are one in ten. That's wrong. Your odds are not one in ten. What they do is they review the tape. The director wants his person, the ad agency may or may not agree. What they do is edit out maybe eight other people from the tape. They show the client or the agency back home their first choice and maybe a backup, and, if they're real insecure, maybe a second back up. So chances are you aren't even on the tape after the callback. The main point is, relax and don't sweat it.

In one spot I was casting, there was a woman who was really wonderful for the part. She had the best look, the right age, all this stuff for a national commercial. And just as she was about to be cast in one of these big meetings with everybody at the agency, the creative director said, "Well, she's totally wrong, so why don't we go over here in this direction and look on the board." And everyone was going, "What the hell's going on? She's the only person that has any life to this character of what we're looking for." The director realized what was going on and told everybody to just settle down, he'd tell them later. And they picked somebody else, the creative director left, and everybody went up to the director and said, "What the hell was that all about? She was perfect." And the director said, "He just broke up with his wife. She looks exactly like this woman. There's no way in the world that he knows this. We can't fight for her on this issue."

How important is a slate in a commercial audition?

Well, usually slates are not important, but what you want to do is tailor your slate to the type of thing it is. If you are doing a high energy McDonald's commercial or a product sell, they want you to be energetic.

The most important thing that I've noticed in terms of the style of casting that I'm hired for—most commercial actors have a habit of being too eager to please. They're there, they want to get the job, they want to get the big bucks and they're out there just going, "Hi! I want to be liked!" and it's usually a big turnoff. Whereas the people that stand their ground and allow us to come to them are the ones that are get our attention.

The worst example of that is when we had this 6-year-old girl come in for a commercial. And she did her audition and she was fabulous. Everybody loved her and they were going, "Oh, thank god. This is the kid." Everybody was totally in love with her. And then she went to the door and she said, "Now you remember. My name is Betty Lou Dink and I'm a trouper." And everybody's jaw dropped, and she left. Now she thought she was doing what her agent and her mother told her to do to be memorable. "Sparkle Shirley," as Shirley Temple's mother used to say before she'd go in front of the camera. The agency producer said, "You tell that precocious brat, that trained frigging seal, you tell her mother and her agent that that 'Betty Lou Dink' shit just cost her forty to fifty thousand dollars. We'll go to our second choice, even though she's not as good. I don't want that bitch on my set." And this was a poor innocent 6-year-old child who basically said, "I'm lying," and that was awful.

Paul, is there such a thing as a commercial type?

There are certain people who hook almost all of the jobs and still have not become stock. I can name three to five in each category between 32 and 45 of people that, out of hundreds of people, will probably get all of these jobs on almost anything. Because there's a warmth about them, and you know what? Forget looks. It's the warmth and the appeal and what you have underneath that is ultimately going to get you cast, because when you're dealing with commercials you're dealing with image.

It's great to be able to have the range to do different characters, but when they want you to do this character, they want you to do this character and forget about all the other stuff. Forget about: "I played Hamlet at the Guthrie Theater." "Yeah fine. Just hold up the dish towel, okay?" The funniest thing is when somebody will say, "Henry, instead of holding it here, hold it here as you smile." And he'll do that and the director will whisper, "Good actor," and he'll mean it. Because a good actor commercially means not just hitting your marks but listening, finding specifics.

If you're holding a product and the name is in your hand, that is not a good idea. There are certain tricks that you can learn in any technique class. How to guzzle Coca Cola with the three bubbles coming in at the right angle and stuff like that.

Where do you go to learn this?

The best thing is to go to a seminar where they have a different casting director every week, so you'll learn the overview. But also techniques like the Wrigley curl, or whatever it's called. When you're chewing gum you have to do it a certain way. These are things you can pick up fairly quickly, or if you have the casting director in the room they can show you.

Are there on-camera workshops for this kind of thing?

Yes, there are. I don't know if PAG still has one—Professional Artists' Group. I know that the Actor's Center has some. I know Estelle Tepper has a technique, Beverly Long has a technique, but there's nothing that I've experienced other than the seminars where you can get that overview.

Bob Lloyd

Bob Lloyd, The Voicecaster, works exclusively with voices.

How did you get into casting voices?

I started as a voice agent back in the times when there were only six agents that had voice departments. For about three years I played that game. I wasn't a very good agent. I'm not very good at feeling good about being rejected, and as an agent you get rejected many, many times a day. But I spent three years doing that before the lady from New York who ran the agency fired me.

A couple of the things that I felt that I learned: number one, advertising agency people didn't really like agents. They didn't like to deal with them. That was the way the system worked out here, and you really didn't have much of a choice. And number two, when you asked for someone who had a Mason Adams sound—the Smucker's voice—these different agents would audition people from their shop. More often than not, they would come back with people who had nothing to do with the Mason Adams sound, so it wasted a lot of the advertising agency's time.

My wife had a pretty good job at the time, and I had a friend who said, "I have an extra room in my building. I'll let you use it." So I decided that I would charge a modest fee to advertising agencies and see if I could provide them with a service that they had never had before, which was simply selecting voices for them. It was an interesting experiment for me because they had never paid for this service before. They did pay for on-camera service.

The advertising agencies had always had the luxury of going directly to agents and saying, "This is what I'm looking for. Give me a tape, an audition tape of people you represent that can do this." And the agents didn't charge them anything. The agents just wanted one of their guys to get the job so they'd get their ten percent.

In my first year—1975—I think I netted $800. The second year was $4,000, which was better. It was just me and an answering machine. Now there are five of us. It's been a growth business, but a slow-growth business because basically the first thing I had to do was get the advertising community to think in terms of spending a little bit of money for casting voices while the alternative was there all the time.

But your services saved them a great deal of time.

Well, that's one of the arguments. The basic, unstated argument was: "If you talk to me, you don't have to talk to these agents." I was an agent. They can't roust me around, I know better. And if you tell me you want Mason Adams types, that's what I'll give you back—because if I don't you won't hire me again, and then I'm out of business. So it became a matter of almost insulating the buyer—the advertising agency—from the seller—the talent agent. It put me in the middle, and they could call one person instead of six or seven. I had no bias—I don't care who gets the job because I have no financial interest in that. I charge the advertising agency an hourly rate. The agents take a percentage of the talent rate. Their interest is different than mine, as it should be.

Bob, what advice would you offer an actor who has never done voice over and wants to break in? Are workshops useful? Courses?

I've never really encouraged people to get in the voice business, but I have never discouraged anybody who wanted to pay their dues, because the dues are pretty hefty today. When I got involved in it, the rap that the voice business had was that just a handful of people did all the work, and that was basically true. The only difference was how big the handful was. Today we're talking, roughly, about 4,000 performers out there chasing the voice dollar, of which 500 of them will probably earn eighty percent of the money. And sixty to seventy-five of them earn well into six figures. I'm talking about scale people, not celebrities. It is the most competitive part of show business because it is the most lucrative part. You can make more money with less work in the voice business than in any other form of show business short of robbing the box office.

Of those sixty to seventy-five people who make six-figure incomes, what percentage are women?

The unions say fifteen percent, and I would guess that they probably know better than anybody else, because the advertisers really don't break it down that way. The last time we measured our business, we measured a full year. During this particular year we did 660 jobs that resulted in 1430 roles that were cast, and twenty-four percent of those were women. I think that's deceptive because we tend to get jobs that may have four or five different people in a spot. Or we get a lot of "Hi Honey I'm Home's," and automatically that's fifty-fifty.

This is particularly true in radio. I didn't break this down between television and radio, but radio will use more women because you can get too many men's voices together and you need to break it up. Plus, many of the story lines in these little thirty-second, sixty-second episodes require male-female banter. And the fact that the female of our species controls so much of the expenditure of the advertising dollar, so you need to appeal to them. What's the most successful automobile commercial on the air today?

Lindsay Wagner.

You betcha! She's dynamite. If you listen to the spots, she never says anything technical or great about the car. That's her deal. She says, "I'll be your spokesman but I won't be your salesman," although in effect she is. She sells cars. She pushes them out the door. And she pushes them to a lot of female purchasers. So the woman is a very important aspect from an advertising point of view.

Why more of them aren't used as spokesmen is a question nobody has really answered yet. The advertising agencies basically say that their research shows that a male voice pushes product better.

Well, there has been some research, as I'm sure you know. The Women's Committee of the Screen Actors Guild a couple of years ago hired a research group to do a study in which two products were analyzed with male voices and female voices selling them. One was Listerine and one was Nestle's Chocolate Morsels. And they found that there was really no significant difference in the response of consumers to these voices. If there was any edge at all, it went to the women. They hired a public relations firm to get the word out. They had articles in newspapers, and yet it has made very little difference in the situation of women in voice overs.

I don't think it will. And I'm all for this. I would much prefer to conduct an audition with women than with men. It's a fact that there is less work for women than for men, and when women come in they're more serious about it. They're more mentally prepared. They get down to work faster and they produce better. And so they make my life easier, and I generally feel better about the end product—the tape that goes back to St. Louis or wherever.

The problem with that survey right on the face of it is, number one, it wasn't in-depth enough. You take two products like that—even if women got half the work doing products like that, they'd still only get about twenty percent of the work, because they didn't test them on the wide variety of things you actually hear on the radio and see on television. They didn't have ... there's no female cowboy up there. Granted, that's kind of a hokey example, but most of the voice work is not Listerine and Nestle's—upscale, big-bucks items that everyone knew.

And it's a given that you can say, "If you do that and I do that, half the people are going to like you. Half the people are going to like me." All it was was kind of scratching the surface of the problem. The research wasn't anywhere near big enough to make the kinds of claims that they did. And the people that made the claims knew that.

I think one of the factors in why men do more things than women is simply the voice box itself. The male voice box is more versatile than the female voice box. You go all the way from here [high voice] to here [low voice]. There's a lot of space in between. But you really don't have that with the female. If you measured it on a frequency spectrum, you'd get a male spectrum about like this and a female spectrum maybe sixty percent of that, on an average.

Let's get back to this question of breaking in. Say I'm an actor with some experience doing stage, maybe some television, some film. I've never done a voice over, but people keep telling me I've got a terrific voice and I should do this. What should be my first step?

You have a step up if you are a performer, even though you haven't done any voice work. We get, easy, fifteen to twenty tapes a week of people wanting to break into the business, and most of them are not performers.

In the first place, you have to be competitive. When you win a role, you don't win it because you have nice big brown eyes. You win it because you read that spot and maybe ten other people or maybe two hundred other people have read that spot and you competed for it. And the only way you can compete is by having someone think highly enough of you that they will ask you to come and read.

Those people are basically agents. Ninety to ninety-five percent of all the voice work that is awarded is awarded through an agent's office. So you have to be able to say, "I can do this well. I can do it as well as this guy or better than this guy and I have a shot." If you can do it, you have to be able to prove it, and you prove it with a demo tape. Most of them today are taking the form of cassettes. They think of the cassettes as being as disposable as a business card because that's the way they are.

It's your résumé.

Yes. It can be expensive, compared to putting a composite together. Depending on how long it takes for you to get enough stuff to put on it or what kind of art work you put on it. And if you are in fact competitive, you can prove it by putting together a demo tape.

How do you get competitive enough to do a demo tape? Are there workshops actors can go to?

There are probably twenty of them around town. It depends on what you want to do—whether you want to get into the commercial business or the animation business—which is a subsection of the voice business—or the narration business, doing industrial sales and training things out there. If you're interested in animation, probably the best place is a girl named Susan Blu.

She has also written a book called Word of Mouth, which is extremely useful.

There is a girl named Kat Lehman who has beginning classes and intermediate commercial classes. Susan also does commercial classes. She sometimes does them with Andrea Romano, who for years was the casting director at Hanna Barbera and now is in animation. She's very good and very straightforward about it. So is Kat. There was a time when Kat had an advanced class, and she had a gal, Kathy Levin, who would do it. It was backlogged for weeks and weeks with people trying to get into it. There's a young fellow named Thom Pinto, who has his own studio facility over on Cahuenga West. And there's a gal who does some things on a much smaller basis, where you get four people at a time and individual instruction—her name is Lou Huffey.

I've watched them all teach, and I feel they know what they're talking about and they are sincere about what they do. And I see people coming out of their workshops who have a better than average shot of getting started in the business.

Basically your workshop will give you the opportunity to perform on different kinds of copy, in different forms of direction, and it will help you find out, number one, whether you are competitive or can become competitive.

You get to hear yourself back?

Record, playback. Record, playback. Take direction from different sources, different kinds of people. If you get into this business, you will find that every time you go out to do a job you have someone that directs you differently. The process of building a demo tape is probably one that you go through after you feel comfortable performing.

Once you've got enough material for a tape, should you try to put it together yourself? Should you hire a professional to put it together with music and sound effects for you?

My feeling is that you need somebody who has all kinds of jingles and things like that, because if you are going to go with what I call a scratch tape, you're going up against this guy that's been in the business for forty years.

What is a scratch tape?

It's all stuff that was fabricated in a studio—nothing was ever recorded and put on the air.

And you know the difference immediately when you hear a scratch tape?

Well, yeah. I'm not certain how important it is that you know whose tape is scratch and whose isn't. It's just that if you do it yourself, it tends to remove all doubt. If it's well enough put together, it will give the impression that you have actually worked these gigs.

How long should a demo tape be?

You ask ten people, you get ten different answers. From my point of view, I don't care. I used to do an exercise where I'd take a tape with Bob Hope and one with Chuck Riley, a funny voice guy who did a lot of animation and that sort of thing. And I would play them in the course of something like this and we'd talk about them and I'd come back a little later and say, "How long was Bob's tape?" And invariably the answer would be: "Four minutes" or something like that. "How long was Chuck's?" Well, that was shorter: "Probably two and a half or three minutes."

Bob Hope's tape was nine and a half minutes, but he was so good at what he did that it captivated you, and you had no idea how long you were hung into that tape. The other guy, Chuck Riley, has basically one act. He does it fast, slow, loud, soft but it's basically an announce act, and his tape was a one-minute tape, but it seemed longer.

So it depends largely on what you do and how well you do it and how diverse you are. If you have one act, then keep it short. Just do what you do well—because if you begin to get beyond that, then you end up putting marginal things on there because you want to be more things to more people. As time goes on and you get very good and very versatile, then don't be afraid to put more stuff on it. The cost factor is negligible.

PART TWO
NEW YORK

CASTING DIRECTOR INTERVIEWS: NEW YORK

GEOFFREY JOHNSON, Independent Casting Director, Johnson-Liff Casting Associates Ltd., Broadway and regional theater, television: *Phantom of the Opera, Les Miserables.*

JAY BINDER, Independent Casting Director, Broadway and regional theater, television: *Rumors, Jerome Robbins' Broadway.*

PAT MCCORKLE, Independent Casting Director, Broadway and regional theater, television: *A Few Good Men, Driving Miss Daisy.*

MARK SIMON, Independent Casting Director, theater: *Tamara, Blessings.*

DEBORAH AQUILA, Independent Casting Director, features and television: *sex, lies & videotape, Last Exit to Brooklyn;* New York casting consultant for NBC.

MARI LYN HENRY, Director of Casting, East Coast, ABC.

BETTY REA, Casting Director, "The Guiding Light."

BARBARA BADYNA, Senior Vice President, Director of Casting, Young and Rubicam, Inc.

LESLEE FELDMAN, Manager of Casting, Saatchi and Saatchi Advertising.

BILLY SEROW, Independent Casting Director, Godlove, Serow and Sindlinger, commercials, television, industrials, voice-overs.

PAT SWEENEY, Independent Casting Director, Reed-Sweeney-Reed, Inc., commercials, industrials.

ALICE WHITFIELD, Independent Casting Director, Real-to-Reel, voice-overs for commercials and animation.

Geoffrey Johnson

G*eoffrey Johnson, a native New Yorker, is a graduate of the Yale School of Drama. He and his partner, Vincent Liff, founded Johnson-Liff Casting Associates in 1976 and that company has been responsible for the casting of such Broadway shows as* The Dresser, Amadeus, Phantom of the Opera, Les Miserables, *and* Sunset Boulevard, *and the television primetime series* "The Holocaust" *and* "Little Gloria ... Happy at Last." *He has also cast many feature films, television pilots, and series, both primetime and daytime (*"Another World"*).*

How did you get into casting?

I was an assistant stage manager for David Merrick, and he had what many Broadway producers had at that time, but which doesn't exist now—in-house casting directors. And while I was an assistant stage manager, David Merrick had a casting director named Linda Otto, who's now a television producer and director. The first year I went to work for David Merrick he was producing eight Broadway shows, plus the shows he already had running. There was a lot of work to be done: casting replacements, casting touring companies. So Linda said to me, "You know a lot of actors. You'd be good as a casting director. Let me see if I can talk them into hiring you as my assistant." And that's really how it happened.

What qualities make a good casting director, from your observation?

The most important thing is doing one's homework, I think. When I say homework, I don't just mean going to Broadway shows and watching television at night and going to off-Broadway, but also attending showcases, the schools and the presentations of the graduating classes, and so on. For example, tomorrow, Juilliard is doing the acting presentation of their graduating class. One really has to keep up, because the acting pool is constantly changing. I'm not talking just about young people, because there are older actors who leave the profession and then come back, California actors who come to New York, regional actors that have been out of New York, and so on. And I think that's just doing one's homework. In addition, one has to be able to recognize good acting, or what a good actor is.

Does it help to have been a performer yourself?

Enormously—but I don't think it's a prerequisite. There are some very good casting directors who haven't been actors themselves. My partner was never an actor, never wanted to be an actor, but he's really an excellent casting director. He has an incredible sense of what makes a good actor.

Could you describe for us the process of casting a Broadway show? Let's take, for instance, a musical like *Phantom of the Opera*.

One should sit down with the director and find out what he wants. We've had the advantage (with shows like *Phantom of the Opera* and *Les Miserables* and *Cats*) of being able to see them in London before we had to cast them in New York, and having the same director, so we know what the director is going for. Then it's a matter of meeting with the director and finding out specifically what he wants. Then we start setting up the auditions. This can work in a number of ways. One way is to start with the Equity-principal auditions. You don't necessarily have to be a member of Equity these days in order to be eligible for these open auditions. If you've performed professionally but haven't yet joined Equity, you can come to these auditions. These open-call auditions last three days.

Is it a waste of time for actors to go to these Equity open calls?

I must say it's difficult for an actor, because one often waits for a very long time, depending on the show. Sometimes you don't always get in to audition. We start at nine or ten in the morning and go 'til six at night, with maybe twenty minutes for lunch. However, these calls are *not* a waste of an actor's time.

How many minutes do you normally spend with each actor?

We're required by the union to spend three minutes with each. And one does find people at these auditions. I'd be lying if I said we cast leads in shows from these auditions, but we often cast a lot of our understudies from them. And we also find people for the chorus. There is also a separate chorus call—that's usually a day or two. It could be a day for singers and a day for dancers. Then we get into what we call "appointment auditions."

These appointment auditions are set up through agents?

Through agents or through our knowledge of performers from the past—not exclusively through agents!

Do you ever, in this situation, see people who are not members of Actors' Equity?

Oh, yes.

So a non-Equity member is not necessarily out of the running?

Not at all. And then there are usually callbacks. If we start out with Hal Prince, by the time we get to the callbacks, the director and musical director are usually sitting in, and a couple of the producers. By the time of the final, final callback, there are quite a few people sitting out front, probably close to a dozen.

By the time of the final, final callback, how many times will an actor have auditioned for that show, usually?

Probably three. After the third callback, you have to pay the actor, according to the union.

What qualities are important for a performer in a musical?

Musicals today obviously put tremendous emphasis on the singing—for example, a show like *Phantom*. A show like *Cats* is more of a dancing show. But it's not enough to have a beautiful voice or just dance well. In the old days, when there were productions of *Blossom Time* and shows like that, you could get by with one skill. Now you must be able to sing, dance, and act. And it's hard, because you have to be able to do a lot of things extremely well. You're really put through your paces at auditions for today's musicals. You should prepare yourself to sing, dance, and act.

How important is the size of the voice? I remember, even twenty years ago, musicals were not heavily miked, whereas now they seem to be. So is a large voice as crucial as it used to be?

Well, I think it's important that one has a "theater voice," because every once in a while someone comes in to sing for us who's basically a club or recording singer—and you can tell, when that person starts singing on a stage. You're not miked when you sing at an audition. Large voices are not as important as they were, because most of the shows are miked now.

Are stage actors really a different breed from film and television actors? You cast both, and you've probably cast the same people in both areas.

Well, I always say good actors are good actors. I've had producers and directors say to me, "She can't do it, Geoff, she's too used to television and film." I think there are rare cases where people can't adjust: they can't go from film or television to stage—if they're on a stage it's too small. Or if they're a stage actor going into film or television, it's too big. But I think most actors can adjust.

What qualities are particularly important for a stage actor? Are we talking about voice, physical agility, stamina, emotional power? What?

I think one has to be able to do all those things on a stage. "You have to be able to move across the stage and not bump into the furniture," as some wag once said—but it's true! I think you've got to be able to project, you've got to have good speech; you've got to have technique, and I think technique is a little different for everybody.

Are there people who have an instinct for the stage, a natural technique without studying and learning? Do you run into "naturals," as we say?

Yes, I think so.

But for those who are not "naturals," what impresses you most in the way of training, when you see it on a résumé?

Well, I must say there are certain acting teachers and schools that impress me more than others, just because, over the years, the students of these particular teachers or schools have emerged as good actors.

Would you be willing to mention a few names?

I think the students that come out of Juilliard are extremely well trained. Also, the Yale Drama School (where I studied as an actor), Carnegie-Mellon, ACT in San Francisco are very thorough and give one a well-rounded theater education. In New York, H-B Studios have turned out some very good people, and I know as soon as I leave here I'll think of other training grounds I should have mentioned.

The generalized wisdom is that if you want to do stage work, the place to be is probably New York. And if you want to make it big in film and television, L.A. is probably the place for a home base. Would you say that's true?

Yes, I would, in general. Unless you want to do stage work in regional theater.

What about an actor who has been in the business for a while and is seeing himself or herself get cast in a particular rather narrow range of parts, which happens a lot in television—and probably in theater, as well.

What would you advise that actor to do, to break out of this pigeonhole that the agent and casting people have put him or her into?

That's a difficult question, because I think it's very, very hard to break the mold. It's perfectly true. People are often typecast. They say, "Oh, she could never do this. She plays the sweet kid sister." And I'm not sure I know what to advise. I guess one has to beat one's agent and say, "Look, I can do things other than the sweet kid sister; I can play a hooker." Maybe one has to try to do a showcase or get into an off-Broadway show, or whatever. It's not easy, I know. I remember Mary Elizabeth Mastrantonio when she first came to New York. She was a singer, and she played a sweet little ingenue in a show based on *David Copperfield.* And she was demure. How she broke out of that and got into *Scarface* I don't know. But that shows it can be done.

Your suggestion of getting into a showcase strikes me as very good advice: an actor, in effect, investing his time and money—because you're not going to get paid for a showcase—to show your agent and any casting directors you can dragoon into coming that you can indeed do this very different kind of role. How can an actor whose work you don't know best get your attention? Say a young actor is in New York, just starting out. Is a showcase still the best approach?

I think the best approach is to try to get in something, no matter where or what. And if there's a flyer, send the flyer to me, and follow it up with a telephone call. And in our office we really keep very extensive files. One tremendous file is a "People We Know" file—for people whose work we know. We also have Dancer and Singer files, and if they do both they can be cross-filed. And God bless the computer age! If somebody sends in a picture and a résumé for *Phantom of the Opera* or *Les Miserables,* for example, because those are ongoing shows with several companies, we have screenings, without the director or associate producer there. Through these general auditions, we put performers in our computer, and file the picture and résumé. We haven't got our system completely in place yet, but it's starting to work very well.

So you've got it programmed in categories for the leading and major supporting roles in the show, and a list of actors you've already determined are possible for that.

Yes. And oftentimes someone will come in and say, "I'm the perfect Cosette." And then we see she's not, but she may be right for something else. And that's happened, and she is cast that way. Actors *don't* always know what they're right for!

But that's your job—to know what they're right for.

That's right.

You were saying the résumé is terribly important—and of course it is. What sorts of things particularly impress you, other than training?

Well, I must say, just that it's a very professional résumé.

What does that mean?

It's a business. Treat it like a business. It's amazing how many actors treat it like fun and games. It's not—it's like being an architect or trying to get a job in advertising or any other business. And it just appalls me sometimes that somebody will send us a picture and résumé and there's no clue of how to contact them.

Now, for the rest of the résumé, I understand that if you're fresh out of school you can't have done that much professionally, and you can't have a very impressive résumé. We cast a lot of young parts, particularly on the daytime "Another World," so training and roles played in school are important for that. I think relative honesty is good. We'll understand a little fudging, but I don't think you should pad the résumé, and I think it must be clearly laid out.

In terms of the format, what should come first on a résumé?

I think probably you have to change a résumé, depending on who you're sending it to. If you're sending it to a television casting person, you'd probably put television first. Most of the résumés I see list theater, then television, and commercials. Usually education is at the bottom, along with special skills, whatever.

A picture and résumé is like a calling card—have it with you all the time. That's another thing actors do—they come to an audition and they say, "I don't have a picture and résumé with me." I'm always happy to take a picture and résumé—I mean, that's what I do. I'm a casting director—I don't resent it if somebody gives me a picture and a résumé. I do resent it if they tell me the story of their life when I'm doing an audition and I've just come out of an audition room, and they say, "Mr. Johnson, may I speak to you a minute?" and then they tell me everything they've done in the last twenty years.

And also, please—why can't actors staple or glue their résumés to their pictures? If you have a picture and it's not attached to the résumé, it can get separated. As long as we're talking about pictures, I'd like to say that you will never get casting directors or agents or managers to agree on what the best picture is. Personally, I think you should get a picture that looks like you!

That would seem to be elementary, wouldn't it?

Yes, but there's a lot of airbrushing that goes on, or actors who go for a sultry look, and so on. Some people are very photogenic and some aren't, but I think it's important that it look like you. There are a few situations in which I call an actor in from a picture, and when they walk in the door I think, *Who is that person?*

For a performer whose work you already know, what's the best way to refresh your memory of that person without being a terrible nuisance? To what extent can one be a bit of nuisance?

I see no harm in writing a note, or even calling in. If I can talk to you, I try to; I realize how difficult it is. But if I can't get on the phone with you, because I'm on another call or whatever, you can always leave a message in our office with whoever answers the telephone. Everything is written down. We don't have those little slips that a lot of offices do; we have a message pad for each day, like a log, and if there's a "G" before it, it's for me, and if there's a "V" before it, it's for Vinnie, and so on, and there are carbon copies made of that, so we can each look at our messages at the end of the day or the next morning. So it doesn't hurt to say, "Just calling in to say hi" or "Just calling in to say I'm back in town," or whatever you have to say.

How do you feel about postcard reminders with an actor's picture on them?

It's okay. I'm not mad about them. I think it can be overdone. But I must say it's more useful for something like a soap.

Are you aware of there being types and age ranges that are appropriate for soaps, in general, that differ from those that are appropriate for the stage shows you cast? Are soap actors generally younger, prettier?

They really go for attractive, young people; there's no denying it. Even if there's no demand in the script for it. I must say, it annoys me, because if I send an extremely good actor to the soap for a part that is not a romantic villain or something—he's just a lawyer—and they call me, maybe after he's worked, and say, "Well, that lawyer wasn't very good-looking," I say, "Well, why does he have to be good-looking?" I mean, this is somebody who's presentable; it's not Scarface. I'm thinking, *Do you know how lucky we were to get him on the show? He doesn't normally do daytime.* If they feel that somebody should be a good-looking lawyer, then they've got to tell me. But they don't always do that. With contract roles—those are the pretty ones.

More so than the day players. And also, what happens with contract roles is that it's casting by committee, real television-casting by committee.

Who has to approve before the person gets cast?

The executive producer, the Procter & Gamble rep, the head writer, about four people at the network—it's too many people, and that many people will never, never agree. Of course, eventually somebody has to be chosen—after months and months and months of going through young girls, or whatever the part is.

How many people will you typically see for a contract role? How many actors?

It does vary, but I would say at least a hundred.

And of that number, how many would get put on videotape?

Well, again, that varies. Sometimes you can get by with one session on videotape, and that could be eight people, but often it could be double that.

Are there special techniques to acting on a soap opera—to doing a videotaped audition for a soap opera?

Well, I think one has to be sort of aware that one is acting for the camera. I don't mean that one should play to the camera or anything like that, but I think there are those camera techniques that one has to observe. Every once in a while, we do get somebody that we tape for a contract role who has never been in front of a camera before. I'm usually in the booth when they're doing those tape tests. And they won't stay still, they're all over the place, and they get out of camera range. They know more-or-less where they have to be, and that on a certain line they need to cross to that chair—they know what their blocking is. But if they haven't been in front of a camera much, they can get way, way off.

Making sudden motions, so that the camera can't keep them in frame?

Yes, so that the test director, who's sitting there with me, is saying, "Why can't he stay still? I didn't tell him to move on that line." But usually that can be worked out. I must say, the test director always takes a lot of time on these tests, and we usually run it dry about two or three times before we tape it. And if they don't feel it's right, then it can be done again.

Or even sometimes the actor will say, "Please, can I do it again? I was awful." Of course I don't think actors ever know when they do a good audition, because more often than not they'll say, "Oh, I was awful," and I'll say, "You were *wonderful*, brilliant." Or they'll say, "It's the best audition I ever gave," and I'll be thinking, *Oh, really?*

Is it useful for an actor who wants to work in soaps and television to take one of those video workshops that allow you to see yourself on camera?

I don't really know about them. I've never been to one, and I don't know exactly what they do. I would think it would be useful for an actor to take a soap audition course, with qualified teachers, seeing yourself on camera—the good things you do and the bad things you do.

I'm a little cautious about answering that question because I'm rather wary of things that exploit actors. I think becoming an actor is a costly business, when you've got to have pictures and résumés, and so on. I know some of those classes are expensive, and I'm sure there are good ones out there, but I'm not really qualified to say.

Somebody like Joan D'Incecco, who's casting director of "All My Children"—she and Judy Henderson, another casting director, teach a class, which I've never been to, but I think Joan is a very down-to-earth lady who knows the soap opera business and has been in it for a very long time. She's right out there, and very honest, and I can't believe she would be teaching a class that wasn't good.

It might be a good idea to check out the background and credentials of anyone who's purporting to teach something. What other mistakes do actors commonly make in auditions, other than jumping around on camera?

People do really strange things. We were doing this pilot, this musical pilot, and an actor I've known for years came in to audition. And he's extremely talented—he's played leads on Broadway, he's done television miniseries, and so on. He's young, but he's really done it all. But he came into this audition (and I've seen him do it before) as if he couldn't have cared less. It was what we call in our office "attitude." And he sort of looked over at me and smiled, because I've known him for years and he's been brought in for shows and he's been cast in many of our shows. And before he even began to sing, he completely turned the producers off, and they just dismissed him.

I think you have to be polite, you have to be nice. You don't have to talk too much—they want to get the part cast; that's all they want to do. People come in and talk about getting stuck on the subway, and how late they were out the night before, and all that craziness, and nobody really wants to hear that.

Oh, and another thing, as long as we're talking about that: People—and I guess it's more younger people—think that casting directors are out to block them, so they don't get the job. And that's so wrong. If I bring you in for an audition, it's because I think you're right, and I think you can do it. But the director may think, *No, that's not it*—for a lot of reasons. Sometimes they tell us; sometimes they don't. But I would be happy if I had a whole day of auditions set up, and you were the first one to come in to audition, and you left and they said, "That's it." I would be *so* happy, because we want somebody to get the job—fast. It makes our life easy, and it's sort of an affirmation of what we do. I think you should get it in your head that even if they're cold people and even if it's not a very nice casting director, you're going in there positively, with the attitude of *I'm very right for this, and I'm going to get it.* Don't *tell* them; don't try and talk them into it. They'll make the decision, the people behind the table.

Do you think people who do extra work tend to get pigeonholed in that classification?

Yes, I think they do, unless they make an effort to break out of it. I know on our soap, we at Johnson-Liff don't cast the extras and the under-fives. There's an assistant casting director, and she does that. There are a lot of professional extras, and they go from one soap to another. There's a restaurant on our show, TOPS, and they use the same waiters every time that restaurant appears, so you can make nice money if you're a waiter in TOPS. I mean, when it comes to the end of a year, you can make quite a bit of money. But it's like anything—you've got to try to get out of that. There are actors who come to me—write notes or send pictures—and say, "Look, I've been working as an extra, but I want to break out of that." I generally try to let them come in and read for me.

What are your major frustrations with the casting process? Is there anything you'd like to see changed or done away with?

That's a great question. I really am frustrated when I'm up against a director or a producer or a writer who will not give an actor a chance, but insist on typecasting—that gets me crazy, and I don't really have much patience with it. And I wish that could change. I think it's something that's been with us forever—it's a losing battle, in a way. I wish there were something I could do about it.

But the fact that you're aware of it, in the first place, and the fact that you fight this battle, it seems to me, is a very good sign for us actors.

Jay Binder

*J*ay Binder is an independent casting director whose Broadway credits include Beauty and the Beast, Damn Yankees, Laughter on the 23rd Floor, Broken Glass, The Rise and Fall of Little Voice, The Goodbye Girl, Jake's Women, Lost in Yonkers, Rumors, Jerome Robbins'

Broadway, *and* Meet Me in St. Louis. *He has also cast many Off-Broadway plays and productions for major regional theaters. He is East Coast Casting Director for Warner Brothers Television, including "I'll Fly Away," winner of a 1992 Artios Award.*

How did you get into casting in the first place?

By a fluke. I don't think anybody—at least anybody I know—wakes up one morning and says, "I have to be a casting director." When I graduated from college I wanted to be a director. I came to New York and was slowly building a directing career but making very little money. Leonard Soloway, who is one of Emanuel Azenberg's general managers, at that time had a producing organization and general management firm of his own. They were doing Edward Albee's play *Lolita,* and the casting situation was very difficult. Leonard called me one day and said, since I knew a lot of actors, why not come in and meet Edward Albee and Frank Dunlop because they were having trouble putting it together. At that time they were looking for a real thirteen-year-old girl to play Lolita. I had met both Frank and Edward socially, so I came and met with them. Edward, who is a terrific man with a dry wit, asked if I had read the play. I said yes, and he said, "Well, you know in the second act there's the best friend of the husband, who has only one arm. Do you think you could find me a one-armed actor?" I said, "Left arm or right arm?" and I got the job.

They'd had a nationwide search to find the young girl to play Lolita, and nationwide searches have never worked, from *Gone with the Wind* up to today. It was a very difficult Edward Albee text, and I kept saying to myself that this was never going to work, seeing all these thirteen-year-old children. I had previously seen a production of *The Glass Menagerie* at the Berkshire Theatre Festival that summer with Blanche Baker, who had just become recognizable because of "The Holocaust," the television miniseries. I suggested to Frank and Edward that we read Blanche, and she was the first actress I brought in when I got the job, and they cast her. That's how it happened.

Do you think having had training as a director and working as a director has been an asset for you as a casting director?

I think it's very helpful, because you come to casting with a directorial eye, and you can see past the audition into some sort of finished product, from the audition. An audition is not a performance, and to have that eye, to see what could be after a rehearsal period, is very helpful. To be able to speak to actors in director-language prior to the audition can help give the director what the director is looking for during the audition process.

Would you describe the process of casting a Broadway show? What goes on when you start to cast something like the revival of *Damn Yankees*?

Well, *Damn Yankees* is a situation where you're dealing with a given. What will make the show work in this day and age is not any updating or changes. What will make it sell is a star. When a major revival happens, it's usually because the producers already have the star.

Once you've set your stars, what is the procedure for casting the other parts?

You begin auditions. The procedure by which a show is cast is basically this: When I am hired, I first do lists—lists of actors that I think would be excellent in each role.

The other thing that happens in the casting process is something called Breakdown Services. It's out in California, but works on both coasts through computers. I write a description of the roles I'm looking for, plus all the pertinent information like dates, director, creative staff, and the like. That is sent to Breakdown Services, and they, in turn, send my description to each agent. The agent reads it and submits their clients via pictures and résumés and a cover letter to my office. Then I choose from their submissions who I think would be suitable. This is in addition to the list I have created, in addition to the lists the producers have given me, in addition to any ideas the director might have.

Then I begin to find out who's available, who's interested, and who will come in. When you're doing a Broadway show the field is more open to you, but there are people who will not play supporting parts.

How many people would you normally see for a major supporting role?

I would hope to see as few as possible: six to ten for each supporting role. In a Broadway show, all you need is the right actor. If the actor is going to take it, sometimes you need only one choice. In *Meet Me in St. Louis*, for the role of the mother I only showed the director four women.

Did he call back any of them more than once?

The woman who was cast as the mother was called back five times, which is what the director thought was required. The girl who is playing the Judy Garland role was called back eight or nine times. After the fourth time on a production contract, the actors begin to be paid. Calling people back an inordinate number of times is valuable only if you work the way Jerry Robbins works. When he calls you back he works with you. If you're called back repeatedly and are continually asked to do it without any adjustment, I think it's a waste of time and a reflection of the director's indecision.

Given the fact that you generally see so few people for the major supporting roles, is there any hope for an actor who goes to an Equity open call?

Absolutely, especially for the large musicals like *Cats*, *Les Miserables*, *Miss Saigon*, and *Phantom*—the shows with ensembles. If you go to an EPA (Equity-Principal Audition), that is a very viable way to get seen. I've cast many people from EPAs.

At an EPA, how long does each actor get to audition?

I don't know if there's an Equity regulation, but as long as it takes to sing a song, approximately three minutes. If it's a play, about two or three minutes.

And the scene or monologue or song is the actor's choice?

Yes, unless it's a revival. With a new play, you have to send a copy to the AEA auditions, I believe. If you choose to read from the play, it is available to you as an Equity member.

Are there scenes or monologues you hope you never have to watch again?

Absolutely. This is just my particular taste, but I am not a Sam Shepard kind of guy. Somebody coming in and swearing and kicking and screaming and throwing a chair—I don't mean to malign playwrights like Mr. Shepard and Mr. Mamet, but it's just not my particular taste.

As for musical auditions, because I'm a traditionalist and like to hear theater music I can make sense of, I'm not overly fond of hearing things from *Cats* and *Les Miz*. They don't appeal to my taste. If I'm doing that kind of show, then I deal with it, but just as an introduction to me, I would rather not see that kind of material.

What advice would you offer an actor who is going for a general audition?

If you are going in on a general, do something—be it a song or a monologue—that will introduce you. It should be something open and charming, something that makes me feel I've gotten to know who *you* are. It has to be something that is very much connected to who you want to project yourself as, something that lets me get to know you as a person. A general audition is an extended résumé.

What sort of length should one go for in this kind of general audition?

A monologue should be no longer than three minutes.

When you do a general interview in your own office, do you offer the actor a chance to do more than one monologue?

Yes. You should have two pieces prepared, and they should be contrasting. One should be comic and one should be serious. If you do one classical work, then the other should be contemporary. I do generals in my office when something on someone's résumé sparks my interest. If I call someone in for a general, I usually suggest the basic parameters of what I want to see. If you're coming in for a musical general, bring all sorts of music. Be as prepared as you can be with as much material as you can. You may not be asked to do it all, but you never know. You don't want to be caught short. And really have the material prepared. There are various coaches and casting directors in New York that offer classes or workshops. Take advantage of them if you need guidance in preparing for auditions.

Are there particular classes or coaches that you have had consistently good experiences with?

Absolutely. In musical theater, Jeffrey Dunn's work is quite good. Jeff teaches out of Weist-Barron. When a student of Jeff's comes in, they really know what they're doing. As a vocal coach, there's a young man named Steven Lutvack who I think is quite good working with singers in all styles. I also think that Barbara Hipkiss, who works for me, is a terrific coach on monologues.

Let's talk for a minute about pictures and résumés. What might catch your attention on a résumé?

If you're a beginning actor, one of the things I look at is training. If your training is on your résumé and if your college background is on your résumé, it may spark something in me. If there is a particular person you've worked with that I respect or have studied with, that's another thing that would catch my eye.

Because our office does a lot of regional theater, we are constantly looking for new young talent. If we're doing a classical play in Boston and there are forty-seven speaking roles and we have to cast a lord, we are looking for new people beginning their careers. When pictures and résumés come into the office and people have worked in interesting places that are not mainstream, I will eventually call them in.

What kind of training or schools might catch your eye?

Any school that I know has a professional training program. We do a lot of musicals, and I'm always looking for singers. If I see that you're a musical performer, I put your résumé in a pile and eventually I will get to it. Things that are necessary to me always get filtered through. If there's a particular play on your résumé that I'm fascinated by, I may or may not call you, but it will certainly get my attention.

What are the biggest mistakes you see actors continually make in auditions?

The biggest mistake is not understanding what an audition is. The audition really is about only the part at that moment, and performing at a level that can convince the director you are the person for that role. When you walk in and read a scene or sing a song, at that moment it has to appear to be a finished product. It isn't, and there's no way it could be, but you have to have the authority and the strength to be able to convince, or to give the illusion to the producer and director that you will have a finished product that's the product they want. Auditions can't be attempts. They have to be choices carried out, and you have to give the impression that you can deliver. People who are not known have to gain that assurance, that trust.

Sounds like it might actually be better to make a wrong-headed choice and do it with conviction than to be half-baked about a good choice.

Right—and if you're not asked to make an adjustment, the director either isn't buying it or likes what you're doing. Nine times out of ten the director will want to see your point of view on it, your take on it. Basically, when you come in, it's yours. It's an attitude—not arrogance—that you have it; it's your job. Do you know what I mean?

Yes, and it's wonderful advice. Jay, are stage actors really a different breed from film and television actors?

People who started their careers as film or television actors are very different. The technique of portraying another human being in front of a thousand people or two thousand people is a whole different technique from portraying another human being in front of a camera. Stage acting, for me, is the true test of real acting because it's unnatural to create another human being that large, so that it comes across the footlights. That's magic, to me.

Are there good stage actors who find it difficult or impossible to work in film and television, and vice versa?

Yes. Take a look at the Lunts. The Lunts were great stage actors who were miserable on film. Then you have the exceptions that prove the rule. Maggie Smith is one of the most flamboyant stage actresses, yet she also has the capacity to be a brilliant film actress. I think that on film no one is more magical than Michelle Pfeiffer; she is incandescent. On stage, because she's not trained and doesn't have the experience to do that, it's flat as a pan-cake.

In your experience, is the transition from film to stage harder to make than going from stage to film or television?

Absolutely.

So it's easier to tone it down than to make it larger?

Right. You can watch certain stage actors get better on film as they gain experience. Bette Midler did certain films where she was far too large, and then there are films where she gives remarkable performances. A lot will depend on the director, too.

When you're casting for theater or television, how important is the role of the agent?

It's important. I would be lying if I said it wasn't. A good agent can get you seen. It's not a guarantee, but if you're with an agency that I have an ongoing relationship with, day in and day out, I trust that agent and I will see a client they recommend.

On the other hand, I know superb agents who really don't help their clients. I see *Cats* every six months or so, just to see if there's anyone on stage that might be of interest to me. I saw this actor I thought was quite good, but how could I really tell how good he was when he was a cat? There was a presence there, and he sang well and moved well, and I wanted to meet him. I called his agent, and they would not let me meet him. I could bring him in to audition for something, but he couldn't come in to do a general. That was "protecting their client": that was their position. I finally got to meet him when I was working on a project with a director I was friendly with, and we brought him in and discovered him together.

Would you have brought him in sooner or for something else if you had met him before?

Had I met him before in a general audition, I would have known more about him and how to showcase him better. I would have had a better idea of what he could do and what he couldn't do.

I find that the best process in casting a show is to have the actors come in and meet first and then audition eventually. It's just a more civilized way of doing it, but some directors don't agree.

What's the benefit for the actor?

It reduces the fear quotient. It is definitely their prerogative to just come in and read if they so choose. There are also actors, generally well known, who don't want to come in and read, although I feel that if an actor really wants a role, no matter how big a star they are, they will ultimately read.

There are directors who have the security just to make offers. I'm doing a play now with John Tillinger, and it's a real joy. He has an in-depth working knowledge of the New York acting community because he directs here all the time. John comes in and says to make an offer to so-and-so. He doesn't need to see them audition, because he's seen them a hundred times on the stage and knows their work.

Do you go to a lot of Equity-waiver or showcase-type productions?

Counting myself, there are three people in our office, and we divide up what we see. We make a list every month from the flyers we get, and we see as much as we humanly can and still get our laundry done.

So the best way for an actor whose work you don't know to get your attention might be to send you a flyer?

That is the best way. As convenient as a general is, it really is not enough. It's a good way to meet, but I feel it's important to know somebody's work. Yes, I have cast people out of the audition room that I've never seen on stage, but it is generally best if I see something finished. That's why I see so much.

Actors also have the right, if they find themselves in a bomb, to say they are proud of what they're doing and that I can leave after the first act, or that their big scene is in the second act and I should only see that. You have to be up-front. If it's a terrible production and you're no good in it, don't ask me to come. It's as simple as that.

Do you ever attend the theater festivals at the regional theaters? Is it a good idea for actors to take part in those?

Let me put it this way: if you are in a position financially to enter into an intern program at a regional theater, by all means do it. You're a slave, but you really learn a lot and you get great training. You are part of the company and are needed in various productions—sometimes even in leading roles. I think that if you want to be an actor, you have to go in the door that says "actor." An internship program in a regional theater is a wonderful way to grow up.

Each regional theater has someone at that theater who's in charge of its casting. If you do a regional tour, you'll get to see every casting director at every regional theater, in-house. There is a person on staff who will see you, and if they think you're terrific they'll recommend you to me. It's another way in.

The Screen Actors Guild and Actors' Equity have committees devoted to the casting of minorities—and in the case of television, women—because they are so underrepresented. Is there anything a person in your position can or should do to have an effect in this area?

In the recent past, the need and desire to broaden minority casting has been a real issue. It's something we are confronted with and want to do as much about as we possibly can, given each individual project. With *Jerome Robbins' Broadway*, we have been in the middle of a situation where Equity has said there's a lack of black people in the cast. Now, given the fact that Jerry Robbins' concept was to re-create these shows, I think that Robbins had the prerogative to do that originally. I do feel strongly that to restrict it to that era now is something that has to be broadened, and is being broadened.

On the other hand, what Equity did not understand, and what I think they do understand now, is that the standard is so high for *Jerome Robbins' Broadway* that very few people are up to that standard. There isn't as broad a base as Equity thought.

I feel strongly there are certain principal roles that can benefit by non-traditional casting. They can be more exciting dramatically, vocally, and in relation to a modern audience. I hope that can be done when we cast the tour.

What are your major frustrations with the casting process? Is there anything you'd like to change or see done away with?

I get frustrated when a director doesn't agree with me, but I get over it. The reason casting directors came into being is simply that the industry is so large. Basically we are a service organization. Directors hire us for our service; they hire us for our taste.

I would like to see a commitment from American actors to divide their time more evenly among television, theater, and film so that theater is not always the lowest priority. It is because you have to make a living. My biggest frustration is that in this country the focus of a successful actor has to be money—as opposed to the British tradition in theater, where one can freely divide one's time. I feel frustrated because actors and agents, more often than not, think they have no real position unless they have some sort of film profile.

Pat McCorkle

Pat McCorkle *has been represented on Broadway most recently with* Philadephia. Here I Come!, Picnic, She Loves Me, Blood Brothers, The Kentucky Cycle, Anna Christie, No Man's Land, The

Homecoming, The Price, *and* A Few Good Men. *Other New York credits include* Remembrance, Driving Miss Daisy, *and* Godspell. *Among her films are* School Ties, Men of Respect, Wizard of Loneliness, *and* Die Hard—New York. *She has cast several television projects for the HBO Lifestories series and PBS's "Ghostwriter." Ms. McCorkle is a member of the Board of Directors of the Casting Society of America.*

How did you get into casting?

Does this sound like a cliché? I wanted to be a director. After an under-graduate major in drama, I did my graduate degree at NYU in directing. I came to New York to direct and fell into casting relatively quickly. I had an office job at Circle in the Square Uptown. I was their subscription manager, and that takes about half an hour a day to do. They had a casting consul-tant, Roger Sturtevant, and I started working with him. Eventually I got promoted to assistant to the artistic director. Roger was an outside consul-tant and I was the inside person. I did that for two years.

Then I left and went to TCG, Theater Communications Group, where I was a casting director for three years. That's where I made all my regional connections. Regional theater is actually much more difficult to cast than Broadway. Eleven years ago I started my own company.

Has your training as a director proved particularly useful?

Yes. Even though I was training to be a director in college, I wasn't con-vinced that I wanted to come to New York to do it. I think being a woman director is very difficult. It's a very, very closed field—even now that it's opened up somewhat.

I wasn't sure that was what I wanted to do, so I was a teacher before I came to New York, and I have a very strong literature background. I taught English—dramatic literature—to high-school seniors in central New Jersey.

Those two things have helped me enormously: the directing background and the literature background. I find most people in the theater are aston-ishingly ignorant about literature. I'm casting *Harvey* right now, and most people don't know what *Harvey* is. Maybe *School for Wives* and *The Rivals* are a bit obscure, but *Harvey*?

Let's talk about the process of casting *A Few Good Men.* Did you have meetings with the director in the beginning?

I had worked with the director before, and yes, we spent a lot of time going over the play. I'm very, very proud of that company, but there are inherent problems that people aren't aware of—though you'd be aware if I cast it wrong. It's twenty-two men and one woman, and when you have twenty-two men wearing Army fatigues who have basically no hair, it's very important that each of those guys be very individual. I also have the problem that all of them have to be fit. Most are supposed to be Marines, so they have to be in good physical shape. I specifically picked appropriate body heights, sizes, and ages. There's age on the stage; we worked very hard at making sure they're not all twenty-two years old.

The other thing about A Few Good Men that's hard is that other than the principals, who are relatively obvious, the "grunts," as we call them—the five guys on the stage who do all the other stuff—also understudy all the principals. Actually, their main function is to cover the principals. They all have to be good enough to play those roles; that's the first priority of those grunts, that they cover X, Y, and Z. Sometimes it's hard to get good actors who are willing to stand at attention for three hours every night.

When some of the leads open up, will the understudies be moving into them?

We hope so. I would say there's a ninety-nine-percent chance of some of them moving up. I can't say for sure because I have to have the playwright's approval—as well as the director's approval, the stage manager's approval, and the producer's approval. There are other parameters which won't affect some of these people, but which have affected others already. When Tom Hulce leaves, although his understudy is very, very good . . .

You need a star name?

Right. That's just the way it is.

How do you feel about actors doing understudy work, in general, in a New York show?

I think it's terrific. You should do it because you'll get to go on and people will see you. You'll get used to being on a Broadway stage. You really have to earn your points. The thing about being an understudy that's difficult is that you have to get yourself into a certain way of thinking. You have to know that every night when you go out there someone else is doing the part you want. You have to be able to live with that for nine months. It makes some people nuts.

It's different with standbys. Can you explain how that works?

Standbys don't have to come into the theater each night. They call in at half hour and ask, "How are things?" It's a difficult job, and you have to have a certain head to do it. It's a paycheck and a Broadway show and all, but you may not get to go on for months.

Going back to the casting of *A Few Good Men*, what's the next step after the conferences with the playwright and the director?

We talk about what parameters need to be defined. In *A Few Good Men*, we talked about the ages of the characters, where they were in the military, who they were.

Then did you contact agents? Use your own files?

All of the above. Anywhere I could get the actors. There are four people who got their Equity cards doing this show, and eleven people in the show are making their Broadway debuts.

In a situation like this, with a large male cast for a Broadway show, does an actor coming to an Equity open call have a hope?

Yes. I'm looking to fill parts. The problem with the open Equity calls is that people don't pay attention to what I'm asking for. With *A Few Good Men*, everyone thinks they can play a grunt, but, as I've said, that's not all they do. I need good actors who can cover principal parts. Sure, you can stand at attention for three hours, but you can't play the doctor, and that's what you need to do.

I just went through four days of Williamstown open call. I listed the season, and I had all these people come in, and I would say that a third of them did Shakespeare. Now Williamstown doesn't do Shakespeare; there's no Shakespeare listed for this season—so why are they doing Shakespeare? Williamstown is doing five contemporary plays. I don't think actors keep in mind that an audition is a job interview. I'm casting X, and these are my needs. Don't give me: "I'm talented and I want you to see that I'm talented"; give me what I ask for.

I am flexible enough that if I see somebody and I really like them but they're not right for the part I'm casting, I'm already thinking of some other role they would be right for.

It sounds as though some actors don't make the connection between what a part is and whether they can reasonably fill it.

That's essentially true. "I'm a good actor; I can do anything." A problem with beginning actors is that they frequently don't understand that directors are not acting coaches; they want directors to show them how to play the part. You should already have an idea of how you're going to play the part, and then—to quote a friend—"the director negotiates between you and the play on how the role will be done." He'll guide you, but you have to bring in the bulk of the work.

If we're talking about something like the Williamstown auditions where you have announced in advance what the shows for the season are, does it make sense to you for an actor to come in with a monologue from one of those plays?

Sure. It helps me. If you're auditioning for *Harvey*, it doesn't help to have a Sam Shepard piece. Pick something from your repertoire that's in the same style as the play you're auditioning for, the same era.

You have to work at acting as a profession, and it's a heavy-duty job. Read the *New York Times*, read *American Theater*, read whatever you can. In New York, especially, if I say Horton Foote you should know who I'm talking about. It's part of your job, the same way it's part of my job. How can you call yourself an actor and say that you don't read plays or go to the theater? If you're still doing Willy Loman for your monologue, get with it! You have to stay on top of the primary material.

How important is networking for an actor?

Networking is important for anybody in this business. I network. Everyone networks. You have to make a distinction between networking—what we call senior gossiping—and junior gossip, which is *gossip* gossip. What you do is find out information and pass that information along. Don't just sit back and wait to be called.

I think actors have to stop thinking of themselves as victims. You have to take a more aggressive, grass-roots kind of small-business mentality. Acting is your business; it's what you do. Actors are in the situation where they have to be asked at the dance, if you know what I mean. However, you can do more than sit against the wall and wait. You also have to be careful not to get into negative thinking. It's very easy to do, especially since there's a ninety-five-percent unemployment rate.

Let's talk for a minute about the question of building a career. At what point should an actor begin to turn down work? Is it harmful for an actor to do episodic television after some point?

I would think that at the beginning of a career an actor would take anything he could get. If you've done the lead in a feature film, you shouldn't be doing episodic television unless it's a wonderful thing. It really depends on the quality of the show. There's been some really good television lately, so it depends on which show you're talking about. When you have people like Robert Loggia doing television, you should be happy to do it—and more and more people are. The bottom line is that it all has to do with money.

Does doing a soap make it more difficult for an actor to do feature films? Isn't there a certain prejudice?

There is a certain prejudice. It depends on what role you're doing and how long you've done it.

How does the length of time come into play?

The problem is that soaps are about plot and character, and not about writing particularly. They're just telling you more of the same story, and soaps are done so fast that you really don't have the time to work on your acting skills. You barely get enough time to even learn the words. Now we have some terrific actors on soaps who go out and exercise those other muscles and do stage work and film. I certainly don't think that having been on a soap is as destructive as it used to be. It also depends on where you are in your career. There are people on soaps who are not our better actors, but if you are a good actor you can still be on a soap and rise above it. There are a lot of very good actors who have done soaps. In New York it's a major way of making a living, especially for day players.

What about extra work?

I think extra work is a good thing to do, because you learn what goes on on a movie set. I don't think you should make a career out of extra work, but if you need it to pay the rent, go right ahead.

What are some of the biggest mistakes people make at auditions?

They forget that it's a business and they're going for a job. They come in and they don't tell you their name; they've forgotten their picture and résumé; they don't identify the pieces they're doing; they mumble; they play it to the wall. I don't mind accents in pieces, but sometimes they're so thick you have absolutely no idea what's being said.

I hate chatting up, being overly friendly. Lack of energy, forgetting your piece. Taking too long when preparing to start. Also doing pieces that have been done to death!

Like what?

Crimes of the Heart, Hilary's speech in *Tribute. A Girl's Guide to Chaos* is the new one. I strongly suggest that you avoid the monologue books. It's not because they're not good; it's because everybody has access to them. Make your own.

I always want people to show me character in a monologue. This is about why I should give you a job and how you're going to play this part. I want to know about your acting. You're the actor; that's your job.

So you want to see a range of emotional colors? You want to see some change?

And conflict. I don't want something passive-reflective. It tells me nothing. It's not terribly useful to me.

Do you have agents that you call regularly when you're casting television or theater?

It depends on what the project is. Agents have styles just like casting directors have styles and writers have styles. There are certain agents who sort of specialize in conservatory-trained actors. If I'm doing a street picture, they're not going to have what I want. If I'm doing Shakespeare, I'll definitely call them. There are other agents who are particularly good when it comes to beauties. You have agencies with strong musical departments, while some have very few musical people.

How important is it for an actor to have a powerful agent?

Powerful agents? What function do you want your agent to serve? A lot of actors need an agent who is really there for them, almost like a manager or a consultant. A lot depends on how the agent responds to you. It's all about personalities and people. It's about relationships. I saw four guys today for one role in A Few Good Men. Three of them I knew, but one I didn't. The agent called up, told me about the guy, and sent me a picture. He looked right, so I called him in.

Is there any chance for an actor who doesn't have an agent? How do they get to you?

They send a picture and résumé along with a cover letter that's specific as to the role they would like to audition for: "I understand you are casting the national tour of A Few Good Men and I think I would be right for the role of X."

So you're not interested in having people send you pictures and résumés on a general basis?

It doesn't do me any good. I'm so involved with problem solving all the time that I don't have the time, really; you also deserve better. You just don't write to IBM and say, "I'd like a job, so please hire me." It's show *business*. It's about being in this profession.

Mark Simon

Since joining Binder Casting in 1993, Mark Simon has worked on Beauty and the Beast, The King and I, City Center's Encores! (Fiorello, Allegro, and Lady in the Dark, in concert), several TV pilots for Warner Brothers, and shows for several regional theatres. His independent casting credits include the New York productions of Tamara and Blues in the Night. With the legendary producer David Merrick and Charles Kopelman, he produced the Broadway revival of Loot, which garnered five Tony nominations.

Mark, how did you get into casting?

I had produced two shows—one very successful and one not so successful—and worked very closely with a casting firm then called Johnson-Liff Associates. Geoff Johnson and Vinnie Liff are close personal and professional friends. When *Loot* closed, I didn't have another show that was ready to go into preproduction, and a producer without a show is unemployed. Geoff and Vinnie were just starting work on *Starlight Express* and knew it was going to be very hairy, and they asked me to come and work for them. We'd had great rapport casting my two shows, and I'd had a basic enthusiasm and interest in the casting process for a long time.

Starlight Express was really my first casting job, and it was a wonderful experience—first, because I think they're extraordinary casting directors who cast the lion's share of Broadway now, but also because the office was very, very busy and it was really like jumping into the deep end of a pool.

While I was at Johnson-Liff, I worked mainly on *Starlight Express* and on the international company of *Dreamgirls*. When I knew that *Starlight Express* was going to be finishing I knew that it was time to move on. The way life works, a friend of mine—the director Sheldon Epps—was just starting on preproduction of an off-Broadway musical called *Blues in the Night*, which was at the Minetta Lane Theater. He said that since I had just finished *Dreamgirls*, and *Blues in the Night* was also an all-black show, how would I like to cast it for him? So, without really much thought or long-range planning, I had some stationery printed and got a second phone line in my apartment and opened my own office. *Blues* was my first show, and I think I'm working on my twenty-seventh show now. People keep calling.

How does having a producer's perspective affect the way you approach the casting of a production?

I think it gives me a particular advantage in that I'm able to see a lot of the different sides of the casting situation. I'm very sympathetic to the needs of a producer who might need a higher visibility cast to sell some tickets, or who might need to see certain people for various reasons, because I've been on both sides of the fence. Also, when it comes to talking about money and negotiating an actor's salary—although it's usually the job of the producer's office or the manager's office—I'm able to make pretty accurate recommendations about what an actor needs, having done so much of that myself. I can say not to bring in Joe Schmoe because he won't work for less than twenty-five hundred a week and you know you can only pay a thousand.

So you save them time by not seeing people out of their price range?

Right, and I can also say that if they're absolutely enthusiastic about this person, it's going to cost them this much. That kind of perspective has helped me tremendously.

What advice would you offer someone who's interested in pursuing a career as a casting director?

There aren't a lot of sure-fire ways to do it. If you're interested, and you have the time and the financial resources, go and intern with a casting director. Identify casting directors you like, or whose work you admire, and call them up, even if you haven't met them, and say, "I'm able to work fifteen hours a week. Is there anything I can do?" Some of that work can be a lot of fun. I always bring in people who are readers, reading against actors who are auditioning. Or if it's a big musical I need someone to help me organize the actual audition room and things like that. That's one way to get in.

I'm intrigued by what you just said about people who are hired to come in and read opposite actors for auditions. Would that be a way for an actor to become known by your office, to call your office and offer him- or herself as a reader?

Absolutely. I always use actors. It's not the easiest work; reading for seven hours can be very, very draining. But if you have that kind of stamina it can be a lot of fun. You get known by all the people sitting on this side of the desk. I always try to use actors because the times I've used nonactors, like an assistant stage manager or sometimes myself, I don't think the auditioning actor gets the best shot. The only danger you run into sometimes with actors is that they forget they're the readers and turn the audition into one for themselves instead. It takes the focus away from the auditioning actor, and we sometimes have to take them aside and explain the situation.

I would also think it's a useful way of learning about what makes a good audition, seeing all those other actors auditioning.

You've literally said what all of my readers say—that they're fascinated by the process and by seeing the wide range. If you're an auditioning actor, you don't often get the opportunity to see what other people do in that room.

Could you describe for us the process of casting a Broadway show—say something like the revival of *Loot*?

Well, once the rights were secured and we had the director signed, we made an appointment with Geoff Johnson, Vinnie Liff, and their colleague Andrew Zerman. I had already provided them with a script, which they had read the week before. We sat down and wrote down our ideal cast. We left that in their hands, and they went out and checked to see if these ideal folks we had written down, our dream cast, were interested, whether they were available. In the case of *Loot*, four out of the five actors on that original dream list did eventually do the show. For me it was absolutely a cast made in heaven.

We had tried out *Loot* at the Manhattan Theatre Club and brought the entire cast to Broadway, with the exception of Kevin Bacon. We replaced Kevin Bacon with a then-modestly-known actor named Alec Baldwin. Alec got his Equity card doing *Loot*.

What's the biggest mistake you see actors constantly making at auditions?

Not being prepared. There is always an opportunity to read a script. You might have to be willing to sit in a casting director's office to read it, or to take it out and photocopy it and bring it back. I see actors over and over again who are just not prepared. It's professional suicide. Read the play. Know the character. Ask questions. I'm surprised how seldom an actor will call me and say he's just read a role and doesn't get something and would I be willing to help. It's my pleasure. First of all, I have a vested interest in an actor doing well at an audition. I get paid to provide good actors.

Would you recommend that an actor memorize a scene if possible?

Absolutely not. First of all, the auditions are often unpredictable. What if the director wants to see a different scene that day? The actor who has memorized one specific scene, or been coached to within an inch of his or her life, falls apart if the director changes his mind.

I would think that if someone was prepared, if someone knew the script and knew the character, if someone knew all about the production from dates to salaries, the more material an actor can bring into the audition, the more successful he'll be.

How can an actor learn all that?

Very simply. All of it is listed with Equity, and the casting director always has it. That's the kind of information that it's my pleasure to provide. If you're being submitted for an audition by an agent, then the agent has all that information.

Is it a good idea for the actor to dress for the part in an audition?

I never tell actors to wear a particular costume. When I was at Johnson-Liff, I did a little work on *Les Miz,* and people would come to open calls wearing burlap dresses, trying to dress for the part. They looked absolutely ridiculous. I always tell actors to keep it simple. Wear nice clothes. Look nice, but don't wear a cocktail dress. Don't bring props. I don't want an actor to look schlumpy. On the other hand—and this seems to happen more with men—I've seen actors come in to audition for *The Grapes of Wrath* in a three-piece suit that's more appropriate for a Chemical Bank commercial audition.

If you're having trouble at an audition, I see no reason on earth not to stop and say to the director, "Give me an adjustment. I'm confused. Tell me where you want to go." I think a lot of actors forget that those fifteen or twenty minutes are their time, and too many are passive in this process.

I think the word "audition" is a tough one, and I'd like to erase it from the show-biz vocabulary. I think of these as work sessions. If someone doesn't do well at an audition, or isn't right for a part, I'm not going to hold that against them. A lot of times people get cast or don't get cast in a show for a lot of ancillary reasons: they're the right age; they have absolutely the right look; the leading lady is over forty and they read too young to play the husband.

How can an actor or an actress whose work you don't know best get your attention?

It's difficult. If the actor is a member of the union, then I encourage them to go to EPAs and EPIs.

Equity-principal auditions, Equity-principal interviews.

Right. I read every single piece of mail I get, so there's nothing really wrong with sending someone your picture and résumé. I can't speak for my colleagues, but I would guess that most of us read our mail. You won't believe how many come in the mail in a blank envelope with just a picture and a résumé—not even a cover letter saying something like "I play the piano beautifully; I'm interested in *Tamara*. I heard you're casting this." Without a cover letter, I don't know what to make of it. Tell me what you want.

So you'd like a cover letter that addresses the things that you are currently working on, or something that might interest you about this person?

Exactly.

Do you go to Equity-waiver theater, showcases, workshops? How valuable are these as sources of exposure?

I think it's valuable for the actor in a couple of ways. First of all, I think actors should work. Forget about whether you're being seen by a lot of agents or casting directors. You should choose to do a showcase if you want to stretch your acting muscles. Do it because you want the work. Do it because you like the play or like the group, not because fourteen agents are going to see you.

What's the best way for a person who's in a showcase to let you know? Send you a note? A flyer? Call you up? All of the above?

Yes. I keep a file, and once or twice a month I take out all the flyers for shows that I've missed and throw them away. I'm only saying that to make light of a terrible situation.

I'm a Tony voter and I take that very seriously, so I see every single show that opens on Broadway. I see virtually every show that opens off-Broadway. I see shows in Los Angeles. I see shows in London. I see shows in Chicago. It doesn't leave me a lot of time. I need something special to get me to leave my very comfortable apartment on my nights off, and if it's a playwright unknown to me, directed by someone I don't know, and cast with people I don't know, it's tough. The whole showcase situation is very tough—which is why I encourage actors to do them as an exercise, like an acting class.

How important is it for an actor to have a powerful agent?

There's no doubt that having an agent helps—almost any agent. There are obviously some that can do more for you than others, but because an agent does this every day for a living, in theory he or she has relationships with casting directors. In theory, he reads the trades and knows when a show is casting. In theory, he gets Breakdown Services every day. It is very important, but I don't think an actor without an agent is hopeless. If an actor doesn't have an agent, they have to compensate for that by faithfully reading *Backstage*, by faithfully reading *Variety*, by finding out what shows are starting to cast, by doing all that legwork.

Does the actor then have to wait for the Equity open call, or should they send their picture and résumé to the producer or the casting person?

I would say start with the casting person. If you know the casting person, call them up. If the casting director knows you, they'll pretty much be able to tell you over the phone whether you're right for the part or not.

But if the casting person doesn't know you?

If they don't know you, go to an open call. It's as simple as that. I've cast lots of people from open calls. I love open calls because they give me an opportunity to see actors I'm not familiar with.

If you're not a member of Equity, is there any hope at all?

Well, a lot of shows, particularly the musicals, have open calls, not just Equity open calls. Equity members are seen first, but then the non-Equity people are seen afterward.

At an open call, besides bringing your picture and résumé, should you be prepared to do a monologue?

Whatever the announcement, it will tell you what to prepare. Usually the announcements in *Backstage* are quite specific about what we need to see. If you're not ready, wait. Be prepared or else it can backfire. Don't waste the casting director's time, please.

Are there certain monologues you hope you don't ever have to endure again?

Lots. It's like fashion fads where suddenly everyone is wearing the same kind of blouse. Last year every actress I knew under forty was doing something from *Women of Manhattan*. I have enormous respect for the work, but by the 150th time you've heard it it gets a little bit monotonous.

Any tips you can offer?

I think there's one mistake and it's a product of those books like *150 Monologues for Actors* or *Great Scenes for Auditions*. There are dozens of books like that, and they're not bad to look at in the bookstore. If you find a monologue you like, don't stop there. Put the book down and go over and buy the script instead. You may even find a monologue you like better. If something finds its way into one of those books, you know that hundreds of other actors are going to be reading it also. What's so bothersome about these books is that people don't read the play and they have no idea what they're talking about.

It's also important to have a monologue that's appropriate for you. I'll give you an example. There's a woman who comes in for every EPA that I do, and she does a monologue that's grotesque and totally inappropriate. She's in her sixties, and the monologue was written for someone in her twenties. It's so wrong for her that it's like fingernails on a blackboard.

Deborah Aquila

D*eborah Aquila is currently Vice-President of Features Casting for Paramount Pictures. Her film credits include* Last Exit to Brooklyn, sex, lies & videotape, The Good Son, The Shawshank Redemption, The New Age. The Brady Bunch *and* Virtuosity. *Before moving to the West Coast she was the New York casting consultant for NBC.*

How did you get into casting?

I studied at NYU. I was trained as an actress and studied with Stella Adler for the four years, and started my master's through the graduate theater program at NYU. I never pursued the profession as an actress, and I went into production for the first four years. I was casting commercials and producing them. Then I switched and was an agent for a while—that didn't appeal to me too much. I worked for Bonnie Timmermann for about a year, and then went out on my own.

Is a performing background helpful for a casting director?

I think it's essential, because you have the ability to communicate with an actor in his own language. You have the ability to see things in a performance that perhaps someone without a trained eye wouldn't see. I think the most important thing is that you're able to break down a script from an actor's point of view, and therefore communicate ideas for auditioning, for presentations to producers and directors. That also helps me to know who the right people might be for a particular project. When I read a script, I usually read dialogue aloud after I've finished the script. That affords me the opportunity to hear the rhythm of the dialogue, so that way I can hear it again from the actors when I'm in readings.

What does it mean to be the New York casting consultant for NBC? What is your relationship to the network?

Basically what we do is keep an eye out for talent in New York, on the East Coast. When there's no casting director assigned to a project on the East

Coast, then we're responsible for making sure everybody in town is seen for the project. We sometimes consult on up to thirty pilots a year, and we have to make sure every person that's right for the part here in New York is seen. It's a difficult process because the volume of work is so great and it's usually concentrated between the end of December and the end of April. It's rewarding because a lot of people have been flown out of New York based on those tapes, and have landed a series.

How much of your time is actually spent on network projects?

A fair amount. I'm blessed with very good staff.

How many people work with you?

Three. I have two assistants, and I have one casting director that works with me. She's in charge of doing the physical taping of the actors, if I have to concentrate on going through submissions, thinking of ideas, and reading scripts.

Would you explain how you cast a pilot or a typical series project?

A typical series or pilot takes about two weeks to cast. If they're having trouble finding the right people, then they'll extend that. Usually, there are no more than four weeks involved. It's the same process as in film, only faster. You put a breakdown out to the agencies in town. They give you submissions. Of course you do your own list; from your previous history you may know a lot of actors who are right for the project. I personally go through a lot of prescreening when time allows me to.

What does prescreening entail?

Prescreening is basically having the actors come in and do readings for me before I tape them. Or producers and directors will come into New York and we'll actually have physical sessions, which I much prefer.

Actually having them there in the room when the actors read rather than seeing them on tape—why do you prefer that?

Because you can get a sense of the human being. You can see things in a room that you can't necessarily catch on tape. Taping itself is a false thing, and there's a certain technique that an actor really has to learn, to make that truthful and alive.

Usually when I'm prescreening, one of my associates is taping at the same time for those people we're absolutely sure are perfect for the parts. For "Dark Shadows" we did thirty-three tapes, full hour-and-twenty-minute tapes, and we must have seen five hundred people for that.

When an actor comes in for a prescreening and then goes on to the final audition, how many times will he have actually read the part by the time he gets the role—if he does?

This is the process we usually follow: For the actors coming in to tape, we try to give them the opportunity to read the script first, because you can't really come in if you don't know your circumstance, if you don't know the history of the project. I like to make sure that the actors have the sides or the material at least forty-eight hours before they're ready to go on tape, so they're familiar with the project. That way they're able to memorize it if they want to go off book.

Is that a good idea?

Absolutely. Then you can forget about the words and you can just concentrate on the action of the piece and on reading with your partner. I read with everybody myself, and if I'm off book by that time, I expect the actors to be, as well. That's especially important in features.

With regard to television, usually they come in and do it once. We have a rehearsal and then we lay it down. Then if the actor doesn't feel comfortable with what he or she just did, we do it again. Then the tape is sent to Los Angeles. The producer, the director, the network look at it, and they make their choices. Then we'll usually tape again. If the creative team and the network like the second tape, they fly the actor out to L.A.

What proportion of the casting comes out of New York for series these days?

It varies a lot depending on the project. I mean, "Dream Street" was almost all New York; there were only two actors from Los Angeles. On a Los Angeles–based project, they'll only look at one or two characters from New York.

Would you describe the general process of casting a feature film—say, something like sex, lies & videotape?

It's the same process. You get sent a script. I read the script once, and then I read it again. I discuss the larger ideas, what I've come away with, with the director and the producer. The first thing we do is sit down and make a list. If it's a low-budget movie we make a wish list.

The people you'd like to have if you could afford them?

Exactly. Sometimes a project comes along with a name already attached to it, and there's little that a casting director can do except try to cast around that person so that the chemistry works.

Talk about that a little bit—this whole question of casting around a star who comes attached to a project. What will you be looking at when you cast other performers?

You have to always keep in mind who's playing the lead role, and then you have to match to that. When you're doing readings you really have to concentrate so you're able to see the film as a whole in your head first. Then you have to see how those performers are going to satellite off the person who's going to be the lead. You almost have to envision the chemistry that's going on between them in your head, and hopefully that's the way it's actually going to come off.

Will an important supporting performer eventually end up reading with the star before the casting is set?

Almost always, especially if it's a male star that's set first. It depends on their contract, whether they have casting approval. In the case of *Wild Orchid*, Mickey Rourke was starring in it and he had approval over the girl. We had to cast and then everyone read with him.

For the kinds of films I work on, I find myself casting a lot of features that are under three and four million dollars.

What is the average cost of films now?

Studios basically can go anywhere between fifteen million up to thirty or forty million dollars. Sometimes more. Relatively speaking, our films are low-budget at three to four million. The costs of shooting in New York are so extraordinarily high that a lot of people think twice before shooting in New York. We're starting a production called *Little Noises* that shoots in New York, and that's a million-dollar film. For the kind of cast we have and the number of setups, I imagine it will be very difficult to come in on budget, shooting in New York. We did manage to cast a hearing-impaired actor from Philadelphia that I'm especially excited about.

How did that come about?

Well, there's the role of a mute person in the script. He's a poet, but he can't speak and can hear very little. He expresses himself through poetry—though nobody believes he's really penned his poems, because he's a street kid with little or no education. We auditioned a lot of actors to play that role, but there was just something wrong about not casting a deaf or hearing-impaired actor for a deaf role. I mean, they did a fine job, but it seemed to me that if you're going to have that kind of a character in a movie, then do the real thing. I suggested to the producers that we start contacting the National Theatre for the Deaf and a lot of the institutions and schools around the country. We found about ten kids that were really right and did a wonderful job. One of them got the role.

How can an actor whose work you don't know best get your attention?

I see showcases on a regular basis; we're at the theater every night. We are booked every single night for the next two months—no exaggeration—because the theater has just exploded in New York this season, and we have to cover everything. While I try for all Broadway and off-Broadway shows, I might not be able to make it to all the showcases I would like to see on a regular basis, so one of my assistants or associates will go down and cover that. I go through every piece of mail that is sent to me.

Including pictures and résumés?

Everything. I have a general From Mailings file, which has been growing during this pilot season, of people I would like to meet. When they are finally scheduled, I'll ask people to do monologues for me so that I can get a sense of their work. I think that's the best way to do it.

When an actor comes into your office to do a monologue, what kind of material should they do?

Contemporary. Knowing the person you're reading for, doing some research, is very important. When I get a script from a writer, I'll research everything that writer has done before—same thing with a director or a producer—so I get to know their minds, their tastes, their history. The same is true for an actor who's going to walk into a casting director's office: know their work, know what they've done, know what they've cast.

How can they find that out?

They should read reviews, especially *Variety*, and find out who's casting certain movies; it's always listed.

Should classical things generally be avoided?

Yes, unless you're auditioning for the Shakespeare Festival. It doesn't help me to hear Shakespeare when I'm casting a contemporary feature. For the kinds of things I cast, I really need something contemporary, and I also like to see a light piece and a dark piece for contrast.

So you want two different selections—one that's more comic and light, and one that's more dramatic?

Right, and keep them short, please: two and a half to three minutes, tops, each one. I like to have an actor direct a monologue to me. A lot of casting directors don't like that, but my feeling is that if you've got another human being in the room, use them. Ask them first, though. It's always very strange to me to see someone talking to the air. I don't get a sense of connection.

Assuming that videotape does play a role in the kind of casting you do—in its proper place, solicited from the actor's agent—how important is videotape to an actor's getting or not getting a role?

For me it's not very important. Say that the actor hasn't done very much, is just starting out. I'd rather have no tape at all than a homemade tape. A lot of actors feel they have to have some sort of tape, and what they'll do is put a monologue or some piece they've worked on on tape, and it's not very professionally done. I would rather not see it because it will hurt the actor. I'd rather see them in the flesh.

If someone does have a good amount of tape from either television or film edited together, they should make sure it's clean and professional. Don't do your own VCR-to-VCR transfer because the quality is terrible. Get professional help.

And it should be in what format?

VHS, mostly.

So you don't necessarily need a three-quarter-inch tape?

It could be either, but keep in mind that most casting people don't have a three-quarter-inch at home. What I do when I have a lot of tapes to look at is take them home.

Assuming that an actor has done a few things—a series or a soap—how long should the videotape be, and what variety of things should be included?

Choose your best stuff, no matter what it is. And keep it really short: ten minutes.

How do you feel about soap opera material on a tape?

If the soap opera material is very good, put it on.

But that might not be first choice if you've done an "L.A. Law" or "Spencer" or a few other things?

I would shy away from it myself. Soaps are done in real time, as opposed to dramatic time or film time. Do you ever watch "Mister Rogers' Neighborhood"? That's real time. He puts his shoes on; he ties his shoelaces, et cetera.

The rhythms are different also, very different. Features are quicker. It's hard to put into words exactly what I mean, but there is a real difference between the soaps and features. If all you have done is soaps, sure, go for it, but go for the best one.

Pictures and résumés: what makes a good picture?

A picture that absolutely looks like you, that really, truly looks like you. The first thing that strikes me about your face is your eyes.

Are there certain teachers whose names impress you on a résumé?

Yes. There are certain teachers in New York City that have a wonderful reputation for accepting and turning out students of extraordinary talent. It sometimes is difficult to get into a class with them, but it's worth trying.

You usually have to audition.

Right, and when you do get accepted in those kinds of classes, by all means put that training first, and stay with them as long as you can. Even if you are a working actor, it doesn't hurt to attend class once a week. You learn on the set, but I think training for an actor is ongoing because it keeps your chops up. It's like a dancer going to class. My brother was a musician and he never stopped studying.

Then there are people who have no formal training at all, like this young man I found for *Last Exit to Brooklyn.* He's unbelievably talented. There are things that just spoke to him "in life," that he just saw from a different perspective. I don't know where he got it. He's from the same neighborhood in Brooklyn that I am, and yet he was able to see above the day-to-day life. I suppose he was a big movie buff and just applied everything he saw on a daily basis to a character, which he was very successful in achieving.

It's important to get formal training, but it's also important to heighten yourself as a human being. It's important to never stop. Never relax. Keep going, because there's a lot out there and there's a lot that you have to know as an actor.

Deborah, what advice would you give to a person just entering the business, with limited credits or no credits at all?

Besides get out? No, no, the best advice I have is to keep spiritually sound and be persistent. Persistence is the key. Just never stop believing in your dream, your personal dream. If that dies, the desire of what you want to achieve as an actor will die, as well.

For an actor, what's difficult is that many times a person's opinion of your work is mistaken for the person's opinion of you. As Stella Adler would say, "the talent is in your choices"—and I believe that one hundred percent.

You have to be able to remove that from who you are as a person. You're putting yourself on the line every second as an actor, and you have to be very strong about your true identity. You have to be able to take the rejection, which will inevitably come in the beginning—or maybe not, if you're absolutely brilliant and someone sees it quickly—since it's not *you* they're rejecting.

You must have seen a lot of actors audition. Are there any mistakes that you see actors commonly make that you wish you could warn them against?

Very, very many. Actors out of professional training programs most often will audition or do a scene as if they were still in a school environment. There's not much you can do about that because you can't put your finger on what they're doing wrong. As they continue to audition, they'll see that they can let go of what was taught in a university environment. There's a definite technique to auditioning and a definite technique in doing mono-logues, and that comes with experience and specific feedback at the moment.

One thing that I caution people about, especially those just beginning, is to know the monologue or piece of material that you present very, very well! You should be able to answer any possible question in your own mind. For instance, if you're playing a woman in her thirties who's sitting at a bar and the scene is about a confrontation between two people, why is she at the bar? Where is she from? What time is it? Has she eaten? What's she drinking? What's the relationship between the two characters? Who are her parents? Her grandparents? Does she speak another language? If it's not in the body of the text or the piece, you have to make this up. You have to do it so well that I can't see you acting. It has to be seamless. The trans-formation has to be very definite when you come in as a person, when you begin your scene, when you leave your character and come back as a person. It's a terribly important sign and signal to me that there's something going on.

Don't comment on yourself. Don't ever comment on yourself after you finish a piece, either verbally or by body language such as a shrug. Just leave it alone and go into neutral. Then come back as you. And certainly don't ever comment on yourself during a piece when you don't have a line. A lot of actors will do that. It can be an uncontrollable gasp of air, a facial gesture, or hand gesture that's not necessary. Some of the most important acting comes when there isn't a line of dialogue.

If you haven't had an opportunity to create a history for a character because you haven't had the script, make sure that your agent asks questions about it or gets a breakdown. Don't take the casting director's time with it unless you need an adjustment, unless you're totally confused by something in the piece. It's your job to make sure that you get some background information on the script, on the character. If it means bothering an assistant and saying that you need to see a breakdown, do it. It's their job. More importantly, it's your job. When I have someone in my office, I truly expect to see a performance. Otherwise, it's a waste of my time and a waste of theirs. If they have questions, I will always answer them because I have the inside scoop on what the director wants, and an actor might not know those specifics from reading a piece. It's my job to prep you for that.

You have to remember that there are casting directors because there are actors. If you don't look good we don't look good. I mean, we're pulling for you guys to be brilliant.

What are your major frustrations with the casting process? Is there anything you'd like to see changed?

The decision-making process seems to me to be intolerably long, but that often depends on whom I'm working with. I spend a lot of time with the director before I hold my first sessions. *Last Exit to Brooklyn,* for instance, took a relatively long time to cast because we were searching for authentic types and required "the real thing" in specific roles. The director's final choices were perfect, so it was rewarding.

I work on a lot of low-budget films, but I don't think this business should be solely about money. Though I'm the first person to recognize that we all have to make a living, it frustrates me when I can't get the kind of attention from agents that I think a script warrants because it's not a sixty-million-dollar project. It gets me very angry. I do think that agencies are starting to turn around. We've gotten a tremendous amount of support from major agencies over the last year, but it wasn't like that when I was casting *sex, lies & videotape.* Four major agencies in New York just told me to kiss off. I understand what they were saying; a lot of people thought it was pornography. They didn't know who Steven Soderberg was. They didn't hear him speak as I had heard him. Although I painstakingly explained his vision to them a million times, they refused to listen and wouldn't give me any help or cooperation. It was demoralizing and painful. But because of that movie and some of the other independents, people are now willing to pay attention to the material even if it doesn't have a high price tag attached.

You mentioned pornography a minute ago. Is it ever a good idea for an actress just starting out to do skin flicks or pornography, given the opportunity?

No. I mean, just the thought of it is repulsive to me. It's ludicrous. Work on Wall Street for a while if you need money that badly. Do word processing.

So it's not going to help you get a starring role in a major film?

Of course not. I mean, you can't even list that as a credit. No, most definitely no.

And it might even prevent you from getting such a role?

Well, do you see very much acting going on in skin flicks? I think the issue is self-evident!

Mari Lyn Henry

*M*ari Lyn Henry, *formerly director of casting for Capital Cities/ABC on the East Coast, continues to serve the network as an independent casting consultant for several nationwide daytime drama talent searches. She is also president of Persona Image Enhancement and co-author, with Lynne Rogers, of* How to be a Working Actor.

How did you get into casting?

I was determined to be an actress, and that was my training as an under-graduate at San Jose State University. I got a B.A. degree there, then went to Catholic University in Washington, D.C., and got a master's degree in theater. I came to New York in about 1969 with all this idealism, and I found that it wasn't the easiest transition, from student to working actress.

I got temporary jobs in various ad agencies, and then a friend suggested that I come to work at Cunningham and Walsh. I was there for six months, and the personnel department knew I was a frustrated actress, from my imitations of various co-workers. There was an opening in the casting department when Maxine Marx needed an assistant.

I knew nothing about casting, but decided to go for it, and I was with Maxine for nine years. It became like a marriage, and it was hard to leave, but I had to move on. When I got the offer to be interviewed for the ABC position, I took it, and I've been there now twelve years.

Do you think having a background as a performer is useful in your work?

I think it's terribly useful. I certainly think it helps you understand the actor's process. Dealing with so many actors in auditions, I am at least able to convey what it is I'm looking for, what I've intuited from the script, what I've learned from the writer and the director, and so forth.

Even reading with the actor, I feel I'm able to be more than a piece of wood that you have to relate to.

Have you ever encountered an actor who looks great on stage and yet comes across badly on film?

Oh sure. The camera just loves certain faces. Film has always been a strong personality business—certainly in the days of the major studios. Some people do fine on the small screen and are just lost in movies. Some people you'll just never see on the small screen. The stage lends enchantment because of the distance; you can't see all the flaws. You can't see the age as much. When you get that person close up in a screen test, you can see everything. That's why plastic surgeons are making an awful lot of money.

Aren't there also techniques that some stage actors find difficult to adjust when acting for film?

I have a phrase that I use sometimes: Getting off stage. Some people come in on stage, and they're just not able to make it more intimate; even their diction is too precise, their emotion too heightened. You don't need all of that on television. I mean, people get away with mumbling on television. I once made the mistake of saying to the casting director of "CHiPS" that one needed subtitles to understand what Erik Estrada was saying, yet it was a big hit.

How important is it for an actor to have a videotape?

Twenty years ago when I started casting, we really didn't know about videocassettes. It just wasn't mentioned. You had audio tapes if you were looking for voice-over talent. You had pictures and résumés to help you decide whether to bring a person in or not. Now, because we're so heavily into how you look and move on camera and how the camera loves you, we really need a videocassette. It's become another tool, and in the second edition of our book we talk about putting a videocassette together if you have no previous experience.

Let's talk briefly about that.

Because so many young actors coming out of the training programs have no videocassettes of their work, we suggest that they first of all get a really good acting coach who understands what the camera needs, in terms of picking material. Many times I'll get these videocassettes from actors with just awful material on them.

You have to pick something that's within your comfortable age range, not something you're trying to get to. You wouldn't pick something from a classic play like *Hedda Gabler;* that's ridiculous. We want to see something that is contemporary, that has humor, that shows you to your best advantage. That's something you as an actor are responsible for finding. Acting teachers who have cast you well in the past and acting coaches are able to zero in on what it is that makes you special.

A short solo piece and one short scene—one that emphasizes you and not your partner—should be included.

What do you mean by short?

A three-minute scene, so that the length of this videocassette is no more than six minutes. In our day and age, nobody is going to look at anything longer than that, and some of them will only look at the first thirty seconds. It's got to be a grabber—but it's got to be an honest grabber, not something that's there for shock value.

Then you investigate the production facilities available in the city you live in, and you find out which ones are the best and most economical for what you need. You have to find ones that are legitimate and have a good reputation.

Time is money, so you'd better be rehearsed and prepared to go on camera and just do it; ideally, it shouldn't take more than an hour. If you need hair and makeup, that's also something you prearrange so you know exactly how much that will cost, and you put yourself in the hands of someone you'd trust with your life. Then you do it.

You then have dupes of it made and proceed to package it carefully so that your picture is on the front of the box, and you include a postcard cutout, contact information, address information, and a mailer so that it can be returned at your expense. You make everything as easy as possible for the person getting it. Otherwise it's going to lie in a stack of videocassettes that nobody is ever going to look at, and when you call three months later they will have lost it. In California they are notorious for that. You must follow up with a phone call to make sure they received it. Hopefully they will have looked at it, and if they don't have time to look at it they can return it to you.

Do actors send these videotapes directly to you, or do they always come through agents?

Sometimes the agents will send them. Sometimes the actors will send them directly.

And if an actor sends one to you directly, that's not the kiss of death?

No, no, no. I'll always look at it, though I'd like to know why they're sending it. I just received a videocassette that said "demo" on it, with a name. It had no information as to the material on the cassette, no address on the front, or even a phone number. Obviously that's not from someone who's terribly with-it in terms of the biz. That says something about whether I want to look at it or not.

Would you look at something from an agent first?

Oh sure, especially if I've requested it. More times than not I've requested the tape. Seldom does one come unsolicited.

What I don't understand is why an actor would send a tape that hasn't been edited yet, and that happens all the time. I've got to fast-forward to try and decipher who that person is. If they've got existing footage, it's got to be edited down just to bare scenes. I'm not interested in anything else. There are plenty of editors around on both coasts.

Would you say there are more parts available for television on the West Coast or on the East Coast?

West Coast. Right now there are as many soap operas shooting on the West Coast as here in New York, and all the prime-time series are shot on the West Coast, with a few exceptions—like Bill Cosby. The last series shot in New York was "The Equalizer" last year.

Why do you think TV shows don't film as much in New York?

We have a lot of union problems. There are overcharges on everything. It costs much more to shoot here, and we also don't have the production facilities they have on the West Coast, and we never will. There's no place to build them.

In casting a new ABC series, at what point do you, as East Coast director of casting, come into the picture?

Right at the beginning, because we service California with the East Coast talent pool. We put actors on tape, and casting directors from the West Coast will send us lists of people who have been submitted to them from here who they want to see on tape for various parts. We are involved right at the beginning with every single pilot that calls for our attention, with the exception of some studios that have their own casting directors in New York.

What part does network approval play in the casting process?

Every regular role on a series, any contract role, has to be approved. In some cases the project has been pulled where studios and networks couldn't find the lead they wanted to make this series work. That's how important it is.

And do the soaps also require network approval for continuing roles?

Absolutely. We have a daytime programming vice president who must concur with the executive producers of the soap opera. The writers also have a say.

My perception of soap operas is that, with some notable exceptions, most are populated with people under forty.

I think that's always going to be the case, because when they break them down into their demographic charts and age ranges that watch the soaps, they're always looking at the group between eighteen and forty-eight, who watch the soaps religiously. While they do have senior-citizen love stories, they're never going to be your front-burner story. Remember, you're looking at your advertiser revenue.

Is soap opera acting different from other television and film acting?

If you say different, it comes from the material and not from the actor. I think it's a way of approaching the material. Everything in daytime is terribly heightened. The situations these characters find themselves in are certainly not real situations. Everything has a certain kind of style within its framework.

What advice would you give someone who's auditioning for a running role on a soap opera?

First of all, anyone auditioning for a soap opera should be familiar with the soap opera they're auditioning for. Do research. Watch it and find out about the characters, find out about the relationships, find out about who your character is going to be relating with. When you get the audition scene, do as much work on it as you possibly can.

If you're auditioning for a recast, the first rule of business I would suggest is not trying to be a carbon copy of the actor or actress playing that role. It's not going to work.

Should you memorize the scene?

For the audition, I would prefer as much familiarity as possible. Now there's a debate going on about this. In California, it appears that if you come in with the lines learned, the casting director is going to assume that that's as much as you're going to do with that role. You're not going to be flexible enough to take other direction, and that can be intimidating to them. The actors there have learned to hold the script even if they already know it.

My feeling here is that I want to see how your brain cells are working. I'd like to know if you can memorize a scene.

What I find is that a lot of people don't know how to audition. It's not about being right or wrong for a part; it's about understanding the audition process. Too many people look at a scene only on its face value and never get underneath it and explore what makes this character tick, why this character says certain things. Is there any humor in these characters? And then there's the use of yourself in that character. It's very important to make those connections.

Is it important for a performer who's auditioning on videotape to be aware of the camera, to use the camera in some way? How much technical awareness do you need?

The best way to develop technical awareness is by commercial auditions. Another thing is to take a video class so that you learn the camera is not your enemy and that it wants to help you. I also think that seeing yourself on camera in a class situation helps lessen the pressure. I used to teach commercial auditioning, and in a ten-week session you would see a profound change just in how the actors felt about themselves in terms of makeup, dress, colors, hairstyle. Also, you can play the reality of the situation in an almost improvisational way, so that you really get a sense of who you are. Working behind the scenes can also give you an awareness of camera.

If you're called back after doing a screen test, awareness of the camera is almost secondary. You should do the scene to the best of your ability. The camera will always find you, so don't worry about it.

What's the best way for a performer whose work you don't know to get your attention?

The first notification I have of any performer is through an agent calling me about that performer to introduce me to that performer, sending a picture and résumé to me, or through the actor sending a picture and résumé directly.

From your point of view, what makes a good picture?

The first rule is that the picture should look like you, not like some photographer's idealized perception. You understand your face and your features, what you're trying to emphasize. For most people it's their eyes. The hairstyle should frame that structure and be neat, the color right, and everything should be in focus. The picture should project your own sense of who you are.

We like to see a nicely cropped, eight-by-ten picture of your face, preferably looking at us. I get a lot of three-quarter shots, tilted heads, the hand in the picture, and all that is not necessary. Lighting is absolutely essential to a good photograph. Some photographers prefer to work outdoors, and I have nothing against outdoor shots, but you can't control conditions out-doors like you can indoors.

What impresses you on a résumé?

The truth is terribly helpful. If you're proud of the work that you've done and you think it's representative of your range, put it down. There are a lot of films going on that are nonunion or local productions. They're of value because they put you in front of a camera and are a credible experience, so list them, as well. Training is vital, and for some people that's most of their background.

What kinds of training would impress you?

Well, certainly there are teachers that I respect. If you have educational degrees, a B.A. in drama or a master's, that's very important. The training is normally an ongoing thing and doesn't just stop in midair. I think that you owe it to yourself to have a coach at the ready, simply because in terms of audition material, if you're up for a major role in a movie of the week, a miniseries, feature film, or daytime drama, you may need to rely on another eye to help you. It gives you more confidence.

There are a lot of contract players on soaps who continue to go to class. For them it's a stretching experience because they're able to do plays and scenes and other kinds of material that they normally would not have time to do with their daily routines.

Dialecticians, singing coaches—you should have a list of these people ready for when you need them.

How valuable are showcases or Equity-waiver theater as a source of exposure for actors?

I don't know how valuable they are as exposure, but usually Equity-waiver showcases give you a sense of commitment to a project, and that sense of purpose is terribly important. As a result of that experience, from the flyers you send to agents and casting directors, you may get attendance by some of them. The ultimate reward, of course, is getting someone interested in you and possibly representing you.

The other side of the coin is that I have been burned badly by terrible showcases—material that never should have been picked, actors who didn't know what they were doing, bad direction, no sense of theme, no conti-nuity, too long overall, and a waste of time.

Do you ever have actors come in and do monologues for you, or do you just see those on tape?

Either-or. I've had actors come in with prepared pieces over the years.

Our philosophy now is that we've seen enough monologues, we've seen enough scenes. If we're going to bring in an actor to audition for us, we assign a generic scene that we're working on from a TV script, sitcom, or whatever, and see how they handle that material.

What are the biggest mistakes that actors make in these situations?

Lack of preparation with the material. They make certain assumptions about the material, even in terms of pronunciation. If you're playing a person in a certain profession, you should know how the person would speak. You've just got to be well prepared. You have to ask questions.

Another thing that happens at auditions is that people talk too much. I know it's a nerve-wracking situation, but they come in and they chatter on and on, usually about nothing, before the reading. You should come in, read it, and if we want to chat with you afterward, we will. To give us too much information about yourself at the beginning serves no purpose.

What advice would you give someone just starting out who's not a union member and doesn't have an agent?

The first thing I would say is that, unless you have wealthy parents, a trust fund, and a place to hang your hat in either New York or Los Angeles, it's useless, futile. It's better to grow up somewhere else before coming here. If you've already made the choice that you have to have New York or you're going to die, then I think you have to be very prudent about your financial resources and use them in the way that makes them stretch farthest. We all know that here desperation is the worst possible thing when you're a young person. This city makes you desperate. There's a constant pull on you emotionally and psychologically, financially and physically. You've got to meet these challenges. You can't do it unless you're prepared in all those areas. You can't devote yourself one hundred percent to acting if you're waiting on tables eight hours a day.

To enter the business, you've got to have a good business head on your shoulders and go about it in an organized fashion.

What are your major frustrations as a casting director?

I guess the major frustration is not getting the person you want for the job. You know they're going to get an Oscar someday, and here's this person saying the acting isn't good enough. I think that pinpoints our major frustration—especially when dealing with West Coast casting directors a continent away who don't know a fourth of the New York talent that we know so well and feel are destined for greatness. These are often theater people, and there's this blind resistance to hiring them for television.

I remember a director from Georgia that I met last year who told me the story of how he was asked for casting suggestions for *Oliver's Story*, the sequel to *Love Story*. He put two names on a piece of paper and sent it to this producer. The producer said that he had never heard of the people. The names were William Hurt and Meryl Streep.

Betty Rea

Betty Rea has for many years been casting director of the daytime series "The Guiding Light."

How did you get into casting?

Well, it was just a fluke, really. I was working as an assistant to Bob LeMond and Bill Treusch, legit agents who were housed at Trainum, which was primarily a commercial agency. A great many of our actors were on "Guiding Light," so I knew quite a few people connected with the show. And the casting director was being elevated to assistant producer, but they wouldn't let her take the job until they'd replaced her. So finally she called me and said, "Why don't you go down and be interviewed?" And I said, "I don't know anything about casting." She said, "That doesn't make any difference. We're desperate. Go down." And I went down and had an interview, and I was quite frank—I said I'd never done this at all, I knew nothing about it—and, much to my amazement, they hired me. And that was about twenty years ago—I'm in my twentieth year.

At one point Procter & Gamble, the producers of the show, tried an experiment. They'd always wanted to see if they could centralize production, and they thought they'd try it out with casting. So for four years I did both "Guiding Light" and "As the World Turns." I don't think it works—it's just too much. So I was very happy when I could just go back to "The Guiding Light." And, of course, if somebody was in one show you couldn't put them on the other show. Even now we don't do that, because they're sister shows—"As the World Turns" comes first, then "Guiding Light." And we do an interchange of noncontract-role names periodically with Geoff Johnson, who casts "Another World," another Procter & Gamble show, so we won't use the same people.

Would you explain what a noncontract role is, as opposed to a contract role?

Noncontract could be a day player, someone who's on for one to three days, or she could have a running part, which might be on for seven months. The difference is that if you were contract, you would be guaranteed X number of shows a week. When you're noncontract, or with a recurring role, whatever you want to call it, they just come on; it's hit-or-miss. And you may lose someone when you want them. If they don't work for a month or six weeks, they may go off to Timbuktu, and that's the chance we take. But it's a less expensive procedure for the producers, who may not know exactly how long they may be using a character. And sometimes a recurring role turns into a contract part, because the character becomes more and more involved with the story line, and the producers realize they can't take the chance of calling up and finding that Jane Smith is not available.

So they'll guarantee Jane that she'll be on at least twice a week?

Twice is the highest. One and a half is much more common. And that doesn't mean that they actually work one and a half shows. But it means, whether they work or not, they receive payment for at least one and a half, on the average, over a thirteen-week or twenty-six-week cycle.

So that, if you're getting, say, six hundred dollars per show, you know that your minimum salary per week, over a thirteen-week or twenty-six-week period, will be at least nine hundred per week?

Yes.

For a new contract part, what kind of commitment does the network usually ask from an actor—how many years?

We never take anything less than three years.

And for how long is the network committed in this situation—also for three years?

The network can get out of the contract like that [snaps fingers]. The actor can't. The network—or whoever owns the show—has to give a warning of a month before they terminate at the end of a cycle. If they don't give a warning, then they have to pay for the next cycle. It's like any contract—there's an "out time" when you can tell somebody that they're through, but if you go beyond that time, then you are liable to pay them until the end of that cycle.

Would you describe the process of casting a contract role on "The Guiding Light"—how you go about it, how many people you see, how it works?

When a new part is coming on, the head writer writes a description of the character, and it's usually very, very precise and sensitive. And then you take that description and pare it down and put it out on Breakdown Services, and then the submissions come in. My associate and I look at the submissions and decide who we want to see. So we bring those people in and audition them.

You read with them yourself?

Yes, if the part is with a female. My assistant is male, so he reads the parts that are with a male. Out of that first group we decide who we're going to call back for the executive producer.

How many would you normally see in that first group?

A hundred, maybe. And then our executive producer decides who he wants to put on tape. And when they're put on tape, they're put on with the person with whom the scene is written, from the show. If they're supposed to have a relationship, you want to see whether people have any dynamics between them or not. If the executive producer doesn't like anybody, then we start again. We often go to California for a very important contract part. Not that the actors are better there, but we feel we should cover as much ground as possible in trying to find the best possible person. And then we put the two groups together, the East and West, and the choice is made by the executive producer, the head writer, CBS, and the client—Procter & Gamble.

Before we leave the whole subject of numbers—and the odds an actor is up against—I'd like to know, out of a hundred people you might see for a contract role, how many you'd typically put on videotape. How many would actually get to come in and do the scene for the camera?

Maybe four, five, six. We try to keep it down to that. And when I said a hundred, that might be just a hundred here—or more—and maybe another hundred from California. And if the part is extremely difficult, and nobody is happy with the first go-around, we would then get submissions from Texas and Chicago, of course—that's a very, very active theatrical community— and in the last six months or so we've been using Florida, because so much is being done in Florida now, with the building of studios and the flourishing of the theaters down there. We go to Canada, too.

What's the most people you've ever seen for a contract role?

Well, I think you see more people for replacements. That's difficult, because everyone has the original face in mind.

Do you try to find a face that's similar?

You try to find somebody who has the same quality. You should start that way. One example is now on the show, the character of Holly, who came back after many years. The original Holly was a unique individual, and we auditioned for a year trying to find the same type. And then this girl came in, and I used her in an under-five, and I liked her immensely. At that point, I was doing the whole show, extras as well.

Would you explain what an under-five is?

The actor has fifty words or less to say. And I loved her. So we were going to go on-camera again, with the pseudo-type, trying to see the same girls. And I said, "I've found somebody I'd like to put on tape with that group." And they said, "Fine." Usually, you have to go through the procedure of bringing them in for the producers, but they were so sick of the whole process at that point they would have seen anybody. And this girl was completely opposite from the original Holly, in looks, persona, everything.

And what was it that made her get the part?

She brought a wonderful quality to the part. And we all said, "Why don't we have *this* quality become Holly? She's older; people change. Why are we sticking to the other, comedic quality?"

Is it true that the camera is in love with certain faces?

Yes.

Would you describe what it is you see when the camera is in love with someone?

I think you see a vitality. With some people, you rehearse them, and they're good. But then you put them in front of a camera and they become alive; they blossom. That, to me, is when they are having a real love affair with the camera. I remember one time that they didn't want this one girl to go on camera. And I said, "We've set it up for X number of people. She's a good actress." And they said, "Yes, but she didn't bring anything to it, really." I said, "Why don't we just try it?" So we put her on camera, and she saw that camera and the camera saw her, and they just *loved* each other. She got the part.

Would you say that the types or age ranges of actors used on soap operas are different from, say, the ranges of actors who might be cast in a typical television movie or feature?

Well, they would all probably be aiming toward the young public, whether it's a TV movie or a soap. I think that the better soaps realize that you really must have different ages on the show. It's not all young people, because we don't just appear out of nowhere. I think it's much better—and I think most writers feel this way—if there's a kind of familial background for as many people as possible. And in each of those families there are different ages, the different generations, which really makes it much more interesting.

How important is it for an actor to have standard American speech?

If you're going to go into all aspects of the business, you should be able to do standard American speech. I mean, if we get someone with too Southern an accent—unless they're playing a Southern part—it's going to be out of sync with the family they're supposed to be in. We have one family in the show that comes from Oklahoma, and they all have a slight Oklahoma accent in the show. But I think you have to have standard American speech.

What about the whole question of minority groups in soap operas? We do see an awful lot of white faces.

It's a disgrace, an absolute disgrace.

Is there anything a person in your position can do—or, indeed, should do—to change this situation?

If we have a day player, or somebody who's going to run for a little while—somebody who is not suddenly going to turn out to be the long-lost cousin of the Savage family in the show—you can ask not to have a white person play it. And I think the majority of shows are very receptive to this.

What's the best way for an actor whose work you don't know to get your attention?

I go to a lot of showcases. For the next month or two, all of us in the business will be going to see the graduating classes of the elite schools. Tomorrow I go to Juilliard, then I'll see ACT, I'll see University of California–San Diego—I'm just mentioning the ones I've already signed up for. I've already seen Syracuse; I'll be seeing Harvard; later on I'll see Yale, NYU, SMU, Carnegie-Mellon. And that's wonderful for people who want to be seen, especially the young people who go to Yale and Juilliard.

The agents go up to see people at Yale before they graduate, and sign them. They do the same thing with NYU, Juilliard, anyplace that's close. And some of the big agencies go out of the city.

So it's an advantage to be studying at one of these schools. You get your work seen without having to scout up little Equity-waiver productions to be in.

Right—and also the American Academy, which is in New York; the Neighborhood Playhouse, which is in New York. So that's the icing on the cake for the kids who go to those schools. There's also the heartbreak if nobody wants them. But at least they're exposed.

For the actor who doesn't have the advantage of being trained in one of these programs, what is the best method—try and get into some sort of showcase production and send you a flyer and a picture?

Yes, and we go. But also have the objectivity to know if you're in a bad show. And if you are, don't invite anybody.

Do you ever hold general interviews or auditions?

Yes, I do one thing through AFTRA. They have a lottery system there, where union members put their names in and they draw. And I usually see people from AFTRA once a month. And then we get pictures sent in all the time. If you see pictures that interest you, you call them in. You see people from every source.

What happens when you call them in from a picture submission, say, that they've sent you directly?

Well, I have a lot of audition scenes from the two shows I've cast. And you know what people look like, obviously, if you've called them in from a picture. And so you get out a scene and ask them to take the scene outside, if they have time, and look it over, and then come in and read with you.

How many people have actually ended up getting cast on the show through that method?

Not a great many, but some. We do that for contract parts too, and for recurring roles. You have your *Players' Guide* and you have your pictures, and that's how you cast your day players and your recurring roles.

What do you look for on a résumé? What impresses you on a résumé?

Training. The people that you're working with. I know that training costs a lot of money, and it's very hard to get that money together to do it. But I have to be honest: it's very impressive if somebody is working with one of the better teachers in the city. You don't have to have gone to one of those schools I mentioned, but if you are studying it helps.

And also, naturally, I notice the work that you've done. If you've spent a summer at Williamstown, for example, that's very impressive.

How important is it to include things like special abilities?

Oh, very. And also put on languages. Or any specialties—if you do bird-calls. I once had to find a man who could do birdcalls. So, be it ever so strange, put it on, because you never know. Put it on that you're a bicycle rider, that you can drive a stick shift. And certainly put on all the athletics.

What is the danger of exaggerating your abilities?

You can get caught. What can be very embarrassing is if you fake the credits. Say, you put down the Guthrie Theatre, such-and-such year. It happened with me, when someone came in. And I wasn't trying to catch the person; it never occurred to me they were lying about it. I said, "Oh, did you enjoy so-and-so, the artistic director? Did he direct you in anything?" A look of absolute horror came on this interviewee's face. And I said, "Well, you've learned a lesson. Don't do it. And as soon as you can, take it off."

So what does an actor without much experience do to have a résumé at all, given this problem?

Just make it absolutely honest. It's amazing how many people we've called in to meet and to talk to, even without credits. Everybody has to get started, and we understand that. There are an awful lot of good people who are just starting, so we're just as anxious to meet them as they are to meet us.

Are there any absolute no-no's for actors in an audition situation? Are there some mistakes you see actors make over and over again in auditions that just kill their chances?

Yes—a terrible audition technique. I'm always amazed, with these elite schools, that they forget about this. You can kill yourself if you take the script and put it down here and say the scene like this.

So the eyes are on the script, the head is down, and the casting director can't see your face at all.

Or if you decide, *I'll show how smart I am, and in the ten minutes I'm outside I'll memorize the scene.* So you come in and you start, and you're groping for words the whole time. I'll stop people when they audition like that, and I'll say quite honestly, "You're killing yourself by doing this. I can't see your face. I don't know what you really want to say in this scene. Why don't you go outside and look at it again?"

And you see that people who have done this for years will look at their lines, and then they'll talk to you, and then they'll look at the lines and talk again—but you always have some kind of eye contact.

There are places you can go to learn auditioning technique, but they cost a lot of money, and most of the schools forget about this. They forget that when their people go out they're going to be brought back for callbacks on the basis of what is seen in that initial interview. Again, I know how difficult it is, but that's what we mean by killing yourself in the interview.

You've put your finger on two of the biggest problems I know of.

And then, never be ashamed of saying, "May I stop, please, and start again? I know I got off on the wrong track." Because you can, out of nerves, begin to garble to such an extent that nothing is happening. The casting person is not going to be annoyed. They'll only respect your ability for recognizing the fact that you are off the track.

What about memorizing the scene for the second audition? Is that important if they've been given the script ahead of time?

I know my boss likes that. But also, it gives you greater flexibility. First of all, just memorize it. Then you can ask when you go in, "Do you want me to use the script or not?" And if the person says, "Yes, please. I don't like to see people not using the script," you use it. But if you're with somebody who says, "Well, if you know it, put the script aside," then you're safe. Sometimes you'll be given some movement in the scene, for a callback. Or you'll be asked to do it another way, because the producer wants to see if you can take direction. Well, if you're still dependent on the script, it's much harder, I think.

Be safe—because you're going to study it anyway, aren't you? I don't mean to say you can't have it with you. But it does show that you have really sat down—which, of course, you should do anyway every time you have an audition—and figured out what is actually happening in that scene.

What the subtext is?

What's the subtext? What's going on? On what levels? You can only do so much of that in a cold reading, although you should certainly look at the scene from that point of view. And for a callback—which can determine whether you have a chance to get on camera—it's extremely important that you know all the things and levels that are happening in the interplay between the people. So if you've gone that far, learn the words, and that will give you an added sense of security—at least for me it would.

And if you get to the videotaped audition?

Of course you have to learn it for that.

Are there any other mistakes you commonly see actors make in auditions?

Sometimes people will audition very well, so then I will ask them to callbacks. But then they will take that scene to a friend or even a person they're studying with and get help with the scene and come back with an entirely different performance, which is all wrong—that's not the reason I called them back. And after they leave the room my boss will look at me and say, "Why?" And I say, "They didn't do that the first time." You know, they'll elaborate on it or build it up.

Oh, and another thing about auditioning: If you've finished a scene and I think you have something, I may say, "Would you please take this scene out and attack it from this angle, and we'll read it again?"—because you're good, but you've gone off on the wrong track. I want to see if you can adjust the other way.

And another thing: When you're reading a scene the first time through and you suddenly say to yourself, "Oh, this is wrong for the part," stick with it—don't change horses in midstream. And then you can say at the end, "That was wrong. That was not my attack. That was not the character." But don't waver, because then you're completely lost and nothing happens.

But you might stop in the middle and say, "May I start again?"

But if you don't, don't waver through it.

There was an article in *Backstage* in which a casting director said that when she's reading with an actor, the actor should never look at her—that the actor should look anywhere but at the casting director. How do you feel about that?

I don't agree with that. It would drive me crazy if I were reading with you and you were looking over there. But I've had people come in who've just had a recent experience with a casting director like that. And they'll ask, "Do you prefer me to look in another direction or to play with you?"

That's a gracious way of doing it, and that might be a smart thing to do. Betty, what are your major frustrations with the casting process? Is there something you would like to see changed or done away with completely?

I wish it were more humane. Everyone connected with the business is trying to think of some way to make it more humane. But you have to see the person; you have to find out if the person can act. You don't just go in and get a part. But my heart aches for people—it's so agonizing.

Barbara Badyna

*Barbara Badyna started her career at Young and Rubicam, Inc. in 1959,
working her way up in the casting department from secretary, casting assistant, and casting director, to director of casting in 1978 and senior vice
president in 1987. Currently she is chairperson on the Four A's Subcom-
mittee of Casting and Talent Agent Relations. [The Four A's is an association of the performers' guilds: the Actors' Equity Association (AEA), the
American Federation of TV and Radio Artists (AFTRA), the American
Guild of Variety Artists (AGVA), and the Screen Actors Guild (SAG).]*

Barbara, how did you get into casting in the first place?

It was quite by accident. I intended to be a teacher. I always took dance
classes, and I went to my class one Saturday, and the teacher said there was
an audition at the Music Hall. I never wanted to dance professionally, but
I wanted to see what the inside of the Music Hall looked like, so I went over
and auditioned. I didn't get into Radio City, but at that time they had a
road company, and I got a job with that. So I went home and broke the
news that I wasn't going on to school. I graduated the next day, and I toured
with them for eight months, doing state fairs. It was a marvelous education,
because I really got to see the country, and I played with Nat King Cole and
Johnny Ray. We played to three to five thousand people in outdoor arenas,
and it was very exciting.

But eventually there came a time when I decided not to perform any
longer—because I had my own style of dancing, and once you learned their
routines, it was just a matter of cutting it up and putting the combinations
together, and if one blinked everybody had to blink. So I made a deal at
home that I would go to school for six months—secretarial school—and
hold a job for six months. At the end of six months, I could go on my merry
way—either pursue a career in that or go back to school and become a
teacher. Young and Rubicam was my first job. I'd been there five and a half
months, and I was about to give my notice when I got transferred up to
casting because somebody went on vacation.

Has the job changed a lot over the years?

Oh, immensely. Casting, like acting, is a craft. I've paid my dues, and
people in my department have paid their dues, and there are a lot of agents
who have. But right now the market has changed—and part of this is
technology; part of it is economics. There aren't many major advertising
agencies that have in-house casting departments; there are a lot more free-
lance casting agencies. There's more quantity than quality.

More quantity than quality in what sense?

You used to have auditions, and you'd prescreen people, and then you'd bring back maybe twenty, twenty-five, and decisions could be made. Nowadays you haven't got time for prescreening. Also, the creatives and clients feel that the more people they see the better, and that's not necessarily so, because usually you come back to your first audition, and somebody is selected from that.

Because there is less prescreening now, is it harder for a new person to break in than it used to be?

No, but your competition is very tough, because you've got so many people wanting it and trying it. I said before that it's a craft. Stage acting is one part of it. Daytime drama is another part. Movies, television commercials. A television commercial is that nice annuity that comes in every thirteen weeks that allows you to take that off-Broadway part that you've always wanted to do, but that you're getting paid no money for. And a lot of people aren't focusing that way. Everybody's thinking, *It's a fast dollar, and I can do it.*

In commercials you're basically putting on a play in less than thirty seconds. It's a very expensive play, and you don't have time to build a character. When you come in to audition, you usually have only a couple of minutes to look at the copy, then you go into a strange room with strange people. You have a storyboard [an illustrated script], a cue card written, and they might have changed the words on you, and they throw all sorts of adjectives at you, and you're looking into the little eye of a camera. And you'll usually get two or three tries, if you're lucky.

That's where the casting director comes into play, because they know the talent. It's our job to make the creative department think it's their idea, because you don't want to step on anybody's toes. But I can say, "You know, maybe she could do it this way. Why don't you ask her? See if she can take the direction off you." And they'll say to you, "Judith, will you do it a little brighter, maybe a little this, a little that." And it turns the whole commercial around.

Would you say, given the fact that most commercials have to get their whole drama across in thirty seconds nowadays, that typecasting is more prevalent in commercials than in plays or films or soap operas?

Very definitely.

You have to see it *right away?*

It's instant, and sometimes it's instant in the look. Again, that's where the casting director will come in. Because an actor or an actress may have three auditions in a day—and if you do, you're very lucky these days—and, say, one is for a fashion kind of thing, and another is for a teenager. They're all different roles. So you're walking out with your wardrobe and your handbag and jewelry. And you've got your hair up, and it's got to come down for one of the roles. And you walk in, and by this time your hair has become frizzy, because of humidity. And they'll say, "Oh, that's the wrong look." And I have to say, "You're creative now, come on. We can do something with the hair." But looks do play a part in commercials; there's no getting away from it. And then the other thing is the acting ability.

Is there such a thing as a "commercial type"?

I think almost anybody is a commercial type, but some people are more usable than others.

What makes somebody more usable?

An overall Americana look. Somebody with a New York accent is not going to sell in the Midwest, even if they're blond and blue-eyed and surfer-looking.

What about age ranges? Is there more work for one age range than another? Where do most of the calls come, in terms of ages?

The twenty-five to thirty-five range.

Young moms and dads? Young career people?

Yes. Career people—that's the new catch phrase. But there's also a big push for minorities, seniors, and women in voice-overs. The woman's role has changed, because we have buying power now—and it *should* change.

Let's talk a little bit about the odds. How many actors do you see for the average commercial?

It's hard to say. Sometimes we've seen as many as two thousand people in a month. I'd say we see about a hundred people for the average commercial.

How many people in the agency have to approve the final choice of an actor for a spot?

Well, you have your art director, you have your copywriter, you have the producer that pulls it all together. And then you have a creative supervisor, and that's within the agency. But then, on the client side, you have account executives. So the layers have substantially increased.

So how many people would there be, in total?

Eight to ten. Sometimes you can get somebody cleared right up to the next-to-highest point, and all of a sudden that client doesn't like somebody for some reason.

What happens then?

We go back to the drawing board. Or we go back to the audition tapes and pull some people that we feel they weren't thinking of in the beginning but should have been thinking of. We do that, in any event. That's part of the function of a casting director—to guide, and to know the scope of talent. But, again, it's all subjective. This whole business is subjective. The person who drew this storyboard has somebody in mind. The person who wrote it has somebody in mind. The client has somebody in mind. The research is proving something else, and we're taking all these factors and trying to get them all together.

When you have callbacks, out of the hundred or so people you've called for the initial audition, how many would you typically call back?

Depends on the client. Probably eight would be average. If I'm doing a mixing and matching of families, I might call more. That's harder for me because I know the actor's point of view: you're sitting out there in that room, and I tell you to stay and let you wait and bring you back in, then tell you to wait a minute, then tell you that you can go. I know what that feels like for the actor, but that's the business part of it. The whole business is built on rejection, and you can't take it personally. You have to get a little bit of a thick skin.

Let's talk for a minute about celebrity casting. I know you do some percentage of this. What percentage of the actors in Young and Rubicam commercials—both on-camera and voice-over—are celebrities?

Probably a quarter. Bill Cosby has been one of ours with Jell-O for a long time, and it's been a long-term relationship, and he's phenomenal, because his credibility hasn't diminished through the years—it's gotten substantially higher. What I'm finding now, which is interesting, is that they want celebrity voice-overs. And, you know, when you separate the person and the voice, many times it makes no difference. People won't recognize the voice, unless it's something very distinctive like a Gregory Peck.

What kind of training impresses you on an actor's résumé?

Nowadays, *any* kind of training.

Is that a rarity?

The résumés are very vague. I like to see a good acting background. And a good actor is not necessarily going to be a good commercial actor. I mean, we've had name celebrities come in and audition, and it's been disastrous. And my people say, "How did he ever get a job?" And you say, "That's not it. It's a different part of the craft."

How is it different? What demand does it make that a good stage actor might find hard to meet?

A good stage actor has an age range of nine to ninety. You have time to develop your character. You're playing to the audience; your voice has to carry. So when you come in to do commercials, it's bigger than life—and you have to learn to pull it back, to be very minute.

What are the biggest mistakes you see actors make over and over again in auditions?

Well, for on-camera, I really think you have to practice in the mirror, because everybody has little personal things they do. Some people squint their eyes too much, and that's probably from trying to read the cue cards. But you see a lot of movement of the eyes, and also with the head. When you're doing an audition, an audition is a very rough idea. You've only had two minutes to look at that copy, and you're doing it on-camera, and we're usually in very close, and if somebody keeps moving their head like this, and you're looking at all these auditions at the end of the day . . .

You're getting seasick?

Yes. You're so distracted.

So we have to learn to hold our heads still?

Yes. You want animation in your face, but sometimes people get nervous and little quirks come out, so I really think you should practice in front of a mirror. You might not even know you have these quirks, and people usually don't have time to tell you.

Are commercial workshops—the kind that allow you to see yourself on videotape—useful in this regard?

Commercial classes have pros and cons. The pros are that they do give you instruction and let you practice, so that you see what is happening. And it's a way of networking, which I think is good—because casting directors do go to showcases. Actors are now finding that this is an easier way of networking than getting work. It's hard to get work.

What is the negative about it? The negative is that most people do exactly what they were told and they all look alike, like cookie cutters. Just because you're told to do it a certain way, you don't have to *keep* doing it that way. This whole business is opinions. You have to sift through those opinions, take the part you like and refuse the part you don't like. You have to keep yourself in there.

A lot of these commercial classes are also expensive.

Yes. And that's another thing: I would not just sign up for a commercial course; I would go and audit a class and see what I personally thought about it, because of the expense involved. It's your investment.

The same with your pictures—look at a photographer's portfolio. Don't just choose a photographer because somebody says, "He's wonderful—here are my pictures." Go look at the different types of pictures he takes.

And don't get gimmicky with your pictures. It's the basic suit, it's the basic black dress you're investing in. It's basically a straight-on picture that looks natural. I wouldn't have too much of a background, because it will detract from you. Again, I would make myself simple, so that it's not dated, so that I could use it for a couple of years, at least. And don't take the opinion of your family.

Whose opinion should you take?

You should bring it around to a couple of agents, a couple of casting people among your contacts, and kind of see who's zeroing in on one or two of the shots. But if you show it to your mom, your dad, your sister, your brother, your boyfriend, your girlfriend, they're going to go for that glamour picture, that high-school picture.

What about the whole issue between head shots and composites? Do you ever like to see composites on an actor?

No, I really think a good head shot works for everything. If you're a character guy or woman, then have a character picture done also. But I think composites are a thing of the past now, even for the models. I mean, their composites have come down to a little index card.

And what's happening with commercial auditions is that a lot of actors don't even bring their head shots, because we take Polaroids. Or, in our case, we have a Mitsubishi camera set up on the video camera viewfinder, so we know that at the audition we can just push a button and get a shot.

You might say, "Why am I spending all this money for this head shot?" Well, the casting people keep them in a file, and many times we'll pull them out and say, "Is this the type you're looking for?" Or they may not like the look you had the day you auditioned, and we give them your head shot and say, "Here, take this over to the client."

Under what categories do you file the pictures?

We do them two ways—alphabetically and by age range. We also have an extra file.

Does doing extra work put an actor in a category that makes it difficult for him to get work as a principal?

Not at our agency. Many times producers have called back and asked for somebody, or somebody has been upgraded. Right now work is so hard to come by, and extra work gives you experience and helps support your benefits with your union.

Should it say on your résumé that you do extra work?

No. I would write that on a separate note if you're sending a picture in to somebody—because not everybody is like our agency. Some people will say, "Oh, I don't cast extras." You have to ask. If you say, "I usually do principal work, but I need it for my hospitalization. Would you mind thinking of me as an extra?" Sure.

Are there any tips you have for actors about professional etiquette? Is there anything they often do that bothers you?

One thing that bugs me—nobody has telephone answering services anymore. They all have answering machines. If I call up, and I get this message with music playing and you doing a monologue—and this happens, believe me—by the time the beep comes, I've forgotten what I wanted you for. I go through that ten times and I get fed up.

If you have an answering machine, make that tape very short: "Hi, this is Barbara. I'm not available at the moment. Leave a message. I'll return your call as soon as I can." Don't do any cutesy things.

Another thing: keep in touch with your telephone. Don't call at nine o'clock in the morning and six o'clock at night. Call it every couple of hours—like nine o'clock, eleven o'clock, one o'clock, four o'clock. Because many times we're calling extras, and if it's a quickie for the next day and it comes to four o'clock and we haven't heard from people, we're going to start replacing them.

What do you like to see on a résumé, other than good training?

The résumé has your name clearly, your telephone number or answering service, your height, your age range, and then your credits. I would avoid listing commercials, because if somebody sees General Foods' Jell-O they think it's current, and if they have another Jell-O product they'll think it's a conflict. So write "Commercials upon Request."

Don't lie on your résumé, either. It catches up with you.

If you don't have many credits—if you're new and starting out—what should you put down on your résumé? School productions? College productions?

I would, because it shows. If we're trying to get you into the union, it's honest. I mean, we will have to send over a résumé and a picture and maybe you yourself. And it's somebody starting out. But this person has training, and in the union code book it says, "sufficient training to qualify, intends to pursue this as a career." So those credits are going to mean a lot—that you went to the High School of Performing Arts, and then you were in your local theater group, and you're taking a commercial acting class, and you did an extra on a soap.

Is there much chance for an actor who's not a member of a union to get a shot at a commercial?

It's very difficult now, because of the numbers. With the mergers of advertising agencies and the mergers of clients, another thing has entered the picture that nobody realizes: they're not making as many commercials. And I think, at the bottom line, it's for many reasons. They're renewing a lot of old commercials. They're doing print.

So for an actor to get seen for a commercial is difficult if he's not a member of a union, if he's not sent by an agent?

Yes, and even finding an agent now . . . The *Ross Reports* [a monthly publication listing advertising agencies, casting personnel, and talent agents] will say, "Do not send your picture; do not phone." Well, you've got to use your discretion. I'm not speaking for anybody else, but I'd say do your homework about who you're going to see, and drop in. Maybe they're not busy. Maybe they will accept your picture. It's all maybes. If they yell at you, you can't take it personally. But take the chance.

In Los Angeles actors are signed with a particular agency for commercials. But in New York many do free-lance. In your view, which is better—to sign with one agent or play the field?

There are pros and cons for both, and I think you have to sort this out yourself. I think in the beginning you have to play the field, and you have to see who's going to be interested in you. In New York you can create energy by making the rounds and by going to see agencies. You have to see who's working the hardest for you. And if somebody is willing to sign you right away, fine, but make sure you have a little bit of an out, too, in case it's not working out.

A couple of questions about how we can present ourselves most effectively: Is it important for a performer to dress for the part, for a commercial?

It's nice, if it can be arranged. It's not always possible, because you're running around. Ask what the part is, and try to do that, but be flexible, because sometimes it changes. Also, remember that by the time the information gets from me to the agent to the agent's assistant, there's a big gap before it gets to you.

But if it is definitely a sophisticated evening look or a career woman, you should dress appropriately. You could have blue jeans on and a blouse and pearls, and if you take the pearls off, you still look right with the blouse and jeans.

You're usually only taping above the waist, anyway?

Yes.

Should you wear the same thing to a callback that you wore to the original audition?

I don't think it hurts.

How important is an actor's slate?

Very important. Take your time. You slate your name and then wait about five seconds, and then go on with your performance. Because if you don't leave some time in there, when we go to edit the audition, part of the slate gets edited off, and then they can't identify you.

And if you get sent out by more than one agent, you don't need to identify the agent on the slate, but make sure when you sign in that the correct agent is on the sign-in sheet.

Since we know that the fast-forward button exists in agencies, if you do a slate badly—if you're lacking in energy or if you're too gimmicky or bright or whatever—can that do so much harm that they won't even watch your audition?

No. We realize that an audition is a very rough form. It's wonderful if you can memorize the copy, because it will put you that much ahead of everybody else. Everybody will be quite impressed, I assure you. But if you can't, that's why the cue card is up there.

And when you do audition, and they say "Thank you very much," and you've had one try, you've got nothing to lose by asking, "Would you like it done any other way?" And if they say, "No, that's fine," you might say, "I have a thought on it, and if you have the time I'd like to put it down." Use your instinct on it. If they say no, then you've tried, and you're not going to go home and say to yourself, "I should have done it that way. Why didn't I ask to do it that way?"

Leslee Feldman

Leslee Feldman, former Vice President, Manager of Casting at Saatchi and Saatchi Advertising, is currently Vice President of Casting for Hollywood Pictures.

How did you get into casting?

I got into it in an unusual way, because I didn't have a particularly heavy background in speech and drama, only a minor one. I went to work for a small advertising agency about ten years ago, in the production department. I was actually hired as a production assistant, and I was secretary to about twelve people. So I learned all different parts of the business: production, business management, talent payments, traffic.

I was lucky enough to be given the opportunity to do whatever I wanted, and I thought casting sounded interesting and fun. I began then to create a casting department, first to do radio commercials, voice-overs, and then to do on-camera casting and celebrity negotiations. And then after a few years I went to work for a much bigger agency—then called Dancer, Fitzgerald, Sample—who, along with half the other agencies in New York, got taken over by Saatchi and Saatchi about three years ago. And I worked there, and became head of the department about a year and a half ago.

Tell us how the staff casting job at an advertising agency differs from that of an independent casting director in commercials.

They're quite different, really, in a lot of ways. As a staff casting director in an agency, we are very involved in a lot of the jobs, sometimes almost from the conception of the idea. We work directly with the creative people—the copywriters and art directors who come up with the ideas. And many times before the story board will be totally conceived, they'll come to us and talk about what kind of people they want in it; if it's a celebrity, then what kind of person would actually be interested and appropriate to endorse the product. And we are involved in the job all the way through. We do all the casting work with the director on the callbacks, and sometimes even after the job has shot and when it's being edited, we are involved in the cutting of the commercial and then, of course, in putting the voice-over on at the end.

When the independent casting directors get the job, they get the story board when it's approved and ready to be shot. And they'll get it maybe a day or two before. Somebody from the agency or the production company will give them the specs. They'll cast the job, give the tape back to agency, and, if the agency is pleased with it, do callbacks. The agency, their client, will choose the final cast, and they're finished with it and go on to the next job.

In my agency we do it both ways. We do a lot of in-house casting, and a lot of independent casting. So, depending on what kind of job it is, what kind of director, what creative director in my agency, we figure out the best way to do it.

You mentioned the negotiation of celebrity contracts. What percentage of the commercials that you do at Saatchi and Saatchi involve celebrity spokespeople?

Well, a very large percentage—maybe thirty percent of the spots that are done—inquire about celebrities. But the deals that are actually closed with celebrities amount to about ten percent. It's very difficult. First of all, the money that celebrities command today for commercials is unbelievable.

Could you give us some idea of the ranges?

It used to be that if you gave somebody $100,000 or $200,000 or $300,000 to do a commercial, that was a lot of money. But today somebody who is not a television personality but a film or rock or music personality will usually look for at least $750,000. It goes up to one and two million—I mean, the numbers are like that.

Even for a television celebrity, if you want one of them today, there are few $50,000 or $75,000 deals anymore, unless you get an ex–sports player—an ex–baseball player or ex–basketball player—or a television personality who isn't really high-profile or who isn't as popular as he or she once was. But anybody who you would recognize as a working and successful television personality would cost more like $200,000 to $500,000.

Since we're on the subject of money, which is of great interest to us all, what percentage of the commercials that you cast are over scale—that is, commercials for which performers are paid above union minimum wages?

Not many. We do many, many scale commercials. A lot of our advertisers do network advertising, buying on specific networks for specific shows, and those network buys make the actors the most money.

Could you explain briefly how that works?

There are two basic ways that the actors get paid: network buys, and what we call spot buys. When we buy network time on specific shows, the actors get paid by the number of uses, and we start out with the first use. I think scale for the first use is $366.60, which is the same as the session fee—what the actor gets for actually performing the spot. Usually the first use is credited against the session fee. And then it goes in descending amounts to the thirteenth use, and then starts again each thirteen-week cycle. And those numbers can add up incredibly. On a strong network buy, an actor can make $10,000, $20,000, $30,000 a year. And also, a lot of times, a voice-over actor may have his voice on a campaign of five different spots, so he gets paid network time at that same scale for each spot.

Another way that we pay is through what's called spot time. Spot cycles run every thirteen weeks, which means that we have four cycles in a year. New York, Chicago, and L.A. are obviously the main markets, and everything is weighted. Houston and Cincinnati would be smaller markets, and then little towns all over would be even smaller. But basically the idea is that if a spot ran in New York and Chicago, plus fifty other units for one cycle, that would pay the actor about $1,500. And the actor gets paid $1,500 whether the spot runs one time or five hundred times. They get paid that amount for the thirteen weeks. So spot buys usually make less than network buys.

When there are spot buys, or when something is testing in only certain areas of the country, some actors will ask for over-scale payments—guarantees of certain amounts of money. And it can be really complicated, but basically the guarantees are based on what category of product we're talking about. For example, if I were testing a fast-food spot in Atlanta, Georgia, for a year, I would have to pay an actor a fairly substantial guarantee, because a spot running in Atlanta would probably make only about $1,500 for the whole year, and that person would not be able to do any competitive advertising for McDonald's, Pizza Hut—any other fast foods. So if you're keeping them exclusive in a very competitive category, you usually have to pay. I have something else that we're doing now for an eyeglass store, which is not a very competitive area. So we'll be able to pay everybody scale for that.

Could we talk a little more about this whole area of conflicts? How do conflicts work? If you've done a spot for Burger King, what does that mean, in terms of your limitation for doing other spots?

It means that while your Burger King contract is in effect you can't do any other fast-food commercials. And there are two ways that it can be in effect.

One is that the spot is on the air and running. The other thing is that when an actor signs a SAG contract for a commercial, it's a twenty-one-month contract, which means that we have the right to use the commercial or hold the commercial for twenty-one months. So we may run it for a couple of cycles—which are thirteen weeks each. If we run it for two cycles, that's six months. And then, if we decide to hold the commercial, we pay a holding fee that will still hold the actor to us and not allow him to do any competitive advertising. However, once we release the commercial—if, after six months, we know we aren't going to use it again, we'll release it—the actor is free at that point to go out and do any competitive advertising.

Would you expect an actor to list commercials on a résumé?

No. "Commercials List on Request" or "Conflicts on Request."

In an ad agency situation, how many people have to approve the final choice of a person for a spot?

Most times it adds up to fifteen or twenty people, including writers, art directors, creative directors, account people, producers, and directors. We try to narrow the choices as we go, so that when we get to the client, we try to show them just one choice and maybe one backup.

How many, on the average, do you see for a commercial in the initial call?

I would say we see at least between fifty and a hundred people for every spot, if not more.

For voice-overs we'd usually see a smaller group, probably twenty-five to fifty people. I use a lot of these people over and over again; a voice-over actor can play many more types.

In terms of categories of on-camera people that are heavily used in commercials, is there such a thing these days as a "commercial type"?

There's always a commercial type, even though everybody says that's what they want to get away from. There are still a lot of clients who feel more comfortable with what they consider an all-American, fair-haired, blue-eyed, professional-looking, warm, friendly, attractive, mid-American look.

So for somebody who is very dark or ethnic-looking in a foreign way, I will have things for that person to audition for—but they're not the "commercial type," and they're not going to be right for as many commercials as the other type. That's just the way it is.

Let's talk about on-camera auditioning. What are the biggest mistakes you see actors make in on-camera videotaped auditions?

You have to be careful about your appearance when you come in for an audition. You don't have to be dressed exactly as you would be in the final spot, but if I'm doing something for a businessman, an executive, and a guy comes in wearing a T-shirt or sweatshirt, looking messy, it's so hard for the people who are looking at the tape to envision this person in the part. And for any audition, you have to look nice. You have to look neat. A lot of people look at those tapes and notice little things—for men, if you wear an earring, you should really leave it home.

For women, makeup is really important—to know how to do your makeup—because the lighting is usually so poor in most of the casting places you go. I think it's really worth it to go to a department store or a salon and have a professional makeup done to show you how to make it light enough and flattering enough for video—and you should obviously tell them that's why you're there. There are some people who come in, and I can see how their makeup would look okay to them, but to the camera it's very dark, and the camera can be brutal.

Anything else you'd like to caution actors about in their auditioning?

Another thing that people do—they'll come in and criticize the copy, or they'll say, "You know, this scene isn't right." And if the writer's sitting there, the casting director might as well say, "I'll just erase that person."

Or you'll give them some direction like, "This is your attitude, and you'll do it that way." And they'll say, "Really? I don't think it should be like that." Basically what you have to do is just go in and do what the casting director says and *listen.*

How important is the slate? Can you do a really bad slate and a wonderful audition, and still get the job?

I don't think the slate is important at all. We just want to know your name. It doesn't matter how you say it.

How important is it to memorize the copy before you come in? Should you even try to do that, given the fact that there is a cue card there?

It's not important at all to memorize the copy. I certainly never expect anyone to memorize it. There's always a cue card right next to the camera, set up in such a way that, even if you're reading it, it kind of looks as if you're looking at the camera. I can only speak for myself and my agency, but what we look for in a first audition is just somebody who seems comfortable in front of the camera, who is relaxed. And I don't even care if you don't say the right copy. As long as you get the gist of it, it doesn't matter.

When you get a callback, then you should probably—and I think most people do this—try to get there a little early so that you do feel more comfortable with the copy. If you feel more comfortable with the words, if you don't have to keep following the part all the time, you will probably give a better performance. But you certainly don't have to memorize it.

Are there certain kinds of colors or patterns that it's a good idea to stay away from in an audition because of the way video cameras and lighting work?

White is usually not good to wear. Pastel colors are good. But as a rule, you don't need to worry about that too much. Obviously, you shouldn't wear anything too severe, too trendy, too low-cut. People come in wearing bustiers for a Procter & Gamble Tide commercial. What are they thinking of? I have models come in sometimes for a shampoo commercial, and they say, "Oh, I didn't have time to wash my hair today." And it's pulled back. It's a *shampoo* commercial—why even bother coming? Those kinds of things are basic.

If you are lucky enough to get a callback, is it a good idea to wear the same thing you wore to the original audition?

A lot of people do that—almost as a superstitious kind of thing—but it is a good idea, because they've seen you that way, and there's something about that look that they like.

How do you feel about commercial workshops—the kind where you do a performance of commercial copy on videotape and the person teaching the class responds and you get to see yourself and maybe do it again? How useful is that?

I think classes are very useful, but you have to be careful. I have to be honest and say that there are things about those commercial classes that really bother me. They're very expensive, and they'll take anybody, and I think it's not always fair to bring people in who will never be successful in commercials and who aren't actors.

There's some exploitation of actors going on here?

Oh, there's no question that there is. I do think they're kind of exploiting the actors when they bring in casting people and agents basically just so you can meet them, and they end up being paid a lot of the time to teach the classes. I have not taught many of those classes, but I have taught a few, and I have found some people in those classes.

I think it's really important to become comfortable in front of a camera, and that is a good way of doing it. You work with real commercial copy, you see yourself on tape, you see yourself played back, so you see how your acting is, you see what you look like, you see how you photograph, how you come across on tape. And you do have the benefit of casting people and agents to critique you, and that really is important. You also get auditioning practice, and sometimes in front of a whole group of people, and those things will relax you and give you experience.

Let's get into the whole question of agents. In Los Angeles you have to be signed to one agent. There's no free-lancing. Here in New York, an actor has the alternative of free-lancing or signing, in an ideal situation. Do you have any feeling about which is better?

Both work. Being signed certainly has its advantages because you usually have a closer relationship with your agents. They know you. And also, if you're signed to them, they will feel more obligated to get you out there, to get you work, and they'll probably work harder to make sure that you get out on auditions, and try to help you as much as possible.

On the other hand, when you're starting, it's sometimes good to be free-lance because you don't really know a lot of agents, and if you can free-lance through some different ones, you can get to know them, see which ones you feel comfortable with, which agents you feel are really interested in you and interested in helping your career.

The smaller agencies usually do a lot of free-lancing, and if you can free-lance through three or four of them, you also have more chance of getting submitted on jobs. Not every small agency is called for every job, but if your name is being sent out through four, there's a good chance that one or two of the agents a casting director calls will submit you.

If somebody in one of the bigger agencies wanted to sign you—if a J. Michael Bloom or a Cunningham or an SEM&M or a Don Buchwald or a Jacobson-Wilder wanted to sign you—I'd say do it, because they get calls for everything. They're not going to sign anybody who they're not going to work for, and who they don't really feel that they can get work for. But sometimes those agencies—a lot of them—will say, "Free-lance with us for a while, and we'll see how it goes." But what happens is, they are obligated to their signed clients first, and they have to make sure that their signed clients get into the auditions. And if they call me and I talk to them and I have, say, eight appointment times that I'm going to give them—I let them submit eight actors—then probably six of those will be signed clients and only two are going to be free-lance. So there's a much smaller chance for you to get submitted.

I think it's good to free-lance at the beginning with small agencies, and then all you have to do is get in a few auditions, get a few first refusals, and if you're lucky enough to book something, the agents will be after you. They make you do all the legwork at first, and then they're happy to represent you when you're working. But you don't even have to sign, because there are many successful actors who free-lance and who just prefer to go out through different agencies.

Can an actor get in to see you if he's not sent by an agent—free-lance or otherwise?

It's very difficult. The truth is, I know how hard it is to get to agents and casting people. And you read the *Ross Reports,* and everyone says, "Don't call, don't call, don't call."

The *Ross Reports* are on our reading list, and they're a very important resource.

Yes, they list all the casting people in New York and what they do. We see it from both sides: I'm sympathetic to how hard it is to get an agent, and it's very hard to get seen. We would like to see as many people as we can and give them as much opportunity as possible. But, on the realistic side, we work mostly through agents—almost totally through agents—because commercials happen very quickly. We get a commercial at two o'clock in the afternoon, and we have to cast it at nine or ten o'clock the next morning, and I have got to be on the phone with the agents, trying to get the actors that I know I want and their other clients. We try to see new people, but I can't go hunting through pictures when I have two hours to prep a job.

A lot of people don't listen to what it says in the *Ross Reports* about not calling, and we get lots of phone calls every day. Most casting people would kill me for saying this, but sometimes if you just call you might get lucky. A lot of times I'll pick up my phone if there's nobody there, and if it's someone whose picture I've seen come across my desk, or if somebody's nice on the phone—not too aggressive—and seems to respect that I don't have very much time to talk, I will try to set up a general interview. But you have to be lucky.

The best thing is to send your picture; send a postcard every month. The pictures come, and we file them. But every day I go through the postcards, and if I see actors that I keep recognizing, a lot of times if there's a job coming up, I'll say, "Bring in this person." Particularly if the actor is in SAG and is willing to do extra work, a lot of times we'll bring them in as an extra, because then we can see if they look like their picture and see who they are.

Do you go to Equity-waiver theater, workshops, showcases? Is that a way people can get you to know their work?

Absolutely. We try to go to as many as we can. We split it up. In my department there are four of us, so not everybody goes to everything, but we try to go to as many showcases and off-off-Broadway plays as we can.

If someone is in a showcase and wants you to come, what's the best thing to do? Call you up? Send you a flyer?

Send a flyer, and then you can follow it up with a phone call. But definitely send a flyer. When you send flyers about showcases, it's probably even better to send them to the assistant casting people than to the head casting people, because the assistants often have time to go to more showcases than the senior casting people.

How can you find out the names of the assistant casting people?

They're in the *Ross Reports*, which are updated monthly.

We were talking about pictures a minute ago. What makes a good picture for commercials?

The most important thing is that it should really look like you. A lot of people have pictures that don't look like them at all. And for commercials, which are very different from legit, it should just be a head shot. A smiling shot—they love to see nice teeth on commercial head shots. And dress very plainly—something that's going to make you look versatile, so that your look can go a lot of different ways. Simple hair. But, most importantly, just something that looks like you.

Do you pay much attention to résumés in casting commercials?

To be completely honest, no. I look at them. I do like to get an idea of who you've studied with—I do look at that. But usually when you come in for a commercial audition I tell you not even to leave a picture, if I have seen you before. We just take a Polaroid, which we use for reference, so the résumé is not really that important.

Is it a big disadvantage if an actor is not a member of SAG or AFTRA?

No, it is not a disadvantage at all. I think it's a big misconception that it's such a problem not to be in SAG or AFTRA. As far as commercials go—and I would think it would be the same in anything—basically what happens is that when we audition people, if I audition fifty or sixty or seventy people for a particular part, and if I want to choose you and you're not in SAG, all I have to do is get a waiver for you. And it's very simple, as long as I can show that I've auditioned a certain number of SAG people—I basically just fill out a standard form and send your picture and résumé. The union just wants to make sure that they're letting someone work who is a legitimate actor or actress, and that we're not taking away work from their members to give it to somebody who's just doing this on the side. As long as I can show that I have auditioned a certain number of actors and that you do have some background, it's an automatic waiver. And then what happens is that for your first commercial they give us a waiver. You don't have to join—and shouldn't join—because you wouldn't have made enough money to cover joining.

The initiation fee is high.

And then the second time you book a commercial, you must join the union. But if people tell you that they won't see you because you're not SAG or that it's so hard—that Catch-22 situation people always describe: that you can't work if you're not in SAG and you can't get in SAG if you can't work—that's not true. The hard part is getting somebody to want to book you for the job as a principal performer. We cannot get waivers for extras; that's impossible. But if you can get someone to want to book you as a principal, they will get you a waiver. And then, of course, if you want to join, you can. And it is good to join, because then you can do extra work. A lot of people don't want to do extra work, but it is a good way of getting to know directors, getting to know people, getting on the set, and getting experience.

Do you think working as an extra in commercials gets you pigeonholed in a bad category—or does that not apply to commercials?

It doesn't apply any longer, I don't think. In the past there were a lot of actors who were known as extra actors—they just worked that way—but it's not really like that anymore. First of all, there's not a lot of work, and everyone needs the money, and extra work pays very well these days.

Also, when you're just starting out and you need to meet people, if you do five or ten extra jobs, it's certainly not going to hurt your career. And it is important to get out there and meet the directors, because they tend to use the same people over and over again. I can't tell you how many times people who have worked with a director time and time again have gotten upgraded on a commercial to a principal, and then they were used as a principal by that director another time. It only can help you.

Is it a good idea, if you have worked as an extra, to put it on your résumé?

It's good to write on the top that you will work as an extra, because even though a casting director may not remember your picture and résumé well enough to bring you in for a principal part, we all keep extra files. Eventually we will call you and you will work. And every time you send a postcard, remind us that you will do extra work.

Billy Serow
-----

*B*illy *Serow is an independent casting director whose firm—Godlove, Serow and Sindlinger—casts commercials, television, industrials, and films. About half his personal casting work is in the field of voice-overs.*

How did you get into casting?

I was an actor from the age of five to the age of twenty-seven. At twenty-seven I decided to shift careers. I'd worked pretty much in the theater—off-Broadway, never on Broadway—did some soap opera work, never auditioned for commercials until after I became a casting director.

I went to work for a place called the Hudson Guild Theater off-Broadway as an assistant director, box-office manager, selling orange juice at intermission, checking hats and coats. Part of my responsibilities included reading scripts, choosing scripts to be produced. And, in working with the executive producer, part of my responsibilities included the casting. I was the reader for auditioning actors, and from that you start getting to know the pool of talent in New York City, slowly but surely. I helped mount plays such as *On Golden Pond* and *Da,* both of which went to Broadway and were made into movies.

When the government grant through CITA that was paying my salary ran out, I didn't know where to turn. I went to the agent that I was signed with as an actor, Fifi Oscard, and said, "Gee, I think I'd like to be an agent." She said, "Well, start at the front desk and answer the phones." I did that for a few months, and the people in the commercial department saw that I was skilled; I have a very good memory, and I am very quick, and they wanted me to work in the commercial department with them.

I had no desire to work in commercials. I had the typical New York stage actor's patronizing view of commercials—at which point the agency said, "You will work in commercials or leave," and I went to the commercial department and found that I enjoyed it very much. I grew to appreciate the art form, and also got exposed to a great deal of talent. But it was very frustrating because it was basically a phone job that also dealt with actors' personalities rather than with the specific audition circumstances, and that's what I missed most.

So I decided to strike out on my own and try to cast. I picked up jobs here and there, and landed a job at a major advertising agency, now called Saatchi and Saatchi. I was on staff there for a couple of years, found the land of Procter & Gamble very limiting, and again struck out on my own.

I landed a job at a place called BCI Casting, which was the largest independent casting firm in the country, with offices in New York, L.A., and Chicago. When it was financially feasible, two partners and I bought that company and formed our own company, called GSS, and here I am.

How many actors do you see for the average on-camera commercial?

There are two schools of thought on commercial casting. There are people who need to bring in a whole lot of people because they are not all that secure with what they're doing. But I pride myself on bringing in the fewest people per role that will be accommodated for the client. Generally, for a big national on-camera commercial, I would probably see between thirty and forty-five people per role, not many more than that—because if the client is specific about what they really want, about that many people come to my mind. That's giving it my best shot.

Out of the forty-five you see for a role in a national commercial, how many would you typically call back for a second audition?

Between three and ten, usually.

Let's talk for a minute about agents. How many agents do you regularly call?

There is a difference between the on-camera world and the voice-over world. For the on-camera world I will usually call between seven, at the very least, and twelve.

In L.A. nearly all the actors sign with a particular agency, but in New York many free-lance. In your view, which is better?

It depends on two things: first, your physical type and age, and second, your recognizability in the industry. What tends to happen is that young people, people that are not established yet, and character people free-lance more than your very down-the-road, straight, wonderful commercial types that you always see on television—your mommies and daddies and spokespeople.

The advantage to free-lancing is that you have a better chance at some-body submitting you. If I give a breakdown to somebody and I say, "I need a sixty-year-old grandma, a nice, sweet old grandma, a little bit sassy, with a little bit of an edge," and I get Rose Goldstein submitted to me on four different lists . . . When I see it the first time I think that maybe she isn't right; I see it the second time and I think, *Well, two people thought that;* I see it the third time, I think, *Boy, maybe I'm wrong.* I see it the fourth time— well, Rose is coming in! That tends to influence a casting director, espe-cially if I don't know the person.

But being signed definitely has it advantages, if you're signed with an agency that gets all or most of the calls. You get better financial protection. They're looking out for you more.

Would you explain in what way the financial protection works?

If I am doing a fast-food commercial, a McDonald's that doesn't run nationally, and I ask for so-and-so, who is the best counter girl in the city, if she is signed with an agent the agent will try to protect her and say, "Well, I need twenty-five hundred dollars per cycle." Which means you get twenty-five hundred every thirteen weeks—a cycle is thirteen weeks long in commercial-land. I have to go back to my client and say, "I can bring in somebody fantastic for you, but she's going to cost you this amount of money." The client decides, "Yes, I can pay that," or "No, this is just going to be a scale job," and I as a casting director have to bring in the best people who will work for scale.

If the person is a free-lance talent, usually they are running their own career, financially speaking, and they have to make that determination. The agent will just say, "Throw them in, I'll submit them, it doesn't matter. If they accept the job, they accept the job. I'll get the money. If they don't accept the job, more power to them." Is that clear?

Yes, that is clear. Is a performer more likely to get called a lot if he or she is with one of the larger agencies?

Yes.

And what might those be? Say the first seven or ten you would call.

J. Michael Bloom, SEM&M, Cunningham, Abrams Artists, JWK, William Morris. That's six just off the top of my head. For adults, mostly adults.

Is there any chance at all for an actor who doesn't have an agent to get in to see you?

Not too much. I open my pictures and look at my pictures and résumés religiously every single day, but it's very hard. Unless they have a very special type or a very special skill: for example, if somebody can juggle five balls or is a gymnast, I save those pictures. If someone speaks fluent Russian or Chinese, I save those pictures. Those are the actors with special skills— that's where it's more applicable. If it's just somebody who is a good commercial type and they are trying to break into the business, they need to get an agent, pretty much, with me.

If an agent calls me up and says, "You have got to see someone, and you've got to make time for it," I do it.

Is there any sense in commercial actors considering having a manager? What use is a manager in an actor's career?

There are many actors who are not good business people, and are also not good salespeople as far as marketing themselves goes. A manager does help in that regard. Of course that comes at a price: a manager takes fifteen percent of your income. An agent takes ten percent, and that's twenty-five percent of your income going right out the door. If you have no income, it doesn't matter. If you have a large income and you're doing well and you have good business acumen, a manager might not be necessary. But for certain people it's very necessary.

Would you explain the difference between a manager and an agent in terms of their relation to the unions and what they do in relation to you?

Managers are under no union jurisdiction; they can charge you whatever they want and set down whatever rules they want. An agent cannot; an agent who works on union commercials is franchised. I only work on union jobs, but there are a great many nonunion jobs out there. The agent is governed by the Screen Actors Guild and its by-laws, and they are allowed to take only ten percent commission, by federal law. If they lose their franchise they can be right out of the business. A manager can last forever.

Let's talk about pictures and résumés or composites. On the West Coast a lot of actors use composites for commercials. How do you feel about the composite versus the picture and résumé?

I hate composites. They're too pat, too stereotypical. And they are usually very badly shot, too, for some reason. Get a good head shot that looks just like you. A picture that is well lit and well shot and represents you at your best.

Are there photographers you know of who do particularly good commercial work?

A woman named Toni Browning, who's wonderful. A guy named Roy Blakey is pretty good. Susannah Gold is also excellent.

What bad things do you often see in commercial pictures that you wish actors would avoid?

Gimmicks. I like something straight-on. In a good picture your eyes have to be alive. They have to say something. Lots of pictures you see are very flat. There is a passivity that makes a picture not jump out of the pile.

And a little touching up never hurts.

So you don't like totally unretouched photographs?

No. I mean, models get retouched in every picture they take, so why not?

What impresses you on a résumé?

That's a good question, because it's not necessarily what they've done. Good training impresses me. Either having gone to a good college and received a degree or having studied with a good person here in the city. Even though we are talking basically about commercials, training really counts with me. Being a good actor really counts. You can be a perfect-looking commercial type, and you can probably work, but you're very limited.

What is a "commercial type," in that sense?

A middle-American, safe, accessible look. For a woman, that means pretty, but you don't have to be a model. And for a man it's attractive, appealing, and likeable.

What about "real people"? I hear that phrase a lot, and I'm sure you do, too.

Yes, there is a trend, and it's a great trend. Thank God people are using more characters and "real people" than ever before, but that's a slow process of change, as far as I'm concerned.

Let's talk for a minute about the whole question of minority groups, racial and ethnic groups. Do you feel that you as a casting director can or should have any influence on helping these people to achieve more work in proportion to their representation in the population?

Yes, most definitely. I'll cite a specific example of that. I do a tremendous amount of casting with children, also. And what you are talking about just occurred. I had to cast an adult and a child to be the same person at different ages. The kid is in a classroom, and there are a number of other children, either extras or principals who are in the background of that classroom with him. When I was doing the casting the agency said, "We need to get some extras, and some kids who will be principals, and we won't have time for casting. Submit a package of pictures to us so we can pick and choose." So I said, "You want ten-year-olds, right?" And they said, "Yes." And I said, "You want white, black, Hispanic, oriental?" And they said, "No, just white." And I said, "Why?" And they said, "Gee, I don't know, let me check." So he called the agency and they said, "Well, sure, give us an ethnic mix." A lot of times they just don't think.

There is an analogous situation with voice-overs. If you listen to voice-overs on TV, you'll hear eighty-five to ninety percent men and ten percent women—the implication being that men sell better than women do, that men carry more authority and weight.

Is that really true?

No, not really. Market research has shown that a woman's voice can sell as well as or even better than a man's. When you're dealing with certain products, there are going to be certain obvious choices. When you're talk-ing about tires gripping the road, or shaving—masculine, macho products—I don't disagree with a man's voice. Everything is demographics, and they sell to who they think is going to buy, and women don't go out and buy cases of beer; men do.

Are you able in your casting of voice-overs sometimes to introduce the possibility of a woman spokesperson rather than a man?

Yes. That happens. And many times the agency is very honest: They call and say, "Well, we are doing a voice-over. It's a man or a woman; we don't know. Bring them both in, and we'll play them against each other." The women come in, and they get so psyched out, they say, "Men are here— great. I have no chance for this at all." In that case—a Liz Claiborne perfume spot—a woman actually got it. The woman's voice was better for it than the man's voice. I personally like women doing voice-overs better than men, because most women do not have this edge or this tendency to hard-sell that many men do have. If I listen to a woman's voice, it's more palatable to my ear, more easy listening than many men.

I'd like to talk about how we present ourselves in auditions. What about dressing for the part—how important is it?

It's pretty important. Advertising people have tunnel vision. Directors don't, creative people don't, but corporate people do. They want to see it on the screen. If I'm auditioning a spokesman, and it's a jacket-and-tie or suit-and-tie situation, and the guy comes in and he's fantastic but he's wearing a T-shirt, he doesn't have a chance in hell of getting the job. So dressing the part really does help—if you can get the instructions on who you are supposed to be.

To what extent should a performer carry this? On the West Coast I know people who drive around with their car trunks full of wigs and costumes and sporting gear.

My viewpoint is that it is so competitive, any edge you can ever get . . .

So it's not a bad idea for a doctor to come in with a white coat and stethoscope?

Absolutely not. I appreciate that. You know you're auditioning against all these other people; if you have an edge that way, take it. The casting director can always say, "Don't worry about it; it's not that important." And maybe it's not, but at least go for it. That's what separates the people who get the job from the people who audition well but don't get the job.

What about memorizing the copy—is it a good idea?

No, it's not.

Why not?

Well, it depends on whether it's long copy. If it's just a line or two, I think it's a good idea to memorize the lines. If it's fifteen or thirty seconds of wall-to-wall copy, I think it's not a very good idea to memorize the copy in the original audition, because you lock yourself into your own idea, and it's hard to have the flexibility to shift gears.

What about handling cue cards? What do you do if the cue card is not near the camera, or if you can't read it?

If an actor can't read the cue card but they are better without glasses, they say their name without glasses. I keep the camera on them for a few seconds so that the client can get a good physical image of what they look like without the glasses, and then they can put their glasses on and read the cue card.

Let's talk for a minute about slates. How important is the actor's personality when introducing himself or herself on tape before the dialogue or the action begins? If the audition is wonderful but the introduction isn't upbeat, how much does this hurt the person's chances?

This really is a bigger question than just slates. The attitude that I like most is when an actor comes in, they do their work, and they leave. And that's it. There are people who come in and have these cutesy ways of presenting themselves or saying their names.

To me a good slate is just saying your name. It does not have to be in character, and it doesn't have to have anything extra to it. Slating your name has nothing to do with the audition, as far as what will get you the job is concerned. I've never seen anybody get a job from an interesting slate. I've seen people lose jobs from stupid slates.

What are some other mistakes that actors commonly make in auditions?

The waiting room sometimes becomes some kind of social club. You find that you see the same people over and over again, you cultivate relationships and friendships, and I find the people coming in are unprepared because they are out there schmoozing and having fun. And when they come in I say, "Have you looked at the copy?" And they say, "Oh, let me look at it now." And that drives me crazy.

What should they have done to prepare the copy?

You get in, you read the script, you look at the storyboard if they have it posted, and you come in with a strong idea of what you think is right and what you want to do.

And listen to the casting director, who should have good solid input either to reinforce what you're doing or to give you enough time to make your own adjustment and do what is required.

Do you ever make the final decision on who gets cast in a commercial?

Sometimes the client will ask me to recommend people. In commercial-land, though, it doesn't happen very often. Casting directors have very little power, and it's a very common misconception among actors that the casting director has this kind of power. I just get them in the audition, I send in the tape and let the client pick, set up the callbacks and let the client pick again, and that's it. I have very little input.

Pat Sweeney

P *at Sweeney is an independent casting director whose company casts commercials and industrial films.*

How did you get into casting in the first place?

I started out as an agent, basically a models' agent, and the burnout rate if you work with models is exceptional. Their entire lives depend on the way they look, not on any kind of acting ability, and they're very insecure people. When I decided that I'd had enough, I just quit. A director I had met through that offered me a job casting. I said I only knew models, not actors, but he told me not to worry about it, that he would take me through it. The first two people I booked were Brandon Maggart and George Irving—which is not bad for a first job. It just built from there. My director friend recommended me to other people. I started going to theater and showcases. I got to know the agents, which was very helpful, and I just moved on from there.

It was something you could do twenty years ago, but I don't think you could get away with that now—going in totally blind and knowing nothing.

Is it important for someone who's casting to have a background as a performer?

I don't think it does any harm, but I don't think it's a necessity. People who were performers and become casting people can find it very hard because it's difficult giving up wanting to perform. The one person I hired who was an

ex-performer started building up a resentment against the actors coming in;
she really could not handle it because basically she still wanted to be
performing. If you are a performer and think you want to go into casting,
you have to be really sure that the desire to perform is out of your system.
Otherwise it's not going to work for you.

How many actors do you see for the average commercial you cast?

I'd say forty to fifty. Because of the state of the industry and everybody being
so insecure, it's gotten to the point where quantity is almost more important
than quality. Not quite, but almost. I do have some directors who will say
they don't have to see the entire city of New York, and I really appreciate
that.

**What have the major changes in commercials casting been over the
years, and what effect have they had on actors?**

With the mergers of the advertising agencies, and the economy the way it
is, the pie is smaller, and more people are trying to cut slices out of it. I
think it's a lot tougher now for an actor than it was twenty years ago—even
five years ago.

You know that cliché—"Don't quit your day job"—well, it's true. One of
the ways actors are supporting themselves is through word processing. It's
something that can be done at night, and it pays well. In fact, a couple of
actors walk around with beepers on, and their calls are not for interviews
but from a word-processing company. It pays top dollar, they can do it at
night, and it leaves their days free. They don't have to be waiters and deal
with the public.

**Of the forty to fifty actors you call in for an average spot, how many do
you usually call back?**

That is also something that's gotten a bit out of control. It used to be that
the director made the choices, or the director and the agency people got
together and made a communal choice. Let's say there were three characters; I would bring back four people for each role. Now what I find is that
the director makes his decision but he's afraid to make a move, so his list is
very long. Then the art director makes his choice, the copywriter makes his
choice, the producer makes his choice, and then the client makes his
choice. You're called back several times, and it's almost like a full session
sometimes.

If you look at the price of a commercial now, it's three hundred to four
hundred thousand dollars for thirty seconds of film. Years ago you could do
a commercial for one hundred thousand. The actor is very important for

that thirty seconds of film, and it's no longer a decision made by one person. Now it's a decision made by a committee.

What I tell actors is to go in and do the best you can and walk out. Don't come out saying, "I should have . . . I could have . . . I might have . . ." You'll drive yourself crazy. Just go in and do the best you can and, if possible, teach yourself to forget about it until the next audition.

What are the biggest mistakes that actors regularly make in auditions?

Not focusing—not paying attention to what they're doing. The copy is always out there for actors to look at, yet I'm always having actors come in and say they haven't looked at the copy. That's your career up there, not mine—although I can end up looking bad because you can't do a good job.

Auditions are set up every ten minutes, and if it's only a couple of lines they'll set it up every five minutes. You're not going to get twelve rehearsals; you're lucky if you get even one.

Another thing I advise actors to do is go to the bathroom or down the hall and read the copy out loud so you can hear it. What you hear coming out of your mouth is not what you hear in your head. They're two different things.

Is it a good idea for actors to memorize the copy?

There are two schools of thought on that. I say no. If you come early to an audition and memorize the copy, when you come into the audition room you don't look at the cue card because you've got the copy memorized. You get halfway through the audition—and this happens to everyone, no matter how long you've been doing it—and you forget a line. The cue card is no good to you because you've never even looked at it and have no idea where you are. If you do memorize the copy, still look at the cue card inside. The way things are placed outside and on the cue card are different.

I also find that when I have clients with me at the auditions, the cue cards change throughout the day. As they hear actor after actor saying those lines, they start to make changes in the copy. The copy you have outside might have been changed several times.

Also, some actors who memorize the copy have it locked in their heads and can't get it out when changes are made in it. That's another problem you have with memorizing copy.

What about dressing for the part? How important is that?

It's more important in California than it is in New York. When I put out breakdowns, I specify: young mom, young dad, casual.

Always ask the agent what you are supposed to be. A lumberjack? House-wife? Businessman? If he's a good agent, he'll tell you. They want you to get the job as well.

Another thing, by the way: always bring eight-by-tens.

If you are called back, should you wear the same thing?

Not really. Some actors do it because they think it's good luck, that the outfit was lucky for them. It's not necessary, though.

Also, don't go out and buy new clothes for an audition. You're not comfortable in them yet, and it shows.

Are there certain kinds of clothes—patterns or colors—that it's not a good idea to wear for an on-camera audition?

Videotape is very weird, and I don't know the technical reasons for it, but sometimes bright reds have a tendency to bleed around the shoulders. Checks might vibrate. I don't get crazy over it, but a lot of the time we are screening these tapes at nine at night when people have the attention span of a flea. They're tired, and I have found that when someone has on a jacket that is vibrating like crazy, instead of watching what the person is doing, you watch the jacket vibrate. That's why I say to avoid bright reds and checks—not all checks, but that's something you find out as you audition.

Are there any general tips about makeup you can offer?

Definitely use makeup: some foundation, some blush, some lipstick. Don't put it on with a trowel, because it looks terrible on videotape. But don't expect to look great with absolutely no makeup, either.

If your agent tells you not to wear makeup for an audition, should you take him at his word?

Yes, he's saying that for a reason. At the session it will usually be explained to you.

Let's talk briefly about etiquette at the audition. Are there certain things actors do that strike you as rude or self-defeating? I'm talking here about common-sense etiquette, not how they read the copy.

I am known as a person who shoots from the hip. I am not known for being subtle, especially when it comes to my office. I don't know why some people do things they would never do at home. I spent a lot of money on my office, and when I walk into one of the waiting areas and find an actor with his shoes up on the couch, I don't care how many people are in the room; I'll tell him to get his feet off my couch.

Respect your fellow performers. The way my office is set up, I have three studios up front and two in the back. Even though the studios themselves are soundproof, there are reception areas in front of each studio, and the soundproofing is not perfect by a long shot. You've got to remember that you are in a business environment. Sometimes I have to come out because everyone is yelling and screaming and carrying on. Everyone is having a good time, but that's not helping the actor who's inside auditioning.

I ran across something recently that struck me as really weird. A girl came in and auditioned. The director explained what he wanted. The girl did it and then went out and proceeded to give her interpretation to all the actresses in the reception room. That was her choice, but two of the actresses decided they couldn't do it and left. Now her interpretation was totally different from what the director was trying to get across. A bit of advice: Go in and hear for yourself; don't listen to what someone else has to say to you.

Also, you're going to run into a lot of copy that is badly written. Keep your mouth shut! A girl was sitting in the waiting area next to a guy she assumed was an actor. She started doing a number on the copy, and I have no qualms about admitting that it was bad. But the man she assumed was an actor was actually the copywriter, who had gone outside for a breather. Needless to say, she didn't get a callback. Watch what you say in the reception area, the elevator, and the bathroom.

Another thing about etiquette: The receptionists at all of these casting offices have a very hard job. Not only do they deal with the phones, but they're typing up cue sheets, dealing with the actors, dealing with the clients. Be nice to them, because they are tomorrow's casting directors and they have memories like elephants. It's part of the job. Look around you and use common sense. If the receptionist has a room that's overflowing, has a phone in one hand while three others are ringing, and is talking to someone, don't ask to borrow the stapler. Be aware of your surroundings.

What about when you get into the audition room?

An agent said this, I didn't—but I think it's a very good way of putting it: You've got to work the room from the time you walk in. That's an old nightclub saying—"work the room." Whether it's just the casting director in there or a line of clients sitting on the side of the room, you have got to be on from the time you walk in. You have to acknowledge everyone there—I don't mean shaking everyone's hand—and you've got to be up and have energy and look like you really want to be there, like you really care about the job. It's energy. It's really caring about being there and having a positive attitude.

The worst thing ever invented for the actor is the fast-forward button on the VCR. In theater and movies you have an hour and a half, sometimes two hours, to establish a character. In commercials you've got thirty seconds. As a start, the visual has to be right. You've got to smile. I've seen them fast-forward past a slate. The slates are very important. Everything you do in that room is important.

What's the best way to do a slate?

"Hi, I'm Judith Searle." Don't get cute on slates. There's no reason for it. Forget about "Good morning" and that kind of stuff. By the time they're looking at it, they don't care.

One of the things we always do in our office on the slate is hands, because they can often save a lot of money using your hands instead of a hand model if your hands are in good shape. It's not going to cost you the job if your hands aren't in good shape, but they always want to see them. If I hear one more time, "Oh, I didn't get a manicure," I'll scream. Keep your hands in good shape. It can only help you.

Is there such a thing as a general commercial type?

Nope, not anymore. Years ago there used to be what they call a P & G type: blond, blue-eyed, middle-American. It still exists—the blond, blue-eyed P & G types will always work—but things have opened up considerably.

Enough people in this industry are going to type you, so don't type yourself. I have on my size cards a blank for age range, and that's something I'm going to strike, because everybody sees age differently. I may see somebody as nineteen, while the director sees her as twenty-four. I just say not to fill it out anymore.

Do you keep files of actors' résumés?

Most of my stuff is in my head. In the office we keep eight-by-tens of SAG members and non-SAG members, but primarily SAG members. If an agent books you as an extra on a commercial, the client has to pay an extra ten percent. If you've got forty or fifty extras in a commercial, that's a lot of money. They would rather pay a flat fee to me, and if they need two or three extras I can just pull the pictures out and do that for them. That's primarily what I use that file for.

Are there any clues you can give us on how to approach acting for commercials?

Let the thought process happen on your face. In other words, you have to think about what you're going to say. You're not an actor; you're a real person, and this is the first time someone has approached you with a camera, and the words would not come out that smoothly. That doesn't mean you stumble or sound retarded. Just let the thought process show on your face.

Somebody who has done nothing but theater can find that very difficult because they play to the mezzanine. When you're working with that video camera in that small room or if you're doing film, it's just you and that camera. I always say that less is more. You are not trying to hit the mezzanine; you're just trying to hit that small camera.

Are there certain faces that the camera is in love with?

Of course. There are the model faces that the camera definitely loves. If a client cannot afford models and asks me to get a beautiful actress, that's terrific. However, there is a difference between the way an actress relates to a camera and the way a model relates to one. It's very difficult to explain; you just have to see it. A model relates to a camera like she's having a love affair with it. An actress treats the camera like an extension of her performance. I have yet to see a model look bad on videotape or film. She can walk in with no makeup and look like a slob, but once that camera is turned on she comes alive. It could be attitude, but there's something incredible there when that camera rolls.

Is there anything a person in your position can do—or indeed should do—to have an effect on the whole problem of minority casting?

If I get a breakdown, especially a large breakdown—a storyboard with a list of characters—I can always say, "Any blacks? Hispanics? Any Asians? Any minorities?" That's about as far as I can go. I don't even think the advertising agencies can fight it. If somebody really wants to fight this, they have to go to Procter & Gamble; they have to go to Bristol-Myers; they have to go to Colgate-Palmolive. That's who makes the decision on that.

Let's talk for a minute about pictures, résumés, and composites. Do you prefer a straight head shot with a résumé, or do you ever like to see a composite for an actor?

I think composites are very L.A. In New York it's eight-by-tens. The way I describe pictures when talking to actors is that it's the kind of picture you'd send home to your mother. You may not love it, but she'll adore it because it looks just like you. It's smiling; it's out there.

Any advice about choosing a photographer?

Talk to other actors as you're going around. Then don't just go see one photographer, but also don't see twenty. I always recommend seeing three. Check their books and check them—see whether you like them and get along with them. Still photography is hard, and if you don't like the photographer it's going to show in your pictures. There are some people out there who are better with men; some are better with women. See about three photographers and remember: Cheap is not necessarily bad, and expensive is not necessarily good.

What should be on a résumé?

I'm not a big believer in lying on résumés. Somebody is going to pick up on it, and it'll get you in trouble.

Don't forget to put your Social Security number on there; once you're in a union, everything is cleared through your Social Security number, not your union number.

Never, ever, put your address on a résumé.

What about your home phone number?

Only if you have a machine on it.

Whatever special abilities you put on there, just be sure you can do them and do them well. If a sports thing comes up for a specific commercial, ask the agent how well you have to do it. If it's Sunday-afternoon touch-football, that's terrific. If it's professional hockey, you had better know what you're doing.

Let's talk for a minute about agents. How many do you regularly call for a typical casting session?

Probably about eight.

And would it be the same eight, time after time?

Yes, because they know me, they know my taste, and I trust their taste. There are always new people coming into the industry, and I don't have time to see them all. The agents do. That's their job. That's how they make their money. They'll find somebody new, and if they're someone I've worked with and trust, and they say I have to see so-and-so, I'll usually say yes, or else look that person up in the *Players' Guide*.

Do you think it's a good idea for an actor to be in the *Guide*?

I do think it's a good idea, because when I'm stuck on a job and not getting it from the agents and not getting it from my own brain, I start thumbing through the *Guide*.

On the West Coast, the *Academy Players Directory* has much the same function. Now, are you willing to name the eight agencies you regularly call?

Oh yes. Abrams, Phoenix, Cunningham, Don Buchwald, Jacobson-Wilder-Kesten, J. Michael Bloom, William Morris, and Schiffman, Ekman, Morrison and Marx, known as SEM&M. That's pretty much it. The others you call when the job is in trouble.

So an actor looking for an agent that gets most of the calls might start by getting in touch with those agencies?

Rarely will you get an agent on the phone. The best advice is to send a picture and résumé with a cover letter, but not a long cover letter. And don't get cute. One picture I got had stardust in it. I had on a black skirt that day, and that picture went right in the trash. A good follow-up is a postcard with your picture on it.

Treat it like a business. Write down who you've sent mailings to and when you mailed them. Say a month later you do your first commercial or your first under-five-line role on a soap. Get your postcards out. Everybody loves a working actor. However you choose to do it—index cards or whatever works best for you—this is show business, but still it's a business. The product you're marketing is yourself.

In Los Angeles, almost all actors are signed with an agency, but in New York many free-lance. In your view which is better—to sign with one agent or play the field here?

If somebody is signed, I don't get them submitted from six people. If an actor is hot and still free-lancing, I'm going to get submissions from six agents. The problem is not as bad as it used to be because lists are now faxed to me, and there's always a time on the sheet. I have to take whoever I get the submission from first.

I fluctuate between signed and unsigned. Sometimes I think it's better for the actor to be signed, because he's going to get better coverage. If you're signed with an agent, that agent is going to make sure most of the stuff you go out on is network or, if it's a local spot, that there's no conflict. The agent is going to watch your career more.

If you are unsigned, they are going to send you out on everything, and it's up to you to make that decision. Do I want to do a local credit card? That will be your responsibility, not the agent's. For a signed client, he will take the responsibility and say that he doesn't want you to do it because it knocks you out of the credit card market.

Agents do not sign people that quickly. They want to see a bit of a track record first. The good thing about free-lancing is that you can find out which agents are going to work the most for you.

If an actor without an agent sent you a picture and résumé, do you ever do general auditions?

Nope, I just don't have the time. Very few casting directors will ever do general auditions. That's why we rely on agents; they will do more than we will.

Do you ever attend Equity-waiver theater, workshops, or showcases?

No, I don't have the time. Sometimes some of the new kids in the office will cover that, but that's more important to give to the agents—not that the agents themselves will attend. When you're sending out a flyer, be sure that the theater is air-conditioned if it's during the summer. If you're doing a show in Secaucus, New Jersey, don't expect the agents to come, because they won't. If you are in the third act of a lousy play, don't invite people. Do it for yourself and for the experience. Be selective. Use common sense. Be careful.

Let's talk for a minute about commercial workshops. For quite a few years, you've given one that's highly reputed among actors. What can you say about commercial workshops in general? What can they do for an actor, especially one just starting out?

The classes give you on-camera experience. You can look up there and see yourself. You have to go in with an open mind and realize that you may have to cut your hair or do something else. Depending on the class, you can have a lot of on-camera time, and that allows you to become familiar and comfortable with that camera. To be able to see yourself up there and get instant critiques can give you confidence. There are a lot of classes out there, so if it's something you want to do, check it out.

What's the best way of checking it out?

Talk to other actors. The way we set it up, I don't permit auditing of classes because I think it's disruptive. Our classes are kept to a maximum of ten. Everyone in the class is already an actor. I will not take people off the street because I think you have to have some background to pull from in order to do this. I will prescreen just to see what you look like and what your résumé is. If somebody comes in and I know it's just not going to happen, I don't want them to spend the money.

What are your biggest frustrations with the casting process?

I'd like to go back to the good old days when it wasn't decision by committee. Nobody has the ultimate say-so anymore. Most agencies will present two sets of actors: first choice and what we call backup, and they have to be just as comfortable with the backup. That's the biggest frustration.

You also have a lot of new directors and producers coming into the business who don't know how to handle actors. It's frustrating to see an actor I know is good not being given proper direction. If you don't understand what a director is saying, tell him you don't quite understand what he needs. Put the onus on yourself, not on him. It's political. Common sense.

Alice Whitfield

Alice Whitfield is President/CEO of Real-To-Reel Recording, Inc., where she writes, casts, produces and directs radio commercials and TV voice-overs. She is the author of Take It From the Top!: How to Earn Your Living in Radio & TV Voice-Overs. *She teaches workshops on voice-overs in both New York and Los Angeles.*

How did you get into casting?

By mistake! Back when I was in theater and whatnot, I did everything once and then I left everything after being very successful. I went to the next thing, and the next thing was advertising. I started writing, and would hear people in my mind as I wrote, so I made sure that I also got involved in the casting. This was back in the time when you could do more than one thing and people wouldn't look at you strangely.

It's become a very compartmentalized business, and people's thinking has become compartmentalized. If you come up for something and you do a child's voice and you leave and the next casting session comes in and they say, "Let's bring in what's-her-name," they'll say, "Oh no, she just does a child's voice." Nobody thinks past the first thing you ever do.

Is a background as a performer particularly useful for a casting director?

Yes—at least from the point of view of empathy with the performer. For the most part, people who are casting today have been moved up from the secretarial pool. That is why, in part, a lot of actors are very pissed off when they go to these auditions and these little kids who are chewing gum say, "Will you try it again, only different?" The actor, who's been a seasoned performer for twenty-five years, says, "Who is this person?"

You must keep files of voice-over performers. How do you categorize voices?

I have a computer program with about thirty categories, and you know something? After designing this elaborate program, I've used it three times—because what happens is that there are crossovers and there are exceptions. I have a little sheet I used to give out. Everyone who came up filled one out so I could put them in the computer. People would check off everything because they think they can do anything—dialects, upscale, light, MOR . . .

What is MOR?

Middle-of-the-road. That's someone who can sell white bread to a nun.

Peter Thomas is MOR. Very credible, straight across the board. He's a deliverer of information.

Deep, gravelly, light—there are about thirty different categories. But then you get someone who has a rasp, but he's also light. He does have a smile, and he can be comedic. That's why it's vital that casting people give actors every chance to try different things.

Do you classify voices at all in terms of age ranges?

You can't really do it that way. Each script is different, each profile is different.

Some people can go from being late teens and early twenties to being an old person. It's amazing, but there are people who can do it. Voice-overs, for the most part—radio, not TV voice-overs—is theater of the mind. You have to create a visual image with your instrument.

A lot of people, when they see an actor, may think that person's too old. Too old for what? We're talking sound here! You may have gray hair, but that doesn't mean you can't do a twenty-year-old. Sometimes the timbre in someone's voice is older, but they probably had that when they were twenty-eight. Voice-over casting people should close their eyes and listen!

How many voice-over tapes, demo tapes from actors, do you keep on file?

I have loads of them. Why do I keep them on file when I rarely listen to them? Because I'm a creature of habit and I have a lot of space.

Might there be a situation where you'd play them for a client who's considering a voice?

Here's what will happen. Sometimes instead of casting sessions they'll ask me to do a talent search. It's different from legitimate casting sessions: I can either go to some work that they've done for us at the studio that I already have on file, or to an audition they came in for, or I can get to their voice-over demo reel and take a section or two.

Understand something—casting directors will pull tapes of people they *know*. They will not pull tapes from people they don't know. Why should they? Part of that is valid. How can they recommend anyone unless they've seen or heard their work or used them?

But then how can somebody whose tape you have not heard break in?

It's terrible, but you have to know someone like me. You could be the greatest person on earth, but I'd never know it. But if someone in my profession, someone for whom I have respect, called me up and said there was someone who was just fabulous and I must hear that person, you bet I would!

What about house tapes submitted by agents? How useful are those for an actor? Do you pay attention to house tapes?

For the most part, those tapes go to out-of-town clients. Those clients will call up an agent and send the agent a script. They say they'd like the agency to send the agency reel so they can pick some people to do it. What happens? One of two things: First the agent will say, "Listen, I'll call those people into my office and have them read. I'll pick some people; no problem." It doesn't cost the client. The agent is hoping that they'll pick one or two of their clients, so it's worth it to them to have people come in and read. And then the agent says they couldn't get Joe Schmoe to come in—but listen to him on our demo reel.

It's important to be on the agent reel. You can be with an agent, but you may not be on the master reel. That could take a couple of years. I know, because I do agents' master reels. I know people who have been signed with agents for a long time, but they're not on that reel.

What advice would you offer to people who have no experience doing voice-overs and who want to break in? Should they take a class? What's the best way to get experience?

Breaking into this business is about as easy as trying to get into the baker's union or the jingle singers' group. Unless you're very close to someone who is *up* there, it's almost impossible. I don't care how good you are.

I warn you in advance: Do *not* go to schools. Do not spend your money on school. Find someone in the business who is offering a class. Find someone in the business you respect, and ask them.

Is there anything actors can do on their own at home—say, with a tape recorder—to work in this area and learn something?

No. I could say listen to television commercials, listen to radio commercials, but I don't think anyone is objective enough to be able to say, "Ah, yes, I sound just like Cybill Shepherd. I even look like her." That's what happens. You sit there and listen and say to yourself that you can do that. Your hearing is very introspective. It's very hard for you—it's very hard for everyone to sit there and step out of themselves.

There are a number of voice-over workshops. With somebody that's good, an experienced voice-over person, can that be a useful thing?

A lot of people who have tremendous experience are terrible teachers. And people who solely teach for a living are out of the mainstream of what's really going on. Working performers doing the teaching—those are the ones I would be more apt to go with, but not all are good teachers. You have to be able to communicate, to motivate, and to be goddamn honest. Nobody wants to hear it's a terrible business and that few are working.

Only a very few are making a lot of money. Nobody just ekes out a living on voice-overs. Either you're rolling in it, or you're not. That's the nature of our business.

Who are the people who are working, who have the six-figure incomes from voice-overs? What percentage are men? Women?

There's an imbalance, but not *such* an imbalance. For spokespeople, usually it's a male announcer talking. If it's a sitcom spot, a spot that has a young girl saying "really" and "awesome," at the end of the commercial it's usually the man. That's where there's the imbalance. But in the situation part of the spot—and those people get paid just what the announcer does—there's no imbalance. There are a lot of women—but as spokespeople, not as many women, even after all those reports came back saying women are just as credible, if not more so. It's getting better, but not great.

Are there certain agents that you will call regularly for voices?

Don Buchwald; J. Michael Bloom; Cunningham-Escott-Dipene; Abrams Artists; Jacobson-Wilder-Kesten.

How do you generally conduct auditions? Could you tell us what a typical session might be like?

When I get a script, what I will do is call for the people I want to see. On many occasions, but not all, I will also say, "Listen, is there somebody new in this category I haven't heard?" I also go to my list of people I've met in all these seminars and classes and through doing people's demo reels. If I feel they are competitive enough, I will call them in—and damn if they don't often book the job!

When somebody comes into your office, how much time do they have to look at a script before they read?

As much as they want. There are certain people who really do need a lot of time. Other people just look at it and spend the rest of the time playing around. Some people just look at it and say, "Let's go."

If a person needs more time, I just let the next person on the sign-in sheet go ahead.

How many takes, typically, will an actor get to do once they're inside your studio?

I won't put anything on tape unless the actor feels really comfortable and I feel it's worth taping. I do dry runs. They'll run through it once and I'll maybe give them some direction, and they'll say, "Let's put one down. You may get lucky." So I'll put one down. I will usually do more than one take to submit to the client, which means I could do three takes and just choose two to send.

So you will edit that tape?

Nothing leaves without being edited—nothing.

Will some of the people who auditioned get edited off the tape entirely?

Absolutely.

Are there certain mistakes you commonly see actors make in voice-over auditions?

There are people who sit there scribbling, and I just have to say, "Stop that! What are you doing?" Walking in and starting to mark your copy is the biggest joke in the world. You could be writing down mistakes, and what you've done is reinforce them.

Another annoying thing is when someone says, "I went to school and they said to stand 2.3 inches from the mike." I ask them, "What? Did you go to engineering school or did you go to school to learn how to do voice-overs?"

So people come in and they mark their copy, and then they come in and measure how far they are from the microphone. *What are you touching my microphone for, you dope? You're supposed to speak into it, not touch it!*

I know you've put together a lot of demo reels for actors. Assuming that an actor hasn't done anything and wants to put together a demo reel, what should be on it?

You have to do what you do best, done the best way possible. What I try to do is pull copy that does have some strong accounts—good regional things. I wouldn't do something everyone has heard, because people would know it wasn't you. I'd find things that are general enough that people wouldn't know that you didn't actually do them.

Each person is individual. Character voices—not cartoon voices but character voices—are very helpful if you do them well, to break up your tape. Animated voices are fine as long as they are part of a commercial. If you're an animated voice in a commercial, you may put that between some of your other stuff. It helps to break it up, and no matter who you are, you still sound like you. Something in that voice is always you.

It's good to have variety. That tape is your portfolio. I'd start your reel off with something that pulls them in. I won't start with a very straight narrative. It just doesn't work. Something that has a great musical punch to it makes everyone's ears perk.

So music helps?

Oh yes. It's tremendous. I use it a lot.

What about dialogue? Should you have a dialogue with another actor? Should I have something with a man?

It depends. Let's say it's a comic thing or a Molsenesque thing. Sure. It's not the first thing and it's not the second thing. Maybe it's the fourth thing.

How long should a reel be?

About two minutes and fifteen seconds of sheer dynamite. Tops.

And how many spots should be on those two minutes and fifteen seconds?

We don't know. We could start off with something that's twelve or sixteen seconds and then, boom, the second thing might be something really short, like an I.D. The next one could be a longer piece. The pacing is imperative. It's always dictated by the piece. I have no idea until I listen to it. It's like a patchwork quilt. You're not going to put the orange with the puce. I lay out all the pieces and start to see what works best. Maybe I'll do a running gag throughout that just keeps coming back in. My reels are always characterized by something fun in them.

What about my making a demo reel by myself? Would that ever work?

Making a demo reel by yourself would be like performing an appendectomy on yourself. You'd have an ass for a doctor and a fool for a patient! It's a waste of tape and money.

Do most voice-over actors do both commercial and animation voices, or are they usually specialized?

No. Animation is a whole different thing.

What are the requirements for animation, specifically?

A voice that doesn't sound human. You turn it into something completely different. You're no longer reading a piece of copy. You're creating a character. That person stands there and begins to read the script, and the animator is there, and the writer is there; they're all sitting there, and things just come out of it. It really is a combined effort. Either the actor plays a very strong part in making an identification for that character, or the writer might say, "This is a witch, but there's something very sweet about her. She really doesn't want to be mean. She has a conscience." So the actor gives her a life.

The guy or gal who's doing the animated voice is making him- or herself out to be a total fool. It's embarrassing. What kind of grownup person does this? These people who go in there to do animation literally leave their dignity down the block. It's very brave—I don't think I could do it.

What percentage of the voice-overs would you say are cast in New York as opposed to California?

I would say sixty-five to seventy percent. What they'll also do is cast in New York and shoot out of town. They'll cast in L.A. and shoot in L.A., but I've gotten a lot of things that were shot in L.A. and they came back here for the voice-overs. For the most part, more of the work is done here in New York—voice-overs and commercials in general. Chicago is getting pretty good, but a lot of times they'll come to New York for the final voice-over.

How many voices do you generally consider for a given role?

What I consider and what I know the client will consider are two different things. What I will never do is overcast. If you give them too many good ones, they'll hate everybody.

What is the optimum number for you to call in?

For an announcer's session, seventeen. Not all of them show up, so you have to cover yourself. I'm very specific, and I don't want people to sit and wait. I will not overbook. Sixteen or seventeen, tops.

And out of that, how many would you present to your client?

If they're all good, sixteen or seventeen. If it's a two-character, maybe twelve sets. Sometimes when I think only six people are good, that's what goes on the tape. If they ask why I only sent six, I say, "Because they're the six best!"

Suppose you've got a dialogue situation that you're casting and one person gives a terrific reading and the other gives a bad one?

I say, "Thank you. John, would you wait? I'd like you to read with Sally." I will never allow an actor who's good to suffer at the mouth of an actor who isn't. It's not fair.

What are the biggest mistakes that actors make at voice-over auditions?

Trying to be smart. Trying to do too much. Trying to be clever. Trying to be tough. I can give you a list of the things they do. The nicest thing an actor can do is to come in and ask what you're looking for.

When you walk in, be who you are. If you do a myriad of things, find a tactful way of letting the casting person know about it.

Are there technical mistakes that actors make that they may not know about?

Yes. When the actor is asked by the engineer to give a level, the actor should start reading the script as if it were a real reading. Don't say "Testing: one, two, three" or any useless chatter, because you're not going to say that when you're doing the reading. Read what's in the script. It's the only way the engineer can set the proper levels.

To what extent should you focus on the technical problems? Or should you ignore them and just do your performance?

Just do your performance. Be careful with your *p*'s so you don't pop them into the mike.

Is there anything a casting person can or should do at least to explore the possibility of expanding categories—for example, recommending that a spokesman role might be done by a woman, even though it's written for a man?

You always suggest: "Gee, this is a great spot. Did you ever think of maybe a woman doing it?" I do that, and I assume that others do. There are people who to this day think that announcers must be male.

What are your major frustrations with the casting process? If you could change something, what would it be?

Oh boy. It's a twofold thing. I think that actors want very much to be loved and appreciated. It takes an awful lot to go in for an audition, whether it be an animated voice or just your voice. A lot of actors do come in with an attitude, and a lot of casting people are stupid. Those are the casting people who did not learn from the masters who understood the process.

I'd like more tolerance from casting people and less compartmentalization in saying someone can only do this or that. I do that myself sometimes.

People aren't nice enough. That goes for actors, too. Even though your ass is on the line, be nice when you go in there. It never hurts. Just remember—whatever you may think, the casting person really wants you to book the job. After all, they called you in.

PART THREE
CASTING:
A PERFORMER'S PERSPECTIVE

Casting: A Performer's Perpective

Over and over, while interviewing casting directors, I found myself wishing I'd had an opportunity to hear what they were saying at the start of my own career. Perhaps because acting is such a competitive field, perhaps because that elusive, critical thing we call star quality is so unquantifiable, a lot of folklore, even superstition, has developed around our profession.

The most valuable piece of advice to come out of these interviews, to my mind, is the casting directors' unanimous insistence that we treat acting as a business. "Most people are confused about the expression *show business*," says Ross Brown, a West Coast casting director. "Most people think it's one word, but it's not—it's two. It's a business, folks, and if you don't take care of business, you're not going to be able to show anything."

An actor who is businesslike will read *Backstage, Variety* and the *Ross Reports* when based in New York, and *Daily Variety* or the *Hollywood Reporter* (or both), along with *Dramalogue*, in Los Angeles. Keeping up with new plays, films, and television shows is essential. If you're being submitted for a role on a soap opera, you'll want to watch the show before you audition.

Business people are constantly networking, and actors who treat their profession as a business will find networking opportunities if they join the Academy of Television Arts & Sciences, The American Film Institute, or Women in Film. If you are a union member, SAG, AFTRA, and Equity will make it possible for you to meet casting directors and other professionals in the industry.

Photographs

"If you don't have a picture and résumé, you haven't even started yet," says Mike Fenton, a veteran West Coast film casting director. Your eight-by-ten head shot (black-and-white) is the key to your career, in a very real sense. It will get you meetings with agents, with casting directors, and finally with the producers and directors who can give you roles. The picture, everyone agrees, must look like you—casting people overwhelmingly prefer a photograph that is straightforward, ungimmicky, and unretouched.

"A picture that intrigues me is somebody I will want to see on a general," says Barbara Claman, who casts films, television, and commercials in Los Angeles. The eyes, everyone agrees, are the crucial element in a good photograph: your eyes must be alive.

Interview several photographers—and see their work—before making an appointment for a shooting session. As always, networking can be an important source of leads.

Some commercial casting directors on the West Coast value composite photographs because they show the actor from several different angles. But the East Coast casting people I talked to have a real aversion to composites, so I'd advise against using them in New York unless you're going for a modeling job. Even in Los Angeles, those who prefer composites are also interested in your résumé, so attach one to any composite you submit. Directors of commercials—many of whom come from feature film backgrounds—want to know that people they hire for commercials are real actors, not just pretty faces.

Since composites are an added expense, I'd suggest you consult your commercial agent before putting one together. Some agencies think they're great and will recommend a printer whose work is good and whose prices are fair; others prefer to use head shots for all submissions.

Résumés

On this point the casting directors are unanimous: Don't lie on your résumé. "If you prevaricate on your résumé," Mike Fenton says, "it can come back and bite you in the bottom—and if it does it leaves teeth marks."

Differences in résumé formats for the East Coast and West Coast reflect the different emphases on the two coasts. New York casting directors are impressed by stage credits, so it makes sense to put those first on any résumé you submit to them, beginning with Broadway shows, then listing off-Broadway, national tours, regional, stock, even (if you're just starting out) college credits. Then list feature films, television, other film (industrial and student films), education, and special skills.

A Los Angeles résumé logically begins with feature film credits, with television second, other film third, and stage fourth. Obviously if you're submitting a résumé to a theater in Los Angeles, you might consider using the format that places stage credits first. I've included my own Los Angeles and New York résumés in appendix B, to show you samples of typical formats.

Commercial casting directors agree that you should *not* list any commercials on your résumé. Because of the situation with commercial "conflicts," you may put yourself out of the running for, say, a Ford commercial if you list a Chevy spot—even one that has been off the air for two years. Most actors use the phrase "Commercial List upon Request," but even that seems unnecessary to me (unless you have a lot of space on your résumé that you're trying to fill up).

Casting directors tell me that the "Special Skills" category is one way to get their attention. If you speak French well, list it (this doesn't mean you've simply studied it for two years in high school); if you juggle or skydive or are a licensed scuba diver, put that on your résumé. If you're a top-flight skier or golfer or tennis player, include that, too. In New York, being able to drive a stick shift automobile is considered a special skill.

If you're just starting out, include under "Training" any college or graduate degrees you have and your field of study (even if it wasn't acting). List any acting programs you have attended (Juilliard, Yale, the Neighborhood Playhouse) as well as private acting teachers or coaches. If you're a musical performer, list singing and dance teachers as well.

Training is something all the casting directors I talked with take seriously, especially on the résumé of a young actor. They're impressed when they see that we're taking scene-study classes or improvisation workshops—it shows that we're trying to develop our craft.

Mailings

The question of how best to submit pictures and résumés to casting directors came up in several interviews. Many actors do mass mailings, and Breakdown Services will even sell you preaddressed mailing labels for casting directors and agents on both coasts. But this kind of shotgun approach may not be very productive. An individually written cover letter—targeting someone who is casting a specific production with a role you feel you are right for—is likely to be a lot more effective. As Mark Simon, who cast the New York company of *Tamara,* puts it, "Without a cover letter, I don't know what to make of it. Tell me what you want."

Also, casting directors don't appreciate actors who ask to borrow their staplers at auditions. Come to the audition with your picture already attached to your résumé. It's not a bad idea to have your name on your photo as well, just in case they do get separated.

Videotapes

All the casting directors I talked with agree that videotapes of an actor's work can be enormously useful. There is much less agreement when it comes to what *kind* of tape, however. Al Onorato, who casts film and television in Los Angeles, says, "If you don't have one, don't manufacture it." Most of the other casting directors feel you should include on a videotape only scenes from films and television shows you've actually done; this may include student films, but not scenes you have had taped at a video production house specifically for use on your demo tape.

On the other hand, Mari Lyn Henry, East Coast director of casting for ABC, suggests that beginning actors go to a high-quality video production house and have scenes put on tape. Such a tape might include two contrasting selections—and, she feels, should be no longer than six minutes. "In our day and age, nobody's going to look at anything longer than that, and some of them will only look at the first thirty seconds."

The way I see it, videotape has become such an important casting tool that any actor who has good film or television footage would be foolish not to go to a first-class professional video editor and have a selection of scenes put together. Many editors who specialize in this kind of work (such as Jan Natarno in Los Angeles) have extensive archives of television shows and may be able to track down footage of your performances that you don't have copies of. A professional editor can also reedit a scene to give more emphasis to you and enhance your performance. This service is well worth the expense involved, since it can get you work.

It's not a good idea to send a casting director an unedited tape of a whole television show or film. They don't have time to fast-forward in search of your performance. And of course you know not to send your only copy of any tape.

Getting an Agent

On both coasts, it's extremely difficult to get an interview or audition with a casting director for film or TV parts unless you're sent by an agent. (A list of agents franchised by the Screen Actors Guild is available from SAG for $1. One of the most important things a good photograph and résumé and an impressive videocassette will do for you is get you an agent, and finding an agent is a major milestone in the life of a working actor. Especially if you live in Los Angeles, your first priority, after getting your picture and résumé together, is to get an agent interested in you.

One reason many actors choose to begin their careers in New York is that it's possible to be seen there for plays and even for commercials *without* being signed with an agent. In fact, many successful commercial actors *choose* to free-lance in the Big Apple. I free-lanced in New York for many years, and I believe I got more auditions—especially for commercials—than I would have if I'd been signed with one agency.

When I moved to Los Angeles, though, it became essential to find both a theatrical agent (a theatrical agent handles film and television as well as stage work) and an agent for commercials. (Though some of the larger agencies have both commercial and theatrical departments, most specialize).

Since I planned to travel back and forth between New York and L.A., I wanted a commercial agent with offices on both coasts—which greatly limited the possible candidates. I already had a good track record doing commercials, so Cunningham-Escott-Dipene was willing to take me on, and I've been with them ever since.

Finding a theatrical agent in L.A. wasn't quite as easy. Before I left New York I wrote to half a dozen agencies to which I had some entrée, either through friends or through contacts I'd made myself when *Hostile Witness* played L.A. I joined an acting workshop and arranged for Fred Amsel to see me in a couple of scenes. Fred had previously worked for an agency that had shown interest in me during the *Hostile Witness* tour nine years earlier; he had just opened his own agency and had not yet signed an actress in my category. He sent me on a few auditions, and we finally signed a contract after I was cast in *Equus* (an audition I'd gotten not through any agent but through the producer, Jim Doolittle, whose theater I performed in during the *Hostile Witness* tour).

Rarely will a theatrical agent sign you without seeing your work, for all the jokes about beautiful young women being promised parts on the basis of something other than their acting abilities. Male or female, if you're young and beautiful, I would strongly advise you not to sign with any theatrical agent who doesn't insist on seeing your work first—a monologue or scene in his or her office, a videotape from a student film you did, a play or workshop you are performing in.

Most agents—like all the casting directors I talked to—try to see plays that showcase the talents of new actors. Performing in a high-quality show at a small theater, either in New York or Los Angeles, is one of the best ways of moving into the category of a working actor who actually earns a living as a performer.

Be careful, though, about inviting agents or casting people to a bad production. Even if you're wonderful in your part, you may be tainted by your association with a show that's painful to watch. I performed in a number of off-off Broadway shows in New York, and soon after I came to L.A. I got a good part in a small-theater production of *Look Back in Anger* that I hoped to invite prospective agents to see. Alas, the show was so poor that I didn't dare invite anyone but my acting coach.

As other actors—and casting directors—will be quick to tell you, not all agents are created equal. The interviews in this book can give you some guidelines as to who the most active (and powerful) agents are; the interviews also suggest ways you can research the subject on your own. The bottom line, of course, is that *any* agent is better than no agent, because— especially in Hollywood—it's virtually impossible to get a reading for a film or television show without being submitted by an agent. Even in New York, where access to stage roles is somewhat easier for the unagented actor, Jay Binder (who casts many Broadway shows) says, "A good agent can get you seen."

Joining the Union

Many beginning actors view qualifying for membership in the actors' unions as a major hurdle on their way to professionalism. Yet, oddly enough, casting directors often see membership in SAG, AFTRA, or Equity as less important. Pat McCorkle, who cast the Broadway play *A Few Good Men*, pointed out that four actors got their Equity cards through being cast in that production. An agent who has seen you give a wonderful performance in a ninety-nine-seat theater and knows you are right for a role in a new TV series is unlikely to be deterred from submitting you by the fact that you are not yet a member of SAG or AFTRA.

Eventually, of course, every working actor must join at least one of the guilds. (You'll find the current membership requirements for SAG, AF-TRA, and Actors Equity in appendix D.) But there are, in fact, some advantages to not yet being a member. One is that you are free to act in nonunion films (such as the student films frequently listed in *Dramalogue* and *Backstage*). Performing in these films gets you the chance to meet student directors who may be the next Steven Spielbergs—and perhaps collect videotape footage on yourself that can help you attract the interest of an agent. Remember, everybody—including Harrison Ford, Meryl Streep, Mel Gibson, and Debra Winger—started out with no credits, no union card, and no agent.

Preparation

What else is involved in treating acting as a business? Preparation, primarily.

Essential preparation may involve taking classes to improve our skills. Workshops and classes are offered in every aspect of our craft. They can get expensive—it's a good idea to audit classes whenever possible before committing to them.

It certainly involves preparing auditions thoroughly—analyzing the scene we are given to read as to our character's underlying motives and emotional processes; familiarizing ourselves with the words; coming to the reading with the right clothes and attitude.

Successful actors *take the trouble to do every audition the best they possibly can.* That means dressing in a way that doesn't contradict the character they are supposed to be portraying. It may also mean arriving early enough at commercial auditions to analyze the script or storyboard, or doing some checking on the credits of the director they are meeting for the first time.

Have I always followed this advice myself? A couple of stories from my own career may be instructive. My first significant professional job was a six-month tour of the United States with the national company of a British courtroom drama called *Hostile Witness,* which starred Ray Milland. New York agent Michael Thomas submitted me for the part of a young woman barrister, and when I saw the show I realized that this was the play's major female role. At that moment in my career, it was a wonderful opportunity.

Did I prepare for my audition? You bet I did: I learned the whole play. When I heard nothing for several months, I assumed they had cast someone else. But then I got a call: they wanted to see me again. I'd forgotten all the lines, so I memorized them again. I got the part and had a great time doing the tour. (I later learned from the wife of the director that the management had wanted another actress, but she wasn't willing to leave New York.)

After I returned from the tour, I continued to prepare thoroughly for all my auditions. Some jobs I got, some I missed—but my average was pretty good. One fine day I got a chance to audition for a television series that was to be shot on the West Coast. It was being cast by one of New York's veteran casting directors, a woman I'd auditioned for several times before. Though I'd never gotten any of those jobs, word had come down that she liked my work.

Excited about the opportunity and more than a little scared, I sought advice from an older actor who was a close friend. "For God's sake, don't overprepare," he said. "Just go in there and read it cold. You're perfect for the part."

I wanted it so much, I felt insecure about my own judgment; I decided to do what he said. The audition went well, and the casting director invited me to come back and read again for the producer. Hadn't I better learn the lines for the callback? "No," my friend told me, "you'll kill your chances. Your reading won't be fresh."

To my sorrow, I listened to him. I didn't do any further work on the part, just showed up and read from the script.

I got a call the next day from my agent: "They've gone with someone else. The casting director couldn't understand why you hadn't prepared for the audition." I never had another opportunity to read for that casting director.

One more story about preparation: I got a call to audition for the Los Angeles production of *Equus*, starring Anthony Hopkins, who was also scheduled to direct. After seeing the show in New York, I'd said to a friend, "I'd give anything to work with Anthony Hopkins." I wasn't going to leave any stone unturned; I learned the lines for all my audition scenes. The director-star read with me himself, and when we finished he said, "I'd like you to do the part." It was my best audition experience, and the show was one of my happiest professional experiences.

I should tell you that there is considerable difference of opinion among the casting directors I interviewed as to whether actors should memorize their material. New York casting directors are more likely to encourage memorization than are their Los Angeles counterparts. The main reservation of those who discourage memorization seems to be that many of us don't learn the script thoroughly enough to make the words our own—while we're struggling to remember our lines, all possibility of an acting performance goes out the window. It is when we have studied a script so thoroughly that the text has become second nature that we are more likely to create a dimensional performance in the audition room.

Certainly, if you are called back for a subsequent audition, knowing the material is likely to be an advantage—though with certain casting directors keeping the script in hand is probably a good idea, if only as a signal that you don't consider this a finished performance. (It had better be close, though, if you expect to get the part.)

Auditions

Being on time is a basic mark of professionalism in any business, and many of the casting directors I talked to emphasized the importance of promptness. Given the fact that the average commercial costs over three hundred thousand dollars to shoot these days, advertising agencies can't afford to hire an actor whose lateness may put the shooting schedule into expensive overtime. If you're late for an audition, you create a question about your reliability, and a reputation for unreliability is the kiss of death for an actor in every area of show business.

The only thing worse than being late is not showing up at all. Elaine Craig, who casts voice-overs on the West Coast, refuses to see an actor again—ever—if that happens even once. (By the same token, Sheila Manning, who casts commercials in Los Angeles, refuses to see again any actor who crashes one of her auditions.)

It's a good idea not just to be on time but to get there *early*, especially for commercial auditions when you need time to look at the script and storyboard. SAG has sign-in sheets on which you must note your scheduled audition time, the time you actually arrived, and the time you left. If you are kept for a commercial audition more than an hour, the advertising agency or casting director has to pay you a percentage of the standard session fee. But if you're more than five minutes late, you lose your eligibility for this payment.

What's worse, you may lose your chance to audition. I was once five minutes late for a commercial reading in New York. "They won't see you," the somewhat embarrassed casting director told me. "They've already cast the spot."

Lack of preparation, a negative attitude, and nervousness are other reasons cited by casting directors for actors losing auditions.

In on-camera auditions, several casting people mentioned the tendency of actors inexperienced in film technique to move off their marks and make jerky head movements that the camera will magnify. A good on-camera workshop—one in which you get to see yourself on videotape—strikes me as basic to any actor's professional education.

People who cast commercials often point out the importance of the actor's slate—the way we say our names at the beginning of an audition. The basic message seems to be, *keep it simple*. Don't get cutesy or gimmicky. Don't give your agent's name, just your own. If you're not straightforward, if you don't project a believable, appealing energy level in your slate, the director may fast-forward through the tape of your audition without even looking at it.

Some casting directors still hold general auditions at which an actor is invited to present brief monologues (usually two contrasting selections). In New York theater casting, the aptness of your material and the skill of your performance may get you an audition for a Broadway play. Nearly everyone I spoke with emphasized the importance of choosing fresh material and of *not* relying on the books of monologues, many of which contain selections that have been done to death. If you are doing an EPA (Equity-principal

Audition), choose a monologue that some relation to the play or season being cast. And never do a spech from a play without reading the whole play.

Who Decides Who Gets the Part?

It's easy to assume that the casting director has the power to decide whether we are cast. But in fact that is rarely the case. Casting directors are essentially go-betweens who mediate between the "talent" (including talent agents) and the buyers of talent (including producers, directors, and advertising agencies). They are hired by the talent-buyers because of their taste and their knowledge of the talent pool. Many of them have backgrounds as performers, and all of them are sympathetic to the actor's problems. Not only are they eager for us to do well because they like us, but their reputations often depend on the quality of our auditions. "If you don't look good we don't look good," says Deborah Aquila, a former New York casting director who currently casts for Paramount Pictures in Hollywood.

The Odds

The odds against getting work are more formidable for some performers than for others. Members of the ethnic minorities, the disabled, and women of all ages are still at a disadvantage—though the examples of such performers as Bill Cosby, Eddie Murphy, and Oprah Winfrey make many people think otherwise.

The 1993 SAG Statistical Survey of Ethnicity, Age and Gender in Film, Television and Commercials tells us that there is still an imbalance in employment for some ethnic groups compared to their numbers in the U.S. population. In television, Caucasians receive eighty-two percent of the roles (though they make up seventy-six percent of the population) and Blacks win thirteen percent of the roles (approximately the same as their numbers in the general population). Asian/Pacifics and American Indians are underrepresented by one percentage point, while the three percent of Latino/Hispanics hired for TV jobs falls short of the census by a full six percent. In features, Caucasian and Black performers are two percentage points ahead of their numbers in the U.S. population, while Asian/Pacifics and American Indians are hired proportionately to the population. The percentage of Latino/Hispanic performers hired is five percent below their U.S. proportion.

Caucasians dominate the commercials field even more than features and television, receiving eighty-four percent of on-camera jobs and eighty-six percent of off-camera jobs. In the voice-over area, Black employment is especially low, while Latino/Hispanics do best in this category by winning nine percent of the work.

But the biggest income disparities are in the area of gender. Men make up fifty-seven percent of the SAG membership, but earn sixty-six percent of total SAG income. As a group, women earn only half the total amount ($341. I million) that men make ($672.4 million). This results in average earnings of $14,138 for men, but only $10,871 for women.

Women work most often in on-camera roles in TV commercials. In this field they receive forty-one percent of all roles, compared to thirty-one percent in theatrical films and thirty-six percent in television productions. They work least often in commercial voice-overs, winning only nineteen percent of these jobs. Even though SAG studies have shown that female voices sell at least as effectively as male voices, women's share of these jobs has dropped slightly from twenty percent in 1986.

For older women, the picture is especially grim. As one long-established star actress I know puts it, "The awkward age for a woman in Hollywood is between forty and sixty." In television, women forty and over get only nine percent (about 3,300 jobs), while men forty and over receive twenty-five percent of all roles. Men under forty receive thirty-nine percent of all roles, and women under forty get twenty-seven percent. In theatrical films, forty-three percent of roles went to men under forty, while men forty and over and women under forty each received about one quarter of all roles. Women forty and over are barely represented on the movie screen with only eight percent of all roles.

I cite these figures not to discourage anyone, but because they give us all a basis for realistic assessment of the odds as they apply to our particular situation. I know many actresses who have dropped out of the profession after age forty and many more whose earnings have been too low (less than six thousand dollars a year) to qualify them for SAG health insurance. A great many of us have, for the first time in our careers, found ourselves looking for non-acting work to pay our rent.

Every casting director I talked with voiced a strong sense of responsibility to increase opportunities for minorities and women. Fern Champion continually works to educate agents and producers: "They forget that a doctor can be a woman. She can also be a minority—she can be Eurasian, she can be black, she can be Hispanic."

But we must recognize that the power of casting directors in this area is limited. Our entertainment media reflect the prejudices of the society we live in. In television, especially, the bottom-line mentality often sees its best interests in reinforcing existing stereotypes.

"I don't think even the advertising agencies can fight it," says Pat Sweeney, who has cast commercials in New York for twenty, years. "If somebody wants to fight this, they have to go to Procter & Gamble, Bristol Myers, Colgate-Palmolive. That's who makes the decisions."

The Casting Couch

Does it exist? Do actors get roles because they're sleeping with the right people?

Maybe one role. Not the lead in the film, certainly. You might get a small speaking part if you're involved with the director, but people will snicker if you're rotten in it. "Word gets around quickly about that kind of thing," says a successful actress I know, "and you'll probably never get cast again—not even by your lover, who's bound to be thoroughly embarrassed by the situation."

The question continues to be asked, and any intelligent answer must take account of the fact that a major ingredient in "star quality" is sexual attractiveness. But most casting directors find questions about the casting couch downright insulting. Casting people think of themselves as professionals, and giving someone a job just because you're involved in an intimate relationship is not something any professional wants to be caught doing.

Even more to the point is the fact that casting directors usually don't have the *power* to cast an actor without approval from at least one other person—and often, especially in commercials, a sizeable group.

Paying the Rent

Whatever you do, don't make porno movies. If you do, and later become a star, you'll have to live them down. If you don't become a star, you'll *still* have to live them down. You can't put porn on your résumé or your videocassette. Most agents will be reluctant to sign you, and casting directors will not consider you a serious actor.

Of course, you need to make money. Acting classes are expensive; so are pictures and résumés; so is living in either New York or Los Angeles. At some point, you are probably going to have to turn to some work other than acting to pay your rent.

Consider word processing (which offers flexible hours and no public visibility) or that old standby, waiting on tables. As Los Angeles casting director Dodie McLean once said to me, "Every actor should have a candy store"—some kind of second career that keeps us from being too desperate to reject an acting job that we have no business accepting. I know actors who sell real estate, actors who teach English as a second language, actors who run catering businesses. It's called paying your dues.

Nobody said this was going to be easy.

APPENDICES

Appendix A

Casting Society of America Members

Casting Society of America
6565 Sunset Blvd., #306
Los Angeles, CA 90028
(213) 463-1925

Abroms, (Rachel)
c/o CSA
6565 Sunset Blvd., #306
Los Angeles, CA 90028
(213) 871-2107

Alderman, (Jane)
Jane Alderman Casting
2105 N Southport, #202
Chicago, IL 60614
(312) 549-6464

Allan, (Robin Joy)
c/o CSA
311 West 43rd St., #700
New York, N.Y. 10036
(516)289-9014

Aquila, (Deborah)
Paramount
Bob Hope Bldg., #200
5555 Melrose Ave.
Los Angeles, CA 90038
(213) 956-5444

Arata, (Maureen A.)
Viacom
100 Universal City Plaza,
Bldg. 506, #104A
Universal City, CA 91608
(818) 777-4410

Aumuller, (Alycia)
Judy Henderson & Associates
330 West 89th St.
New York, NY 10024
(212) 877-0225

Ayer, (Simon)
Glen Larson Productions
3400 Riverside Dr., 3rd Floor
Burbank, CA 91505
(818) 972-0303

Barylski, (Deborah)
Disney Studios
Zorro Bldg #1, Room 9
500 S Buena Vista
Burbank, CA 91521
(818)560-2896

Bascom, (Fran)
CBS Studio Center
Bldg. 5, Room 104
4024 Radford Avenue

Studio City, CA 91604
(818) 760-5895

Basker, (Pamela)
c/o CSA
6565 Sunset Blvd., #306
Los Angeles, CA 90028
(213) 851-6475

Bayer, (Cheryl)
Cheryl Bayer Casting
2020 Avenue of the Stars, 5th floor
Los Angeles, CA 90067
(310) 557-7014

Beach, (Lisa)
HBO
2049 Century Park East, 41st floor
Los Angeles, CA 90067
(310) 201-9490

Belajac, (Donna)
Donna Belajac & Company, Inc.
247 Fort Pitt Blvd.
Pittsburgh, PA 15222
(412) 391-1005

Benson, (Annette)
Kushner Locke
11601 Wilshire Blvd., 21st floor
Los Angeles, CA 90025
(310) 445-1111

Bentley-Griffin, (Shay)
Chez Casting, Inc.
572 Armour Circle
Atlanta, GA 30324
(404) 873-1215

Bernard, (Chemin Sylvia)
Chemin Bernard Casting
4435 W. Slauson Ave, #146

Los Angeles, CA 90043
(213) 507-7400

Bestrop, (Juel)
Gracie Films, Sony Pictures
Poitier Bldg.
10202 W. Washington Blvd.
Culver City, CA 90232
(310) 280-5691

Bialy, (Sharon)
Pagano/Bialy/Manwiller Casting
Trailer 767
10202 W. Washington Blvd.
Los Angeles, CA 90035
(310) 203-3153

Billik, (Tammara)
c/o CSA
6565 Sunset Blvd., #306
Los Angeles, CA 90028
(818) 560-4087

Binder, (Jay)
Jay Binder Casting
513 West 54th St.
New York, NY 10019
(212) 586-6777

Bluestein, (Susan)
c/o CSA
6565 Sunset Blvd., #306
Los Angeles, CA 90028
(310) 203-1296

Blythe, (Eugene)
Disney Studios
Team Disney Bldg. 417E
500 South Buena Vista
Burbank, CA 91521
(818) 560-7625

Boldin, (Jo Edna)
Third Coast Casting
Studio B Productions
501 N. IH 35
Austin, TX 78702
(512) 472-4247

Bowdan, (Jack)
Binder Casting
513 West 54th St.
New York, NY 10019
(212) 586-6777

Branman, (Megan)
Universal
100 Universal City Plaza,
Bldg. 463-112
Universal City, CA 91608
(818) 777-1744

Brinkley, (Barbara)
Brinkley/Perkins Casting
P.O. Box 167157
Irving, TX 75016
(214) 986-0427

Briskey, (Jackylnn B.)
NBC Productions
330 Bob Hope Dr.
Burbank, CA 91523
(818) 840-7727

Brody, (Jane)
Jane Brody Casting
20 West Hubbard
Chicago, IL 60610
(312) 527-0665

Brown, (Deborah)
Deborah Brown Casting
160 West End Ave., #15P
New York, NY 10023
(212) 724-3447

Buck, (Mary V.)
Buck/Edelman Casting
4045 Radford Ave., #B
Studio City, CA 91604
(818) 506-7328

Bullington, (Perry)
MacDonald-Bullington Casting
3030 Andrita St., #A
Los Angeles, CA 90065
(213) 550-4505

Burch, (Jackie)
c/o CSA
6565 Sunset Blvd., #306
Los Angeles, CA 90028

Cagen, (Irene)
Liberman Hirschfeld Casting
5979 West 3rd St., #204
Los Angeles, CA 90036
(213) 525-1381

Cannon, (Reuben)
Reuben Cannon & Associates
1640 S. Sepulveda Blvd., #218
Los Angeles, CA 90025

Capizzi, (Anne)
c/o CSA
6565 Sunset Blvd., #306
Los Angeles, CA 90028

Carlson, (Marta)
c/o CSA NY
311 W. 43rd St., #700
New York, NY 10036

Carrow, (Lynne)
Box 93011
W. Vancouver, BC V7v 3GA
Canada
(604) 983-5391

Cassidy, (Alice)
c/o CSA
6565 Sunset Blvd., #306
Los Angeles, CA 90028
(310) 574-5500

Cavallo, (Lucy)
Stephen J. Cannell Productions
7083 Hollywood Blvd.
Hollywood, CA 90028
(213) 856-7573

Chamian,
c/o CSA
6565 Sunset Blvd., #306
Los Angeles, CA 90028
(213) 525-2790

Champion, (Fern)
c/o CSA
6565 Sunset Blvd., #306
Los Angeles, CA 90028
(310) 301-0158

Chappelle, (Aleta)
c/o CSA NY
311 W. 43rd St., #700
New York, NY 10036
(212) 941-2405

Chavanne, (Brian)
c/o CSA
6565 Sunset Blvd., #306
Los Angeles, CA 90028
(818) 244-4704

Chenoweth, (Ellen)
c/o Werthemer Armstrong
& Hirsch
1888 Century Park East, #1888
Los Angeles, CA 90067
(310) 333-4552

Claman, (Barbara)
BCI
8281 Melrose Ave., #300
Los Angeles, CA 90046
(213) 951-1010

Cobe, (Lori)
3599 Cahuenga Blvd. West, #322
Los Angeles, CA 90068
(213) 876-2626

Cohen, (Andrea)
Warner Bros.
4000 Warner Blvd.
Burbank, CA 91522
(818) 954-6709

Cole, (Richard)
McCorkle Casting
264 West 40th St., 9th floor
New York, NY 10024
(212) 840-0992

Collinge, (Patricia)
Collinge Pickman Casting
138 Mt. Auburn St.
Cambridge, MA 02138
(617) 492-4212

Collins, (Annelise)
Annelise Collins Casting
1103 El Centro Ave.
Los Angeles, CA 90038
(213) 962-9562

Colquhoun, (Mary)
c/o CSA NY
311 West 43rd St., #700
New York, NY 10036
(212) 333-4552

Conforte, (Ruth)
P.O. Box 4795
N. Hollywood, CA 91617-4795
(818) 760-8220

Cowitt, (Allison)
Mike Fenton & Associates
14724 Ventura Blvd., #510
Sherman Oaks, CA 91403
(818) 501-0177

D'Incecco, (Joan)
c/o CSA NY
311 West 43rd St., #700
New York, NY 10036
(212) 333-4552

Da Mota, (Billy)
P.O. Box 4795
Glendale, CA 91222
(818) 243-1263

Daniels, (Glenn)
c/o CSA
6565 Sunset Blvd., #306
Los Angeles, CA 90028
(310) 449-4071

Dann, (Anita)
270 N. Canon Dr., #1147
Beverly Hills, CA 90210
(310) 278-7765

Dawson, (Eric)
Ulrich/Dawson Casting
6421 Coldwater Canyon
North Hollywood, CA 91606
(818) 763-1388

de Oliveira, (Patricia)
c/o CSA
6565 Sunset Blvd., #306
Los Angeles, CA 90028
(213) 463-1925

Dennis, (Leslee)
Chanticleer Films
1680 N. Vine St.
Los Angeles, CA 90028

Dimeo, (Diane)
Diane Dimeo & Associates
12725 Ventura Blvd., #H
Studio City, CA 91604
(818) 505-0945

Dinman, (Dick)
c/o CSA
6565 Sunset Blvd., #306
Los Angeles, CA 90028
(213) 469-2283

Dixon, (Pam)
Pam Dixon Casting
P.O. Box 672
Beverly Hills, CA 90213
(310) 271-8064

Dockstader, (Donna)
Universal Studios
100 Universal Plaza
Universal City, CA 91608
(818) 777-1961

Doster, (Jo)
Jo Doster Casting
P.O. 120641
Nashville, TN 37212-0641
(615) 385-3850

Dudley, (Carol)
Cannon, Dudley Associates
33 Great Cumberland Place, Top floor
London, England WlH 7LF
071 262-8546

Dunas, (Dorian)
9021 Melrose Ave., #301
Los Angeles, CA 90069

Dutton, (Nan)
c/o CSA
6565 Sunset Blvd., #306
Los Angeles, CA 90028
(213) 951-9214

Edelman, (Susan)
Buck/Edelman Casting
4045 Radford Ave., #B
Studio City, CA 91604
(818) 506-7328

Ekholdt, (Donna)
c/o CSA
6565 Sunset Blvd., #306
Los Angeles, CA 90028
(310) 394-3964

Ellers, (Penny)
Aaron Spelling Productions
5700 Wilshire Blvd., No. Lobby, #116
Los Angeles, CA 90036
(213) 525-3524

Farberman, (Rachelle)
P.O. Box 5146
West Hills, CA 91308
(818) 972-0533

Fenton, (Mike)
Mike Fenton & Associates
14724 Ventura Blvd., #510

Sherman Oaks, CA 91403
(818) 501-0177

Fertig, (Steven)
Steven Fertig Casting
8271 Melrose Ave., #28
Los Angeles, CA 90046
(213) 655-5737

Feuer, (Howard)
c/o Altman, Greenfield
& Selvaggi
120 W. 45th St., 16th floor
New York, NY 10036

Finger, (Leonard)
Leonard Finger Casting
1501 Broadway, #1511
New York, NY 10036
(212) 944-8611

Finn, (Mali)
Warner Bros.
4000 Warner Blvd., Trailer 10
Burbank, CA 91522
(818) 954-4411

Finnegan, (Bonnie)
Bonnie Finnegan Casting
12 West 27th St.
New York, NY 10001
(212) 725-3505

Fogel, (Alexa L.)
Alexa Fogel Casting
157 Columbus Ave., 2nd floor
New York, NY 10023
(212) 456-3631

Foy, (Nancy)
c/o CSA
6565 Sunset Blvd., #306
Los Angeles, CA 90028
(310) 824-6220

Franks, (Jerold)
c/o CSA
6565 Sunset Blvd., #306
Los Angeles, CA 90028
(213) 874-1901

Frazier, (Carrie)
c/o CSA
6565 Sunset Blvd., #306
Los Angeles, CA 90028

Frost, (Jean Sarah)
c/o CSA
6565 Sunset Blvd., #306
Los Angeles, CA 90028

Garcia, (Risa Bramon)
Alomar Pictures
6404 Hollywood Blvd., #309
Los Angeles, CA 90028
(213) 469-7303

Gartzman, (Melinda)
c/o CSA
6565 Sunset Blvd., #306
Los Angeles, CA 90028
(818) 840-7606

Giella, (David)
Reuben Cannon & Associates
1640 S. Sepulveda Blvd.. #218
Los Angeles, CA 90025
(310) 996-1885

Gilburne, (Jessica)
Hughes Moss Casting
311 W. 43rd St., #700

New York, NY 10036
(212) 307-6690

Ginsberg, (Shani)
c/o CSA
6565 Sunset Blvd., #306
Los Angeles, CA 90028

Glaser, (Jan)
Concorde/New Horizons
11600 San Vicente Blvd.
Los Angeles, CA 90049
(310) 820-6733

Gleason, (Laura)
c/o CSA
6565 Sunset Blvd., #306
Los Angeles, CA 90028

Glickman, (Susan)
Susan Glickman Casting
12001 Ventura Place, #400
Studio City, CA 91604
(818) 766-2610

Golden, (Peter)
Cannell Productions
7083 Hollywood Blvd.
Hollywood, CA 90028
(213) 856-7317

Golden, (Pat)
c/o CSA NY
311 West 43rd St., #700
New York, NY 10036
(212) 496-0146

Goodman, (Elisa)
c/o The Mirisch Agency
10100 Santa Monica Blvd., #700
Los Angeles, CA 90067
(310) 772-0722

Gordin, (Alixe)
129 West 12th St.
New York, NY 10011
(212) 664-0640

Gordon, (Lynda W.)
P.O. Box 4611948
Los Angeles, CA 90046
(818) 501-3160

Gordon, (Lillian)
Lillian Gordon Castings
13103 Forest Hills Dr.
Tampa, FL 33612-3335
(813) 931-3252

Gorman, (Christopher)
CBS
7800 Beverly Blvd., #231
Los Angeles, CA 90036
(213) 852-4489

Greenberg, (Jeff)
Paramount
Marx Bros Bldg. 102
5555 Melrose Ave.
Los Angeles, CA 90038
(213) 956-4886

Greenspan, (Harriet)
9242 Beverly Blvd.
Beverly Hills, CA 90210
(310) 246-7628

Greer, (Michael)
Universal
10 Universal City Plaza, 32nd floor
Universal City, CA 91608
(818) 505-7644

Hamer-Tumaroff, (Yonti)
Unique Casting Company, Inc.
1613 Alton Road

Miami Beach, FL 33139
(305) 947-9339

Hamerman, (Milt)
c/o CSA
6565 Sunset Blvd., #306
Los Angeles, CA 90028
(213) 463-1925

Hann, (Theodore)
Warner Bros. Television
300 Television Plaza,
Bldg. 140, #139A
Burbank, CA 91505
(818) 954-7642

Harbin, (Robert W.)
20th Century Fox
Executive Bldg 335
10201 W. Pico Blvd.
Los Angeles, CA 90035
(310) 203-3847

Hart, (Natalie)
Sunset Gower Studios
Bldg. 13 Box 27
1438 N. Gower
Los Angeles, CA 90028
(310) 575-5630

Hendel, (Karen)
HBO
2049 Century Park East, 41st floor
Los Angeles, CA 90067
(310) 201-9309

Henderson, (Cathy)
Cathy Henderson Casting
3025 W. Olympic Blvd., #207
Santa Monica, CA 90404
(310) 828-7477

Henderson, (Judy)
Judy Henderson & Associates
330 West 89th St.
New York, NY 10024
(212) 877-0225

Herold, (Paula)
c/o CSA NY
311 West 43rd St., #700
New York, NY 10036
(212) 399-3222

Hirschfeld, (Marc)
Liberman Hirschfeld Casting
5979 West 3rd St., #204
Los Angeles, CA 90036
(213) 525-1381

Hirshenson, (Janet)
The Casting Company
7461 Beverly Blvd., Penthouse
Los Angeles, CA 90036
(213) 938-0700

Hochberg, (Alan C.)
Alan C. Hochberg Casting
4063 Radford Ave., #103
Studio City, CA 91604
(818) 505-6600

Holstra, (Judith)
c/o CSA
6565 Sunset Blvd., #306
Los Angeles, CA 90028
(818) 503-2238

Howard, (Stuart)
Stuart Howard Associates
22 West 27th St., 10th floor
New York, NY 10001
(212) 725-7770

Huff, (Vicki)
c/o CSA
6565 Sunset Blvd., #306
Los Angeles, CA 90028
(310) 821-8609

Huffman, (Phyllis)
Warner Bros.
1325 Sixth Avenue
New York, NY 10019
(212) 636-5023

Hughes, (Julie)
Hughes Moss Casting
311 West 43rd St., #700
New York, NY 10036
(212) 307-6690

Hymson-Ayer, (Beth)
Glen Larson Productions
3400 Riverside Dr., 3rd floor
Burbank, CA 91505
(818) 972-0303

Isaacson, (Donna)
20th Century Fox
Bldg 12, #225
10201 W. Pico Blvd.
Los Angeles, CA 90035
(310) 203-1824

Jacobs, (Steven)
c/o CSA
6565 Sunset Blvd., #306
Los Angeles, CA 90028

Jacoby, (Justine)
Auroa Productions
8642 Melrose Ave., #2
Los Angeles, CA 90069
(310) 854-6900

Jacoby, (Ellen)
Ellen Jacoby Casting, International
420 Lincoln Rd., #210
Miami Beach, FL 33139
(305) 531-5300

Jenkins, (Jane)
The Casting Company
7461 Beverly Blvd., Penthouse
Los Angeles, CA 90036
(213) 938-0700

Johnson, (Mel)
Mel Johnson & Associates
Bldg. 22, #235
1000 Universal City Plaza
Orlando, FL 32819
(407) 363-8582

Jones, (Caro)
Caro Jones Casting
P.O. Box 3329
Los Angeles, CA 90078
(213) 664-0460

Joseph, (Rosalie)
Rosalie Joseph Casting
1501 Broadway, #2605
New York, NY 10036
(212) 921-5781

Kalles, (Patti)
Patti Kalles Casting
Smith Tower 1525
506 Second Ave.
Seattle, WA 98104
(206) 447-9318

Kanner, (Ellie)
Warner Bros. Television
300 So. Television Plaza, Bldg. 140
Burbank, CA 91505
(818) 954-7644

Kaplan, (Darlene)
Darlene Kaplan Casting
P.O. Box 261160
Encino, CA 91426-1160
(818) 981-3527

Katcher, (Michael A.)
Liberman/Hirschfeld Casting
5979 3rd St., #204
Los Angeles, CA 90036
(213) 525-1381

Kaufman, (Avy)
c/o CSA NY
311 West 43rd St., #700
New York, NY 10036

Keigley, (Liz)
Liz Keigley Casting
121 North Hall
Sugarland, TX 77478
(713) 242-7265

Kent, (Rody)
Rody Kent & Associates
5422 Vickery Blvd.
Dallas, TX 75206
(214) 827-3418

King, (Ramsay)
Heartland Casting
P.O. Box 6025
Gulfport, MS 39507
(601) 864-5193

Kleinman, (Marsha)
Marsha Kleinman & Associates
704 N. Gardner St., #2
Los Angeles, CA 90046
(213) 852-1521

Klopper, (Nancy)
c/o CSA
6565 Sunset Blvd., #306
Los Angeles, CA 90028
(213) 463-1925

Knight, (Eileen)
Mack Casting
12009 Guerin St.
Studio City, CA 91604
(818) 752-1994

Koehler, (Joanne)
Warner Bros. Television
Bldg. 140, #140
300 S. Television Plaza
Burbank, CA 91505
(818) 954-7636

Kressel, (Lynn)
Lynn Kressel Casting
445 Park Avenue, 7th floor
New York, NY 10022
(212) 605-9122

Kurtzman, (Wendy)
c/o CSA
6565 Sunset Blvd., #306
Los Angeles, CA 90028
(310) 204-0404

La Padura, (Jason)
c/o CSA
6565 Sunset Blvd., #306
Los Angeles, CA 90028
(310) 581-6874

Landsburg, (Shana)
Shana Landsburg Casting
11811 W. Olympic Blvd.
Los Angeles, CA 90064
(310) 996-9534

Larroquette, (Elizabeth)
Port Street Films, Inc.
Producers Bldg 1, #102
4000 Warner Blvd.
Burbank, CA 91522
(818) 954-2605

Laughlin, (Kathryn)
Independent Castings, Inc.
8313 West Hillsborough Ave., Bldg. 4
Tampa, FL 33615
(813) 884-8335

Lear, (Sally)
Nevada Casting Group, Inc.
100 Washington
Reno, NV 89503
(702) 322-8187

Leder, (Geraldine)
Warner Bros. Television
Bldg. 140, #139
300 South Television Plaza
Burbank, CA 91505
(818) 954-7635

Letterie, (Kathleen)
Witt/Thomas
6311 Romaine
Los Angeles, CA 90038
(213) 962-5575

Leustig, (Elisabeth)
c/o CSA
6565 Sunset Blvd., #306
Los Angeles, CA 90028

Levey, (John)
Warner Bros.
Bldg. 3A, #26
4000 Warner Blvd.
Burbank, CA 91522
(818) 954-4080

Levine, (Marion)
c/o CSA
6565 Sunset Blvd., #306
Los Angeles, CA 90028

Levitt, (Heidi)
1020 N. Cole Ave., 2nd floor
Los Angeles, CA 90038
(213) 467-7400

Lewis, (Carol)
c/o CSA
6565 Sunset Blvd., #306
Los Angeles, CA 90028
(213) 960-4770

Lewis, (Ellen)
130 W. 57th St., #12E
New York, NY 10019
(212) 245-4635

Liberman, (Meg)
Liberman/Hirschfeld Casting
5979 W. 3rd St., #204
Los Angeles, CA 90036
(213) 525-1381

Liebhart, (Vince)
"As The World Turns"
524 W. 57th St., #5330
New York, NY 10019
(212) 975-5781

Liebling, (Terry)
c/o CSA
6565 Sunset Blvd., #306
Los Angeles, CA 90028

Liff, (Vincent G.)
Johnson/Liff Casting Associates
1501 Broadway, #1400
New York, NY 10036
(212) 391-2680

Lilienfield, (Tracy)
c/o CSA
6565 Sunset Blvd., #306
Los Angeles, CA 90028

Lippin, (Robin)
330 Bob Hope Dr., #C110
Burbank, CA 91523
(818) 840-7643

Litt, (Leslie)
N.B.C.
3000 Alameda, #231
Burbank, CA 91523
(818) 840-4142

London, (Lisa)
c/o CSA
6565 Sunset Blvd., #306
Los Angeles, CA 90028

Lopata, (Molly)
Molly Lopata Casting
4043 Radford Ave.
Studio City, CA 91604
(818) 753-8086

Louden-Kubin, (Cheryl A.)
The Casting Crew, Inc.
1948 Tyler St.
Hollywood, FL 33020
(305) 927-2329

Lowry Johnson, (Junie)
Paramount
Von Sternberg Suite 104
5555 Melrose Ave.
Los Angeles, CA 90038
(213) 956-4856; (310) 203-1296

Lyons, (John S.)
John Lyons Casting
110 W. 57th St., 5th floor

New York, NY 10019
(212) 765-7670

MacDonald, (Bob)
MacDonald-Bullington Casting
3030 Andrita St., #A
Los Angeles, CA 90065
(213) 550-4505

Mackey, (Amanda)
c/o CSA
6565 Sunset Blvd., #306
Los Angeles, CA 90028
(310) 449-4078

Maisler, (Francine)
Francine Maisler Casting
7813 Beverly Blvd., 3rd floor
Los Angeles, CA 90036
(213) 852-2875

Manwiller, (Debi)
Pagano/Bialy/Manwiller Casting
10201 W. Pico Blvd., Trailer 767
Los Angeles, CA 90035
(310) 203-3153

Margiotta, (Mary)
Margiotta Casting
8265 Sunset Blvd., #200
Los Angeles, CA 90046
(310) 288-2502

Mariano, (Irene)
Warner Bros. Television
300 S. Television Plaza,
Bldg. 140, 1st fl.
Burbank, CA 91505
(818) 954-7643

Marin, (Mindy)
Casting Artists, Inc.
609 Broadway

Santa Monica, CA 90401
(310) 395-1882

Marx, (Elizabeth)
c/o CSA
6565 Sunset Blvd., #306
Los Angeles, CA 90028
(213) 463-1925

McCaffrey, (Valerie)
New Line Cinema
116 N. Robertson Blvd., 6th floor
Beverly Hills, CA 90048
(310) 967-6656

McCorkle, (Patricia)
Patricia McCorkle Casting
264 West 40th St.
New York, NY 10024
(212) 840-0992

McDermott, (Beverly)
923 N. Golf Dr.
Hollywood, FL 33021
(305) 625-5111

McRae, (Vivian)
Vivian McRae Casting
P.O. Box 1351
Burbank, CA 91507
(818) 848-9590

McSweeney, (Tom)
Tom McSweeney Casting
3025 W. Olympic Blvd., #207
Santa Monica, CA 90404
(310) 828-7477

Merlin, (Joanna)
c/o The Disney Channel
477 Madison Ave., 5th floor
New York, NY 10022
(212) 735-5342

Meshel, (Jeffrey A.)
NBC
3000 W. Alameda Ave., #231
Burbank, CA 91523
(818) 840-4729

Meyer, (Ellen)
Sar-Jen, Inc.
11811 W. Olympic Blvd.
Los Angeles, CA 90064
(310) 444-1818

Meyers, (D. Lynn)
P.O. Box 3277
N. Hollywood, CA 91609
(818) 703-5254

Michel, (Adriana)
c/o CSA
6565 Sunset Blvd., #306
Los Angeles, CA 90028

Miller, (Barbara)
Warner Bros. Television
300 Television Plaza, Bldg. 140, 1st
floor
Burbank, CA 91505
(818) 954-7645

Miller, (Dee)
Dee Miller Casting
1524 N.E. 147th St.
N. Miami, FL 33161
(305) 944-8559

Millikan, (Rick)
c/o CSA
6565 Sunset Blvd., #306
Los Angeles, CA 90028
(310) 203-2772

Mionie, (Lisa)
c/o CSA
6565 Sunset Blvd., #306
Los Angeles, CA 90028

Mock, (Patricia)
c/o CSA
6565 Sunset Blvd., #306
Los Angeles, CA 90028

Moran, (Pat)
Pat Moran Casting
805 Park Ave.
Baltimore, MD 21201
(410) 385-2107

Morones, (Bob)
KCET
4401 Sunset Blvd.
Los Angeles, CA 90027
(213) 953-5657

Moss, (Barry)
Hughes Moss Casting
311 W. 43rd St., #700
New York, NY 10036
(212) 307-6690

Mossler, (Helen)
Paramount Television
5555 Melrose Ave.
Los Angeles, CA 90038
(213) 956-5578

Mussenden, (Roger)
The Casting Company
7461 Beverly Blvd., Penthouse
Los Angeles, CA 90036
(213) 938-0700

Myers, (Elissa)
Elissa Myers Casting
333 West 52nd St., #1008

New York, NY 10024
(212) 315-4777

Nassif, (Robin S.)
ABC
2040 Avenue of the Stars
Los Angeles, CA 90067
(310) 557-6423

Nayor, (Nancy)
MCA/Universal
Bldg. 508, 1st floor
100 Universal City Plaza
Universal City, CA 91608
(818) 777-3566

Newberg, (Bruce H.)
c/o Edward Rada
5670 Wilshire Blvd., #1450
Los Angeles, CA 90036
(213) 463-1925

Novack, (Ellen)
Ellen Novack Casting
20 Jay St., #9B
New York, NY 10013
(212) 431-3939

O'Loughlin, (Meryl)
c/o CSA
6565 Sunset Blvd., #306
Los Angeles, CA 90028
(818) 953-5371

Oberst, (Gary)
c/o CSA
6565 Sunset Blvd., #306
Los Angeles, CA 90028
(213) 463-7872

Openden, (Lori)
NBC
3000 W. Alameda, #231

Burbank, CA 91523
(818) 840-3774

Orenstein, (Fern)
Fern Orenstein Casting
5433 Beethoven
Los Angeles, CA 90066
(310) 302-9149

Oshen, (Jeffrey)
Paramount Studios
Gower Mill 117
5555 Melrose Ave.
Los Angeles, CA 90038
(213) 956-5969

Overwise, (Jessica)
Jessica Overwise Casting
17250 Sunset Blvd.
Pacific Palisades, CA 90272
(310) 459-2686

Pagano, (Richard)
Pagano/Bialy/Manwiller Casting
10201 Pico Blvd., Trailer 767
Los Angeles, CA 90035
(310) 203-3153

Paige, (Marvin)
Marvin Paige Casting
P.O. Box 69964
West Hollywood, CA 90069
(818) 760-3040

Palo, (Linda Phillips)
Palo/Haklar Casting
650 N. Bronson Ave., #144
Los Angeles, CA 90004
(310) 396-8328

Papsidera, (John)
Casting Artists, Inc.
609 Broadway St.

Santa Monica, CA 90401
(310) 395-1882

Parada, (Dan)
The Casting Group
1020 N. Cole Ave. #4267
Hollywood, CA 90038
(213) 461-3399

Parks, (Ellen)
Ellen Parks Casting
c/o Soundstage
630 Ninth Ave., 14th floor
New York, NY 10036
(212) 315-9800

Patton, (Cami)
Witt-Thomas Productions
Bldg. 35, #577
1438 N. Gower St.
Los Angeles, CA 90028
(213) 960-8276

Paul, (Joey)
Joey Paul Casting
28165 Avenue Crocker
Valencia, CA 91355
(805) 294-8410

Pemrick, (Donald Paul)
Don Pemrick Casting
3520 Hayden Ave.
Culver City, CA 90232
(310) 838-7800

Piccione, (Nancy)
Manhattan Theater Club
453 W. 16th
New York, NY 10011
(212) 645-5590

Pickman, (Carolyn)
Collinge Pickman Casting
138 Mt. Auburn St.
Cambridge, MA 02138
(617) 492-4212

Pincus, (Warren)
c/o CSA NY
311 W. 43rd St., #700
New York, NY
(212) 989-3230

Powell, (Holly)
c/o CSA
6565 Sunset Blvd., #306
Los Angeles, CA 90028
(213) 655-2970

Praggastis, (Cate)
Cate Praggastis Casting
4760 S. Highland Dr., Box 205
Salt Lake City, UT 84117
(801) 461-5843

Rack, (Pamela)
c/o CSA
6565 Sunset Blvd., #306
Los Angeles, CA 90028

Ray, (Johanna)
Johanna Ray Casting
1022 Palm Ave., #2
West Hollywood, CA 90069
(310) 652-2511

Ray, (Robyn)
c/o CSA
6565 Sunset Blvd., #306
Los Angeles, CA 90028

Rea, (Karen)
c/o CSA
6565 Sunset Blvd., #306
Los Angeles, CA 90028

Rea, (Betty)
Betty Rea Casting
222 E. 44th St.
New York, NY 10017
(212) 983-1610

Reed, (Robi)
Robi Reed & Associates
8170 Beverly Blvd., #202
Los Angeles, CA 90048
(213) 653-6005

Reich, (Joe)
c/o CSA
6565 Sunset Blvd., #306
Los Angeles, CA 90028
(213) 465-3929

Remsen, (Barbara)
Barbara Remsen & Associates
650 N. Bronson, #124
Los Angeles, CA 90004
(213) 464-7968

Rennell, (Gretchen)
c/o CSA
6565 Sunset Blvd., #306
Los Angeles, CA 90028

Rhodes, (Shari)
c/o CSA
6565 Sunset Blvd., #306
Los Angeles, CA 90028
(213) 654-2141

Rich, (Shirley)
Shirley Rich Casting
200 E. 66th St., #E1202
New York, NY 10021

Rosen, (Stu)
Stu Rosen Casting
7631 Lexington Ave.
Los Angeles, CA 90046
(213) 851-1661

Rosenberg, (Vicki)
Vicki Rosenberg & Associates
1438 N. Gower, #1406
Los Angeles, CA 90028
(213) 460-7593

Rosenstein, (Donna)
ABC
2040 Avenue of the Stars, #500
Los Angeles, CA 90067
(310) 557-6423

Ross, (Marcia)
Marcia Ross Casting
12725 Ventura Blvd., #1
Studio City, CA 91604
(818) 980-3022

Ross, (Eleanor)
c/o CSA
6565 Sunset Blvd., #306
Los Angeles, CA 90028
(213) 463-1925

Rothfield, (Jodi)
Rothfield, Ryan &
Roth Casting
2033 6th Ave., #306
Seattle, WA 98121
(206) 448-0927

Rousselot, (Renee)
c/o CSA
6565 Sunset Blvd., #306
Los Angeles, CA 90028

Rubin, (David)
David Rubin Casting
8721 Sunset Blvd., #208
Los Angeles, CA 90069
(310) 652-4441

Rubin, (Tara Jayne)
Johnson-Liff Casting Associates,
Ltd.
1501 Broadway, #1400
New York, NY 10036
(212) 391-2680

Rubinstein, (Debra)
Spelling Entertainment
5757 Wilshire Blvd., #670
Los Angeles, CA 90036
(213) 525-2856

Ryan, (Suzanne)
Lynn Kressel Casting
MCA Universal
445 Park Ave., 7th floor
New York, NY 10022
(212) 605-9122

Saks, (Mark)
Warner Bros. Television
Bldg. 140, 1st floor
300 S. Television Plaza
Burbank, CA 91505
(818) 954-7326

Sandrich, (Cathy)
c/o CSA
6565 Sunset Blvd., #306
Los Angeles, CA 90028
(310) 449-4078

Sanitsky, (Ellen) Lubin
Universal TV
Bldg. 463, #108
100 Universal City Plaza
Universal City, CA 91608

Schaeffer Stockton, (Irene)
Irene Stockton Casting
261 Broadway, #2B
New York, NY 10007
(212) 964-9445

Schecter, (Amy)
Stuart Howard Associates
22 W. 27th St, 10th floor
New York, NY 10001
(212) 725-7770

Scoccimarro, (Jean)
Jean Scoccimarro Casting
6565 Sunset Blvd., #306
Hollywood, CA 90028

Scudder, (Susan)
Susan Scudder Casting
6565 Sunset Blvd., #306
Hollywood, CA 90028

Seff, (Sherie)
400 W. 43rd St., #9B
New York, NY 10036
(212) 947-7408

Selzer Kaplan, (Julie)
c/o CSA
6565 Sunset Blvd., #306
Los Angeles, CA 90028

Sepulveda, (Anthony)
Warner Bros. Television
Bldg. 140, #137
300 S. Television Plaza
Burbank, CA 91505
(818) 954-7639

Shaner, (Dan)
Wilshire Court Productions, Inc.
1840 Century Park East, #400
Los Angeles, CA 90067
(310) 557-2444

Shannon, (Barbara)
Barbara Shannon Casting
1537 Rosecrans, #G
San Diego, CA 92106
(619) 224-9555

Shaw, (Susan)
1501 Broadway, #2605
New York, NY 10011
(212) 354-4207

Shepard, (Bill)
c/o CSA
6565 Sunset Blvd., #306
Los Angeles, CA 90028
(818) 789-4776

Shull, (Jennifer)
c/o CSA
6565 Sunset Blvd., #306
Los Angeles, CA 90028

Simkin, (Margery)
c/o CSA
6565 Sunset Blvd., #306
Los Angeles, CA 90028

Simon, (Meg)
Meg Simon Casting
1600 Broadway, #609
New York, NY 10019
(212) 245-7670

Skoff, (Melissa)
Skoff Casting
11684 Ventura Blvd., #5141
Studio City, CA 91604
(818) 760-2058

Slater, (Mary Jo)
Slater/Brooksbank Casting
MGM
2401 Colorado Ave., 3rd floor
Santa Monica, CA 90404
(310) 449-3685

Soble, (Stanley)
Center Theatre Group
601 W. Temple St.
Los Angeles, CA 90012
(213) 972-7374

Soble, (Sharon)
Jeff Oshen & Assoc.
Paramount
5555 Melrose Ave., Gower Mill 117
Los Angeles, CA 90038
(213) 956-4850

Sparks, (Pamela)
c/o Chelsea
3859 Lankershim Blvd.
Studio City, CA 91604
(805) 266-9671

Steinberg, (Dawn)
c/o CSA
6565 Sunset Blvd., #306
Los Angeles, CA 90028

Stephenson, (Ron)
MCA Universal Studios
Bldg. 463, #100
Universal City, CA 91608
(818) 777-3498

Stiner, (Sally)
12228 Venice Blvd., #503
Los Angeles, CA 90066
(310) 827-9796

Stokes, (Stanzi)
c/o CSA
6565 Sunset Blvd., #306
Los Angeles, CA 90028
(818) 508-6485

Stone, (Randy)
20th Century Fox
Bldg. 54, #6
10201 W. Pico Blvd.
Los Angeles, CA 90035
(310) 203-4115

Stratton, (Gilda)
c/o CSA
6565 Sunset Blvd., #306
Los Angeles, CA 90028
(213) 463-1925

Sturtevant, (Roger)
BSB
405 Lexington Ave.
New York, NY 10174

Swann, (Monica)
Monica Swann Casting
12009 Guerin St.
Studio City, CA 91604
(818) 769-8564

Swee, (Daniel)
Lincoln Center Theatre
150 W. 65th St.
New York, NY 10023
(212) 362-7600

Taylor, (Judy)
Taylor Casting
P.O. Box 461198
Los Angeles, CA 90046
(818) 501-3160

Taylor, (Juliet)
Juliet Taylor Casting
130 W. 57th St., #12E
New York, NY 10019
(212) 245-4635

Teschner, (Mark)
General Hospital
4151 Prospect Ave.
Hollywood, CA 90027
(310) 557-5542

Tichler, (Rosemarie)
New York Shakespeare Festival
425 Lafayette St.
New York, NY 10003
(212) 598-7100

Tillman, (Mark)
c/o CSA
6565 Sunset Blvd., #306
Los Angeles, CA 90028

Todd, (Joy)
c/o CSA
6565 Sunset Blvd., #306
Los Angeles, CA 90028

Ulrich, (Robert J.)
Ulrich/Dawson Casting
6421 Coldwater Canyon
No. Hollywood, CA 91606
(818) 763-1388

Valko, (Nikki)
c/o CSA
6565 Sunset Blvd., #306
Los Angeles, CA 90028
(213) 463-1925

Vice, (Karen)
Karen Vice Casting
12001 Ventura Place, #203
Studio City, CA 91604
(818) 760-5263

Villaverde, (Jose)
c/o CSA
6565 Sunset Blvd., #306
Los Angeles, CA 90028

Waite, (Dava)
Universal Studios
Bldg 463, #104
100 Universal City Plaza
Universal City, CA 91608
(818) 777-1114

Warren Jr., (Samuel)
Warren & Assoc. Int'l Casting
Services
2244 - 4th Ave., #D
San Diego, CA 92101
(619) 531-0107

Webster, (April)
April Webster Casting
513 Wilshire Blvd., #196
Santa Monica, CA 90401
(310) 285-8631

Welden, (Rosemary)
c/o CSA
6565 Sunset Blvd., #306
Los Angeles, CA 90028

Wieder, (Susan)
c/o CSA
6565 Sunset Blvd., #306
Los Angeles, CA 90028
(213) 463-1925

Wilkinson, (Nick)
ABC
2040 Avenue of the Stars, 5th floor
Los Angeles, CA 90067
(310) 557-6511

Williams, (Kim)
HBO
2049 Century Park East, 42nd floor
Los Angeles, CA 90067
(310) 201-9402

Wilson, (Judy Blye)
ABC
320 W. 66th St.
New York, NY 10023
(212) 496-3354

Windsor-Fischer, (Geri)
Geri Windsor & Associates
11333 Moorpark St.
P.O. Box 402
Studio City, CA 91602

Woodman, (Liz)
Woodman Casting
11 Riverside Dr., #2 JE
New York, NY 10023
(212) 787-3782

Wyatt, (Darlene)
Darlene Wyatt Casting
1138 E. Highland
Phoenix, AZ 80014
(602) 263-8650

Wyman, (Lori Sheryl)
Wyman Casting
16499 N.E. 19th Ave., #203
N. Miami Beach, FL 33162
(305) 354-3901

Yeskel, (Ronnie)
c/o CSA
6565 Sunset Blvd., #306
Los Angeles, CA 90028
(213) 851-8123

Young, (Dianne)
Dianne Young Casting
15001 Calvert St.
Van Nuys, CA 91411

Young, Rhonda
10350 Santa Monica Blvd.
Los Angeles, CA 90025
(310) 556-2235

Zaluski, (Joanne)
Joanne Zaluski Casting
405 S. Beverly Dr.
Beverly Hills, CA 90212
(310) 456-5160

Zane, (Debra)
Debra Zane Casting
DDF Films, Inc.
8157 Lankershim Blvd.
North Hollywood, CA 91605
(818) 771-9206

Zerman, (Andrew M.)
Johnson Liff Casting
1501 Broadway, #1400
New York, NY 10036
(212) 391-2680

Zuckerbrod, (Gary M.)
c/o CSA
6565 Sunset Blvd., #306
Los Angeles, CA 90028

Appendix B

Résumé Samples: Los Angeles and New York

TYPICAL ''LOS ANGELES'' RÉSUMÉ FORMAT:

JUDITH SEARLE

Height:	5'9"	Eyes:	Blue	Unions:	SAG
Weight:	135	Hair:	Lt. Brown		AFTRA
					AEA

FILM

WALK PROUD: Universal (Directed by Robert Collins)

TELEVISION

MOWs,
Mini-series,
Specials:

CONCRETE BEAT (Directed by Robert Butler)
RAINBOW (Directed by Jackie Cooper)
THE DEATH OF RICHIE (Directed by Paul Wendkos)
CRASH: THE TRUE STORY OF FLIGHT 401 (Directed by Barry Shear)
HAROLD ROBBINS' 79 PARK AVENUE (Directed by Paul Wendkos)
THE CASTAWAYS ON GILLIGAN'S ISLAND (Directed by Earl Bellamy)
DISNEY'S ALL-STAR VALENTINE PARTY (Voice of Chip)

Episodic:	MOONLIGHTING REMINGTON STEELE FAME (Directed by Peter Levin) ARCHIE BUNKER'S PLACE HARDCASTLE & McCORMICK THE ROCKFORD FILES
Daytime:	SOMERSET: NBC (Contract role) SEARCH FOR TOMORROW: CBS (Contract role) LOVE IS A MANY-SPLENDORED THING: CBS (Contract role)

S T A G E :

Broadway:	ANGELA with Geraldine Page (Directed by Jack Ragatzy) THERE'S A GIRL IN MY SOUP (Directed by Robert Chetwyn)
Off-B'way:	THE WINTER'S TALE (Hermione): Jean Cocteau Theatre HERE COME THE CLOWNS (Connie): Equity Library Theatre
Nat'l Tour:	HOSTILE WITNESS with Ray Milland (Directed by Reginald Denham)
Los Angeles:	EQUUS (Hester) with Anthony Hopkins (Directed by Anthony Hopkins)
Other:	STRANGE INTERLUDE (Nina): Theatre Lobby, Washington D.C. A DELICATE BALANCE (Claire): Woodstock Playhouse, Woodstock, NY THE DEVIL'S DISCIPLE (Judith): Woodstock Playhouse, Woodstock, NY LOOK BACK IN ANGER (Helena): Joker's Playhouse, Pasadena, CA THE TYPISTS & THE TIGER (Sylvia/Gloria): The Actor's Company, Washington, D.C.

C O N T A C T : Fred Amsel & Associates (213) 939-1188
C O M M E R C I A L S : Cunningham, Escott, Dipene & Associates: (213) 855-1700
M E S S A G E S: (213) 472-1630

TYPICAL "NEW YORK" RÉSUMÉ FORMAT:

JUDITH SEARLE

Height:	5'9"	Eyes:	Blue	Unions:	SAG
Weight:	135	Hair:	Lt. Brown		AFTRA
					AEA

STAGE:

Broadway: ANGELA with Geraldine Page (Directed by Jack Ragatzy)
THERE'S A GIRL IN MY SOUP (Directed by Robert Chetwyn)

Off-B'way: THE WINTER'S TALE (Hermione): Jean Cocteau Theatre
HERE COME THE CLOWNS (Connie): Equity Library Theatre

Nat'l Tour: HOSTILE WITNESS with Ray Milland (Directed by Reginald Denham)

Los Angeles: EQUUS (Hester) with Anthony Hopkins (Directed by Anthony Hopkins)

Other: STRANGE INTERLUDE (Nina): Theatre Lobby, Washington, D.C.
A DELICATE BALANCE (Claire): Woodstock Playhouse, Woodstock, NY
THE DEVIL'S DISCIPLE (Judith): Woodstock Playhouse, Woodstock, NY
LOOK BACK IN ANGER (Helena): Joker's Playhouse, Pasadena, CA
THE TYPISTS & THE TIGER (Sylvia/Gloria): The Actor's Company, Washington, D.C.

FILM

WALK PROUD: Universal (Directed by Robert Collins)

TELEVISION

MOWs,   CONCRETE BEAT (Directed by Robert Butler)
Mini-series,   RAINBOW (Directed by Jackie Cooper)
Specials: THE DEATH OF RICHIE (Directed by Paul Wendkos)
               CRASH: THE TRUE STORY OF FLIGHT 401
               (Directed by Barry Shear)
               HAROLD ROBBINS' 79 PARK AVENUE (Directed
               by Paul Wendkos)
               THE CASTAWAYS ON GILLIGAN'S ISLAND
               (Directed by Earl Bellamy)
               DISNEY'S ALL-STAR VALENTINE PARTY (Voice of Chip)

Episodic: MOONLIGHTING
               REMINGTON STEELE
               FAME (Directed by Peter Levin)
               ARCHIE BUNKER'S PLACE
               HARDCASTLE & McCORMICK
               THE ROCKFORD FILES

Daytime: SOMERSET: NBC (Contract role)
               SEARCH FOR TOMORROW: CBS (Contract role)
               LOVE IS A MANY-SPLENDORED THING: CBS
               (Contract role)

CONTACT: Michael Thomas Agency: (212) 867-0303
COMMERCIALS: Cunningham, Escott, Dipene & Associates:
                       (212) 477-1666
MESSAGES: (212) 799-5254

Appendix C

Breakdown Services Samples

(File 1/19B2) L

Carolco Productions
"Total Recall"
Feature Film
Dec. 16, 1988

Producer: Buzz Feitshans
Director: Paul Verhoeven
Writers: Ronald Shusett & Dan
   O'Bannon
Revised by: Gary Goldman
Casting: Fenton/Taylor Casting
Start Date: April 1
Location: Mexico

Written Submissions Only To:

Valorie Massalas
Fenton/Taylor Casting
Universal Studios
100 Universal City Plaza
Trailer 78
Universal City, CA 91608

RICHTER: A large, imposing, menacing man, he's a top agent who furiously pursues the renegade Quail. An arch-rival of Quail, he is determined to wipe his nemesis off the face of the earth, and he becomes progressively more dangerous and upset when his quarry persistently eludes him. Merciless, conscienceless and relentless, Richter is a formidable opponent . . . LEAD (31)

DR. EDGEMAR: A non-threatening, intellectual looking fellow in tweeds, this physician claims that he works for Rekall, Inc., and that he has been implanted in Quail's "schizoid embolism" in order to try and talk him back into sanity. In reality, Edgemar is actually an agent who has been dispatched to further confuse and disorient Quail . . . 21 speeches & 11 lines, 1 scene (84)

HELM : Richter's partner, he's a little, vicious man who is as tenacious and ruthless as his compadre. He's also determined to track Quail down at any cost, but he's content to play second banana to Richter, obeying his every order without question . . . 1 speech & 7 lines, 28 scenes (34)

BOB McCLANE : A jovial hustler with a vigorous manner, he's a top salesman at Rekall, a futuristic technological company which offers a unique service to its customers. Sensing that Quail is a potential customer, McClane really gives him the hard sell. Later, however, when Quail freaks out during a routine procedure, McClane realizes that he and his associates have a killer tiger by the tail . . . 23 speeches & 11 lines, 4 scenes (12)

DR. LULL : A bird-like middle-aged woman, she "is too skinny, and her hair is too red." The doctor who has been assigned to perform a routine implantation on Quail, she treats her patient with impersonal conviviality. When Quail freaks out during the procedure, she's obviously terrified . . . 10 speeches & 14 lines, 3 scenes (17)

HARRY : A middle-aged, likeable guy with a beer belly and a Brooklyn accent, he's Quail's buddy and co-worker on a futuristic construction site. Later, it is revealed that Harry is actually a highly trained agent who has been assigned to monitor Quail—and who has absolutely no compunction about blowing his pal away if his programming should go awry . . . 6 speeches & 13 lines, 6 scenes (10)

STEVENS : This moustachioed soldier of fortune is an old friend of Quail from their days as special agents on Mars. He helps Quail out of a tight pinch, but is later blown away by Richter . . . 8 speeches & 5 lines, 3 scenes (44)

CABBIE / JOHNNY : A smiling robotic mannequin in an old fashioned cabbie's uniform, this mechanized taxi driver is the automated Checker cab of the future. A relentlessly cheery automaton who takes everything a bit too literally, he picks Quail up as a fare and is subsequently blown up in a desperate car chase—a disaster that doesn't perturb him in the slightest . . . 4 speeches & 6 lines, 3 scenes (24)

C A P T A I N : This spaceship captain is preparing to depart for Mars, and is annoyed when Richter delays the launch for security reasons . . . 3 speeches & 4 lines, 1 scene (61)

S U I T : This agent in a conservative suit greets Richter when he arrives on Mars . . . 2 speeches & 3 lines, 1 scene (64)

S C I E N T I S T   # 1) These scientists, seen in Quail's trance-
S C I E N T I S T   # 2) induced flashback, discuss the nuclear
S C I E N T I S T   # 3) reactor they have found in a Martian mine . . . 2 speeches & 3 lines, 1 scene; 1 speech & 2 lines, 1 scene; 2 lines, 1 scene respectively (106)

E R N I E : This hyperactive young lab technician assists Dr. Lull in the implantation procedure. A character who "has the air of an acid-head who's still out there," he's also frightened by Quail's violent outburst . . . 1 speech & 5 lines, 2 scenes (17)

C L E R K : This clerk at the Mars Hilton welcomes Quail, whom he obviously recognizes as a regular patron . . . 1 speech & 3 lines, 1 scene (70)

D O C T O R : This doctor prepares Quail for his reprogramming . . . 2 speeches & 1 line, 1 scene (115)

T I F F A N Y : A bored, ornamental receptionist who is sitting at the front desk doing her nails, she welcomes Quail to Rekall . . . 1 speech & 2 lines, 1 scene (12)

B A R T E N D E R : This bartender works at a Martian whorehouse. He tells Quail that the whore he's asking for is pretty particular about her choice of patrons . . . 1 speech & 2 lines, 1 scene (74)

B U R L Y   P A S S E N G E R : This burly former miner, who is traveling on a Mars subway car, fills Quail in on recent events at the Pyramid Mine . . . 1 speech & 1 line, 1 scene (68)

J A K E   T H E   P A W N B R O K E R : This pawnbroker is suspicious of Quail's odd behavior when he redeems a satchel . . . 2 lines, 1 scene (47)

A G E N T : This agent is helping Richter track Quail . . . 2 lines, 1 scene (55)

R E P O R T E R : This television reporter questions Cohaagen about the recent civil unrest on the planet Mars . . . 1 line, 1 scene (7)

M I S S   L O N E L Y H E A R T S : A lonely, middle-aged lady who is also a prospective client of Rekall, she's scandalized when she over-hears the news of an internal company crisis . . . 1 line, 1 scene (20)

G O O N : This large, thuggish looking agency goon is helping Harry "eliminate" the troublesome Quail, but gets wiped out himself in-stead . . . 1 line, 1 scene (26)

F A T   C O M P L A I N E R : This fat man complains when Quail forces his way on a subway elevator . . . 1 line, 1 scene (36)

O L D   L A D Y : This irate old lady chews Quail out for hogging a phone booth . . . 1 line, 1 scene (46)

F I R E M A N # 1)	These firemen check the blazing cab's
F I R E M A N # 2)	wreckage for Quail's remains . . . 1 line, 1 scene apiece (53)

S E C U R I T Y # 1)	These security officers check out the
S E C U R I T Y # 2)	space shuttle for intruders before lift-off . . . 1 line, 1 scene apiece (60)

S T E W A R D E S S : This stewardess shows Richter and Helm to their cabin aboard the space shuttle . . . 1 line, 1 scene (62)

Y O U N G   S O L D I E R : This hapless young soldier is brutally slugged by Richter . . . 1 line, 1 scene (67)

M A R T I A N # 1)	These Martians complain about the con-
M A R T I A N # 2)	ditions on their planet . . . 1 line, 1
M A R T I A N # 3)	scene apiece (67)

P U N K   C A B B I E : A punked out cabbie in his 20s, he bawls Benny out for stealing his fare . . . 1 line, 1 scene (72)

M I N E R : This miner is shot by the furious Richter . . . 1 line, 1 scene (97)

N A R R A T O R : This commercial announcer extolls the wonders of a Rekall, Inc. vacation . . . 2 speeches, 1 scene (9) May be voice over only.

S T O R Y   L I N E : DOUGLAS QUAIL, a happily married construction worker in a futuristic America, begins to piece together his past life: He is a former government agent who has been "reprogrammed" to forget his past and assume a completely new identity. A hunted man, Quail stays one step ahead of his tenacious pursuers, led by RICHTER, while he tries to solve the frightening puzzle of his origins . . .

(File:3-6R3) L
BASED ON THE SCRIPT, THE FOLLOWING SYNOPSIS WAS WRITTEN BY A BREAKDOWN SERVICES STAFF WRITER.

20TH CENTURY-FOX TV
L.A. LAW
"UNTITLED"
EPISODIC/NBC
STORY #19
DRAFT: MARCH 6, 1990

Exec. Producer: David E. Kelley
Co-Exec. Producer: Rick Wallace
Supv. Producer: William M. Finkelstein
Producers: Elodie Keene Michael M. Robin
Coord. Producer: Alice West
Co-Producer: Robert M. Breech
Director: Miles Watkins
Casting Director: Beth Hymson
Casting Assistant: Peggy Kennedy
Dates: 3/14–3/23
Location: L.A.

WRITTEN SUBMISSIONS ONLY TO: HARBIN/HYMSON
                                 CASTING
                                 20TH CENTURY-FOX
                                 10201 W. PICO BLVD.
                                 PICO APTS. #5
                                 L.A., CA 90035
                                 ATTN: L.A. LAW

Twentieth Century-Fox Film corporation is an equal opportunity em-
ployer with an affirmative action plan and policy. All roles to be cast
are open to any sex or race unless otherwise specifically stated in this
breakdown. We are asking for your support in helping 20th Century-
Fox to display the "true American scene" when you are casting. Where
there are opportunities for senior citizens, handicapped, minorities, and
females, please utilize their talents and skills. Please refer qualified people to our casting directors with that understanding.

MURRAY MELMAN: Roxanne's father, in his late 60s, Murray has just been thrown out of his retirement home for a strange reason: he thinks he's Ralph Kramden. Sometimes Murray is able to
reason cogently and angrily, but suddenly he will veer into his replica-
tion of Jackie Gleason. He refuses to move in with Roxanne, and is
quick to remind her of all the times she has failed to visit him. Arrested after stealing a bus, Murray slowly comes to admit that maybe he
has a little problem . . . LEAD (8) POSSIBLE RECURRING ROLE

PETER REYNOLDS: A man in his 30s, Peter Reynolds was a
student activist in Argentina in 1979. Arrested for his activities, he
was repeatedly tortured by horrific nightmares and unable to hold down
a job. He is now suing the guard who once was his torturer, and is now
a successful businessman in America. An anguished man whose nerves
are still stretched to the limit, he pulls a gun on Mendez after the trial
is over, and threatens to transform his victimizer into one of the victims . . . LEAD (11)

ORLANDO MENDEZ: An Argentinian in his 30s, Mendez
was a torturer with the Argentine Army in 1979, but has since come to
this country and made a success of himself. Sued by Peter Reynolds, he
claims to have been forced to do the dirty work, and avers that he too
suffers from nightmares. After a rough grilling by Markowitz, he is
found not guilty, and tries to make up for his past actions by offering
Peter Reynolds a job . . . LEAD (11)

M A R T I N   H U M M E L L : A little man in his mid 60s, Martin was riding a roller coaster when his wife passed out. Now he's suing the roller coaster company, and relishes recounting his testimony, complete with sound effects. A feisty, peppery man, Hummell goes along when Van Owen decides the jury must ride the roller coaster, and makes it clear that he loves every thrill-packed minute of the harrowing ride . . . LEAD (1) ACTOR *MUST* BE WILLING TO RIDE MAJOR ROLLER COASTER, I.E., COLOSSUS.

C A R L   D I E T R I C H : The attorney for Orlando Mendez, he/she presents his defense of his client's actions that Mendez was forced to commit at the behest of his superiors, and was only following orders. Dubious when Orlando offers to make restitution by giving employment to Peter Reynolds, he is appalled when Reynolds threatens his client with a gun . . . LEAD (11)

E T H Y L   H U M M E L L : A little woman in her 60s, Ethyl sits at the plaintiff's table along with her husband, having filed suit against the roller coaster company. Ethyl passed out after riding their roller coaster, and as her husband recounts his testimony, a feisty Ethyl insists on repeating her own version of the story, despite Judge Van Owen's admonitions . . . LEAD (1)

K I M   P E R R I N : An attorney in his 40s, he represents Mr. and Mrs. Hummell in their suit against the roller coaster. A competent lawyer, he is able to keep his cool under strenuous conditions, and can even counter objections while cresting the top of a roller coaster . . . LEAD (1) ACTOR *MUST* BE WILLING TO RIDE A MAJOR ROLLER COASTER, I.E., COLOSSUS.

R I C H A R D   R E D D : The attorney for the defense in the roller coaster case, he is forced to object repeatedly when the Hummells continue to interrupt one another's testimony. During the roller coaster ride itself, Redd continues to pepper Van Owen with objections . . . LEAD (1) ACTOR *MUST* BE WILLING TO RIDE A MAJOR ROLLER COASTER, I.E., COLOSSUS.

B A R T H O L O M E W   M I L L E R : A man in his 40s, he is a witness for the defense in the roller coaster case. He claims the roller coaster is extremely safe, and becomes defensive when the ride's reputation is attacked. Later, he goes on the roller coaster with the others, shouting that it is completely safe . . . LEAD (17) ACTOR *MUST* BE

WILLING TO RIDE A MAJOR ROLLER COASTER, I.E., COLOS-
SUS.

DR. DIANE KRAVITZ: She is a competent, professional
psychiatrist in her 40s, whose patient is Orlando Mendez. Called to
testify for the defense, she asserts that although Mendez is sane, he was
powerless to stop himself from torturing Peter Reynolds. She is harshly
cross-questioned by Markowitz . . . 2 speeches & 8 lines, 1 scene (20)

DAN NYSTROM: In his 40s, Nystrom is the director of a retirement home. With Murray present, Dan tells Roxanne about the
problems Murray has been causing, and insists that Murray leave before
he disturbs more people . . . 1 speech & 9 lines, 1 scene (8)

SCOTT PEROT: A corporate head in his 60s, Perot is one of
the law firm's biggest cash cows. At lunch with Leland, he is asked
about his relationship with Rosalind, and gives her a firm vote of confidence. After being told that McKenzie is thinking of ousting her, Perot
is very dubious, but reluctantly loyal to his old friend Leland . . . 3
speeches & 6 lines, 1 scene (34) VERY NICE SCENE

STENOGRAPHER: This court stenographer goes on the roller
coaster ride, and has a hard time transcribing the proceedings . . . 3
scenes (36) ACTOR *MUST* BE WILLING TO RIDE A MAJOR
ROLLER COASTER, I.E., COLOSSUS.

FOREPERSON: The foreperson in the Mendez trial, he/she finds
Mendez not guilty . . . 1 speech & 1 line, at least 1 scene (43)

POLICE OFFICER: This police officer escorts Murray in to
see Roxanne, and addresses Murray as "Ralphie boy" . . . 1 line, 1
scene (52)

(1100)
ALL COMMERCIAL EXPRESS AGENTS

CASTING: SHEILA
MANNING

US POSTAL SERVICE
Shoots: Aug. 23–30
(1 day)

NATIONAL
Interviews: Tomorrow

PIX BY 3 TODAY TO: SHEILA MANNING
508 S. SAN VICE-
NTE
L.A., CA 90048

SEEKING:

Supervisor: 50, white male, Robert Duvall type . . .
Computer Operator: 25–30, Asian woman . . .
Systems Controller: 25–35, black male . . .
Letter Carrier: 25–30, woman, all ethnicities . . .
Letter Carrier: 25–35, man, all ethnicities . . .
Woman Receiving Letter: 25–35, white . . .
All Talent Should Look Healthy, Attractive, Friendly

COMMERCIAL EXPRESS   8/16/90   BREAKDOWN #7

(1105)
ALL COMMERCIAL EXPRESS AGENTS

CASTING: SHEILA
MANNING
Shoots: TBA

CHEVRON
Interviews: Tomorrow

RUN: TBA

PIX BY 3 TODAY TO: SHEILA MANNING
508 S. SAN VICENTE
L.A., CA 90048

SEEKING:

Man: For 6:15 sec, spots. Spokesactor, 30s.
               Friendly, affable, smart, with some
               levity . . .

Carpoolers: 2 men/1 woman, late 20s to early 30s . . .
Chevron Mechanic: Age open . . .

(400)
ALL COMMERCIAL EXPRESS AGENTS

                                    CASTING: TEPPER/
                                    GALLEGOS
WEIGHT WATCHERS   Shoots: Aug. 27 & 28
NATIONAL

PIX BY 10 A.M. MON. TO: TEPPER/GALLEGOS
                           7033 SUNSET BLVD.
                           L.A., CA 90028

N O T E : ALL WOMEN SHOULD BE REAL PEOPLE, PEOPLE THE
TARGET AUDIENCE CAN IDENTIFY WITH. SHOULD BE
SLIGHTLY (5–15 LBS.) OVER THEIR MODEL WEIGHT. SHOULD
LOOK LIKE THEY CAN BE FROM ANYWHERE IN COUNTRY
EXCEPT EAST OR WEST COAST.

S E E K I N G :

Mom: 34–36, best reflect look of mom, not too old or
                   too young . . .
Businesswoman: 35–45. Should look like a go-getter, gets things
                   done. No time for meals . . .
Party Girl: 27–32, should not look like a kid. Mature look-
                   ing. Very social with bubbly personality . . .

Appendix D

Union Membership Requirements: SAG, AFTRA, AEA

UNION MEMBERSHIP REQUIREMENTS

As I mentioned earlier, beginning actors often assign more importance than they should to union membership. You should understand that once you join any performers' union you will not be allowed to work in any amateur production—including community and college theater—and this can prevent you from getting valuable experience. So it may be wise to hold off joining AFTRA, SAG, and Equity, if you have a choice

The simplest way to join any of the guilds is to get a job under their jurisdiction. You will need to present proof of a signed contract for a specific role in a specific production at a specific salary, and then pay the required initiation fees There are also some other roads to membership.

AMERICAN FEDERATION OF TV AND RADIO ARTISTS AFTRA

AFTRA is an open union To join, all you need to do is plunk down the initiation fee and first dues installment. Each AFTRA local sets these fees individually: in Los Angeles and New York the initiation fee is currently $800.00. Dues are assessed on a sliding scale based on your previous year's income from acting. In Los Angeles and New York, semiannual dues for actors in the lowest income category who are not members of another guild are $42.50.

Under the Taft-Hartley Law, you are entitled to do your first AFTRA job and work in television for up to thirty days without joining the union After that, membership is compulsory

SCREEN ACTORS GUILD (SAG)

Actors used to be able to join SAG after a year of membership in AFTRA or Equity simply by paying their initiation fees and first dues. This situation no longer exists. Now you must have worked at least once as a principal (under AFTRA or Equity) or three times as an extra under SAG jurisdiction. The Screen Extras Guild (SEG), which used to govern union extras on the West Coast, has now been absorbed into SAG.

SAG's initiation fee is $1008.00 and the first semiannual dues are $42.50—so the total joining fee comes to $1050.50.

ACTORS' EQUITY ASSOCIATION (AEA)

If you have belonged to any Four A's union [AEA, AFTRA, AGVA, or SAG] for a year and have performed work comparable to Equity-principal work, you are eligible to join Equity.

You can also join through Equity's Membership Candidate Program, which allows you to credit fifty weeks of work at accredited theaters toward Equity membership. (You can reduce the number of required weeks to forty if you pass a written exam about AEA.) Contact an Equity office for further details about this program.

Equity's initiation fee is currently $800.00 for actor's whose parent union is AEA, SAG, AGVA, or AFTRA. For those already in AGMA as parent, the initiation fee may be reduced by up to $400, depending on the fee paid to the parent union. Basic semiannual dues are $39.

SCREEN ACTORS GUILD

NATIONAL HEADQUARTERS
5757 Wilshire Boulevard
Los Angeles, CA 90036-3600
(213) 954-1600

ARIZONA
1616 E. Indian School Road #330
Phoenix, Arizona 85016
(602) 265-2712

ATLANTA
455 East Paces Ferry Road, N.E. #334
Atlanta, Georgia 30305
(404) 239-0131

BOSTON
11 Beacon Street, #515
Boston, Massachusetts 02108
(617) 742-2688

CHICAGO
75 E. Wacker Drive, 14th Floor
Chicago, Illinois 60601
(312) 372-8081

*CLEVELAND
1030 Euclid Avenue #429
Cleveland, Ohio 44115
(216) 579-9305

DALLAS
6060 N. Central Expressway
#302, L43604
Dallas, TX 75206
(214)363-8300

**DENVER
950 S. Cherry Street, #502
Denver, Colorado 80222
(303) 757-6226

* AFTRA offices which also handle SAG business for their areas.

**Denver is a regional office which also covers Nevada, New Mexico and Utah.

DETROIT
28690 Southfield Road
Lathrup Village, Michigan 48076
(810) 559-9540

FLORIDA
7300 No. Kendall Drive #620
Miami, Florida 33156-7840
(305) 444-7677

HAWAII
949 Kapiolani Boulevard, #105
Honolulu, Hawaii 96814
(808) 538-6122

HOUSTON
2650 Fountainview, #325
Houston, Texas 77057
(713) 972-1806

*MINNEAPOLIS/ST. PAUL
708 N. 1st Street #343A
Minneapolis, Minnesota 55401
(612) 371-9120

NASHVILLE
1108 17th Avenue South
Nashville, Tennessee 37212
(615) 327-2958

NEW YORK
1515 Broadway, 44th Floor
New York, New York 10036
(212) 944-1030

PHILADELPHIA
230 S. Broad Street, 10th Floor
Philadelphia, Pennsylvania 19102
(215) 545-3150

*ST. LOUIS
906 Olive Street, #1006
St. Louis, Missouri 63101
(314) 231-8410

SAN DIEGO
7827 Convoy Court, #400
San Diego, California 92111
(619) 278-7695

SAN FRANCISCO
735 Pine Street, 11th Floor
San Francisco, California 94104
(415) 391-7510

*SEATTLE
601 Valley Street, #200
Seattle, Washington 98109
(206) 282-2506

WASHINGTON D.C.
The Highland House
5480 Wisconsin Avenue, #201
Chevy Chase, Maryland 20815
(301) 657-2560

AFTRA OFFICES

NATIONAL OFFICE
260 Madison Avenue, 7th Floor
New York, New York 10016
(212) 532-0800

ALBANY
Mr. Bill Barran, Shop Coordinator
c/o Station WROW-AM
341 Northern Boulevard
Albany, New York 12204
(STA) (518) 436-4841
(H) (518) 271-8322

ATLANTA
Ms. Melissa Goodman, Acting
Executive Director
455 East Paces Ferry Road, #334
Atlanta, Georgia 30305
(404) 239-0131

BOSTON
Ms. Donna Sommers,
Executive Director
11 Beacon Street, #512
Boston, Massachusetts 02108
(617) 742-2688

BUFFALO
Mr. Rick Pfeiffer, President
c/o WIVB-TV
2077 Elmwood Avenue
Buffalo, New York 14207
(716) 874-4410

CHICAGO
Mr. Paul Wagner, Executive Director
75 East Wacker Drive, 14th Floor
Chicago, Illinois 60601
(312) 372-8081

CLEVELAND
Ms. Joan L. Kalhorn, Executive
Director
1030 Euclid Avenue, #429
Cleveland, Ohio 44115-1504
(216) 781-2255

DALLAS—FORT WORTH
Mr. William McCright, Acting
Executive Director
6060 N. Central Expressway, #302
Dallas, Texas 75206
(214) 363-8300

DENVER
Mr. Jerre Hookey, Executive Director
950 South Cherry Street, #502
Denver, Colorado 80222
(303) 757-6226

DETROIT
Ms. Barbara Honner
Executive Director
28690 Southfield Road
Lathrup Village, Michigan 48076
(313) 559.9540

DETROIT BRDCST DIV.
Mr. Dave Gebard, Broadcast Rep.
3172 Cedar Key Drive
Lake Orion, MI 48360
(313) 391-1999

FRESNO
Mr. Chris Ward, President
P.O. Box 11961
Fresno, California 93776
(209) 222-7065

HAWAII
Ms. Brenda Ching, Executive Director
949 Kapiolani Blvd., Ste.#105
Honolulu, Hawaii 96814
(808) 538-6122

HOUSTON
Mr. Jack Dunlop, Executive Director
2650 Fountainview, #325
Houston, Texas 77057
(713) 972-1806

KANSAS CITY
Ms. Laurie Jenkins, Executive Director
P.O. Box 32167
4000 Baltimore, 2nd Floor
Kansas City, Missouri 64111
(816) 753-4557

LOS ANGELES
Mr. Mark A. Farber,
Executive Director
6922 Hollywood Boulevard, 8th Floor
Hollywood, California 90028-6128
(213) 461-8111

MIAMI
Ms. Diane Hogan, Executive Director
20401 N.W. 2nd Avenue, #102
Miami, Florida 33169
(305) 652-4824
(305) 652-4846

Orlando Office
Major Building
5728 Major Blvd., Suite 264
Orlando, FL 32819

Ms. Lorraine Lawless
Central Florida Rep.
(407) 354-2230
1-800-330-AFTR (Miami)

MILWAUKEE
Mr. Mike Donovan, Bus. Rep.
5004 West Burleigh Street
Milwaukee, WI 53210
(414) 442-7000

NASHVILLE
Mr. Randall Himes, Executive
Director
P.O. Box 121087
1108 17th Avenue South
Nashville, Tennessee 37212
(615) 327-2944
(615) 327-2947

NEW ORLEANS
Mr. Bob MacDowell, Executive
Director
2475 Canal Street, Suite #108

New Orleans, Louisiana 70119
504) 822-6568

NEW YORK
Mr. Stephen Burrow, Executive
Director
260 Madison Avenue, 7th Floor
New York, New York 10016
(212) 532-0800

OMAHA
Mr. Bob Horder
3000 Farnham Street, Ste.3 East
Omaha, Nebraska 68131
(402) 346-8384

ORLANDO
(see Miami)

PEORIA
Mr. Garry Moore, Treasurer
c/o Station WEEK
2907 Springfield Road
East Peoria, Illinois 61611
(309) 699-5052

PHILADELPHIA
Mr. John Kailin, Executive Director
230 South Broad Street, 10th Floor
Philadelphia, Pennsylvania 19010-
1229
(215) 732-0507

PHOENIX
Mr. Donald Livesay
Executive Director
1616 East Indian School Road, #330
Phoenix, Arizona 85016
(602) 265-2712

PITTSBURGH
Mr. Mark Wirick, Executive Director
625 Stanwix Street

The Penthouse
Pittsburgh, Pennsylvania 15222
(412) 281-6767

PORTLAND
Mr. Stuart Pemble-Belkin, Executive
Director
516 S.E. Morrison, #M-3
Portland, Oregon 97214
(503) 238-6914

ROCHESTER
Mr. Michael T. Harren
Executive Director
Chamberlain, D'Amanda, &
Oppenheimer
1600 Crossroads Office Building
Rochester, New York 14614
(716) 232-3730

SACRAMENTO-STOCKTON
Mr. Michael McLaughlin, President
836 Garnet Street West
Sacramento, California 95691
(916) 372-1966

SAN DIEGO
Mr. Tom Doyle
7827 Convoy Court, #400
San Diego, California 92111
(619) 278-7695

SAN FRANCISCO
Ms. Rebecca Rhine
Executive Director
235 Pine Street, 11th Floor
San Francisco, California 94104
(415) 391-7510

SCHENECTADY
Mr. Jim Leonard, President
170 Ray Avenue
Schenectady, New York 12304
(518) 381-4836

Mr. Peter Rief
Shop Coordinator
(518) 381-4848
c/o WGY/WGY-FM
1430 Balltown Road
Schenectady, NY 12309

Mr. Jack Aernecke & Peter Brancato
Shop Coordinators, c/o WRGB-TV
(518) 346-6666
1400 Balltown Road
Schenectady, NY 12309

SEATTLE
Mr. Anthony Hazapis, Executive
Director
P.O. Box 9688
601 Valley Street, #200
Seattle, Washington, 98109
(206) 282-2506

ST. LOUIS
Mr. Larry Ward, Executive Director
906 Olive Street, #1006
St. Louis, Missouri 63101
(314) 231-8410

STAMFORD
Mr. Len Gambino, Shop Coordinator
c/o Station WSTC
117 Prospect Street
Stamford, Connecticut 06901
(203) 348-1308

TRI-STATE
(Including Cincinnati, Columbus,
and Dayton, Ohio;
Indianapolis, Indiana; and Louisville,
Kentucky):
Ms. Herta Suarez, Executive Director
128 East 6th Street, #802
Cincinnati, Ohio 45202
(513) 579-8668

TWIN CITIES
Ms. Colleen Aho, Executive Director
708 North First Street, Ste.343A
Itasca Bldg.
Minneapolis, Minnesota 55401
(612) 371-9120

WASHINGTON—BALTIMORE
Ms. Pat O'Donnell, Executive Director
4340 East West Highway, #204
Bethesda, Maryland 20814
(301) 657-2560

Recommended Reading

BOOKS:

The Agency Guide, Los Angeles: Breakdown Services. Published biannually.

Blu, Susan, and Molly Ann Mullin. *Word of Mouth: A Guide to Commercial Voice-Over Excellence*. Los Angeles: Pomegranate Press., Ltd., 1987.

Brouwer, Alexandra, and Tomas Lee Wright. *Working in Hollywood: 64 Film Professionals Talk about Moviemaking*. New York: Crown, 1990.

The C/D Directory. Los Angeles: Breakdown Services. Published four times a year.

Caine, Michael. *Acting in Film*. New York: Applause Books, 1990.

Cameron, Julia. *The Artist's Way: A Spiritual Path to Higher Creativity*. New York: Tarcher/Putnam, 1992.

Eaker, Sherry. *The Back Stage Handbook for Performing Artists*. New York: Back Stage Books 1991.

Henry, Mari Lyn, and Lynne Rogers. *How to Be a Working Actor*, 3rd edition. New York: Back Stage Books, 1994.

Hunt, Gordon. *How to Audition*. New York: Harper and Row, 1979.

Kallan, K. *The Los Angeles Agent Book*. Studio City: Sweden Press, 1989. *The New York Agent Book*. Studio City: Sweden Press, 1989.

Lewis, M.K., and Rosemary R. Lewis. *Your Film Acting Career*. Los Angeles: Samuel French, 1993.

Logan, Tom. *How to Act and Eat at the Same Time*. Washington, D.C.: Communications Press, 1982.

Monos, Jim. *Professional Actor Training in New York City*. New York: Broadway Press: 1989.

The New York C/D Directory. Los Angeles: Breakdown Services. Published biannually.

Shurtleff, Michael. *Audition*. New York: Bantam, 1980.

Small, Edgar. *From Agent to Actor*. Hollywood: Samuel French, 1991.

PERIODICALS:

Backstage. New York: published weekly.
Daily Variety.
Dramalogue. Los Angeles: published weekly.
The Hollywood Reporter. Published daily.
Ross Reports. Long Island City, N.Y.: Television Index, Inc. Published monthly
Variety. Published weekly.

Index

INDEX TO NEW INTERVIEWS

About the Author

Judith Searle's acting credits include Broadway and off-Broadway theater, film, television, commercials, and voice-overs. She is the author of a novel, *Lovelife,* and her articles on theater and the entertainment industry have appeared in *The New York Times, Cosmopolitan,* and *The Drama Review.*